'A fascinating read, both as an o[...] punk – it's hard not to like the sound of the Filth, a Sydney quartet whose audition for a major label involved their lead singer repeatedly head-butting a door – and a kind of rake's progress' **Alexis Petridis,** *Guardian*

'Ostensibly the story of Nick Cave's formative years, it is so beautifully constructed that one is not just delivered besides the young Cave, but also next to the modern version' **Ted Kessler,** *The New Cue*

'There is plenty of humour in *Boy on Fire*...and beautiful moments, as well as delinquency and sadness...Hopefully Mordue will write a follow-up to this highly engaging biography very soon' *Buzz Magazine*

'[H]is access to Cave and associates also creates an unusually intimate account' *Mojo*

'Mordue's book offers total immersion in the artist's early years... paints a vivid portrait of an artist in the process of becoming' *Uncut*

'Beautifully written...Mark Mordue expertly guides us on a journey as he narrates memories of Nick Cave from a middle-class background, trying to find his way in life in those wilder, often destructive early years' *Louder Than War*

'An indispensable read for dedicated Cave heads' *Irish Times*

'A powerful and unusually focused biography' **David Fricke, The Writer's Block, SiriusXM**

Mark Mordue is an Australian writer, journalist and editor. He is a co-winner of the 2014 Peter Blazey Fellowship, which recognises the development of an outstanding manuscript in the fields of biography, autobiography or life writing. He is the author of the acclaimed poetry collection *Darlinghurst Funeral Rites* and the memoir *Dastgah: Diary of a Headtrip*. His journalism has been published in *Rolling Stone, Vogue, GQ, Interview,* the *Australian* and the *Sydney Morning Herald*. He was the winner of a 1992 Human Rights Media Award and the 2010 Pascall Prize for Australian 'Critic of the Year'. His poetry was shortlisted for the 2016 WB Yeats Poetry Prize and, together with his fiction, essays and memoir work, has appeared in literary journals including *HEAT, Meanjin, Griffith Review* and *Overland*. He lives in Sydney.

BOY ON FIRE

FIRE THE YOUNG NICK CAVE

MARK MORDUE

ALLEN&UNWIN

First published in Great Britain in 2021 by Allen & Unwin
First published in Australia in 2020 by HarperCollins*Publishers*
Australia Pty Limited
This paperback edition published in Great Britain in 2022 by
Allen & Unwin

Allen & Unwin
c/o Atlantic Books
Ormond House
26–27 Boswell Street
London WC1N 3JZ
Phone: 020 7269 1610
Email: UK@allenandunwin.com
Web: www.allenandunwin.com/uk

A CIP catalogue record for this book is available from the British Library.

Photographs by Peter Milne appear courtesy of Peter Milne and
M.33, Melbourne
Typeset in Bembo Std by Kelli Lonergan

Paperback ISBN: 978 1 83895 372 0
E-book ISBN: 978 1 83895 371 3

Printed by CPI Group (UK) Ltd, Croydon CR0 4YY

10 9 8 7 6 5 4 3 2 1

For my children,
Atticus, Franny and Levon

And for Bryan Wellington,
Anne Shannon and Eddie Baumgarten,
and all the boys and girls next door

'At the end of it all, it was difficult to decide which was the
more romantic, the more exciting: the real man or
the myth he has become.'

Colin F Cave, *Ned Kelly: Man and Myth*

Nick Cave singing 'I'm Eighteen', Boys Next Door gig,
Swinburne College, 1977 *(Peter Milne)*

CONTENTS

AUTHOR'S NOTE

Quotes by Nick Cave are from interviews and phone conversations between us from 2010 to 2018. These are used throughout the text – and without endnotes – unless additional context is required.

Interviews that occurred earlier with me over the course of Nick Cave's career – and published stories of mine about him and his work – are referenced in the endnotes and acknowledgements.

Interviews I carried out with Nick Cave's family, friends and peers – along with material drawn from books, essays, articles and reviews, and Nick Cave's own journals, notebooks and letters archived at The Arts Centre, Melbourne – are referenced in endnotes.

In areas where published material and my own interviews overlap, I have chosen the more articulate version, and delineated between a published quote and an elaboration based on my own conversations. This was made easier by well-worn anecdotes, even the verbatim retelling of certain events.

I have tried to be wary of entrenched perceptions – and their opposite, the elision or rewriting of history, in content or emotion, to fit with a new point of view. Certain truths, even 'facts', remain in the province of the group more than the individual. History is still alive to those who lived it.

Un pour tous, tous pour un
One for all, and all for one.

The
Journalist
and the
Singer

The first time I ever spoke to Nick Cave was in a phone interview to promote his second solo album, *The Firstborn Is Dead* (1985), an ominous, blues-affected work that sanctified the birth of Elvis Presley and thereby rock 'n' roll itself in quasi-religious, apocalyptic terms. Our conversation around the recording was as dry as spinifex, so slow and spacious it sometimes ceased to exist. As if Cave could not be less interested in what I was asking or saying and never would be. Given his notorious hatred of journalists back then, this made for an uphill experience. I put the phone down with sweating palms and a sinking feeling in my heart. What a failure.

Dealing with Cave again, let alone meeting him in person, was not something I looked forward to. In 1988 I nonetheless lobbied to interview Nick Cave for Sydney's *On the Street*. Second time lucky, I must have been hoping. Face to face he had to be more approachable than that distant voice on an echoing telephone line. Besides, he was the pre-eminent Australian rock 'n' roll artist of his day. This made him hard to ignore.

Cave was in town to read from and preview a much anticipated literary work in progress, a book that would become known as *And the Ass Saw the Angel* (1989). He'd already gone so far as to declare himself 'more of a writer now'[1], disowning rock 'n' roll for its lowbrow qualities and Pavlov's-dog audience responses.[2]

I was given a laneway address for a warehouse located directly behind Sydney's somewhat alternative and bohemian gay strip, Oxford Street. Cave was apparently holed up there with a girlfriend or a dealer or criminal acquaintance: rumours varied, depending who I spoke to. As always with Cave, rumours were all around him, as if his every movement across town were hot-wired into the gossip chambers of inner-city Sydney conversation. The only other wave-making machine of this kind that I would ever know was Michael Hutchence. It was as if you could feel their presence rippling through the city from the moment their flight hit the tarmac and they entered, half in secret, into our closed little world.

When I knocked on the door of what looked like an old garage, a key was hurled to the road with a vaguely familiar shout hovering invisibly on the Sunday-afternoon air. As I let myself in, I heard footsteps on the wooden ceiling and the creak of a trapdoor above. At the top of the ladder-like stairs that rolled down to meet me with a thud there was now a hole in the ceiling where Nick Cave himself stood, bathed in backlight. He beckoned me upwards like some awful figure in a B-grade horror film about a journalist come to interview a terrifying rock 'n' roll vampire. I gulped and set forth on my way to meet my Nosferatu.

Once I arrived upstairs, the atmosphere changed immediately. Cave was a solicitous host, while a young woman I took to be his partner bossed him about as if I had just entered a Goth version of the British comedy *George and Mildred*. 'Get Mark something to eat, Nick,' she said briskly. A large serving of the very best fruits was put before me – grapes, lychees, melon, apple – all prepared and presented in a grand manner.

As Cave was about to seat himself and enjoy some of this banquet, his partner said, 'Did you offer Mark some coffee, Nick?' Again he rose, mock lugubrious, stick-insect angular. He went over to an old metal funnel attached to a wooden workbench, poured in some coffee beans and began to slowly turn a handle: 'Grind, grind, grind, it's the story of my life.'

With a variety of expensive biscuits now also arrayed before me, I was soon thanking the couple for their surprising hospitality. Cave asked me why it should be so unexpected. An evasive answer seemed tactically unwise, so I mentioned the Prince of Darkness thing around him, and his reputation for treating journalists poorly. 'Who says that?' he asked, a little surly. 'Why, the *NME* [*New Musical Express*] ...' I began to say, in reference to the influential British music paper of the day. 'The *NME*!' he barked. Cave began to grind the coffee beans with much greater intensity. His partner looked at me and said, 'Don't get him started.' To Cave she called out in a calming voice, 'Now, Nick ...' Cave ground on, taking it out on the beans: 'The *NME*!'

Finally he came back over to us with a large silver coffee pot steaming with his efforts. A set of fine china cups were ready on a matching silver serving tray. Mid-pour, Cave lost focus, the coffee slowly streaming out of the spout and around – but not into – the cups in an ever-widening circle, the tray filling with black liquid as if it were a swimming pool, until he snapped back into consciousness and finally found the cups as well. Completing the task at last, Cave then asked me with all the decorum he could muster: 'Would you like milk or sugar with that?'

The next two and a half hours felt rather like an interview taking place under similarly dark water. Each question seemed to demand huge reservoirs of concentration from Cave, not to mention frequent pauses and micro-sleeps. Cave's sometimes thin and creaky, sometimes sonorous and self-consciously refined speaking voice certainly had its hypnotic qualities. I felt suspended, unsure of what to do, or even how to leave. To be honest, I'm not sure the encounter ever quite ended so much as faded away. With everyone heavily relaxed, I departed once more through the floor.

It was yet another Cave interview in which I felt I had somehow failed, despite Cave's very best efforts to help me. This was largely because I didn't really understand how to write up what had happened. I also dreaded sitting down and transcribing the interview tapes, a process that would demand even greater leagues of passing time from me all over again.

Two nights later, on stage at the Mandolin Cinema in Sydney's Surry Hills, Cave would recite from sections of his work in progress while an ambient soundtrack rose and fell with suitably ominous and dreamlike effect around his reading voice.[3] Looking every inch the 'Black Crow King' (one of many self-referential character songs that would add to his mythology, despite the satirical swipes it took at his image and those who subscribed to it), Cave did not so much walk onto the stage as dangle, stoop and hang in the air as if from unseen strings. He would eventually fall off the stage. And yet the cinema was full to the brim with his fans, a sellout performance over two nights, and a success in terms of the mood created by him reading from what appeared to be a credible, black-humoured, Faulknerian work of fiction well on the way to completion.

In 1994, six years after these readings and our warehouse encounter, the boot would be on the other foot, when I once again spoke to Cave, this time over the phone. He'd been living in São Paulo, Brazil, and – by all public accounts at least – was as clean as a whistle. For me it was an early-morning interview.

Very early. Unfortunately, I'd broken up with my girlfriend the previous night and not been home, to sleep or otherwise, barely brushing in the door to take Cave's call. Thank God I'd prepared the previous day. When Cave asked me how I was, I told him at great length: that I'd been out wandering all night, that I'd been here and there, felt this and thought that, a long, wild, emotional ramble that ended with me saying I loved his new record, *Let Love In*, and finally asking if he had a favourite walk he liked to take in São Paulo.

Cave took this all in with a long pause and slight grunt – and we began to talk. It was a great interview and I liked him a lot. He seemed completely non-judgemental about my 'condition'; in fact, I'd say he was both courteous and curiously amused throughout. As for his answer to my opening question: 'Well, I make my favourite walk daily. Which is up to my local bar. Out the door, up the street, past the junkyard where the chickens and the old junkyard dog sits. And up a steep hill to my favourite bar, San Pedro's. There's this giant barman there who is the fattest guy I've ever seen. He is constantly described by locals as a huge woman, but he's a man with a moustache. He looks more like a giant baby to me. I sit there and read, drink and contemplate the meaning of life. Then I walk back down.'4

A few years on I would meet Cave again, in 1997 in a rather sterile, fluorescent-lit room at the offices of Festival Mushroom in Sydney. Cave remembered me well enough, but his mood was odd and, I realise now, highly vulnerable, as *The Boatman's Call* – a raw and revealing album that revolved around his break-up with Brazilian partner Viviane Carneiro and a wounding affair with PJ Harvey – was about to be released. None of that was public knowledge yet. I nonetheless asked him, almost randomly, if he thought the love of a good woman could redeem a man. It was a question that seemed to arise out of his lyrics and what they implied across the record. Cave looked at me as if I were a total fucking idiot, and then away at the white wall as if he were a hopeless and godforsaken case himself. 'How the hell would I know?' he said. And then he looked back at me and waited for the next question.

More than a decade after that last experience, I began work on a biography of Nick Cave's life. Biographies are strange beasts, underlined by a cautionary wisdom that dates back to artists of the Italian Renaissance and their understanding that the portrait painter always paints something of his or her self.[5]

Nick and I met to discuss the project at his Brighton and Hove home office in the United Kingdom in 2010. I was told he could give me a few hours. We would spend the next three days talking intensely, then speak often in person after that, as well as on the phone, on tour and via email over the years to come. I still remember that first meeting outside his office, a very warm day. We were so close to the beach I could hear the waves washing back and forth over the stones. I had on a new pair of Havaianas branded as 'Brazilian blue', a good-luck purchase for my opening encounter. Nick noticed them immediately. 'Great colour! Mine are pink. I will wear them tomorrow.'

He was bright as a button, his office charged with creative energy and an apparent zeal that year for the works of American poets John Berryman and Frederick Seidel. Later, I would become intrigued by Berryman's sense of multiple selves and his use of them to create a performance on the page, interrogating himself through actors that were variations of his own personality. Seidel was very different: commanding and privileged, savage and song-like as he moved through his world. It was not hard to understand why these voices appealed to Nick. He encouraged me to investigate Jerome Rothenberg, whose collection *Technicians of the Sacred* had become a foundational text for him. It gathered together a global array of shamanistic ritual songs and chants and their contemporary equivalents. The radical leaps in logic, the sense of magic at work, the veneration of sound (over language itself) as a form of meaning or feeling – all resonate in everything that came along from *Push the Sky Away* onwards. As I write, I can see how Rothenberg's work changed Nick's thinking about music as much as lyrics, affecting the spiritual journey he would go on to make *Ghosteen* with Warren Ellis and the rest of The Bad Seeds.

On the second day of our meetings in Brighton, we went upstairs to Nick's family home, a rare act of trust. While Nick was answering phone calls, his wife, Susie Bick, asked if I was hungry. She made me a sandwich for lunch, then offered me tea and biscuits she scrabbled to find in their fridge. Susie had an aristocratic, almost nervous, energy that struck me as eccentric and vulnerable and wild, not quite of this earth. Something about Susie finding those extra biscuits for me felt particularly kind and thoughtful. And though she did not want to be interviewed for the biography, I liked her from that moment on for making me feel so welcome in her home, where others may have been more defensive or suspicious.

Nick told me later that Susie had a habit of moving the furniture around. He would return from a visit to London or a tour, even just a night out, and not be able to find the lounge and the television. 'Sometimes she's moved the entire bedroom to another room and I can't find that either.' He seemed to accept this with a shrug. 'I've mentioned it in song. People think it's some poetic image I've made up. I'm just documenting a straight fact.'

There was a guy downstairs whom Nick had recently helped clear out some space. 'He was like those people you see on TV shows about hoarding.' It had been almost impossible to get inside his apartment. The debris had begun to collect outside in the hall. Nick felt a sense of achievement when he convinced him to surrender a number of old and rusty pushbikes, as well as the more general rubbish he'd accumulated. It was all a matter of giving the poor fellow encouragement. 'I told him, "C'mon, you can do it."' Nick laughed. 'I know he will collect the same kind of stuff and it will all just come back in the door and I will have to do the whole thing again a year from now.'

Perhaps fame necessitated the same house clearing. I would see how forcefully some people sought to attach themselves to Nick, as well as how wounded and resentful those left behind could feel. I set my own terms of intimacy and distance as best I could, embarrassed by the way people would disempower, even disenfranchise themselves, just to be in his company.

As a biographer, I came to define the cloudy territory I found myself in as akin to a working friendship. I understood that when the work was over, the friendship would likely pass. This was the dilemma Nick left behind for people as their life story got sucked up into the slipstream of his, forever measured against his adventure and the songs that marked it. I vowed to avoid this fatal attachment. Though, of course, as you get to know people over time, things are never so straightforward. The act of maintaining a little distance can be confusing, perhaps even two-faced. So too can opening up.

On the third day of our meetings, the end of a school day, Nick and I went out for pizza with his ten-year-old twin sons, Arthur and Earl. Like many fathers who worked from home, Nick struck me as attentive and involved with his children, and very close to them, a good father. Earl seemed quieter and shyer, nearer to Susie in his tender demeanour. Although Arthur was fair in his looks, he took more after Nick and was robustly social. He was interested in magic and a bit of a performer. Arthur had an impressive rope trick he could do. Even when he showed me how he had managed the finale, a dramatic and quick untangling, I still could not work out how he had done it. Arthur tried to show me again a few times and

I failed to see the revelation each time he explained it. Eventually, Nick waved his hand at him to stop him and said, 'I think your secret is safe here in England, Arthur. Mark won't be able to take the rope trick back to Australia with him.'

By the summer of 2013, I was deep into the biography. Nick and I met in Melbourne at his mother Dawn's house. It was twilight and we walked with his sons to a nearby park. The boys shared a skateboard and what looked like a very good digital film camera. I was under the impression Earl was more accomplished on the skateboard, but it was Arthur who rode it slowly inside and around a hazily lit park rotunda while Earl climbed onto railings and filmed him. Nick called out to be careful. They explained they wanted to avoid showing the skateboard, to create the illusion that Arthur was floating like a bird or someone in a dream.

The loss of fifteen-year-old Arthur from a cliff fall on 14 July 2015 was a terrible tragedy for Nick and Susie and Earl and all the extended Cave family. By then my biography project had long unravelled as the quantity, quality and depth of Nick Cave's output overwhelmed me. What I had started writing became a baggy and unfinished monster with all the scope and cornucopia of *Moby Dick*. My idea for its form had involved conventional chronology and the nine lives of a cat, but also a symbolic under-structure pinned to Milton's *Paradise Lost*, a work Nick had referenced repeatedly with allusions to 'the red hand' of God.[6] I could see many easy parallels: God casts the rebellious Satan out of Heaven (Nick is banished by his father from his country home of Wangaratta); the Fallen Angel gathers his demonic cohorts to build Pandemonium (Nick meets the members of The Boys Next Door and they forge themselves at the Crystal Ballroom in St Kilda); Satan travels across space to wreak revenge on Eden (Nick travels to England to begin his assault on the garden of culture) … Such connections were loose and incidental, but also well mapped in song, as if Nick had been writing and reinforcing his own mythology all the way. Which, of course, he had.

After the death of Arthur, Nick felt he had been changed entirely. There was only before and after. 'I'm a different person now,' he said to me on a few occasions. In his opinion, this rendered what had been said in our conversations 'entirely redundant'.

Our communications dissipated and ceased. I occupied myself with my own struggles and life story, a messy and tangled narrative all its own as, by then, my grand Miltonian plans for a Nick Cave mega-biography had well and truly collapsed. I must say Nick was only ever kind and understanding over the period when I went off the rails, expressing concern for my wellbeing and encouraging me to rebuild myself, as well as offering good-humoured conversation and a few spikes of pragmatism. But the road we were on was parting, as I always knew it would. The ride was over.

I lamented that I nonetheless did have a biographical volume almost done, a portrait of the artist as a young man and all that he promised ahead of him. A book that, with just a bit more work, was even more important in the wake of what had occurred. This book keyed itself in to Nick Cave's childhood and youth, from Wangaratta to the Crystal Ballroom scene in Melbourne, through the early landscapes, novels, artists, loves and friendships that shaped him. Much of which Nick would continually refer to in his songs, books, poetry and films. I believe this Australian youth, this Australian being, to run deep inside him. I also believe it relates to something paradoxical about the nature of 'Australianness' itself: how we undervalue and disguise, and even dismiss what we are as we look outward from our culture for international affirmations, losing sight of our history in a sometimes brutal and ongoing act of forgetting. The older we get, however, the more we begin to reach back to our youth as essential to who we are and who we still can be.

What emerges in this biography is a remembering of that world. Not just Nick Cave's story of growing up, but the memories and stories of all those around him. The life and times of a boy on fire, with all that he absorbed in order to dream himself into becoming one of the darkest, and then one of the brightest, of our rock 'n' roll stars. Light enough for the many to share.

Nick Cave backstage at the Tiger Lounge, Royal Oak Hotel,
Richmond, 1978 *(Phill Calvert)*

PART I

THE
RIDER

Such
Is Life

MELBOURNE & SYDNEY

2007

'Too little, too late,' he says. Nicholas Edward Cave has just turned fifty, and old wheels are grinding inside him.[1] His car pulls forward at the traffic lights and makes its way further down his former stomping ground, Fitzroy Street, St Kilda. The silvery light of an encroaching Melbourne dusk settles over the peak-hour traffic and he catches a glimpse of the waters of Port Phillip Bay at the street's bottom end, as if he could drive into this same silvering and disappear.

It is 28 October 2007 and Nick Cave is about to fly to Sydney to be inducted into the ARIA (Australian Record Industry Association) Hall of Fame. The singer describes it as 'the seventh circle of hell', then 'a bad party you can never escape. Let's face it, it's really a form of punishment.'[2] For a moment he considers stopping the vehicle so he can hop out on Fitzroy Street and run away. The ARIA Awards! He puts his head to the glass as if he has a headache. *Thump.* 'God, I'd rather just go and get a kebab.'[3]

The only people he'd care to associate with in this Oz Rock Valhalla to which he is being condemned are The Saints and AC/DC, he reckons. There's Michael Hutchence too, of course, 'a beautiful guy', but Cave's friendship with him was not about halls of fame or even music, not INXS anyway; that was quietly understood. There was something else between them. Something brotherly only people in their shoes could share. Those stoned afternoons they'd spent trying to pull their lives together as well as having fun. Mornings when the pair would take their respective son and daughter, Luke and Tiger Lily, to a local park. The Portobello Café, which they bought together in London in 1995; that place never made a profit. The phone messages Michael left him two years later, so wild and funny, and in retrospect so in need of contact. Michael's voice on his answering machine saying, 'I'm coming to see The Bad Seeds play in Sydney, Nick. I'll be up the front throwing rotten fruit at you.'[4] Nick still has the hotel number jotted down in an old diary somewhere, along with a note to call Michael back in Sydney.[5] 'Ask for Murray River's room,' Hutchence said with a laugh.[6]

November 1997. Ten years earlier. What a bad month that was. Beginning with Kevin 'Epic Soundtracks' Godfrey – the former drummer for Swell Maps, Crime and the City Solution, and These Immortal Souls – turning out the lights in his West Hampstead flat and never waking up. Nick can only shrug when Epic's name comes up. He didn't know him that well. 'And to tell you the truth, I was never a big fan of his music, but people I rated always rated him, so I had to respect that.' Epic died in his sleep, cocaine and heroin in his system, autopsy results inconclusive. The information would reach Nick through mutual friends, including his Bad Seeds collaborator and bandmate Mick Harvey and the singer Dave Graney, both of whom were troubled by Epic's death and what could have been a decision or plain bad luck.

A few weeks later Michael Hutchence passed away at a five-star hotel in Double Bay, Sydney, under similarly cloudy circumstances. Ten years ago, almost to the day. Nick ended up writing out a set of lyrics when he got the news: 'Adieu, adieu, kind friends adieu, I can no longer stay with you ...' The words were drawn from an eighteenth-century west-country English ballad called 'There Is a Tavern in the Town': the lament of a suicidal woman destroyed by her lover's insensitivity. It is also known in some quarters as 'The Drunkard's Song'. In Nick's diary version, various lines are reworked as the narrator's voice slips uneasily between a method actor's empathy for what is happening and a storyteller's detached insights.[7]

Looking from the outside, who'd have thought Nick would have been the good influence in this friendship, the one who learned to swim while Michael was going under? 'I liked Michael a lot. He was very passionate. There was a truth to Michael that was very impressive. When I knew him he was going through a really bad period, being hounded night and day by the English press. He couldn't move a muscle. I didn't understand the extent of it till we went out to this club together. We got in fine. But when we left there were paparazzi everywhere. Someone pushed me. In a rage I pushed them back. Michael pulled me away. Then we left. He said to me, "You can't do that, it's a waste of time." It was criminal what they did to Michael. They hunted that guy to his death.'

These weren't the first or last people Nick would witness leaving this world unexpectedly. Not by a long shot. Ever since his father, Colin Cave, was killed in a car crash, he had been learning what it meant to live with the dead. The road accident happened on the first Sunday of 1979, just a few months after Nick turned twenty-one. It took him a long time to accept how much it affected him, Nick says, 'to engage with it or even understand it'. Between his mother's pain and the thrill of leaving for London a year later, in February 1980, with his fine young band, The

Boys Next Door, Nick had pushed his own feelings aside. He only saw later how the loss of his father intensified something that went back to his boyhood days in Wangaratta. Not even the town as it was, really, more the way he would remember it and then mythologise it. Things like the railroad tracks, the slaughterhouse, the river where he swam and its willow trees had become the stuff of songs such as 'Red Right Hand' and 'Sad Waters' for him, a real and yet imaginatively transformed land akin to William Faulkner's Yoknapatawpha County.[8]

As if to confirm a rural Gothic streak straight out of a novel by the likes of Faulkner or Flannery O'Connor, Nick had even found a body when he was a kid. Someone from the old people's home had stumbled down in their pyjamas to the shade of the riverbank and lain down to sleep in the mud. For the twelve-year-old Nick and his friends it had been the thrill of their day, astride their bikes on a narrow strip of road staring down at the still figure. Amid their excited chatter, one of the boys silenced everyone. '"Show some respect for a dead man," he said. I really remember that.' Nick could not wait to get home and tell his mother about their discovery. 'She wasn't very happy with the way the police had spoken to us, actually. They told us all to piss off when they arrived.'

Nick Cave's old friend, photographer and journalist Bleddyn Butcher, is driving him to the airport in Melbourne today so Nick can get to the ARIAs on time. Bleddyn's black suit and bolo tie accentuate a bright face and bob of unruly white hair that faintly suggest the appearance of a frontier-town Tennessee judge. An exceptionally long fingernail on the pinky of Bleddyn's right hand serves him well for playing guitar at home; it has Oriental overtones too, symbolising a man of culture and breeding who is above manual labour. In *Taxi Driver*, a much-loved film of Nick's teenage years, Harvey Keitel's pimp character has a similarly long talon, painted red and used for the convenience of sniffing heroin on the go.

A figure of almost enraged intelligence, Butcher is made of more affectionate materials than such associations might indicate. 'I think I can call Nick a friend,' he tells me later, touching his chest. 'I think so. I feel it in my heart.'[9] Having photographed Nick for the *NME* ever since the singer's arrival in London with The Birthday Party in 1980, and run an official Nick Cave fanzine called *The Witness* in the late 1990s, the London-born, Perth-raised Butcher can lay claim to knowing Nick's work as well as anyone. Unlike many in Nick's orbit, he's never shy of making his judgements, or his appreciations, known, something that moves Cave to drolly comment, 'You don't go to Bleddyn for a response when you have something at a sensitive stage of development.'

Even so, here Bleddyn Butcher is, back in Melbourne and driving 'The Dark Lord' (as he likes to call Nick) around again. It amuses him that the singer did not apply for a learner's permit till 2001 in the United Kingdom, which is where Cave continues to reside today, in the seaside community of Brighton and Hove. The driver's licence might be interpreted as yet another marker of Nick's drug-free lifestyle. Let's face it, the 1980s was not a time when you wanted to see The Dark Lord behind the wheel of any vehicle coming your way. Bleddyn can only arch an eyebrow and observe, 'Nick is still a little prone to lose focus behind the wheel if he's talking to you.'[10]

Bleddyn has picked Nick up from his mother's place, where he sat around over tea and homemade cheese scones with Dawn Cave while her son packed his bags. The sparring intelligence between mother and son has the light touch of comedy: Nick's lugubrious, 'Yes, Mum'; Dawn's wry comebacks; the jolts of affection that unite them and pull you closer to them when they are together. It is surprising to Bleddyn, but there is one word that is rather underused in critical appreciations of Nick's work, yet is present throughout a host of his songs, and in the way he sings them: *tenderness*.

Dawn Cave's present happiness is a matter of long-term relief as much as anything else. After all the years of turbulence, her son 'has settled down so well' with his wife, Susie, an English former model and Vivienne Westwood fashion muse. 'And he's such a good father to the twins, Arthur and Earl. If Nick's father, Colin, were alive today he'd be so proud,' she says later in an interview. 'And Nick's free of the drugs, too.' Dawn holds her hands together in an unconscious prayer motion as she contemplates it. Being with Susie made all the difference in the end: 'They saved each other, I think. I could have run down the street and jumped up and kicked my heels together, I was that relieved and happy when Nick first told me he was going into rehab. Little did I know how hard it would be, how long it would take, but I will always remember that first time [in 1988]. At last, I thought, at last.' [11] Ten years on, and four more rehab centres later, Susie Bick finally came onto the scene. At last, at last.

Dawn waved goodbye to Nick and Bleddyn from the door of her home and closed the security grille. Nick had told her the night before that a few old friends were ribbing him about an exhibition of his life and work coming up in Melbourne, entitled, appropriately enough – 'and with all due humility!' he says – Nick Cave: The Exhibition.[12] Pennants showing his face are already fluttering from flagpoles around The Arts Centre in the heart of the city to promote the show, which opens in another week. Together with the 2007 ARIA Hall of Fame induction this evening, it contributes to a rather uncool impression that this one-time punk rocker and wild man of Australian rock 'n' roll is being institutionalised and tamed.

The putdowns are endless, a few quite barbed. Nick's ex-girlfriend and first great muse, Anita Lane, will be there with the others on opening night, going through room after room, heckling him and comparing Nick Cave: The Exhibition to a game of *Where's Wally?*

Anita Lane. She always had a way of shaking Nick out of himself. Old friends sometimes refer to her as 'his first wife'. You can barely see the scar she left on Nick Cave's face two decades ago. He touches it, almost without thinking, as he sits in traffic and Bleddyn edges their vehicle forward. Fitzroy Street in St Kilda makes him think of her, especially with the night coming on. It's where their adventures began in the late 1970s, with art and music, with heroin too, and a whole way of being that carried on across the world, to London, then West Berlin and a few other cities as well. On the cover of *Tender Prey* (1988), the scar looks as fresh as a rapier slash from a duel. It was a vegetable knife, prosaically enough, a middle-of-the-day domestic in West Berlin during which Anita took a chunk out of his cheek and went at him for another piece. Nick had unwisely decided to end their relationship once and for all by telling her that he had a new girlfriend. The relationship would recover, sputtering on for another year.

Amphetamines could do that to you back then. The drugs flowing from the East were very high-grade. Speed addictions would send half the city mad, leaving people damaged and broken just as the Wall was falling and Germany was being reunited. Nick would hear the crowds shouting in the streets while he and The Bad Seeds were working at Hansa Studios on the night of 9 November 1989. He would not allow the band to leave the studio to take a look, relenting only to let them watch the television news. In truth, the band were not that interested. Like many West Berliners they anticipated people from the East bringing down the tone of their neighbourhood, breaking through the Wall and singing about freedom – yeah, sure – but mostly screaming out for stonewash denim, Coca Cola and 'buying bananas', Nick says. For him it was time to finish the album – and get out of town permanently. Owing money to various dealers only added to his motivation to leave while everything was falling down.

Ever since Nick had left Australia, he had lived in a wilful state of exile, and more than a little like a man on the run. Having used up Melbourne, London and West Berlin, he'd made the city of São Paulo, in Brazil, his next port of call after coming out of a legally enforced stint of rehab for the first time in England. On a tour of Brazil at the end of 1988 he'd met a new lover, Viviane Carneiro, and found fresh inspiration in the culture he encountered there. Brazil had quickly become his new home and marked a new direction in his music. *The Good Son* had been recorded there, and he'd only skulked back into West Berlin in late 1989 to finish the sound mixes at Hansa, his drug debts and the temptation to relapse with friends making it a necessarily brief return.

Fleeing back to Brazil was what old hands in NA and AA referred to as 'doing a geographic' – running elsewhere, only to discover you took your problems with you. He wrote 'The Ship Song' not long after coming out of rehab, farewelling Anita and longing for what Viviane and a new world promised. After enjoying a celebrity welcome to Brazil, Nick thought he liked the day-to-day of being 'nothing but a gringo' in São Paulo. But even outsiders can get tired of things. He was never that great with foreign languages. Viviane felt that Nick's dependency on her to speak for him drained him of his enthusiasm for her country.[13] That and the fact he was drinking like a fish, the classic ex-junkie way to self-medicate. Nick tried New York as an alternative base, but it was too crazy there to set up a family. São Paulo, West Berlin, São Paulo, New York, London, São Paulo, London again, then back to São Paulo ... it was getting hard to keep track of where Nick lived. He made firmer plans to relocate to England, and Viviane, now his wife, and their young son, Luke, followed him to try to make another home together.

Back more or less living in London by 1993, and much the worse for wear from drinking and drugging again, Nick found himself being interviewed by *MTV Europe* in a bar. Sitting beside him was The Pogues' sacked singer, Shane MacGowan, perhaps the most famous booze-hound in rock 'n' roll since the early days of Tom Waits. Nick and Shane had put together a Christmas song the previous year, a sincere version of Louis Armstrong's 'What a Wonderful World' that swam out of their shipwrecked reputations. Many critics found it hard to distinguish its pained idealism from drunken karaoke. MacGowan's profoundly Irish music had made Nick aware of a great loss in his own life – and the lost horizon he felt was lurking below their interpretation of 'What a Wonderful World'. 'The older I get,' Nick told *MTV,* 'the more inclined I am to think that you need some kind of roots and you need to think that you belong somewhere ... I've kind of destroyed that part of me as a person. I really don't feel I do belong anywhere anymore.'[14] It was a sad confession to make on camera. But Nick was bullshitting himself. He was always going to have to answer to home sooner or later. Or if not quite home exactly, the gravitational pull of a past he'd yearn for in his songs and buck against in his life as if there were something way back in time to be ashamed of.

Home. There were days when Nick had 'this awful intuition of Melbourne' looming over him. When it felt as if everybody was trying to own him and 'any sign of me enjoying success is construed as me getting too big for my boots'. It makes coming back to Australia hard, even a little suffocating. It is not so far away from the ideas he played with in the old Birthday Party song 'Sonny's Burning'. Crime and punishment in his work were as ambiguous as the sadomasochistic twist to his heart in those days. 'Sonny's Burning' enhanced the demonic sexual presence glowing around him in 1982, irradiated in the song by repressed desires that consume him. The narrative positioned the listener as complicit in a torture scenario, enjoying the warmth and light that comes from burning Sonny alive. Birthday Party performances would be incited by a ritual shout-out before it began: 'Hands up who wants to die?!'[15]

Though he played the seductive predator in the song, a carny-like presenter of a sinister peepshow, Nick was slyly sanctifying himself as the victim of an audience revelling in his self-destructive impulses. Twenty-five years later and here he is, no longer destroying himself, which seems to invite greater resentment from some quarters. His crimes in 2007 are health and happiness; his punishment delivered by friends who once supported him. Susie chides Nick for putting up with their snide comments at the Melbourne social events they are invited to: 'Why do you bother with these people when they behave this way towards you?' Nick is unusually silent and unable to answer. But he definitely broods on it. Friends of a world he had left behind.

As Nick left his mother's house for the ARIA Hall of Fame induction, Dawn sensed his troubled mood and pulled him aside to give him a tight hug and a pat on the back. 'Hold your head up high, Nick,' she told him, 'and fuck them all!'

———

Nick Cave laughs in the car about what he describes as his then 81-year-old mother's 'sage advice'. She's a retired librarian, and it's not her usual manner of speaking. He'll pocket it away for future reference, 'a maxim to keep in mind', even tell Dawn later, to her horror, that he is thinking of getting it translated into Latin and put on a family coat of arms in England. Fuck them all! He wishes he had it emblazoned on a T-shirt right now – *Fuck lemma totus*? That isn't quite right. If his old friend, the Boys Next Door and Birthday Party bassist, Tracy Pew, were alive, he'd translate it in a snap – and probably come up with a suitably ribald T-shirt design as well.

An epileptic fit killed Tracy Pew on 7 November 1986. Nick thinks that after years of heavy drinking Tracy's sobriety may have brought on the seizures that eventually ended his life at age twenty-eight. 'I don't *know* that for sure, but it can happen,' says Nick, like he does know. It was yet another event that made the month of November chime with dark anniversaries. 'Tracy's death was a really sad business.'

And if Tracy were alive today, what would he make of Nick Cave: The Exhibition? Ah, Nick suspects, he would probably give him shit for being a wanker. *Pennants, you prick!* Nick laughs at the thought, questions, 'How you can love someone so much – and yet have so many punch-ups with that same person? We used to hit each other all the time. I don't even remember why now.'

Despite the gibes he's been getting, Nick says, 'I'm actually very proud of the exhibition at The Arts Centre. Trying to look at it from the outside, as a show about this guy called "Nick Cave", I think it is kinda interesting.' But the 2007 ARIA Hall of Fame induction is harder for him to come to terms with. He looks over at Bleddyn and realises his friend is rattling on about TS Eliot and the artistry of theft, a much worked-over topic between them whether they're talking about blues music or Greek mythology or, as Nick likes to put it, 'my favourite subject, me'.

Bleddyn shifts his conversation to Cormac McCarthy's novel *The Road* and asks, 'What did you think of that vision of the fish at the end?' Then it's back to TS Eliot and how the world will end 'not with a bang but a whimper'.[16]

Nick feels a vague headache coming on, one of the by-products of the insomnia he suffers when he has had a bad night. 'Yes, Bleddyn,' he says. 'Cheer me up already, and no more end-of-the-world stuff, please.' But Nick is only half-listening as he starts to jot down ideas for the acceptance speech tonight. 'Look, do you know any good dirty jokes I can use? I think I'd like to be funny.' He hunches over his notebook and scratches away. Bleddyn says something crude in French as their car hauls to a stop again, caught in traffic barely half a block further down the road. Nick begins to sing The Loved Ones' 'Sad Dark Eyes' under his breath, till it trails off into an embarrassed croak while the car shunts along.

The song is all mixed up inside him, the words of Gerry Humphrys merging with his own lyrical improvisations. It's yet another bastard marriage in a classic interpretative repertoire that includes Cave's diabolically violent 'Stagger Lee', a drastic rewrite of an old blues ballad formerly known as 'Stack O' Lee', and a raucously possessed slant on Bob Dylan's 'Wanted Man'. Over the years, the way Nick Cave reworks songs and makes them his own will almost be as important to understanding him as his originals. Maybe the covers are even more revealing, as Bleddyn implies when speaking of TS Eliot's ideas about theft and transcendence. How does one define a voice you can call your own anyway? It comes from everything you've borrowed.

'Sad Dark Eyes' still sounds good to Nick. It makes him think again of being a kid in Wangaratta, of his eldest brother, Tim, coming back to their home town from yet another moratorium march in Melbourne against Australia's involvement in the Vietnam War. Tim was the real wildcat in the family. A young Nick relished hearing his teenage brother's tales of the big smoke, as well as the black wafers of vinyl Tim returned with: LPs by Cream, Jimi Hendrix and, yeah, The Loved Ones.

Wangaratta slides over Nick's vision of St Kilda today and overwhelms it. Wang! The heat haze of summer rippling off the bitumen, the subzero winter mists chilling a wire fence so cold you couldn't touch it in the morning. It's like the country town is floating, and him as a boy along with it. 'That town was all about walking,' Nick says, with undisguised affection, 'just wandering around on foot.' More random thoughts roll by: a teacher holding up a Bic biro and explaining to the class they won't need their fountain pens anymore; his school stopping to witness grainy black-and-white satellite footage of the first man on the moon. The closest Nick ever got to sex education, he says, was a documentary in biology class on the birth of a kangaroo. Left to his own devices, Nick liked to contemplate 'how hot Elizabeth Montgomery looked on *Bewitched*, the way she wrinkled her nose' to cast a spell. Oh boy. 'I couldn't work out whether it was her or Carolyn Jones as Morticia on *The Addams Family* that first aroused my interest in women.' Talk about patterning behaviour. The secretarial types and the Goth girls imprinted on his formative desires – thank you, crap sixties television. Nick looks startled and says, 'Oh my god, I married Morticia!' Then he relaxes again and says, 'Please stop me. I am really talking rubbish now.'

These days, whenever journalists ask him about his past he tells them to 'just Google it!'[17] They usually do. But it's mostly half-truths and data, not much inner life or mystery; it all seems inadequate or wrong. It took Nick a long time to get over his disgust with himself about doing interviews during the 1980s, and the awful truth that they were among the few times he allowed intimacy into his increasingly drug-fucked life. No wonder he was so ambivalent about the process. Then to have things he said ten, twenty, even thirty years ago quoted back at him like he would never change his mind, let alone remember it? If he even meant what he said in the first place? His mother tells him that it's his own fault. 'You do like to exaggerate when you tell these people your stories, Nick.'[18]

Dawn was right. Nick would develop a practice of rehearsing his quotes in casual conversations till he had them sounding exactly how he wanted them to be in print. Once he had them down, he'd mostly stick to the script – and would often regret it when he didn't. Like all contrary artists, Nick Cave wants his tale told on multiple levels: larger than life, yet right on point; how it was, but always through the prism of how he sees it now.

In his Birthday Party days Nick regarded his audience with something approaching disgust; these days he appreciates the communal energy that rallies around him. Now and again the old confrontational edge will rear up, of course, giving people a frisson of how it feels to be attacked as much as entertained. But the beast in Nick is well reined in. It's getting easier and easier to forget he was never an Oz rock hero at the start; you will discover that quickly enough on Google. If anything, Nick Cave cast himself as the villain to succeed: the prince of darkness, the junkie Hamlet of rock 'n' roll[19] ... yak, yak, yak ... God, how the press can go on. And having become a drug-free family man, driver's licence and all, 'I am suddenly "Quiet and Contented of Hove"!' Living one's life under other people's slogans can be a laborious business, especially when some of them have sprung, well practised, from your own lips.

After a while the stories run on without him and seem to be about someone else. Decades of this have made him obsess about controlling his own narrative. He admits he finds it impossible to say much in public without seeing the words appearing in black and white before his eyes. 'It can make you a little self-aware.'

In any case, here he is in late 2007, not doing so badly: on his way to Australia's rock 'n' roll hall of fame. An international star with million-selling recordings, including 'Where the Wild Roses Grow' (his duet with fellow Australian Kylie Minogue) and classics such as 'The Ship Song', 'Red Right Hand', 'Into My Arms' and 'The Mercy Seat'. The résumé is so rich as to be boundless:

writing a row of film scores and award-winning scripts such as *The Proposition* (2005); soundtracks for theatre and dance projects from London to Reykjavík; invitations to curate arts festivals and give lectures; the odd bit of acting over the years ('I think I've proved it's not my forte; I'm stiff as a board'); and even a set of violent, white-trash, one-page plays he worked on with Lydia Lunch when he was off his head in his twenties. It has been a long journey from those chaotic early days to singing with the likes of Johnny Cash[20] and creating songs that people ask to be married and buried to. And yet in so many ways it is all of a piece.

'There's more to come, more to come,' Nick says, hinting at a veritable deluge: another film script in development about a sex-addicted door-to-door salesman[21]; more soundtracks; and a collection of poems tracing the history of violence in literature that he plans to edit if the copyright issues can be ironed out. As if that's not enough, the singer launched a side-band project in 2006 called Grinderman. Their sexed-up, prog-rock, blues-metal and what Nick thought were some pretty satirical lyrics are earning him a fresh round of misogyny charges from critics, as well as plenty of midlife-crisis comments. Even from his mother. Dawn told Susie, 'I think Grinderman is Nick's change-of-life record.' Nick rolls his eyes. The porn-star moustache he has taken to sporting only encourages such impressions. Even so, Nick wonders how anybody could regard a Grinderman song such as 'No Pussy Blues' as anything other than self-mocking. A friend messaged him earlier in the day from Los Angeles about the last Grinderman show there, saying he had never seen so many girls in miniskirts in one place before. It really makes Nick laugh. He texted back: 'It's sexy music, man! The girls love it! I tell you, Grinderman are the rock 'n' roll equivalent of chick lit!'[22]

As usual Nick feels the old reactive surges sparking extremes in him, the desire to take things even further now that people are angry or upset. 'If people think what I say in Grinderman is bad, wait till they see what I am doing next.' In this Nick has long felt an unlikely bond with a renowned feminist thinker and fellow Australian expatriate. 'I love Germaine Greer, if only for the fact she just stirs things up again. I don't always agree with everything she says but I understand, to a degree, where she's coming from: that it's not always necessary to be right. Sometimes just to provoke is enough.'[23]

While the self-titled Grinderman release continues to dominate Nick Cave's life over 2007, a fresh album of songs entitled *Dig!!! Lazarus Dig!!!* is ready to go with his main band, The Bad Seeds. Like the gridlocked traffic Cave is caught in today, this new Bad Seeds album has been postponed by his record label, Mute, until people digest the Grinderman recording and the plethora of interests the singer is unleashing on the world. Mute label boss Daniel Miller is worried about how to manage it all: the range and quantity of Nick's output verges on a mania.

What's driving this creativity? An ex-junkie's need to stay busy, perhaps? This theory has been doing the rounds for ages. It's a post-rehab 'condition' that may have added velocity to Cave's output since the late 1990s, but a close look at the singer's life shows the raging work ethic was always there. For a time in the 1980s you could argue Nick Cave was the hardest-working heroin addict in showbiz. At his personal worst, during the West Berlin years, his output was just as phenomenal, even frenzied.

People say Nick is a driven man: all those records, books, films and live shows across the planet; all the people who have fallen in his wake. Cave seems to share in Keith Richards' hardy rock 'n' roll voodoo in that respect, standing where others have dropped like flies. Again and again friends will note how ridiculously lucky Nick is. The guy always lands on his feet. Nine lives like a cat. Others say you make your own luck. But there was something Shane Middleton, the roadie for Cave's teenage group, The Boys Next Door, observed a long time ago that struck a deeper nerve: 'I don't think Nick's a driven man, but a fleeing man, running from the fear of failure.'[24]

It's true there's a need to prove his talents are still there, to show that he hasn't stopped moving forward. Maybe he is striving to prove something to his long-dead father, too? The pop psychologists would love to hear him admit to such thoughts. 'We Call Upon the Author to Explain', a song on *Dig!!! Lazarus, Dig!!!*, goes right to the heart of that material: rock stardom, fan worship, dead-father hang-ups, disputes with God, the full technicolour yawn.[25]

'It's all good.' That's the shorthand Nick's older sons, Jethro and Luke, use on him whenever he bugs them about how they are going. The boys were born to two different mothers in two different countries – Beau Lazenby in Australia and Viviane Carneiro in Brazil – ten days apart in 1991.[26] It's one way to start a decade. Distance would strain and complicate the relationship with Jethro as Nick reached out and tried to be a father when he became older. He would be much more involved with Luke's day-to-day upbringing in London, and was in some ways saved from addiction by having to look after Luke. Nick valued being a father more than anything else in the world, though he may not have appeared to be the most orthodox of parents. He started making changes; he was fighting to get a few things right. But it wasn't all good before he met Susie in 1998. Not at all. PJ Harvey ditching him over the phone because of his heroin habit had caused him to break down and cry.[27] 'Just say you don't love me,' he'd demanded as she gave him the bad news. 'Just say that you don't love me.' She did. And that was really that. He'd half-joke that he almost dropped his syringe when she told him it was over, but that kind of honesty was as much some bravado to mask the hurt. It was a devastating wake-up call for Nick. That and Susie Bick refusing to see him till he got clean.

Jethro and Luke needing him, losing in love with PJ Harvey, knowing that heroin was blunting his ability to create as he got older, the sheer boredom of feeding a habit, the work that scoring involved, then meeting and keeping Susie, and the birth of Arthur and Earl – at last, at last, his world was changing, step by step. It can take a while to see that happening when it's your own life, like starlight reaching you long after the fact. People would ask him if his music had changed because his life had changed, but they did not understand how the songs could be things made to will yourself into another state of being. It's why art is so dangerous as well as inspirational. It can make things happen, terrible things. It can be your liberator. But it can be your gaoler, too, if you're not careful. It reminded Nick of that old Tarkovsky film *Stalker.* You needed to develop an understanding of the difference between your deepest wish and your most powerful desire, and how much your work could fuel one or the other, if you were ever going to survive the journey you set out on as an artist.

Sitting in the passenger seat, Nick Cave grows agitated once more about this 2007 ARIA Hall of Fame induction. He says that he has been told they won't include The Bad Seeds because there are 'foreigners' in the band. Nor will they include Cave's first great band, The Birthday Party, the Melbourne group that evolved out of The Boys Next Door and shotgunned Cave onto the English stage as the underground music icon of the post-punk era, a successor to the vaudeville viciousness of the Sex Pistols' Johnny Rotten and the tense interior realms of Joy Division's Ian Curtis.

Like Rotten and Curtis, Cave became a true Romantic figure on the UK cultural scene – mad, bad and dangerous to know.[28] He did not do it alone. The Boys Next Door, The Birthday Party, The Bad Seeds – all had given him his wings. Nick Cave considers his solitary honour tonight, and says that he regards the exclusion of his bandmates as an affront 'typical' of an Australian music industry against which he has always battled, an industry that has never really understood him. 'We always had this thing, too, way back then, that anybody the Australian music industry liked just couldn't be any good,' he admits. 'We didn't want to be a part of it.'

And now he has made it, the belated pat on the back. That is how it seems to him. Onya, mate! 'Foreigners!' Can you believe that? Nick re-examines his attitude from every side, the good and the bad of it, as he sits stuck here in Bleddyn's Mercedes a few hours before the ceremony. Yet it is obvious the coming evening means a great deal to him precisely because it is much-longed-for recognition from home, the one place his Australianness can at last be understood. 'We're an Australian band making Australian music,' he will say of The Bad Seeds at the ARIAs. All Nick's emotions centre on these simple words as he puts pen to paper in the car and jots them down.

Bleddyn brakes suddenly, almost rear-ending the truck in front, flinging everyone forward for a moment. 'Sorry,' he says. Tram bells ring once more. The traffic finally moves. And Nick Cave is released from Fitzroy Street, St Kilda, and all his thinking at last.

Fuck them all.

That night in Sydney, Nick's attention is drawn to the press release that has gone out prior to the induction. Ed St John, chairman of the ARIA Awards Committee, is quoted fulsomely: 'Nick Cave has enjoyed – and continues to enjoy – one of the most extraordinary careers in the annals of popular music. His contribution over the past thirty years was never limited by geography or nationality and nor could it ever be described in terms of hit records, chart positions or radio airplay. He is an Australian artist like Sidney Nolan is an Australian artist – beyond comparison, beyond genre, beyond dispute. As an industry we should be immensely proud and humbled by Nick Cave's achievements; I know I speak for the ARIA Board when I say it's a real pleasure to be inducting this artist into the Hall of Fame.'[29]

The comparison to Nolan strikes a chord in Cave's heart just before he strides out to accept the honour and receive a standing ovation. He feels surprised, even overwhelmed, which is not what he expected after brewing over the event all day back in Melbourne. Ed St John must have known Nick nursed ambitions to be a painter. Cave's biggest living hero as a teenager was actually the flamboyant wunderkind of Australian art, Brett Whiteley. But Sidney Nolan, eh? The reference is oddly more on point. Whiteley flamed out on heroin; Nolan grew old and grand and endured. Cave's almost at the microphone, and those phenomenal Ned Kelly paintings by Sidney Nolan rise up like phantoms in his mind.[30]

Oh well, here I am, he thinks. Centre stage right. The ARIA gallows! Such is life.[31] But there's something brash to Nick Cave's manner as he begins to speak, something overly theatrical and forced about his speech. 'I cannot really accept this until we get a few things straight,' he says.[32] He then wonders loudly – too loudly, it seems – why The Birthday Party and The Bad Seeds are not included in the Hall of Fame. And he takes it upon himself to induct them all along with him, one by one – but leaving out The Birthday Party's vital original drummer, Phill Calvert. Despite Cave's insistence on giving due credit to his bandmates, the exclusion of Calvert will leave a less-generous impression in the minds of some of those who saw both The Boys Next Door and The Birthday Party in their flaming heyday. Had Nick just forgotten Phill, as he would later claim, or was it true that even thirty years after a rupture, the singer could not bring himself to thank an old comrade?[33] Oh yeah, people will tell you, Nick really knows how to hold a grudge. Don't be fooled by the charm. Wait till he cuts you down, they warn; everybody gets their turn.

Despite the praise that will be heaped upon *Dig!!! Lazarus, Dig!!!* in reviews, Nick Cave tends to hear the compromises that were made between him and Warren Ellis and Mick Harvey during the recording process. Mick would turn things down when mixing in the studio, seeking out subtlety and depth; but, when he left, Nick and Warren would turn them back up, wanting power and dynamism. It got a little childish. The tensions with Mick are only going to grow.

Nick loves Daniel Miller and Mute but he thinks they underestimated Grinderman as a side project, and it has been 'a bit of a lost opportunity'. His homecoming to Melbourne, the ARIAs in Sydney, the exhibition about his life, turning fifty a few weeks earlier – all reinforce a deep unease rather than any sense of achievement. Nick leaves the triangular-shaped award behind on his mother's mantelpiece. 'ARIA ICONS: HALL OF FAME' it reads on a plaque at the base, above his name and the date, '28 October 2007'. He will wonder about it as he departs for the United Kingdom a few weeks later. How hard it was to maintain a hold on what was occurring as he stepped up to the microphone with his trophy and the stage seemed to skew away from him. 'As if I had somehow stumbled into the wrong movie,' Nick says, 'and I was playing the wrong part.'

King
and
Country

As he passes through Mount Buffalo National Park, then drops out of the coolness of the high country altogether, descending into the valley below, the heat becomes hard to take. It's in the high thirties out there, a stinker of a day, the sky a pale, hurtful blue that loses its colour in the glare. His tired eyes are as grey and mineralised as the road ahead; he blinks to water them. The time is headed towards 4 pm on Sunday, 7 January 1979, and he is in a hurry to get home. His white Ford Fairmont is not fitted with air-conditioning. He keeps winding the window up then down, an oven-temperature breeze offering little relief.

A former English teacher and amateur director for the Malvern Theatre in Melbourne, Colin Cave can reel off entire stretches of the Bard, a little Dostoyevsky, and Nabokov too, as a moment may demand. There is a lot preying on his mind this afternoon. The weekend's triumphs are fading, and the troublesome question of Nick is coming back into view. Most immediately, what to do about the police charges that look like being laid against his youngest son? A bandaged cut on Colin's right thumb irritates him as he grips the wheel.[1]

Colin takes consolation in the words of Vladimir Nabokov. A line from *Lolita* about life being like a work of art, its moments gathering together obscurely and strangely to form something greater that we can't quite see because the work is still unfinished. Yes, there is plenty ahead for him and Nicky, and for the whole family yet. A passionately held philosophy of 'continuing education', in both life and work, connects these thoughts with the Russian author's vaguely ironic words. Fate versus will: it's an interesting theme to consider.

The bitumen continues to waver before him, transforming what should be a three-hour return to Melbourne into what feels like one long drive into a heavy dream. The land around here is parched. On the horizon a few wispy rain clouds are struggling to form.

Colin is not far outside the town of Wangaratta, where he and his wife, Dawn, and their four young children – Tim, Peter, Nick and Julie – lived from late 1959 till the end of 1971. He doesn't push on into Wang. Instead Colin tears off the bitumen and onto the dirt of the Dockers Road, wrenching the steering wheel out of a gravel slide as he lead-foots the accelerator. Dust trails behind him and he disappears.

Seven years may have passed since he lived here, but this is an old, familiar realm. Later, questions will be nonetheless asked about what he was doing on these hazy excuses for roads. Visiting a thirty-acre block of land the family had purchased as a holiday place and was yet to build on? Going to see someone on an impulse? A look at the map suggests Colin Cave may have been taking a short cut, but the story of his movements will become as faint as the legend of these roads.

Summer always made for a difficult start to the year when he worked out here in the 1960s. Trying to keep students alert in the drowsing heat. As an English teacher in Wangaratta, he had enjoyed playing with the roots of language, striding into his first classes and chalking 'CAVE' then 'COLIN' side by side on the blackboard, then 'cave' and 'canem' below it, 'Latin for "beware" and "dog"!'[2]

His friend Bill O'Callaghan, the former mayor, recalls that 'like many teachers there was a bit of the thespian in him. Students ... never knew what to expect'.[3] A flamboyant, boom-voiced lover of literature with memorably bushy eyebrows – and 'nostrils that flared like a thoroughbred when he was excited'[4] – Colin Cave would not just recite *The Merchant of Venice* for his class, he would act it out, almost weeping the lines 'the quality of mercy is not strained'. Thirty years later his students would not only remember these displays vividly, they would describe them as life-changing.

It was as a galvanising and sometimes over-the-top high-school teacher, then as the founding chief executive officer of the town's new adult education centre, that Cave would make an impression – with enough energy left over to be both the director and sometime star of The Wangaratta Players. He also wrote the high-school anthem and submitted satirical verse to the local newspaper. Dawn Cave recalls how 'Colin really loved to shake things up wherever he went', but there was a faint feeling among his children that sometimes Dad had enough energy for everything except a family.

Because it was the first attempt of its kind outside Melbourne, the Wangaratta Centre for Continuing Education was used as a test case for the expansion of adult education across the entire state. Colin Cave was not unaware of this significance, or of the commitment needed to make it work. The caretaker who lived nearby remembers hearing the door frequently bang shut at 10 pm as Cave ended his day. His hands would be stained red and blue from the inks of the spirit duplicator he was forced to wrestle with so that the secretary could copy his furious output of letters and reports.[5]

Son Nick would inherit this obsessive work ethic. He would also soak up other influences that came through his father's agency. In the refurbished old school that became known as 'The Centre', Colin oversaw courses, talks, screenings of European films and exhibitions that took in such unlikely subject matter as 'Mexican Popular Art' and 'American Psychodelic [sic] Posters'. As a boy, Nick treated The Centre like a second home, wandering through the rooms and events almost at will.

Colin Cave rehearsing *Dinner with Family* with The Wangaratta Players, 1966. A classic Cave pose. *(courtesy of the Centre for Continuing Education, Wangaratta)*

It was here that Colin set up a workshop for the construction of small fibreglass boats known as Mirror-class dinghies. Locals loved to sail them of a weekend on the nearby, artificial Lake Mulwala. Colin even made one for Nick, the son who seemed to feel his father's absences and lack of attention the most. Nick proudly notes that Colin built it 'all by himself. He painted it bright yellow and named it *Caprice*.'

Nick was too young to make much use of it, and not particularly interested in sailing. 'I just hung around on the foreshore of the lake,' Nick says. 'Got a crush on a girl there, though, a skinny thing called Libby Meek – mostly because she wore a Jimi Hendrix T-shirt.' He would end up spending hours, either alone or in his mother's company, watching his father and his older brothers and younger sister on the water calling out to each other. Years later, Nick Cave would say, 'Dad loved that boat.'[6]

When Colin Cave announced his imminent departure from Wangaratta in 1971 to become Director of the Council for Adult Education (CAE) in Melbourne, many locals were saddened. He had only recently been named Wangaratta's 1970 Citizen of the Year.

Colin suggested another local teacher, Adrian Twitt, as an appropriate successor at The Centre. Unfortunately, Victoria's rigidly conservative Liberal premier, Henry Bolte, sought to overturn this nomination. Twitt's face had been recognised from an old newspaper photo that showed him leading a moratorium march against the Vietnam War in Melbourne. Colin opposed the premier and fought to see his colleague given the job on merit. As always, Colin Cave proved a very hard man to resist. To many people's amazement, Colin got his way and Twitt was approved.

A full-page photo of Colin Cave was duly published in the *1971 Report from the Wangaratta Centre for Continuing Education,* with these words printed boldly underneath to mark the end of an era: 'The King is Dead – Long Live the King!'

Cave's promotion to Director of the CAE was an acknowledgement of his determination and abilities. It has led him to spend most of the 1970s cultivating a blossoming network of centres across the state, all based on what has become known as 'the Wangaratta model', part of a revolution in community education he helped set in motion.[7] On the first weekend of January 1979 he is typically hard at it, the year barely started. A classical-music 'song camp' has been organised in the hill town of Harrietville. For a man of Cave's dynamism, the long drive from Melbourne to launch its debut is no obstacle. That Harrietville is a satellite of Wangaratta only adds to his interest.

Tourism brochures refer to the region he passes through on his drive home as 'Kelly Country'. A sign back on the Hume Highway entices visitors with the slogan 'Legends, Wine and High Country'. Colin Cave has long been fascinated by the convergence of myth and fact in the life of Ned Kelly, the rebel hero who formed out of this frontier and continued to ride on through history as an apparition of everything from Australian Republican sentiments to something eternally independent and anti-authoritarian in the national consciousness. Back in the Easter of 1967 Colin organised a national symposium in Wangaratta that would affect perspectives on the outlaw in everything from historical writings through to art, film and literature. Comparisons were made to Robin Hood, William Tell and Jesse James. The great Australian historian Manning Clark gave the keynote address.[8]

Something of a frustrated storyteller, Colin Cave wrote a florid introduction to a book that came out of that weekend, entitled *Ned Kelly: Man and Myth*. It is one of the best and most entertaining things in the collection. Colin highlights the moment Kelly was captured wearing the homemade armour he had forged out of melted iron ploughshares. A bizarre vision protected from gunfire, Kelly was shot in the leg and downed while searching for his younger brother outside the Glenrowan Inn at the height of the siege, his gang burned out and brutally slaughtered in a melee that saw some 15,000 bullets rained down upon them. The bodies of Steve Hart and Dan Kelly were found scorched almost beyond recognition inside the Glenrowan Inn. Fellow gang member Joe Byrne, Ned Kelly's second in command, was in good enough condition to be dragged outside and strung up against a wall like a marionette for press photographs.

Colin Cave likens this series of events to a western by the American director John Ford.[9] And he writes about it in a similar spirit of high-plains drama and regal fatality. Colin's eldest son, Tim, would later caution against reading too much into a performance on the page that was as much about 'Dad's passion for theatrically expressing himself'[10] as any inner obsession being revealed. It is a son's subtle distinction between public performance and the private man. But it is undeniably true that you hear a highly excited voice stirring out of what would normally be a more sober historical appreciation, a voice distinguished by a rush of exclamation marks and a zeal for bloody fantasies of crime and murder that borders on the unseemly as Colin Cave enthuses over all things Ned Kelly from start to finish:

> There is something in us which makes us forgive a man
> his sins so long as he is chivalrous. Moreover, Kelly rode a
> horse. This makes a man ten feet high, something to look

up to, something quick to come and go, something with
that air of mystery and mastery which stirs us all ...

But above all, Kelly was clad in armour. Here is the
impregnable disguise for which the civilized soul yearns ...
In the imagination of all who think of Kelly stirs that
faceless thing in iron, like Sidney Nolan's image of Kelly,
Iron with Eyes. What reckless jaunts, what romantic
exploits, what criminal escapades would we indulge in if
only we could be unrecognized! What would we not do
if only we had some armour to climb into which would
hide us, disguise us and protect us?[11]

You could hardly call this assessment 'subdued'. In *hearing*
that voice you are immediately struck by just how much these
rhetorical qualities – and the attraction to masks, as well as
violent or chivalrous freedoms – would resound in the songs of
his son.[12] Nick, then nine years old, never forgot seeing the suit of
armour on display at his father's symposium: the presence of the
breastplate; the headpiece that looked like an upturned billycan or
a welder's visor; the iron that Kelly had beaten into shape for his
last showdown at Glenrowan. Dented by bullets. 'It really made
quite an impact on me,' Nick says. So too the photograph of dead
Joe Byrne, disfigured and blackened by flames, his body held up
with guy-ropes, the gruesome historical precursor to Nick's song
'Sonny's Burning' and other works.[13]

When he became an art student in Melbourne, Nick could
truly appreciate why Sidney Nolan had made such a mysterious
icon of Ned Kelly in his paintings, as if the outlaw were a
medieval knight adrift in a colonial Australian Dreamtime. The
connections become even more vivid when Nick speaks of his
youth wandering the countryside around Wangaratta: 'It would
be fair to say that, unlike much nature I have experienced, the
Australian bush has always felt haunted to me, and the ghosts of

its bloody past felt ever-present and still speaking to us and had yet to be laid to rest. The enduring image of Ned rising from the mist in his armour was a powerful symbol in our household, and I was often told that story by my father when I was a boy.'

Inevitably, Colin Cave's book and the stories it contained would assume their own ghostly presence in Nick's library. Footnotes to a vast, obscure, unfinished masterpiece that Nick would try to bring together in the mock-heroic title of an Australian tour that marked his first ever steps onto the stage as a solo artist in the summer of 1983–84: 'Nick Cave – Man or Myth'.

Out on what has become the Dockers Road, Colin Cave drives on alone towards the Glenrowan tourist site and the Hume Highway that will take him back to Melbourne. Many will remark later that he always liked to flatten the accelerator. Tunnels of dust fly from the wheels behind him, sheep graze in the sparse shade of the gum trees. Colin hopes the charges against his youngest son – drunkenness, vandalism and petty theft – will be dismissed as nothing more than youthful tomfoolery before they are ever brought to court. They have shaken him as a parent. Always trouble with Nick, now twenty-one, so much trouble, starting from when he was a boy. It was why they had to send him away from Wangaratta to a boarding school in Melbourne when he was thirteen. If only juvenile pranks and unruliness were the issues confronting Colin and Dawn today. He hurries the car along. Getting back to Melbourne has begun to feel imperative, with the police pursuing their enquiries into Nick's behaviour.

Two images of Nick performing with The Boys Next Door linger in Colin's mind. The first from when he snuck along to watch them on New Year's Eve in 1977. A host of young bands had set up on Faraday Street in Carlton and started performing without any permission. As he was arriving, they were already playing. It took him a while, though, to see where his son was. It turned out Nick was rolling round in the gutter, groaning about somebody watching him.[14] There were teenagers drunk everywhere. The most awful noise. 'Punk Gunk' they had called the night. The scene was chaos. Colin departed, unimpressed. Nick had only to leave The Boys Next Door's set list on the kitchen table to prompt further reservations: 'Sex Crimes', 'Masturbation Generation' ... Despite this coarseness, Colin decided to take another look. The boys were playing at the Tiger Room, where they'd got themselves a residency. They'd been given a record contract. It was all becoming more serious. When a surprised Nick saw his father mingling with the crowd, Colin Cave gave him an encouraging smile. As this happened, Nick, wearing a white shirt, was hit by the spotlight. Colin later told Nick, 'You looked like an angel up there,'[15] surprising his son, perhaps reminding him of something better within

He has lost count of the number of times he has tried to tell Nick it was beauty that would save the world – 'education and beauty, Nicky'. He hoped the message might stick. Nick had always been a fine drawer. But he had dropped out of art school and got caught up with the band. He still thought his son's interest in art might lead him to become a writer and illustrator of children's books one day.

Colin Cave is even deeper now in a network of country back roads. The far-off Warby Ranges, where the Kelly Gang once rode into hiding, are clothed in a smoky blur. The car slips again on the gravel. He rights the wheel. Just by Bobinawarrah Memorial Hall someone comes driving towards him out of nowhere. Their dust consumes him in a cloud. Then he is out the other side of it and on into the silence again.

Some dead trees arch over the road just ahead. Countless small, brightly plumed parrots are gathered in the roadside ditches, flocks of musk lorikeets fluttering upwards and away as his car approaches. The road is long and straight.

A local farmer is out repairing a fence near the edge of his property when he sees a strange cloud starting to spread. Fearing a bushfire, Michael Conroy heads down towards it, only to discover it is just dust dispersing. Then he sees a badly damaged vehicle that appears to have come off the road and overturned before rolling back onto its wheels. The passenger looks seriously injured. Conroy rushes back home to call the police. 'That's all I can tell.'[16]

Senior Constable Brian Erskine receives the call at nearby Whitfield. 'From something I was told I believed it to be a fatal accident.'[17] A heavy and surprising burst of afternoon rain forces the police vehicle to slow on the Dockers Road as the officer rushes to get there. At the scene of the accident Erskine notices a fallen branch on the gravel and wheel marks that indicate the car might have swerved, losing control and running off the road.[18] He sees a logo for the Council of Adult Education on the buckled door, an owl with a folded wing and a sprig of leaves beside it. The roof is badly crushed. It's clear the man behind the wheel is deceased. The officer finds a metal ID tag hanging from a chain around the driver's neck. Unable to locate his family in Melbourne despite repeated phone calls, Senior Constable Erskine summons Adrian Twitt to the hospital in Wangaratta. Twitt formally identifies the body as 'Colin Francis Cave', relationship 'friend'.

'There was nothing to show that anything had happened to him at all, apart from a bandage around his head,' Twitt says. 'You'd think he was just asleep, there was not another mark on him.'[19]

A coroner finds that Colin Cave was killed on impact. Colleagues use phrases such as 'the prime of his life' and 'the peak of his career' to express their dismay at his death. Descriptions such as 'meticulous', 'hard working' and 'man with a vision' are also used. The formalities behind such words sound clichéd, but his presence was so vital that Adrian Twitt is stunned to be told Colin Cave was fifty-three; Twitt presumed him to be a decade younger, as most local people did. 'I never would have thought he was that old,' Twitt says, 'not even close!'

Eventually, a room will be set aside at The Centre and renamed The Colin Cave Gallery to honour a figure who still looms large in the town today, even as his name fades with the lives and memories of a generation who knew him as the dynamo who changed their world and the shape of adult education across the state.

The gallery was opened by Dawn Cave in 1994. Tim drove her to Wangaratta for the occasion. Peter and Julie were bound by work commitments in Melbourne. Nick was overseas and also unable to attend the ceremony.

Inside the gallery there is nothing much to show today but a bare foldout meeting table, stacked rows of plastic chairs pushed against a wall, and a large black-and-white photo of Colin Cave, framed and tucked into a seemingly neglected corner.

PART II

THE GOOD SON

Man
in the
Moon

WARRACKNABEAL

2008, 1957–59

'I was climbing up over the fence of the chicken coop to try to have a look at the chooks,' says Nick. 'That's my first memory, really. Next thing I was falling. I cracked my head open. There was blood everywhere, apparently. Whenever people ask me about Warracknabeal, that's all I can remember. I must have been about three. Ask Mum, she'll know.'

In 2008 it appeared Nick Cave had descended upon the town of his birth, Warracknabeal (pronounced 'Warrick-na-beal'), in far north-western Victoria, merely to torment it: a larger-than-life figure making his crooked way homewards, as if out of one of his own dementedly fabulous songs. Those inclined towards a less-fancy prose style put it rather differently: he was just an arsehole making fun of a country town going through a drought.

In any case, the *Wimmera Mail-Times* – 'the voice of Wimmera since 1873' – was alight with a front-page story by Michelle Dryburgh for its weekend edition dated Friday, 20 June 2008. It ran with a sharp one-two headline punch to the eyes: 'I'm serious.' Pictures of actor Russell Crowe and a heavily 'blinged' hip-hop musician called Snoop Dogg featured above the headline. Nick Cave had commissioned a statue of himself and hoped to place it somewhere in the town for an official unveiling. 'Russell Crowe, my mate, has promised to attend,' he said. 'Snoop Dogg ... says he'll come if they let him into the country.'

Thanks to the wonders of Photoshop, a life-size image of Cave dressed in nothing but a loincloth and seated atop a rearing horse was shown in a mock setup outside the Warracknabeal Library. It was surrounded by gravel and clumps of cosmetically arranged spinifex grass. The image was drawn from a maquette designed by English sculptor Corin Johnson, best known for his work on the Princess Diana memorial in London. That the model existed at all suggested a grain of truth to the story, which Cave had been flirting with as a possibility in various interviews since at least 2001. The rumours had made their way to the Warracknabeal town mayor, who finally asked the local paper to investigate.

Cave was happy to oblige with their enquiries via email. He admitted to the *Wimmera Mail-Times* that the rumour was true, and that things had progressed more than anyone might realise, though he had 'probably jumped the gun' by inviting famous friends along before the plan was complete. He revealed that it would cost $60,000 to cast a 'ten-feet high' version of this horse-and-rider in bronze.[1] Nick would then need to ship Corin Johnson's work from the United Kingdom to the port of Melbourne, from where a U-Haul truck would take it by road to Warracknabeal, so the costs were becoming personally prohibitive. He was now 'looking for a wealthy benefactor who would be interested in investing in an historical monument that will make Frank Rusconi's *Dog on the Tuckerbox* pale by comparison'. The off-the-cuff reference to Frank Rusconi was itself impressive: here was a man who knew his Australian roadside icons and their creators by heart.[2]

As if to incite sympathy for the project among the men of Warracknabeal, Cave told the reporter: 'Kylie Minogue said she wouldn't miss it for the world; she even promised to wear her gold lamé hot pants.' A photo on the front page from her 'Spinning Around' video whetted appetites further as she leaned back provocatively in high heels on a cocktail bar. A headshot of Cave also appeared, his dark, thinning hair swept back, a broad moustache above a somewhat crooked smile: here was the kind of B-movie villain you would expect to tie sweet Kylie to some railroad tracks. And this guy had sung with her? Was even rumoured to have got it on with her? No way.

Maquette for 'Homecoming', Warracknabeal statue of Nick Cave, by Corin Johnson *(courtesy of the artist)*

A series of vox pops indicated that most townsfolk thought Cave should pay for this thing himself, but he was welcome to put it up – and a concert would be a great way to say thank you. A number of citizens preferred, though, that the statue be located 'somewhere more quiet' than the location proposed in the newspaper. Jono Price was one of the few locals keen on the statue appearing anywhere: 'He is a legend and a great songwriter.' Jamie Sevenich saw the upside of down: 'It's a good idea because this town is dead.'[3]

The Age in Melbourne picked up the story, as did the *Sydney Morning Herald* and a number of international publications. Talkback radio in Melbourne also saw the statue proposal gain further amplification, much of it critical. This Nick Cave character was just making fun of a country town experiencing hard times. Who the hell did he think he was? Dawn Cave got on the blower from Melbourne to her son in the United Kingdom. 'You've got to put a stop to this, Nick. It's getting out of hand.'[4] Nick promised he would do something about it. He had honestly not known about the drought affecting the Wimmera region when he'd told the journalist of his extravagant plans and star-studded guest list. And so the very next day Nick contacted Michelle Dryburgh to set the record straight.

For a start, he told her, he had never intended to imply that the town should pay for the statue. The economics of it would be entirely his concern. After a few other points of clarification, Cave received some breaking news from Dryburgh – the local council was now considering a monument with an indigenous theme – a dingo and her pups – to be situated at a roundabout on Scott Street, effectively gazumping the only free site that might suit his memorial plans. Cave seemed to grow irate in his reply. Displaced by a dingo and her pups! 'I ask you,' he said, 'what could be more indigenous to Warracknabeal than me? I was bloody born there.'

He then apologised for all the misunderstandings he had created. Kylie would not appear wearing her gold lamé hot pants, as he had hoped, but she would certainly come along to the unveiling as he had promised. Snoop Dogg, however, was indeed likely to have visa problems entering Australia, and this sadly made him a no-show. 'But fear not, I've heard from my friend Mike Tyson and he is willing to organise some bare-knuckle boxing matches in the centre of Lions Park ...'

And on it went. Cave smiles when he tells his monumental yarn later. The issues of the *Wimmera Mail-Times* in his library are precious. He grins and folds the papers away with an air of satisfaction and says, 'I just couldn't help myself.'

Does all this then mean that his plans for a statue in Warracknabeal were just some elaborate practical joke or twisted fantasy? No. Cave still has hopes of doing something about his statue, though he remains vague about when and how. Like some proverbial ghost rider, Nick's dream of himself immortalised on horseback has ridden on for another decade since, rearing up periodically then disappearing into the sunset again. As he first told *The Age* when they asked what was really happening, 'I'm an Australian – even we don't know when we're joking and when we're not.'[5] In the same news story he insisted that if Warracknabeal were to refuse his statue a place on their streets, he would 'drive it out into the desert and dump it somewhere, *Planet of the Apes*-style'.[6]

Nick's old artistic hero, the painter Sidney Nolan, might have sympathised with this gesture. He'd been posted to another part of the Wimmera region as an army conscript back in the 1940s. Isolated and miserable, Nolan began painting a series of self-portraits inspired by tribal masks, scarification and indigenous art of the Pacific. Eventually Nolan became a deserter and fled the area. But the experience and the self-portraits were a step on the road to what became his iconic Ned Kelly series. Nolan's psycho-geography and artistic obsessions prefigured Colin Cave's own movements from Warracknabeal to Wangaratta. By the time Nick Cave was contemplating his own grand return to the Wimmera region, the stories of the outlaw and the painter, the teacher and his son, overlapped as if by cosmic design. All that the sculptor Corin Johnson first remembers when he began making a model for a statue is Nick wanting the maquette to look like a bushranger from a film he was writing: 'Aussie cowboy but a bit sad.'[7]

There are many descriptions of Warracknabeal. 'A whole lotta nothing' and 'flat as a pancake' are two of the more notable. 'Very flat' is another.

A former local, preferring to remain anonymous, explains it more subtly. 'Everything changes slowly out there. Because farming is ninety per cent of everything, so it's natural everything would change slowly. To weather the storm, to deal with a few bad years of drought, you gotta be able to take it. And put things in a bigger arc of time … There's this saying about a nation that takes over another nation – which is what we white Europeans did a long time back to the Aboriginals – that it becomes like the original nation within three generations. I really think there is something to that when you look at the people out there.'[8]

Around the time Nick Cave was developing an outback Australian western with the director John Hillcoat, which they would eventually call *The Proposition* (2005), his birthplace of Warracknabeal came up in early interviews as an inspiration. There was an implication Cave had arisen out of a frontier land himself. It was a notion fuelled by Nick, who fancifully described Warracknabeal as 'a re-housing town for ex-cons who want to go straight, only nobody has gone straight, and it's turned into this strange, lawless place'.[9]

Located on the bone-dry banks of the Yarriambiack Creek, approximately 330 kilometres north-west of Melbourne, the 'strange' and 'lawless' Warracknabeal has a relatively crime-free population of 3300 people. It functions as a service centre for a spread-out wheat-farming district that survives on the moisture-holding grey soils that run in a thin strip through the arid red landscape of the Mallee scrub region.

An ambitious young high-school teacher, Colin Cave arrived here in early 1957 with all the zeal of a pioneer. Accompanying him were his pregnant wife, Dawn, and their two sons, Tim and Peter, then aged five and three, respectively. Nick would be born later that first year in Warracknabeal, and Julie, the Caves' only daughter, in 1959.

The family took up residence at 72 Jamouneau Street, where Dawn was housebound looking after Nick, then Julie as well, while Tim and Peter attended primary school. 'It was a housing-commission area,' Dawn recalls glumly, 'with all the streets given these unbelievable French names – it was so incongruous.' Feelings of stir-craziness would set in. 'You would go for a drive,' she says, 'but the landscape never changed. You'd be in the car and you'd wonder what you were doing and where you were going.'[10]

In summer the temperature could reach well into the forties. In winter it just got 'very cold', especially at night, when the place could feel as barren as a moonscape. Colin's father, Frank Cave, dubbed the town 'Warrackna-bloody-beal', a name that would catch on in family parlance. Known to one and all as 'Poppa', Frank was a formidable presence. Nick says, 'Mum always had to call his beloved wife [Colin's mother] "Mrs Cave", never Imogen. He used to make Mum feel so uncomfortable with things like that.'

Dawn Cave confesses: 'I'd get in such a lather when he and his wife, Imogen, were coming [from Melbourne]. She was very intelligent, one of the first women to get into the Victorian College of Pharmacy in Melbourne. I really respected her. But it was very hard to relax with him.' As if still sensing Frank's disapproval of her domestic abilities to this very day, she says, 'They would never stay the night with us, never. You should have seen the hotel they preferred to stay at, too; it was such a dump.'[11]

Frank Cave was a First World War veteran, and later became head of public relations for Shell, the petroleum corporation. His position had led to his own Sunday-night radio show in Melbourne during the 1940s, 'The Shell Show'. Frank played popular tunes and interviewed international guests – most famously, in Cave family lore, the British comedy musician George Formby. Formby's risqué songs on the banjo ukulele greatly amused Frank, who relished Formby's double entendres and inane catchphrase, 'It's turned out nice again, hasn't it!' The first man in Australia to broadcast live-to-air music on radio, Frank would round out his show by telling a ghost story every week, amusing or frightening listeners.[12] Dawn Cave thinks it's through Frank, then Colin, that Nick inherited 'the showman thing'.

Despite Frank Cave's high public profile and relatively glamorous career, he had a secret: Frank was not the man he claimed to be. His extended family would learn through Imogen (née Chambers) that 'Cave' was not the real family name. By then Poppa had established himself as such a towering and acidic figure they were all simply too afraid to ask him for the truth. Only after he passed away did anyone dare attempt a genealogy. This project was comically referred to as 'The Lost Caves'. A group effort finally unearthed the true family name: Landvoigt.

Although he had fought in the First World War under his own name and on the side of the British, growing anti-German feeling during the build-up to the Second World War convinced Frank Landvoigt that a change of moniker was a good idea. 'Landvoigt' was not just German, it was Prussian in origin, carrying all the aristocratic and military connotations of that kingdom. 'Cave' was Frank's English mother's maiden name. There is speculation that Frank's decision was also taken in belated reaction to his father, who walked out on the family when Frank was just a boy. He is known to have been using his mother's maiden name in varied circumstances well before it was changed by deed poll in 1940. In any case, it was then that a sign went up over the doors of the car yard he opened in Melbourne, and 'Frank Cave' was officially born.[13]

Nick Cave recalls staying with Poppa and 'using a wind-up stereo to listen to all his old 78s. There was a song he had, called "Can I Sleep in Your Barn Tonight, Mister?" It was this hard-luck narrative of a guy who has had his wife and kid stolen away from him by a handsome stranger he took into his home. And how he's wandering now, looking for them, telling people his sad story wherever he goes.' Nick sings a fragment of the song in a cracking, old-timey voice, '"May I sleep in your barn tonight, Mister? It's cold lying out on the ground."'

A traditional country ballad, this song has been covered by everyone from America's Hank Thompson to Australia's Slim Dusty, the provenance blurred by the various interpretations and accompanying claims of authorship. The lyrics are underlined by an eerie suggestion that the wandering stranger might well be the one who stole away the woman and child he laments as lost to him. 'It's a bit of a stretch,' Nick says, 'but when I think about how often I listened to it, it probably sowed the idea somewhere in my head for "Song of Joy" on *Murder Ballads*.'

Frank Cave would prove fertile territory in other ways, forming the basis for the 'granddad' figure in the closing section of *The Death of Bunny Munro*. 'Poppa had a wind-up mechanical bird like that grandfather character in that book has. A what-do-you-call-it? An automaton? It used to fascinate me,' Cave says. 'He used to go, "Don't break that thing!" every time I went near it. He even dressed the same way as the character does in my novel, except Poppa's fly wasn't always undone. That's an important difference.

'I remember how Poppa would sit there in his chair with a whisky; his bald head like a big skull. I also remember how I had done this painting while I was at Caulfield Grammar School, just a picture of an old guy with a skull-like head. It was called "The Voice". Very obviously influenced by Edvard Munch. But, coincidentally, it did look a lot like Poppa sitting there. Every time we knew he was coming round Mum and Dad had to take the painting off the living-room wall and hide it.'

Nick laughs. 'He was a real old cunt. But I liked him. I actually always remember Poppa smiling when I was a kid. He was quite the practical joker when he was younger, or so I heard. Drove his car all the way up the steps of Parliament House in Melbourne for fun. Another time a friend left him his car and went away north for a holiday. Poppa disassembled it and took it piece by piece into his friend's bedroom where he reassembled the whole car. I used to hear those kinda stories about him ... It was only after Mrs Cave died that he got angry and nasty. I remember him being quite sweet when she was alive.

'A big story in the family is when Mum and Dad went to visit Poppa in Melbourne – they were still living in Wangaratta at the time – about a year after his wife had died [in 1966[14]]. They hadn't seen him for a while and thought it would be nice to go pay him a surprise visit. Cheer him up. Anyway, they drove all the way down to Melbourne to see how he was, and when they knocked on the door he opened it and shouted, "Piss off!" And shut the door again in their faces. Yeah, Poppa was a real old cunt.'

Dawn Cave's family lineage casts its own light and shadow on the Nick Cave story. Her father, Edward Cooper Treadwell, ran a printing business and published a racing paper, *The Sporting Judge*, and served as an alderman on Melbourne City Council. Her mother, Florence Kench, was an English immigrant who arrived in Australia in 1911 at the age of sixteen without much education. She went to work at 30 York Street, St Kilda, keeping house for Treadwell, his mortally ill wife and their five children.

Treadwell lost his wife, Mary Jane[15], in 1917, then his eldest son, Edward Junior – who died in 1918 at age twenty-one in a propeller-blade accident on a British airstrip during the last days of the First World War – and finally his eldest daughter, Maisie (May Jane), from peritonitis in 1919. By strange coincidence they all died in September, which Edward Treadmill would refer to ever after as 'my bad month'. He still had two younger daughters, Ruby and Alice, to look after, as well as his older boy, Frank, out in the world. By this stage Florence had ceased working for them and been employed by others, but in the circumstances she was recalled to the house where her services were required full-time. Treadwell, almost inevitably, fell in love with and proposed to his young housekeeper. Florence and Edward married in 1922 and had two more daughters, Gwendolyn in 1923 and Dawn in 1926.

After so much tragedy, one would imagine Edward Treadwell to be a rather distant and melancholy figure, but Dawn Cave describes him as a personality of great determination, always able to talk about the family members he had lost and yet never overwhelmed by sadness. Nick caught hints from his mother that her father 'enjoyed a drink or two at the Council meetings when he was an alderman. He'd take all the leftover cakes and stuff them in his pockets and bring them home for the kids. All these smashed-up cakes falling out of his pockets.' Dawn Cave says, 'My father was a very strong man. I think that's why I lived in that

St Kilda house with him and Mum till Colin and I got married.'[16] The loss of such a warm and charming character in 1950 was keenly felt. The cause of death was pneumonia, but Edward Treadwell had suffered for quite a while, says Dawn, 'blind for several years, and in his latter years bedridden completely'.[17] Though a relatively young widow, Florence stayed on at the home and never remarried.

Julie Cave, Dawn's youngest child, recalls how she and Nick would stay with Grandma Treadwell during their school holidays in the 1960s – and what a great adventure it was. The big old house had been divided into flats by then, and a changing retinue of boarders, part of a great European influx of migrants into St Kilda, provided the children with many colourful characters to observe. 'We just loved visiting her,' Julie says. 'Grandma would vamp away at the piano playing songs she picked up by ear listening to the phonograph and the radio.'[18]

An otherwise tiny and quiet woman, Florence would come alive at the keys, continuing to belt out her favourite song, The Beatles' 'Hey Jude', in rousing fashion well into her eighties. 'That's where Nick really first learned the piano,' Julie Cave insists, 'the way Grandma did it. I see it in the way he moves his hands and how it sounds, and feels. He still plays like Grandma now. She would have loved it.'[19]

Nick is surprised to hear the description. 'Julie said that, did she? It's awful, that left-hand thing I used to do,' he says, beating a barrel-house rhythm out on an imaginary keyboard in the air beside him. 'I don't play like that anymore,' he emphasises. 'Mum's sister, Auntie Gwen, who I absolutely adore and love, floored me once, scarred me for life, with something she said in relation to all this,' he laughs. 'I was just eleven. Just chording stuff out on the piano. I couldn't play that well. We were all around the piano singing songs and taking turns to play something. My turn. And I'd hardly got going before Gwen said, "Oh, get off, you're just vamping." Every time I hear that word come up in association with my playing I still get a chill. It suggests you don't know what you are doing, that you're just faking it. Vamping!

'Actually, I got very distressed about my grandmother's hands when I was a kid. Her fingers were bent almost at right angles. Literally. She did play beautifully, almost any song by ear, but her fingers …' Nick shakes his head as he pictures them, making a snapping gesture across each of his own fingers. 'I told Mum I didn't want to play piano because I was so afraid my fingers would go like Grandma's. I was really scared. "I don't want to have fingers like Grandma." That's when Mum told me, "She got them scrubbing floors, Nicholas."'[20]

Before becoming a librarian, Dawn studied violin for a year at the Conservatory of Music in Melbourne. 'I was never that good,' she says dismissively. 'They told me to go do an Arts degree.'[21]

Dawn Treadwell would receive her BA in 1949, the same year that Colin Cave completed his BA Dip Ed and they became engaged. An ailing Edward Treadwell would die just a few months after their engagement party in December. Colin and Dawn would eventually marry in 1951, and then move westward into the state's interior, following a series of country town appointments to advance Colin Cave's career. Though only a junior teacher, Colin had a vision that was more far-reaching than that of most young men his age.

For a pregnant young woman with two boys in primary school, Warracknabeal proved to be a very lonely place in the late 1950s. 'People were very self-contained up there. They didn't welcome us into their arms,' says Dawn. 'I think we were regarded as oddities. And it was a fact we weren't there for life,' she admits, straining to be fair, before adding, 'The Vicar of Warracknabeal told us later that people like us were referred to as "birds of passage". That's what the locals called us. "Birds of passage."'[22] More than fifty years on from the experience, she repeats what could sound like a pretty phrase with distinct acidity.

As well as teaching English and mathematics at the high school, Colin Cave immediately set about establishing a theatre group in the town. According to the stories Nick heard, 'I think they thought he was a weirdo, putting on plays and things like some overeducated homo.' Remarkably, by September 1957 the Warracknabeal Dramatic Society was not only in existence – less than a year after his arrival – it was staging a Colin Cave–produced and directed version of *Rope*[23] for the locals. Colin had also entered the play into a regional theatrical festival in Ballarat, some 230 kilometres away, a good four hours' drive on an outback highway at the time.

Dawn was by now heavily pregnant with Nick. 'But I was always late [before],' she says, referring to her two previous sons' births. 'The weekend they were to take the play to Ballarat was looming and it was the same weekend I was due. We had this old Peugeot station wagon; it was the only car that could take the coffin-like chest that the body was put in as part of the play. Colin went to our doctor and said, "What shall I do?" The doctor said, "Colin, what do you consider more important?" Colin went to Ballarat.

'Anyway, I had Nick very early on [the] Sunday morning. Ballarat to Warracknabeal is quite a trek. Colin packed everything in the play up and headed back as fast as he could. He came in late looking terribly anxious. Fortunately he made it in time. But he wasn't present at Nick's birth. Fathers weren't allowed to stay in the delivery room in those days.'

Dawn still gets people with an interest in astrology asking her the exact time of Nick's arrival. 'I can't remember,' she says with a wave of her hand. 'But some people are very persistent. I just make up a time, it keeps them happy.'[24]

───────

'As a little boy, Nick loved to talk. He loved to engage you in a conversation. He was a little chatterer,' Dawn says. 'Everyone seemed to love Nick, those big eyes of his looking up at you. When we visited Melbourne, Nick would sleep in Grandma's [Florence Treadwell's] room, and she'd say she'd see him there in the cot when she woke up, just standing there, looking at her with those eyes of his.

'They'd have these long conversations just lying there at night when he got a little older. Anything he admired, she gave it to him. The only things he said he really wanted were this wooden chest, which she used to tell him he could have after she died, and a huge leather-bound Bible. He must have been around eight when he showed an interest in her Bible. Anyway, she let him have it and he put a family tree in the front in great big kids' handwriting and completely defaced it.

'I was only asking him this last weekend if he could remember much of his life in Warracknabeal. He said something about when he was three and trying to climb a fence to look at chooks and he cut his head open. And that's about it. But it was a good childhood in Warracknabeal, and Wangaratta after that. Nick would just wander out the door and up the street sometimes and someone would bring him back. That's life in a country town. It's a great way for children to grow up.

'He was always easy to have around the house, and very affectionate – he still is very affectionate now. When I had Julie and she was a baby and I was bathing her, he would never wander off and play then. He'd just sit there patiently, wanting to have a conversation. "God, I wish he'd shut up, I just need to think for a minute!" – I'd feel that way sometimes, he'd chatter so much. But Nick would sort of demand your answer. Later, when he was growing up and a teenager, there'd be family arguments and you'd think it was all over, but Nick always had to have the last word. You'd think it was finished and done and Nick had a way of just saying one more thing, even as you were leaving the room. And then of course it would start up again. Colin found it very hard to take.'[25]

Down
by the
River

'One of the many things I regret about writing *And the Ass Saw the Angel* was that I didn't set it in Australia. It could just as easily be set in Wangaratta rather than an imaginary part of the American South. I don't know why I didn't do that. I wish I had. For sure that book comes from growing up in the country, from living a life in country Australia. It's not from listening to murder ballads. The river was the sacred place of my childhood and everything happened down there.

'On the edge of the river there's willow trees, just like it says in "Sad Waters". The plaiting of the willow vines – that happened. So, a song like "Sad Waters" is a remembrance of that childhood scenario. The tree roots all torn out of the ground. The river was fucking muddy too, not one of these glistening, glacial waters people imagine. You never knew what terrible things you might be swimming towards. We used to jump off the railway bridge into the river – there was only one place where you could jump off safely, between these two pylons where we knew it was deep enough; pretty exhilarating stuff as the trains were coming.

'People look at these things as academic exercises, like I am just sitting around listening to country and blues songs. As if there's no life experience behind them. And it's just not true. I'm not sure, though, about the line in "Sad Waters" about the carp darting about. I always thought carp were little fish. But when I was shown one recently it turns out they are these great big, ugly motherfuckers,' Cave says, holding out his hands in horror to indicate their size. Then he shrugs his shoulders and laughs. 'Anyway, the thing is, I always have a very strong visual idea of where the songs that I write are set. And invariably it is in a small town and that town is Wangaratta. But it's a mythical version, not an actual version.'

When the Cave family arrived in Wangaratta towards the end of 1959, the population hovered at close to 14,000 people.[1] Compared to Warracknabeal, where Nick was born, it was a veritable metropolis, almost five times larger and experiencing what regional historians would describe as 'a cultural flowering', driven by an influx of European migrants labouring in the increasingly successful vineyards and the recently opened Bruck Textiles factory.

The flour mill and its pale silos towered over a railway line that made 'Wang', as the locals called it, an important rural link between Melbourne and Sydney. Wool prices were good and sheep farms were numerous in the valley. Cattle were still being herded through Phillipson Street towards the saleyards well into the late 1960s. Wang's abattoir was an economic mainstay, its presence marked by a stench that wafted over the new suburbs across the railway tracks on the western side of town. A smell of blood and bone would ooze out like clockwork towards the end of each working day.

It was a pretty town nonetheless, poised at the junction of the Ovens and King rivers, which flow down from the Victorian Alps, their cold waters gathering farm soil from the banks and darkening on their journey. The rivers, the railway tracks and the French Gothic architecture of the Holy Trinity Cathedral dominated the town's heart, vaguely conjuring the postcard atmosphere of an inviting French village transplanted into the broad-brimmed, knockabout Australian outback. Built of granite taken from the nearby Warby Ranges, the Anglican cathedral would take on a warm, almost pinkish glow in the afternoon sunlight.[2]

Wangaratta's name reputedly stemmed from a local Aboriginal word that meant 'nesting place for cormorants'. Appropriate, then, that 'birds of passage', as the Vicar of Warracknabeal had so disparagingly described the Caves, should find it an ideal place to settle. They'd already moved from Melbourne to the far-western Victorian towns of Hamilton and then Warracknabeal to advance Colin Cave's teaching career. But they had never felt much sense of welcome in those tight little communities. Wang was different from the start.

The town's population had doubled in the fifteen years since the end of the Second World War. A bursting Wangaratta High School was relocated to a freshly built site, energising efforts to establish what would become the Centre for Continuing Education in the old school buildings just off the main street. Colin was in his element here, both as an English teacher at the newly expanded school and as a community dynamo behind the foundation of 'The Centre'.

Dawn Cave was much happier too, far less isolated socially and culturally than she had felt in Warracknabeal. When her children grew to school age, she was able to recommence work as a librarian at Wangaratta High in 1968. Colin continued to teach part-time while running The Centre, in between producing and directing seasons of amateur theatre for The Wangaratta Players. In private, Colin pursued his literary interests, writing short stories, which he unsuccessfully submitted to journals such as the *Reader's Digest*, and satirical verse, some of which appeared in the local paper. Notable among these published verses was an anonymous piece entitled 'Ode to the Evening Air', an attack on the foul smells of the abattoir: 'My only wish is those who / This nauseation every eve perpetrate / at eight / Should have themselves / immersed within sewers / Buried neck-high with various manures.'[3]

The Cave family lived on the western side of town at 31 Mepunga Avenue. 'When we lived there,' says Nick, 'there were constantly new houses being built, the foundations of which I loved climbing on and falling off. The local swimming pool was nearby, where many an hour was passed lying on the hot concrete. I was always practically black as a child and we never wore shoes. Next to the swimming pool there was a [sports] field we had to cross, where magpies would dive-bomb us and the grinderman would park his van to sharpen the neighbourhood knives.'

If you were to 'Take a little walk to the edge of town' and 'Go across the tracks / Where the viaduct looms like a bird of doom' – as the song 'Red Right Hand' would later have it – 'Past the square, past the bridge, past the mills, past the stacks'[4] – then you might find yourself stumbling westwards and even down Mepunga Avenue itself. 'So, yes,' Cave admits, '"Red Right Hand" is set in a reconstructed version of Wangaratta.' Not the real place, as he invariably emphasises, but still somewhere real enough for those lyrics to serve as a map that could guide you from one point to another with an eerie familiarity.

Childhood friend Bryan Wellington refers to himself as 'Nick's first boy next door'. 'I lived at number 27 Mepunga Avenue,' he says proudly. 'The street name actually has two different spellings at either end written on the signposts: "Mepunga" and "Mupenga". It's only a hundred metres long! The different spellings were a constant amusement to us as kids.'

The feel of the surrounding area was – and still is – lower middle class, the lawns mown, the gardens well tended, a sedate, even bland oasis penetrated by the sounds of passing trains running every second hour. At the western end of Mepunga Avenue, where it intersects with Phillipson Street, the suburb starts to give way to warehouses, factories and the nearby racecourse and cattle saleyards. In the 1960s this was 'the edge of town'. Bryan Wellington recalls the verandah of the Robinson brothers' house down the road, where he and Nick would compete against them in lengthy table-tennis tournaments; the 'necessary season tickets' for the swimming pool; and climbing the massive pine trees in Wareena Park, where he, Nick and their friend Eddie Baumgarten forged a childhood gang that would 'climb higher and higher to test ourselves'.

Wellington's view of Nick's father, Colin, however, is less enchanted. 'I don't have fond memories of him personally. Nick's mother was fantastic. Nick's father may have been a great man, but he liked things to go his way. I thought he was an authoritarian in his own home. I dunno what Nick thinks of this, but I have often got the feeling his song "Red Right Hand" is about his dad, that it comes from being bent over and disciplined. Nick was scared of his dad, no doubt about that. Nick's two older brothers, Tim and Pete, they toed the line where Nick didn't. Nick was like … like a branch of Colin's anger; they clashed. Colin was an enigma to me, when I look back. He could produce plays, he could teach and inspire people, but he could be a bully too.

Nick riding Bryan Wellington's horse in Wangaratta c. 1968
(photographer unknown; courtesy of Bryan Wellington)

'I should say that my own father was not an educationalist, let's put it that way. I had to leave home in order to finish high school at age sixteen. So, my father always tried to keep me away from Nick – because of the fact Nick's parents were a teacher and a librarian and they had degrees. My dad found all that threatening, and he had great difficulty communicating with them. Alcohol was a big part of my family life, and it was a big part of Eddie Baumgarten's family life too. That made it easy for my dad to talk to Eddie's dad. Nick's dad didn't drink! But Eddie wasn't brought up with the fear that I was; or the fear that I believe Nick was brought up with too. That thing of wanting to please, and not knowing how to ...' Wellington pauses at what seems like an inadequate summary. 'It's a very intricate situation to explain.'[5]

Eddie Baumgarten lived a couple of blocks away from the Mepunga Avenue boys. Nick freely refers to him as his best friend when he was young. The Baumgarten family are writ so large in Nick's tales of growing up in Wang they emerge like some childhood reminiscence out of a novel by Cormac McCarthy or Harper Lee. Dawn Cave remembers the family well: 'Mrs Baumgarten had her own hairdressing salon. She was a very religious woman ... She used to like singing "Popeye the Sailor Man" around her own home.[6] Mr Baumgarten was nice too but there was something strange about him.'

'Eddie's dad was a wonderful, shambling man,' Nick says fondly. Mr Baumgarten would take Nick and Eddie out on trips hunting rabbits. 'He just drove us up to the Warby Ranges, gave us a shotgun each, some cartridges and a six-pack of beer, then went off somewhere and came back later on and picked us up,' says Nick. 'I was twelve or thirteen. Eddie and I would sit up there and talk about stuff, walk on the great hot boulders, shoot the myxo rabbits[7], which you could actually walk right up to and blow away, executioner-style, or just clap your hands and watch them run blind and bash themselves on the trees. Awful, really ...' The sound of his clapping hand as Nick tells the story is as sharp as a rifle shot into the memory. 'On the rare occasions Eddie and I would actually shoot a rabbit that was not diseased, Mrs Baumgarten, a tough, kind and generous woman, would skin it, remove the pellets and cook it. I would like to add that my mother knew nothing of these activities and would have been appalled if she did.

'Eddie had a homemade sterno still in the backyard, where he boiled sugar and potato skins. It had a coiled clear plastic hose, the works ... I can't, in truth, remember ever drinking any of this, or whether the still he made was actually successful at all. It's the thought that counts! Have I told you about the Triple A Club? It stood for Anti Alcoholics Anonymous. It was a Gentleman's Club of two – just me and Eddie,' Nick says proudly. 'We'd pay taxi drivers to go buy us a bottle of Stone's Green Ginger Wine or Marsala or some other godawful thing. We would meet in a shed somewhere between his place and mine that we had set up – I can't recall where; it was almost falling down even then – and we'd play music there [on a radio] and drink ourselves sick. I remember throwing up green grenadine all over Mrs B's carpet. She took it in her stride.'

Anne, Eddie's older sister, looks back at their friendship with Nick and is still surprised at how strong the connections proved to be. 'My family were not nearly as high status as his family. But Nick seemed to like being around. My brother Eddie was a very charismatic kid, I guess; he was one of those people able to get away with things and make people laugh. He and Nick were alike in that way.

'Nick was a pixie-looking little kid till he shot up tall when he was older. Nick used to have a lisp too when he was young; it made him even cuter. He was a great friend to have. Everyone else in town was so boring. Nick was just out there, bizarre, and very intuitive. He could go off on any crazy tangent you liked. We'd play that card game Strip Jack Naked a lot, except we didn't take our clothes off. We were only kids.

'He used to be really affectionate with my mum. Nick'd put his arm around her and call her Mrs B. She loved that. She was a really eccentric woman, not everyone understood her: she'd grown up on Mount Buffalo and never saw another child till she was ten. Her family hosted well-known tourists who came to stay on the mountain. She'd met all these artists who used to go up there and paint, like Arthur Streeton and Tom Roberts. Her mother was a writer and her aunt and an uncle were painters. Percy Grainger visited. Well-to-do tourists from Melbourne were attracted to the natural environment. I have photos of mum as a child with General Sir John Monash.

'Dad had suffered a breakdown after his farm was burned out by bushfire in the early 1950s. The fire was started by a spark off an old tractor at a neighbouring farm. He and Mum had only been married six months. He never adjusted to life away from the land. He became an alcoholic. He was a lovely, gentle man. Nick was always very respectful to Dad.'[8]

Anne describes how she, Eddie and Nick set up a special listening room out the back of the Baumgarten home after her mother decided her teenage daughter needed a space of her own. 'We painted the ceiling black, and stapled netting to it. Then we got newspaper and stuck it to the wall with flour and water, and painted that all blue,' says Anne. 'We had an old second-hand record player and lounges and we'd sit around with the lights off and have candles and incense burning and turn up the music. My favourites were *Bridge over Troubled Water* and The Beatles' *Let It Be*, and lots of Dylan; I was really into the lyrics of songs. Nick and I used to talk about Leonard Cohen. Just how there were so many different levels to his voice. I'd read that he said he wasn't a very good singer, but we thought he was like Dylan, just the feeling he could get into a single word was amazing. I think Nick's the same now as a singer when I listen to him. He can really get that feeling into one word. I think he's a really great singer, just like they are.'[9]

Nick says, 'I spent a lot of time in the back room at Eddie's wonderfully ramshackle house with his sister Anne, listening to music. This is where I first heard Leonard Cohen. Again, I must have been around twelve or thirteen. *Songs of Love and Hate*, still Leonard Cohen's greatest record, in my opinion. Staring for hours at that most uncompromising of covers and listening to all the dark, violent and very beautiful songs. Anybody who tries to tell you Leonard Cohen is not depressing obviously hasn't listened to *Songs of Love and Hate*.[10] Anne Baumgarten was only a few years older than Eddie and me. What a gal! Owning that record in Wangaratta! The first track, "Avalanche", was the most extraordinary lyric I'd ever heard – still is, really. For me, doing it as the first song on *From Her to Eternity* [Nick's debut as a solo artist] was as much a calling forth of my childhood years in Wang as a tribute to the master poet–songwriter.[11] Eddie died some years ago of cancer.' When Anne called Dawn Cave in Melbourne in 2004 to pass on the news that Ed had died, Nick was home with his family, visiting his mother for Christmas. That was the last time Anne and Nick spoke.

'Oh yes,' Dawn Cave says, whenever the Baumgartens come up in conversation, 'Anne and Eddie had quite an influence on Nick.'

Below the railway bridge where Nick and his friends used to leap into the Ovens River, there is some graffiti scrawled on a viaduct archway: 'You'll Always Live and Rock in Our Hearts.' It's not meant for Nick Cave, and could be no more than a decade old, but he might sympathise with the tone of nostalgia and grief it announces as you walk by it and on down to the river of his past. There, the sheared-off tree trunks still jut out from the water. The sun still glitters on the green-brown surface, its depths and currents varying and deceptive. A constant hum of locusts gives the air a fullness of space. Birds clicking and whistling add to the atmosphere. The periodic sound of town traffic just a few blocks away, coming in gusts with the breeze, is the only thing to intrude on this secret world – though even that sound adds to a sense of this world being hidden away and separate.

Directly above on Faithfull Street a boy rides his pushbike, hands free, his arms held lazily behind his head. You can cut

Anne Baumgarten and Nick Cave in Anne's front yard, Wangaratta, 1972. Anne is holding her dog, Cindy; Nick has her cat, Woodrow Wilson, in his arms. *(courtesy of Anne Shannon, née Baumgarten)*

down to the river here at the end of Faithfull Street, or walk up the gravel siding onto the railway line and over the bridge itself. The height of the bridge, once you are on it, is a shock. It is not just a big jump into the Ovens – it is a daunting one, some twenty metres perhaps. It is hard to believe anyone would take the plunge. Standing on the tracks, you can see quite a distance, the perspective dissolving into a smoky blue haze. Judging the spot where the depth of the river was deep enough to absorb your fall, and avoiding the tree trunks that open up below like savage mouths, must have been quite an art. So must the timing of the jump as a train approached.

Chris Morris, a high-school friend of Nick's brother Tim, remembers how 'jumping off the bridge was the "tough" thing to do. Just hearing that sound of the train before it came into view and feeling that rumble on the tracks beneath your bare feet.' He says, 'Nick back then was a little brat. We'd always be hearing about his exploits second-hand. Both his parents worked at the school, and they knew Nick was really bright. He'd get bored shitless after doing the work in five minutes, so he'd cause trouble. I think it's harder for offspring when their parents are teachers at a school. The parents are harder on you, too – to make the point that you are being treated equally. Tim and I used to nick off for a few cigarettes; other than that, our behaviour was pretty tame. Their other brother, Peter, was into motorbikes and things. Nick was always more anti-authoritarian and out there than his brothers. Several times he got suspended at school. He had that very strong will of his father. Later on, when we heard about Nick in The Birthday Party, being off his head and falling over on stage, everyone in Wang thought, What a dickhead. But little by little the story started to change. A bit of awe crept into the way people started to speak about what Nick was up to.'[12]

Schoolteacher Adrian Twitt concurs with Chris Morris. 'You teach so many children, it gets hard to recall what members of any family you did or didn't have in your classroom. But I can say with confidence that Nick was so bright he was almost unteachable!'[13]

As for Nick's bad reputation, Adrian Twitt relates it to a broader family scenario. 'Nick was probably too much like his father, and I'm guessing they didn't get on too well,' he says. 'I remember how there used to be all these announcements over the school PA system by the principal's secretary in this high-pitched, piercing voice. They'd come every five minutes sometimes. I taught in the classroom next to Colin. Apparently he had been in the middle of a soliloquy from Shakespeare when one of these announcements came over the PA yet again. We all watched from the classrooms as Colin stormed down to the principal's office and ripped out all the leads in a fury. I think most of the staff were very glad he had done it. But Colin could be bombastic and put people offside without meaning to, particularly women. The way he would stride into the staff room and start making announcements. But there was an enthusiasm too, almost like a little boy sometimes, the way he would get so excited about things. Personally I never found Colin overpowering in his energy, maybe because we shared a lot of interests, like chess and amateur theatre. When I first came to town as a single man, he and Dawn made me feel very welcome in their home. I saw Dawn as a fairly sensitive person by comparison. She was the centrepiece of the family. Only a sensitive person can fulfil that role, I think. She was always calm, collected, some say quiet. The only two members of the household being openly extroverted were Colin and Nick.'[14]

'My father believed to his core in the power of education to elevate lives, and thought it was nearly a divine calling to be a teacher,' Nick says. 'There is a letter my father wrote to a friend – my mother has it – where he is talking about a theatrical production he is involved in. It goes on for three pages with incredible enthusiasm about the actors and the production. By the end, you realise that he is describing a student play he is putting on at the high school. It's about love, really. And whether you're writing a song or choosing curtains, it's the same thing if that's what you put into it.

'Anything my father involved himself in he did obsessively. Except, possibly, child-rearing. Huge energy.' The memories of his father tumble out as Nick looks not so much back to the events as inwards to something he can see. 'He was a teetotaller who took "the Pledge" when he was in the army. Never found out why. For a treat, we used to stop at the pub and he would drink a cold glass of Solo lemonade at the bar. Hard thing to do in an Australian country town in the sixties. He was gutsy like that, and very much his own man.'

Despite any authoritarian shadows that loom over such admiring family impressions, it is important to remember that Colin Cave was a product of the post-war 1950s. The stern patriarch and passionate arts lover, the domineering yet inspiring teacher, the ambitious bureaucrat and eccentric theatre lover are more a paradox than a contradiction. In a very black-and-white time, these character traits hinted at a man who was difficult to categorise, and perhaps difficult to know. Daughter Julie remembers her father teaching her how to read which way the wind was coming by watching the surface of the water as they sailed on Lake Malawa, and learning how to spell the word 'biscuit' by writing it on his back with her finger.

Even Bryan Wellington acknowledges an innate poetry to the man that flowed into his children. Wellington tells a story about Nick arriving at his home one afternoon with a handful of photos of the Milky Way. Colin had given Nick a camera passed on from Frank 'Poppa' Cave. Father and son had spent ages in the backyard one evening as Colin taught Nick how to photograph the night sky on a slow shutter speed.[15]

Colin Cave conducting a salesgirls' course in Benalla, Victoria
(courtesy of the Centre for Continuing Education, Wangaratta)

Woken by his insomnia after a Grinderman performance in 2011, Nick lay in bed wrestling with his complicated sense of who his father was. Eventually it was easier to just work. It may be that certain questions about those we love are never answered. 'I fell asleep for just two hours till five o'clock in the morning,' he says. 'What a bummer. I woke up with Grinderman's "Man in the Moon" in my head. Don't know what you make of this song, but to me it's important and one of my better songs. It crystallises something that I have written about a lot. The relationship I have as an artist towards my father, in particular, and the potential to both paralyse and energise that the ghosts of the dead can have on you. It is one of my themes, man! I mean that also in the collective effect of the dead on our world, their ghosts – I'm thinking of Ned Kelly here again – if you are writing about Wang, not just as a literary artifice but a very real thing that was passed down in the Cave family. A presence.

A story. Anyway, it often feels to me like the dead are everywhere sometimes, showing the way.'

Nick continues: '"Sitting here and scratching in this rented room" refers obliquely to heroin use, but it is also "scratching" out songs, "scratching and tapping" – writing on paper and on the typewriter – "to the man in the moon".[16] Grinderman play a mammoth version of this song, on the organ, followed by a superb, super-long and super-heavy mandocaster solo by Warren [Ellis]. It is seriously epic in a punked-up Prog sort of a way! It's Warren's solo that wakes me in the middle of the night.'

Nick's musical education began at age eight, when he joined the choir at Holy Trinity Cathedral. Anne Baumgarten says, 'You have to understand what an important social and intellectual hub the cathedral was for many people in Wang. We're talking High Anglicanism, and life in a country town. It possibly sounds silly these days, especially if you live in the city, but we'd go to church just to listen to the sermons and get ideas to talk about. It was never just about being religious. Church attendance was also a cultural experience. I think that for both Nick and me, this kind of spirituality has been an essential force in our lives.'[17]

The choirmaster was Father Paul James Harvey, one of many unrelated Harveys who would pop up and play a crucial role in Nick Cave's life. Years later, when *The Boatman's Call* was released in 1997, the Bishop of Wangaratta would read a news article mentioning the influence of a PJ Harvey on the album's songs, and would proudly mention the enduring impact of Nick's old choirmaster to an appreciative congregation.

Father Harvey was by all accounts a sharp-tongued perfectionist whose rigorous approach would preserve the foundations of what was then – and remains – the last cathedral boys' choir left in existence in Australia outside the capital cities. Their repertoire included masses by Mozart and Haydn, with an emphasis on the grand liturgical performances at Christmas and Easter. Hymns such as 'Jerusalem', based on William Blake's poem – 'And did those feet in ancient time' – were given a rousing treatment, summoning up an Anglican vision of England that was righteous and blissful.

Nick slyly describes Father Harvey as 'having a feyness about him' and being 'a little like an irritated Stephen Fry, though perhaps I shouldn't say that'. He recalls being put at the back of the choir, where for three years he would 'grow taller and taller' in his lowly black cassock, while other boys would arrive and be promoted forward, where they would then wear purple and be allowed to sing solos – an honour he never received. Nick refers to this experience as 'scarring' to his confidence, the first of many encounters that would ingrain a feeling that he could not really sing. Somewhere in the vaults, nonetheless, there is a 1971 live recording of 'Silent Night' and 'O Little Town of Bethlehem' by the Australian Broadcasting Commission (ABC) that marks Nick Cave's debut as a recorded performer.

To some extent, what mattered most in Nick's time with the choir was the physical involvement with the Holy Trinity Cathedral itself. Rehearsals, and the need to attend mass at least twice a week to sing, would make him deeply familiar with both the rituals of the Church and the artistic architecture of the Anglican faith surrounding him. It is easy to imagine a young boy staring – if only in the throes of boredom – from the rear of the choir, where he would have been afforded a view of an elaborate stained-glass work that wove together images of early settlement, land clearing and modern life in Wangaratta.

Choirmasters were renowned over the decades for exhorting the boys to sing to the back of church, where this historical diorama dominated their gaze. It is topped by a scene of a vested priest and his altar boy, their backs turned at an altar, offering up the Eucharist in praise. A liturgical text blossoms forth in capitals below them: 'HERE WE OFFER AND PRESENT UNTO THEE O LORD OUR SOULS AND BODIES.' The images and the moral are unmistakably theological and social: the life of the town offered up to God as an ongoing story of sacrifice to ensure His good graces. Nick would subvert this theme with grimly humorous irony in songs such as 'God Is in the House', the tale of a fundamentalist community possessed by devilishly claustrophobic moral certainties.

Elsewhere within the Holy Trinity Cathedral is more artwork that influenced Nick's later passions for religious icons, Gothic painters and Biblically inclined lyrics. A small set of stained-glass windows in the antechamber of the Lady Chapel, which depicts the four evangelists of the gospel, Matthew, Mark, Luke and John, is especially noticeable. Set beside the main altar, the chapel is a shadowy place where errant choirboys would retreat in whispers, less out of prayerful reverence than childish conspiracy. There is a distinct side-of-stage feeling to it. Of the four evangelists depicted, only Saint Mark is blessed with a luminous blue robe, which attains the most striking lustre when the sunlight penetrates it from outside. Nick would later write an introduction to *The Gospel According to Mark* for the Pocket Canon series of books from the Bible, emphasising how 'Christ came to me' through Mark's Gospel 'with a dim light, a sad light, but light enough'.[18]

Looming over the main altar of the church is a figurine, *Christus Rex*, by mid-twentieth-century Austrian-Italian wood carver Leopoldine Mimovich. Directly below it is where the choirboys performed, beside a huge and highly resonant church organ. Rather unusually, the carving that hung above the boys depicts Christ in priestly robes, not in any way bloodied or pained by the Crucifixion. Instead, the carving is serene and powerfully monumental, exuding an intense dignity. It is a portrait of a king unbowed by death: his palms open as if in the middle of a sermon, his fatherly teachings continuing.

A memory of Anne Baumgarten's gives this carving even more interesting associations. She recalls 'how well respected Colin was at school. That's why he taught the senior classes. I can still remember him standing on a ladder, to play God with a booming voice, in a school play. It was the first time I'd seen that sort of creative thinking and involvement from a teacher. Usually we had standard Shakespeare or Noel Coward plays.'[19] Colin in his element again, a God calling his students to the divine possibilities of art, theatre and literature.

'Nick always enjoyed sitting at the piano when he was young,' says Dawn Cave. After enrolling him in the choir, she arranged piano lessons for him from around the age of nine. Nick remembers the lessons well, but not so much for musical reasons. 'I did piano lessons for two years; it was just across the road from The Centre, where Dad worked. Next to the piano teacher's house was a place where the town paedophile used to waylay us young boys when we walked past, suggesting we go into his house and play on his "organ". I went in once and never again!

'This was back in the good old days when being molested was simply a rite of passage. Back when you had cigarette ads on the telly and seatbelts were just being fitted but people were too suspicious of them to wear them. Ah, there is so much to miss! But let's not make too much of the local tamperer – he never molested me, but he did wait for me after my piano lessons and would always ask me if I wanted to go into his house. He explained to me, one time, that masturbation was very good for you and that if you did it in the right way, it was the equivalent to a five-mile run. Helpfully, he offered to show me how.

'Anyway, one day he talked me into going inside the house to play the organ and, indeed, he had a little Farfisa set up. He sat next to me on the stool. I tapped at the notes. Suddenly I felt really creeped out and got the hell out of there. I was about ten years old. This is back before the media hysteria about these things, when the local paedophile was just a part of the social network, along with the lollipop lady and the policeman and the guy at the fish-and-chip shop and whoever else makes the town go around – a bent little cog in the communal machine – but one of God's creatures, just the same. So, no, I wasn't fondled and damaged, I'm afraid.'[20]

For Nick's fourteenth birthday, Colin Cave treated Nick, Bryan and Eddie to a screening of *Planet of the Apes* (1968) at the local movie house. Nick was gripped by the sci-fi fable from the opening moments when George Taylor (Charlton Heston) and his two fellow astronauts crash-land into a lake on a strange planet, after which the three men stumble across backward human beings living under the yoke of simian rule. Rod Serling, best known for *The Twilight Zone*, had dreamed up the Darwinian inversions on which the final script was based – a satire of racism and social stratification, and any notion that Man might be the superior species. Serling also came up with some startling scenes, including an iconic closing image of the Statue of Liberty, its snapped torso emerging from the shoreline of a deserted beach. It was an apocalyptic revelation to Heston's character – and to the audience – that this was no alien world, but our future Earth. For the astronaut George Taylor, there would be no escape 'home'.

Planet of the Apes' surprisingly avant-garde soundtrack would earn composer Jerry Goldsmith an Academy Award nomination.

Atonal and percussive, with aggressively orchestrated strings and instrumental moans, it immersed the viewer in primitivism and terror. Colin Cave thought he heard elements of Stravinsky in the music the boys excitedly described as 'weird'. And didn't the actors dressed as monkeys look real? Dining on hamburgers and Cokes afterwards, he and the three boys had plenty to discuss. They all pictured themselves as the stranded astronauts, though each boy imagined he was the one playing the lead part of George Taylor. Only one of them would get to play that role.

In January 2012, Nick Cave would recall his first viewing of *Planet of the Apes* and 'that fucking bitch-slap of an ending'. He'd been reminded of it while watching Lars von Trier's *Melancholia* (2010) on DVD at home with Susie. 'We loved it. It has always been a theme of mine – more and more, actually – of the ordinary human trauma reverberating apocalyptically.'

If Leonard Cohen's *Songs of Love and Hate* was Nick's ultimate musical bonding experience with Anne and Eddie Baumgarten, then the *John Lennon/Plastic Ono Band* album would prove similarly significant in his friendship with Bryan Wellington.

The Wellingtons had moved out of Mepunga Avenue by 1970, to a small property on the eastern edge of town. Nick and Bryan would play in the shed, learning how to set off all the hunting traps without ever using them. The idea of hunting repulsed Bryan, and the .22 rifle his father had bought him for his twelfth birthday sat in the corner of the shed unused but for target practice. Nick says: 'Bryan had a couple of old horses we would ride, past the "Pop. 18,000" sign, across the bridge over the Ovens River, where we used to swim, into town. I remember listening to John Lennon's Plastic Ono album there at his place over and over again – the one with "Mother" and

"Working Class Hero" on it and poring over those lyrics. That brutal vocal and the pounding piano of "Mother" used to blow me away. All of us trying to be transported elsewhere, out and away from this town, to where we thought the world thrummed with excitement!'

It was a dream Bryan Wellington shared. 'I do remember this one day very, very well,' he says. 'Nick and I both would have been about twelve or thirteen years old. I was at the Rovers Football Ground. Not that I cared much for football. It was just another of my dad's ways of trying to keep me away from Nick. I'd hang at the front gate mostly, wishing I could leave. Anyway, Nick came looking for me at all our usual meeting places; eventually he came riding up on his bike to the football ground where he knew I'd probably be, standing there at the gate like I did. And he had this black armband on. When he got close and stopped I said, "What are you wearing that for?" He said, "Don't you know? Jimi Hendrix died today."'[21]

By then Tim Cave was becoming an influence too. Everything from Hendrix to English progressive-rock recordings by Yes and King Crimson were entering the family home, as well as pioneering Australian music acts such as The Loved Ones and The Master's Apprentices. Tim was also being politicised by the Vietnam War. Anne Baumgarten says, 'Tim was like the Brad Pitt of the town. He used his cool status to lead a student moratorium opposing Australia's involvement in the Vietnam War. Tim got dozens of students to abandon their classes, march with him and stage a sit-in right there on the middle of the school's football field.'

At home, Tim and Nick were thrilled watching the first episode of *The Johnny Cash Show* on television in June of 1969. A poised and sober-looking Bob Dylan would make a great impact on them, singing 'I Threw It All Away' in the show's debut. Tim would seek out a copy of the countrified

Dylan album *Nashville Skyline*, and it would become one of the sweetest albums in Nick Cave's memory, despite the critical drubbing it has always received. As a solo artist in his own right, Nick would reflect on 'I Threw It All Away' in the most laudatory terms some forty years after first hearing it. 'There was always something about that song that was so simple,' he says. 'And an audacity to the simplicity of that song. But it was so, so powerful at the same time – for me at least. I was always ragingly jealous of that song.'

The impact of Johnny Cash was even more profound. 'Up until then,' Nick says, 'I was just listening to children's music. I saw and thought that rock 'n' roll could be about something else ... I got that rock 'n' roll could be evil, it could be a bad thing; he seemed like a real bad man. Dressed in black. At the start of the show he stood there with his back to the camera, then he swung around and said, "Hello, I'm Johnny Cash." I think some people thought he was selling out, but I don't think that's true. I think it was a brave thing for him to do. Generous.'

Something akin to Cash's romantic, if threatening, stoicism was native to the local character of many Australian country towns. Wangaratta took great pride in having been the home base where the 2/24th Battalion of the 26th Brigade of the Australian Army was billeted during the Second World War. Many local young men had signed up with them, earning the battalion the informal soubriquet 'Wangaratta's own'. It was this 2/24th Battalion that became better known as 'The Rats of Tobruk', fighting against overwhelming odds to frustrate the progress of Rommel's undefeated Afrika Korps and change the course of the war. Along with the vagaries of flood and drought, this set piece of Australian military history almost rivalled that of Gallipoli, wedding itself to the Ned Kelly myth and an ongoing Wangaratta fable of male resistance and strength under pressure. This same stoicism and bravery could take on a mangled, thuggish form when there was nothing to genuinely fight for and boredom took hold in the town. People could draw on it as an excuse for anything.

Nick watched as Tim and Peter grew older and began to fall foul of the Wangaratta law. It was not uncommon for inexperienced police, or what Dawn Cave calls 'hard cases' with a bad reputation, to be posted away from the city to rural towns, where local youth could be on the receiving end of rough justice. As teenagers, Tim and Peter started to stand out, their long hair distinguishing them from most clean-cut country boys. In 1969, when Tim was seventeen, he left for Swinburne College of Technology in Melbourne. Peter stayed in Wang and weathered the difficulties, by all accounts a loner who preferred riding about on motorbikes in the bush and tinkering with their engines at home.

'I saw my brothers badly treated by the police, Tim especially,' says Nick. 'I was too young to suffer any of that.'

On the cusp of becoming a teenager himself, Nick was nonetheless poised for serious trouble in Wang. 'It was your typical country town,' he says, 'in that everyone headed down to the main street on Saturday night and hung around and got into fights. I saw my first real fist fight outside the Greek fish-and-chip shop. This little guy was just about to start eating a hamburger when it happened. He was a nasty little fucker. I saw him stuff the whole hamburger into his mouth and start swinging. That really impressed me. Very exciting.'

Later, Nick would eulogise his brother Tim in the Grinderman song 'Fire Boy' (2010). '"Fire Boy" is about the loss of ideals and its effect and is a ramped-up version of my brother's escapades, for sure,' Nick says, 'with a bit of Baader–Meinhof thrown in!'

Dawn Cave says 'it's a myth' that Nick Cave was expelled from Wangaratta High School. Given she was a librarian there, and

Colin Cave was still teaching English part-time, it would be truer to say they could see the writing on the wall. Polite hints that it might be better for Nick to leave came to a head when he was involved in an incident with two older boys who pulled down the underwear of a fifteen-year-old girl in the school playground. Nick raises an eyebrow when discussing the incident. 'The parents of the girl tried to have me charged with rape. But I was only twelve years old, so the charge didn't stick. The other boys weren't much older than me. It was just a silly prank that got out of hand.'

Nick was in second form. Dawn says, 'He was made to go round with a conduct card in his pocket all the time. Every class, the teacher had to sign it to say he was good. And he had to wait outside at the end of each class to have it signed. I'd go to the staffroom and teachers would always be saying, "I've just had your son." Eventually one night one of the teachers I was friends with, Joy Star, was driving me home. I must have sat with her in the car outside our house for two hours while she persuaded me to get Nick to leave Wangaratta. She felt he had much more to offer, that he was too bright. "But he loves the reputation he is getting," she said, "and he is going from bad to worse. For heaven's sake, get him out!"' Something about this story coats Dawn's eyes with tears that don't fall. 'I can still see us sitting there in the car as it got darker and darker,' she says, 'till there was no daylight at all. She really cared.'[22]

'I do remember Joy Star,' Nick says, though he never knew she played such a crucial hand in changing his life. 'She passed me on my Tea Making Badge at Cub Scouts even though the cup I made her was cold and horrible. I didn't boil the kettle long enough. You make someone a cup of tea and if they think you have done it successfully you get the badge. I just remember doing a botched job of it and Joy saying, "Don't worry, Nicky boy, you'll get your badge."'

Something else was beginning to make its appeal felt to Nick: a mix of music, landscape and literature stirring up a new sense of language within him. 'The first book that I read where I felt a real quickening of the heart in regard to language was when I was ten years old, when I was reading a Tarzan novel by Edgar Rice Burroughs – and it described a lion resting in the jungle and "spasmodically" moving its tail. I remember very clearly getting a physical charge from that word – loving it but not knowing what it meant,' he says.

Nick had a makeshift bedroom arrangement, sleeping in what was effectively a sunroom. 'It was the room you went through on the way to the toilet. Where I lay, I had my head right beside this old boiler.' An adjoining room functioned as Julie's bedroom. She'd cry out, 'Nick, tell me a story.' And he would relish the opportunity almost every night. The deal they brokered was that Julie would make him a hot chocolate each morning in exchange for a tale. Julie recalls Nick had to 'almost shout the stories out to me. Or speak quite loudly, anyway.'[23] They both refer to what Nick calls 'a favourite one' about a deep-sea diver 'going down deep into the water looking for gold'. At various moments during the dive, sharks and other forms of danger approach. Nick would provoke shrieks of fear in Julie. Eventually the diver finds the bar of gold he is seeking and comes to the surface. 'And it turns out it is just a little kid in the bath with a block of soap, imagining it all.' Nick looks a little sheepish when he retells the story now. 'I was only twelve!' he adds defensively. In fact, Julie is not sure Nick actually came up with the story on his own, or if he absorbed it from somewhere and forgot its origins. Not that it mattered. He developed a litany of horror stories and scary tales, delighting in Julie's terror. 'Yeah, I cut my teeth on her,' he says, smiling.

'One of my favourite contemporary authors is the crime writer James Lee Burke,' says Nick, 'who writes the most beautiful descriptive prose about the town of New Iberia in Louisiana: Spanish moss, the Bayou Teche, antebellum houses, purple mists, rattling lightning, et cetera, et cetera ... I loved the way he wrote about it so much I went there on my honeymoon with Susie. We drove around Arizona, Colorado, through Texas and down South – saw New Iberia on the map and headed there, all the way me telling Susie how beautiful this place would be because of what I had read in his twenty or so novels. When we arrived, it was actually full of Burger Kings and McDonald's and all the rest of the shit that American small towns consist of these days, but beneath it, deep down, you could sense Burke's ghosted vision of his home town rising up – it was a deeply selective representation and all about memory and its spirits; and so it is with me and Wangaratta. James Lee Burke says, "I have come to learn that memory and presence are inextricably connected and should never be seen as separate entities." This is so true. The past is always there, calling to us, whether it be Ned Kelly rising from the fog or my father crunching down the garden path late at night or the spirits of our absent friends reminding us that there is still much to know and much to learn.

'In my memory Wangaratta is a magical place, where only good things ever happened. The swinging rope, the willow trees, the railway bridge, the pylons, the roots of half-submerged trees rising out of the muddy water – all that stuff – it's there in "Bluebird", "Carry Me", "Sad Waters", "Your Funeral ... My Trial", "Where the Wild Roses Grow" ... if a song has a river in it, it's that spot in Wangaratta just under the train tracks where we used to go as kids,' he says. 'It's an idyllic substructure that sorrowful tales of corrupted innocence can rest upon. I wouldn't trade all that for anything.

'I was both terrified and excited when I left, but I remember feeling deep down that I was being sent away. I was always under the impression that I was asked to leave Wangaratta High School, but now I wonder if that's true. Mum says she sent me to Melbourne to "save me from Wang", but I remember it as being kicked out of high school. Whatever the reason, I certainly felt at the time that I was being sent to Melbourne because I was in too much trouble. That's not to say I felt like my mum and dad didn't love me. I always felt that, I always felt supported by them and that they had a special place in their hearts for me. The "trouble" thing was supported by the fact that at the first class I was in at Caulfield Grammar School, the teacher came into the classroom, pointed straight at me and said, "Sit down, Cave. We've heard all about you!" I felt this comment very deeply because it supported the notion that I had left Wangaratta under a cloud of strife – and as I knew no-one there, I felt very isolated. So I felt ashamed and lonely, but also I remember feeling angry, like, "Who the fuck are you? You don't know anything about me."

'So, like I say, Wang represents a childhood ideal – the river, the ghost gums, magpies, the ranges, the swimming pool, the paper run, my bike, the mighty trees we would climb, the footpaths that would fry our bare feet hard, storm drains, yabbie dams, the high bridges we jumped off, swim holes, vast star-filled skies, the living moon, the smell of a storm coming in the dust, the stench of the abattoir as you came into town from the Glenrowan end, the nests of red-backs [spiders] out in the compost, snakes, the wool mills – they're all symbols of my childhood that come up repeatedly in my song writing and that connect to a sense of childish wonder that was lost or at least changed when I left to go to boarding school in Melbourne at age thirteen. I caught the train to Melbourne and the world changed into something different, complicated and ultimately adversarial for me. It would never be the same again.'

PART III

SONNY'S BURNING

The Word

MELBOURNE

1971–75

The fields of Caulfield Grammar School stretched out in the early summer morning like a burning lake, the sun igniting the dew. Nick walked the green edges on his way to class, still thunderstruck to be there. Founded in 1881 as 'a thoroughly Christian' school, the Anglican college took as its motto the Latin phrase *Labora ut requiescas*: 'Work hard that you may rest content.'

Despite this familiar Protestant ethic, and the school's reputation for progressive teaching in the arts, Nick felt no contentment on the horizon. Instead, he sensed the geometry of a prison, the brute hierarchies of a boys' boarding school closing in around him from the very first day. Skinny and awkward, like some goofy fallen bird, he must have looked an easy mark for bullying. Closer examination would have revealed broad shoulders, a country boy's sinewy strength and dauntingly large hands that were as good as clubs when he formed them into fists. Cave had something else, too, in his favour when it came to defending himself: what might be called a killer instinct, a way of never giving up no matter what odds were stacked against him.

His future bandmates in The Boys Next Door and The Birthday Party, Mick Harvey and Phill Calvert, had also started at Caulfield Grammar. The three would slowly become friends, forming what would be their own little clique inside the school's Art House. Mick and Phill managed to avoid the periodic fights and bullying that broke out; Nick drew this bad energy to him like a magnet. 'Trouble seemed to be part of my DNA,' Nick says. 'I don't know why.'

He arrived to repeat second form in 1971, his reputation from Wangaratta High School trailing after him. Both Mick and Phill recall early sightings of Nick on the sports fields enmeshed in fights, often against older or bigger boys who had targeted him or found his smart-arse comments insufferable. The pecking order could be ruthless, exacerbated by conflicts between the boarders and 'day boys' like Mick and Phill, who lived in the surrounding suburbs. An encounter with one of Caulfield Grammar's more intimidating figures, the almost comic-book-sounding 'Beaver' Mills, was typical of what happened in a brawl. 'Nick's incredible under adverse conditions,' says Phill Calvert. 'He has incredible strength when he is under duress. It's this absolute driven, animal-type strength. I just could not believe it when the teacher broke it up: Nick was winning, he was on top and he was gonna kill Beaver.'[1]

Nick may have 'looked like an Art House wimp', to use Calvert's words, but to see him in a fight was, Mick Harvey agreed, 'quite scary'.[2] When Nick returned home to Wangaratta for the holidays, his old friend Bryan Wellington sensed the changes. Nick told him about it, how he had to fight. 'How unhappy it made him. There was no violence in our growing-up time in Wang; Nick was not a toughie or an aggressive personality,' Wellington insists. 'With Nick I saw how that came into his life later, when he was forced to leave and go down to Melbourne. I often think it wasn't Wang so much that influenced him, it was leaving Wang.'[3]

The gaps between each visit home were growing longer. When Nick did come back to town, Wellington says, 'we used to spend a lot of time writing out the lyrics to songs. I remember that being an important activity for us. Leonard Cohen, Dylan, John Lennon ... just listening and writing down all the words.'[4]

On one of these visits, Nick stayed with Bryan for a weekend. He brought with him from Melbourne a copy of *Fillmore East – June 1971*, a live album by Frank Zappa and The Mothers of Invention. Nick and Bryan blasted out the track 'Bwana Dik' on the record player again and again, partly to aggravate Wellington's father. Both boys thought the song's double entendres to be the height of wit. The absurdist jazz mania of the music, and the vocals – alternately cartoonish, operatic, orated or yelled – impressed them greatly: a compound of avant-garde style and crude humour cast in the mock form of a seduction taking place between a rock star and a groupie. 'Each time we played it Nick turned it up a little louder. I took great delight [in that],' says Bryan.[5]

The weekend over, Nick caught the train back to Melbourne. Bryan says he and Eddie had in the meantime 'became better friends after Nick left town, as it was then that the wagging, drinking, smoking and porn began at another friend's garage'. The duo would later fall out, arguing over a local girl. When she died unexpectedly of cancer, the rift became something deeper. Bryan Wellington was only sixteen when he fled from his 'anti-intellectual' father to live with his uncle and aunt in Wangaratta so that he could finish high school. Eddie Baumgarten signed on to join the navy at age fifteen. Bryan says that 'Eddie was sent away', but Anne remembers her brother being an adventurer and 'a pretty charismatic kid who drew people to him. That was how he and Nick connected. When Ed came back from the navy he had all these amazing stories about his trips around Asia. Bryan was a bit of an outsider. A nice kid, but not particularly cool and not in any group.'[6]

Bryan followed Nick's career from afar as he dealt with his own profound feelings of exile, then similar problems of addiction. After a long patch away from the town, he would end up back at the Holy Trinity Cathedral in Wangaratta, finding accommodation there as a groundsman and listening to rehearsals by the various boys' choirs as he went about his work over the years.

Asked what he most identifies with in Nick's lyrics, Bryan Wellington can only respond with jet-black humour: 'Maybe the drug-induced, not-caring attitude.' A little more genuinely, he adds, 'All this stuff is really hard to talk about.' The songs he can relate to most are like a dream of what it was like to be young: a dream of never being able to go back, or never really leaving. 'Music,' says Wellington, 'was always our escape from Wangaratta.'

He would obsess over Nick's 'The Hammer Song' as a key to something that happened to Nick in particular, and to all of them in some broader way. But when Bryan discusses why the song is so important, he is elusive and imprecise, suggesting its meaning without wanting to fully state what he feels privy to behind the lyrics. 'That is very autobiographical if you know the story,' he says. 'Nick talks about the hammer coming down and how it squashed all dreams. But it made no sound! It means a secret. To me the song is about Nick being sent off to boarding school. He's had a dream life and his tortured life began. It's Nick's idea of a bit of a joke, too. He likes to say things are true that no-one can say are true. There's a mystery to it. Failure is what it's about. A major failure in his eyes. The hammer coming down could be a God reference, but I don't think Nick means it that way.'[7]

It was during his first year as a boarder at Caulfield Grammar that Nick was summoned to his father's study after provoking Colin's ire yet again on a weekend visit home. Nick would write about this experience in his 1996 BBC radio essay 'The Flesh Made Word', in which he describes his father confronting him as a twelve-year-old and asking him what he had done to make the world a better place or improve the lot of his fellow man. Fairly obviously, Nick felt strange about this, and rather confused. He was just a kid. Unable to answer, he threw the question back at his father a little defiantly. Colin cited a few short stories he had written and pulled out the journals they appeared in. There was a moment of reconciliation between father and son as they shared in what they meant. But Nick could see the publications were at least a decade old, and any promise in them of something greater had long ago faded.[8]

Nick later described these stories as 'light and comic, the kind of thing you get in *Reader's Digest*. One was this humorous, quirky tale about a lady in a hat shop. It was clever and funny and quite lightweight. The other was a rewrite of *Snow White*. An adult rewrite,' he adds with a curious emphasis.

'My father and I became quite competitive as I got older,' Nick says. 'It was in some ways just me needing to assert myself against this giant personality my father had. So I actively sought out areas of knowledge he didn't have. And began reading things like Alfred Jarry. My father would usually have a withering reply about that kind of thing. I was also getting into painters, and that was not his area. I still remember telling him, "I've just been

looking at Mondrain." He looked up and said, "It's Mon–dri–an."
Then I backed out of the room.'

Despite this competition, there is no doubt that father and
son shared a profound love of literature. 'With *Lolita*, my father
actually sat me down and read the first chapter to me out loud –
I think he knew it by heart, actually. He unlocked the words
for me, explained why it was such a forceful first chapter, taught
me what alliteration was, the way the opening chapter drew you
in. He saw it as the greatest novel of the twentieth century. He
also recommended I read the murder of the pawnbroker scene in
Crime and Punishment, which I later studied in final-year English
Lit, and that had a huge impact on me. He got me to read *The
Old Man and the Sea* – Hemingway – that was cool – short and
sweet! Also *Lord of the Flies* …

'I can still remember the things he would say where he placed
an emphasis on the importance of style. Style over content. I'm
the same now. I've always been a style-over-content man, really.
It's not so much the content that interests me as the way it is said.
Anyway, when Dad first read me *Lolita* he was excited by the
sheer use of language, not what it was about. In some respects,
it's very inappropriate to turn a twelve-year-old boy on to *Lolita*.
It's an adult book. But my father would say there is more benefit
than harm in it.'

Cave's friend and English writer Will Self would hear of this
childhood encounter with *Lolita* via a journalist in 2010. One
would expect Self, a master of hyper-grotesque satires, to be a
relatively unshockable figure, but the idea of introducing a young
boy to *Lolita* seemed to do the trick. When Nick heard of this
misconception, he had to call Self personally and explain, 'No,
my father wasn't grooming me, as the journalist might have
implied! It was only the first chapter that Dad concentrated on
when he read to me. My father saw it as a brief lecture on the art

of the English language. I did go and look up what "loins" meant in the dictionary, though.'

After his father's first-chapter-only briefing on *Lolita*, Nick recalls 'reading a murder mystery novel of some kind. I must have been fourteen by then … My dad said, "If you're looking for blood and guts, read this," and tossed me *Titus Andronicus*. "Huge body count!" At a stretch my songs "O'Malley's Bar" and "The Curse of Millhaven" could be seen as responses to *Titus* for the ridiculously high, comic, horror-show death ratio. Just trying to please my old man, is all!'

In the wake of these experiences Cave admitted later, 'I will sit down together with my sons now and watch a hugely inappropriate film, usually some kind of horror story. They love it. They love having the shit scared out of them[9] … I can still remember an experience like that myself in that house in Caulfield North, when I was old enough to have graduated from sitting on the carpet to the big brown armchair. I sat there one night watching *Division 4* with my parents. It was all about a dead hooker. At the end there was this deathly silence, then all this uncomfortable shifting around from my father and mother. Finally Dad says, "I guess you're happy we let you watch that one."'

Amid all these thoughts and memories, Cave suspects, lies 'something that is driving the force of my songs'. Or some seed, at least, for the way his self-expression has developed. 'Definitely I'm excited when I write violent and sexual stuff by the details you can insert. That create this jarring effect, or have a telescoping effect: envisaging a scene then adding a detail that zooms in. I can think of other people's songs that do that too. An old traditional ballad like "Knoxville Girl", where it talks about killing a girl and then the lyric comes, "I drug her by the hair". The intimacy of detail: the songwriter is there. It isn't an objective, voyeuristic thing. Suddenly the writer is right there in the bloody guts of it.'

Even the novel he was reading when his dad tossed him *Titus Andronicus* had its virtues, he says. 'I think it was a fifties-style crime book with one of those raunchy fifties cover illustrations on it actually.[10] And on the very first page there was something about "the wicked little gun". There was something about the way that gun was described and I think it was the use of the diminutive, something so sinister about the use of the word "little". I've done that type of thing all my life. To me there is something quite beautiful in it.'[11]

Dawn wept each time she waved Nick goodbye from the railway station during 1971. She was not unaware of his unhappiness as a young boarder – she could see it in his face at the window as the train pulled out. Had she and Colin done the right thing? Dawn was not so sure anymore.

Nick would watch the world pass him by as his journey accelerated. In winter it was hard to see anything at all. The train would be very cold of a morning, his feet resting on a metal foot-warmer as the carriage rattled along, the mist outside so thick and cloudy it was as if Wangaratta had floated away. It made him think of ghost towns and tourist sites such as Glenrowan. The past could overtake the present and even be *more* alive. He cried too, of course.

Her son felt cast out, but, as Dawn Cave recalls it, her husband had visited 'every possible' boarding school in Melbourne to find one with the right mix of academic and 'human qualities'. What struck Colin Cave most about Caulfield Grammar School, he told Dawn, was that 'it was the only place where they had asked him what Nick was like as a person rather than just about his grades'.[12]

In retrospect, Nick is sanguine about the changes forced upon him. 'When I think about Wang, it's more about the freedom you can have as a child. I could go where I wanted to go: I lived my childhood by the river, under the railroad tracks, in the mountains. It's not so much a state of bliss as a child that I remember, more the way it could be as a child compared to how it is now. When I think about my own kids it grieves me that they don't have that freedom, that they can't experience it. Small country towns are beautiful to grow up in – and then to get out of by the age of twelve.'

When Colin Cave received news of his promotion to become Director of Adult Education in Victoria, Dawn was glad it would require a move to Melbourne from the start of 1972. Though they would miss Wang, it was an opportunity for the family to regroup. Nick was still boarding at Caulfield Grammar and clearly lonely; Tim was at Swinburne College of Technology studying sociology, and by his own account 'going to moratoriums and throwing rocks, getting up close and personal with police horses during protests'.[13] Though Dawn and Colin were not privy to their sons' wild worlds, they knew enough to sense more trouble brewing. Getting Peter out of Wangaratta was another benefit of the change.

So it was that Colin, Dawn, Peter and Julie shifted into a two-storey, five-bedroom house at 6 Airdrie Road in the middle-class suburb of Caulfield North. Tim agreed to move back in with them. Australia's involvement in the Vietnam War was winding down; a passion for Marxism was making way again in his life for musical obsessions such as The Moody Blues and Genesis. Nick returned to the fold in Caulfield North as well, absorbing big brother Tim's Molotov cocktail of rock 'n' roll and politics on a vaguely heroic level.

This was Tim Cave's heyday. Led Zeppelin had kicked open the year with a hugely powerful tour that asserted a long overdue generational shift in the wake of the 1960s. Their sound hit young people like the proverbial hammer of the gods. When Gough Whitlam's Australian Labor Party (ALP) swept to power in late 1972, it represented the stunning end to twenty-three years of unbroken conservative rule under the former Liberal and Country Party coalition governments. The ALP campaign slogan, 'It's Time', caught the public yearning for change. Whitlam immediately set about withdrawing the last troops from Vietnam, abolishing the death penalty, taking the sales tax off the contraceptive pill and making universities accessible to working-class youth by getting rid of exorbitant tertiary entrance fees. He also personally approved what seemed then to be the wildly extravagant $1.3 million purchase of Jackson Pollock's *Blue Poles* by the National Gallery of Australia in 1973.

Nick – as apolitical as his brother Tim was radically inspired – took almost no interest in anything outside of art and music. Looking back on the times, he says, 'I must have been at rehearsals a lot.' It would be naïve, however, to presume that this attitude meant he was unaffected. No artist escapes the landscape out of which they rise. For a start, it was the combination of free tertiary education and generous, as well as easily accessed, unemployment benefits that allowed a hedonistic and bohemian youth culture to flourish. Tim, and then Nick, revelled in this climate. Whitlam's electrifying victory and a favourably disposed attitude towards the arts launched a visionary charge into the future that also opened Australia up to the world. A tour by the Rolling Stones in 1973 crowned this cosmopolitan zeitgeist with a jet-set thrill. Lou Reed's 1974 tour brought a more poisonous glamour to the table, with both AC/DC and Stevie Wright acting as his supports. It was as if someone had flicked a switch from black and white to colour, a mood captured when television literally began to broadcast in colour in 1975. A relaxation of the licensing laws in Victoria in the early 1970s – associated with the voting age being dropped by Whitlam from twenty-one to eighteen – added to this youthful wave. Gigs were suddenly everywhere. A post-sixties, post-hippie sense of national identity flourished in the venues, theatres and art galleries, as well as universities where left-wing student unionism – and its entertainment tastes – seized the day. The advent of community and alternative radio across the FM bandwidth was another crucial element.

It would become a cliché that the sixties did not start till the seventies in Australia. When punk arrived in the late 1970s it may have distinguished itself in reaction to an early-seventies 'hippie' scene, but the truth was that it continued to deal in the same questions of cultural identity – if from the more aggressive and pessimistic vantage point of having seen the fleeting Whitlam-era renaissance terminated in 1975 and a conservative government and its agenda reinstalled. A young, hard-drinking audience was pumped up and ready to rage. The pub rock music they wanted got faster and tougher with them. By then, AC/DC were the yardstick by which all other live bands in Australia were measured. Their ability to convert parochial brutalism into a globally transcendent rock 'n' roll vernacular was not easily matched. The left-leaning wit and lyrical promise of inner Melbourne's Carlton music scene seemed feeble by comparison. Australian punk would struggle with a lack of local roots as its reactionary stance towards both the industry and past countercultural models intensified its internationalism and an inclination towards exclusivity and separatism.

Nick papered the walls of his bedroom with images that revealed a burgeoning interest in everything from German Expressionist cinema to El Greco's *View of Toledo*. 'I lifted a print of it from an art book in the school library. Best thing El Greco ever did. It was the only piece of art I had on my wall, apart from all the usual religious crap of suffering saints and the like.'[14] A group photo of The Boys Next Door taken in 1979 by his friend Peter Milne gives a good idea of how his room eventually looked.[15] 'In that picture,' Nick says, 'I think there is [also] a pretty bad Brett Whiteley-esque etching of Adolf Hitler that I did at school – basically John Christie with swastikas – that everyone thought showed great promise and which Mum hung up in the house at Airdrie Road, which is only further testament to my mother's undying love for her child – particularly as we lived in Caulfield North, the Jewish heartland of Melbourne.'[16] Also on Nick's wall was a large, framed painting of an old lady in Victorian-era garb, who seems to stare down aghast at the chaotic state of the room. 'It may have been a relative of some sort. I just liked it because the woman looked kind of retarded and spooky.'

Such decorations were more sophisticated than the usual 1970s teenage boy's predilection for posters of *Kiss Alive!* and *Charlie's Angels'* Farrah Fawcett – not that Nick was unaware of the latter's appeal.[17] One of his favourite sex symbols of the era was Abigail, who played Bev Houghton on the risqué Australian soapie series *Number 96*. Blonde and busty, Abigail Rogan became such a sensation she never needed to use her full name again. Her autobiography, *Call Me Abigail*, sold an astounding 150,000 copies in 1973. Abigail even managed a Top 10 smash the same year with her breathy, orgasmic cover of the Serge Gainsbourg song 'Je t'aime … moi non plus'. Despite the overt eroticism, Gainsbourg always claimed that it was an 'an anti-fuck song', dealing in physical love as an act of desperation, and ultimately something impossible to attain. Nick saw and heard something he liked, to which he would later return as a singer in 1995 on a recording with his first great (and by then estranged) muse, Anita Lane.[18]

Living at 6 Airdrie Road gave Nick a degree of pop-culture kudos that he bragged about at school. The house had been the former home of *World Championship Wrestling* and all-round Saturday-morning TV hero Mario Milano. Nick enjoyed telling people that when the family moved into Caulfield North there was 'a suspicious ball of wiry black hair in the shower cubicle that everyone was afraid to go near'. He was mightily pleased with the wrestling connection, though he claimed later, 'It would have been even better if the house had belonged to "Haystacks" Calhoun!'[19]

His troubles at nearby Caulfield Grammar School, however, were not over. Nick proved he was a force to be reckoned with among the boarders. But in third form he found himself a member of their hated opposition, the 'day scabs'. Allies were thin on the ground and he lived under a thuggish cloud. Nick had now been put through the pecking-order rituals three times: commencing high school in Wangaratta, recommencing his second year as a boarder at Caulfield, then again as he joined the day students. The cycle felt endless. His unruly attitude continued in class, the rebel-and-clown act a typical adolescent bid for popularity. As Mick Harvey noted, 'He was quite an extrovert at school; everyone knew him and he made a show of himself.'[20]

Busted for carving his initials into an old dining-hall table, Nick was made to stay back after school, sandpapering the wood clear of all its marks and restoring it completely. The restoration took him two weeks of detention. When it was done, he was told to turn the table over and inscribe his initials again underneath. Nick's mother was mortified by Nick's vandalism. The wisdom of the punishment convinced Dawn and Colin they had made the right choice with Caulfield Grammar, despite Nick's problems.

Wendy Stavrianos, Nick Cave's art teacher in 1971 and 1972, saw a very different young man to the class troublemaker and schoolyard rabblerouser. 'Nick had this wonderful energy that not many kids have. He was engaged with things. There was a sort of intensity, an excitement there. I remember a drawing that he did, a beautiful pen-and-ink drawing of a baby in the womb. For a boy that age to do something like that, I mean it would be uncool. But Nick was never worried what anyone thought. At that time he was really all over the place – I think he was trying to work out who he was and what he was on this planet for. He was at that point where he was reacting to everything – literature, art – and trying to find a path. He was never defiant to me. I never saw him in any other capacity than being really easy to get on with. We talked; it was just like friends in the class. But I know that he probably crossed a lot of other members of staff because he was going through that stage. One day he even came in with a bit of make-up on and said, "How do I look?" It was gorgeous! I didn't say, "That's disgusting" – I said, "I think it looks great!", going along with what he was actually experiencing.'[21]

Nick says Wendy Stavrianos is the one who inculcated a lifelong passion in him for the paintings of Edvard Munch. 'At school, when I was a pimply, cum-encrusted teen, my art teacher Wendy Stavrianos, who I lusted after horribly, leaned over my desk and explained the erotic symbolism of *The Dance* [*of Life*] and I was blown away. The moon and its reflection as a phallus, our dark selves and better selves in a dance or grapple to the death, the picture swimming before my eyes, her rich, Greek cigarette laugh … We were all floundering and she inspired us.'

It was during his third year that Nick finally began to settle into a stable peer group, a collective of outsiders and oddballs who 'mostly liked to hang out around the Art House', Mick Harvey recalls. 'We certainly weren't interested in playing sport during the lunch hour. We'd listen to music a lot. There were probably a few good spots around the Art House as well where we could smoke without getting caught.' It was from this Art House gang that a band started up. Mick Harvey says they were playing together as early as mid-1972, albeit in highly tentative form and without a singer. Phill Calvert was the most skilled musician by far, having taken drum lessons since the age of ten from Les Tasker, who had been a member of the Moscow

Circus. Brett Purcell joined on bass and Mick handled guitar duties. Chris Coyne began playing sax soon after. With bands like Iron Butterfly and Led Zeppelin popular, they started calling themselves Concrete Vulture as a joke. 'There just seemed to be all these bands around at the time with these ridiculous names based on opposites,' says Mick Harvey.[22]

Concrete Vulture started rehearsing in a classroom, then on weekends at a parish hall in Ashburton that was in the care of Mick's father, the local Anglican vicar. Eventually, Nick tried out as a singer, arriving at the parish hall one Saturday afternoon in 1973 with a memorably surly, defensive attitude and a hip flask, from which the fifteen-year-old vocalist kept swigging vodka. Mick Harvey laughs: 'He wasn't that great as a singer, in fact he couldn't sing at all, but [he] looked and acted like a front man, so he was in. Like I said, he was always a bit of a show-off.'[23]

The school band at Caulfield Grammar, 1973. Left to right: Mick Harvey (seated), John Cocivera (guitar), Chris Coyne (sax), Phill Calvert (drums), some random guy on vocals who had just joined, and Brett Purcell (bass).
(Wayne Purcell; courtesy of Phill Calvert)

Cave brought someone else along to the rehearsal, a guitarist by the name of John Cocivera, who was quickly recruited. With the band gaining a much more serious lead guitarist in Cocivera, Mick Harvey could focus on his first love, playing rhythm. Things really started to move along. The boys felt excited by what they were doing. It started to all seem real.

Back in Wangaratta, Anne Baumgarten received a letter about Cocivera she never forgot. 'Nick told me about having met this new friend at school and how he had this incredible record collection and a record player with the biggest arm on it he had ever seen, a needle arm as big as a cannon, he said. Nick went on and on about it. He was really crazy about music by then and everything to do it with it, from magazines to clothes to record players. He'd always tell me that English music was better than American music because of how skinny the guitarists' legs were.'[24]

Nick says John Cocivera was 'the absolute sweetest guy. He based his smooth guitar style around David Gilmour [of Pink Floyd]. Music was his absolute life. A beautiful-looking guy – the girls adored him, but he was painfully shy around them. He had a very sensitive, drifty style on the guitar. He played a maroon Gibson SG copy. All we did was listen to music together, after school and on the weekends. We were very close.'

The question of what to name the band took years to resolve. After Concrete Vulture they decided on Madwich. Then they tried Quaker Lady, Caliban, and S-Bend. Heavy Freedom was floated as another possibility by Nick. Grasping at straws, an end-of-year high-school concert in 1974 would see Nick tell organisers they were called The Magic Pudding.[25] Mick Harvey explains that 'Norman Lindsay was something of an obsession for Nick at the time.' By 1975 things really hit bottom when the band started calling themselves Café. 'A really shit name,' says Mick. 'So shit I had put it out of my mind entirely.'[26] Then it was

Kissy Loftus Band and, at least in stupid conversations, Nicky Danger and the Bleeding Hearts.

There were more. But these seem to be the significant ones. Calvert and Harvey claim the band had a different name every second week, usually at Nick's prompting. Once they had well and truly mastered 'a few West, Bruce and Laing covers'[27], along with standards like 'Johnny B Goode' and 'Boney Maronie' – and realising they were incapable of playing the intricate filigrees that prog-rock demanded the band began to pursue a passion for glam rock. The possibility of playing a few shows at nearby Shelford Girls' Grammar School provided further motivation for everyone to improve and show off even more. It may have been at one of these shows they tried calling themselves Suffragette City. Mostly they can't remember exactly what they were called across these early years. All agree, however, that they are heartily sick of reading that it was Concrete Vulture, when that was the first name they came up with and it barely lasted six months.

Nick was fixated on David Bowie and The Sensational Alex Harvey Band. He remembers 'rushing home from school, locking my bedroom door and putting *David Live* [1974] on the stereo, pretending I was singing to all those people'. Bowie's *Aladdin Sane* (1973) had caused a rift with Tim, who was still heavily into Yes's *Close to the Edge* (1972) as well as blues-influenced, psychedelic equivalents such as Australia's Madder Lake. Tim's music tastes fitted the dope-smoking mood of the era: an ethos of mind expansion and good times, with a hard-partying edge on the rise. Nick was stepping out of the shadow of his big brother's authority and defining his own stomping style, even if Hawkwind's 'space rock' still provided them with some common ground.[28] Glam rock versus prog rock was the teenage culture war of the period, a case of pop-art trash overtaking neo-classical pomp. In simpler terms, singles rather than albums were starting to drive the market again as a younger generation of music buyers entered the fray. Eventually they had their own albums to listen to as well. Before long Nick cut his hair Bowie-style, appearing at home with a rooster-ishly feathered coiffure à la 'Ziggy Stardust'.

Dawn says that she and Colin 'reacted with amusement, I guess, and wondering what was going to happen next. We were never judgemental or disapproving, as it was all done light-heartedly and a bit of a joke. Tracy, Mick and the boys were such nice boys [and] they were always good to have around, whatever way they chose to look.' Julie recalls seeing her brother dress up 'in little tight shorts and fishnets, a tight green shirt, braces and lots of make-up. The suits were the next thing he got into after that.'[29]

Phill Calvert, drums, 1973 *(Wayne Purcell; courtesy of Phill Calvert)*

Apart from the brilliant cosmic strut of Marc Bolan's T-Rex, it was Nick's hero David Bowie who dominated glam, giving it a sophistication missing in the likeable but essentially bubble-gum thrust of everyone from Slade to Gary Glitter and Australia's own Hush. Bolan and Bowie exuded a more poetic and androgynous style with ease – the other chart-makers mostly looked and sounded like men with five o'clock shadows who wore make-up and tinfoil as the latest pop fad demanded, all the while thumping out brash and reverb-drenched hits.

Bowie had the magpie art of appropriation and a cooler intuitive intellect in his favour, absorbing lessons from past countercultural masters: the late 1960s multi-media Pop Art happenings known as Andy Warhol's Exploding Plastic Inevitable; the associated songs of The Velvet Underground (with Lou Reed exploring everything from S&M to heroin as subject matter); and the outrageous garage-rock energy of The Stooges, fronted by a boyish, coiled and animalistic Iggy Pop This combination of references had already led David Bowie to develop his breakthrough concept album *The Rise and Fall of Ziggy Stardust and the Spiders from Mars* (1972). According to Bowie, 'It just seemed perfectly natural for me to put together all these odds and ends of art and culture that I really adore.'[30]

For most fans of pop music the baggage behind this cultural transformation would remain obscure. But for hardcore music lovers like Nick Cave, Bowie acted as a bridge – within his music and lyrics, as well as through his flamboyant interviews – taking inquisitive teenagers from the mainstream into the rock 'n' roll avant-garde and beyond. 'Bowie was supposed to be a chameleon, that's the theory. He was anything but that,' Nick says. 'The idea that he disappeared into his work and whatever persona he created for each record he did is just ridiculous. Bowie was many things, but the one thing you can say for sure is that he never disappeared from view.' Bowie would later admit that in putting on his Ziggy Stardust mask, 'I found my character – one man against the world.'[31] It was almost everything Nick could have asked for in a rock star at the time.

The Sensational Alex Harvey Band, or SAHB as they were commonly known, were something else again as a teenage influence during the mid-1970s. On the one hand they rode the glam craze, but there was none of Bowie's androgynous and self-consciously arty vibe about them. A tough Scottish rock 'n' roll band, they were spearheaded – as their name suggests – by Alex Harvey, a brilliant showman capable of delivering over-the-top rock 'n' pop outlaw monologues such as 'Framed', followed by a piece of highbrow European cabaret such as Jacques Brel's 'Next'. It was an audacious combination best witnessed live, but Nick adored the recordings.[32]

Almost a quarter of the school band's set list would come from the first two SAHB albums, including 'Framed', 'Midnight Moses', 'Isobel Goudie' and 'The Hammer Song'. Nick admits Bowie's music was mostly too complex for the teenage band to master, despite their best efforts. SAHB had a bluesy directness that was much more available to the boys' playing and Nick's basic singing abilities.

There's an argument that SAHB's theatrical music was a showy precursor to the noir aggression of the punk era in the United Kingdom. Harvey said he abhorred any violence at his shows, but there was no denying the ferocity of a SAHB performance or Harvey's delight in being intimidating. Harvey's own band would admit he even frightened them now and again. At a time when glam promoted a feminised masculinity, the only pantyhose Alex Harvey wore was pulled down over his head to look like the Glaswegian hoodlum he mythologised while

Nicky Danger, vocalist, c. 1974
(Ashley Mackevicius)

singing 'Framed'. Nick took to Harvey's story-like songs of romantic thuggery like a duck to water, inhabiting their natural drama on stage.[33] There was also something defiantly camp about Harvey's performing style, a malevolent humour that only added to the edges. Reading about his larger-than-life personality in rock magazines provided irresistible material for the teenage Nick Cave. If Bowie was the androgynous alien, Alex Harvey was the erotic criminal.

Nick would cover Harvey's 'The Hammer Song' again for posterity on his album *Kicking Against the Pricks* (1986). Never shy of taking a phrase or an idea and making it his own, he would even write an original song with the same title on *The Good Son* (1990). It is interesting to also reflect on a SAHB tune called 'There's No Lights on the Christmas Tree, Mother, They're Burning Big Louie Tonight': the tale of a criminal being sent to the electric chair, it has a West End musical theatre feel with some exaggerated rock 'n' roll snarl. Magic Pudding did not play it, but Nick enjoyed singing along to it at home. Though more of a joke song, it may have helped seed a later Nick Cave classic, 'The Mercy Seat'. Listening to SAHB, a young Nick Cave was learning many things: among them the possibilities of a theatricality that maximised a take-no-prisoners aggression, matched by the power of narrative song writing and a fearless lyricism that drew on base masculine resources and a goodly dose of aggressive street humour as much as any refined poetic interests.

On a Grinderman tour of the United Kingdom in 2010, Nick Cave would have an opportunity to express his gratitude to the late and greatly underestimated Alex Harvey by dedicating a show at the Barrowland Ballroom in Glasgow to the memory of his former hero. 'The Barrowlands is this vast old-school venue. Alex Harvey would have played it many times,' Cave says. 'I explained to the audience how he changed the trajectory of our young lives. His stuff is the shit! "Midnight Moses" ...

great song. Anyway, a journalist reviewing the show took this to mean Grinderman were heavily influenced by AH. Not true, but man, did he blow my mind when I was about fifteen. "Isobel Goudie", "Faith Healer", "Gang Bang", "Hammer Song" were all real life-changers for me. Especially his lyrics and phrasing. Of course, he sings in a heavy Glaswegian accent, but I didn't really understand that at the time. I just thought he sang like someone from outer space! And the words! There was nothing like [the song] "Shark's Teeth" around. Wow!'

Nick says, 'I had my first kiss with a girl called Penny in Wang when I was twelve. It was to the song "Venus" by Shocking Blue.' When pressed, he can still echo the sentiments with enthusiasm: 'You're my desire!'

He speaks of another budding romance that began by correspondence at age thirteen. Nick had cultivated a sixteen-year-old pen pal in England called Dorothy. 'I may have exaggerated my age by a few years in my letters. Anyway, the moment came when she asked to exchange photos. Mum took a picture of me in the backyard. I had this stripy jumper on that Mum had knitted me, tucked into my jeans. I looked like the kid I was. Once I sent that I never heard from Dorothy again,' he says, laughing.

Though Anne Baumgarten describes their relationship as 'mostly platonic', she received a stream of letters from Nick, especially when he was struggling to stave off loneliness as a boarder at Caulfield Grammar. There's something inherently romantic about this communication, as if lifted straight from a classic Australian coming-of-age film like *The Year My Voice Broke*.

Nick's correspondence with Anne continued well into his teens, maintaining his links with the Baumgartens and

Wangaratta. 'We'd write really crazy letters to each other,' Anne says, laughing. 'One of the things I really liked about Nick [was that] he wasn't your average friend – he could be very intuitive and go off on any tangent or thinking. He had a lot of warmth and humour.'

Now and again Anne would catch a train and visit Nick in Melbourne, or vice versa. He would return to Wang bearing vinyl gifts and they'd sit again in Anne's blue-painted listening room, its window busted by a football, the wind blowing through, day into night, and no-one caring. 'Nick introduced to me to all these bands. Especially the British ones – Yes, Genesis, Pink Floyd and even The Moody Blues. But more than Cohen or any others, his main obsession became David Bowie. He really liked the cover of *Diamond Dogs*, but it irritated me. He gave me his copy of *Ziggy Stardust*. I felt uneasy about this because the album I gave him in return wasn't as good.

'Nick embraced glam-rock fashion too. I still have a gold-coloured crushed velvet jacket he used to borrow when we went to The Kettle, the local coffee shop for youths, situated in the main street of Wang. He liked to wear eye make-up and bracelets, but he also wore ripped jeans and tight jumpers.'

Anne also remembers Nick's growing interest in 'sketching, musical theatre, pottery and other forms of art. There was one stage when he was very much into Ray Bradbury's books. It seemed to me that Nick wanted to cram as much experience of art and ideas as he could into his teenage years. Nick was really into the I Ching too. Zen Buddhism. He must have been about sixteen by then. It's a very random religion.'[34]

Visiting Nick in Melbourne, Anne felt very welcome, but she was slightly less comfortable at the Caves' Caulfield North home. 'After dinner the family would sit around the table playing civilised games of Scrabble. I agonised over these games because the family, especially Colin, had such terrific vocabularies. I struggled to find

School band Madwich mixed Bowie, SAHB, Genesis and garage-rock influences, 1975 (Ashley MacKeulrius)

one- or two-syllable words to play. Colin had a strong character, that's for sure. He was very committed to the subject of English. Some people could find that daunting, but I wasn't frightened of him. Holding back his irritation in Scrabble is pretty minor stuff. Dawn was always very even-tempered, absolutely gorgeous, a really gracious lady. Julie was pretty extroverted; she had a bizarre sense of humour. Tim was right out there – with his politics, his girlfriends. Peter was quieter, he wore glasses, I got the feeling he was quiet with the others. He was studying electrical engineering. Peter was nice. They were a really nice family.'

During the day while she was in Melbourne, 'Nick and I used to go shopping in Bourke Street. He'd take me to The In Shop opposite Myer's. And then to a coffee shop down the Spencer Street end. It was so atmospheric.'

They were about sixteen when these visits and their letters finally faded. 'We grew apart,' Anne says matter-of-factly, before adding, 'Nick *really* got into the music. I've still got his *Ziggy Stardust* album. Maybe I should have given it back to him.'[35]

Some forty years later, Anne Shannon (née Baumgarten) wants Nick to know she's been out living at Lajamanu in the Northern Territory's Central Desert, 'teaching with my husband, teaching very young Aboriginal children to read and write, and about things like nutrition and a better quality of life'. It's been a wonderful experience, no regrets. 'I was just happy to have known Nick and see him go into music like the people we listened to and dreamed about.'[36]

Julie Cave remembers her brother showing her a tiny six-line Leonard Cohen poem that he liked at the time entitled 'For Anne'. It was not hard to figure out why Nick was so fond of it. It's a love poem and the name matches. With typical economy, Cohen subtly references the famed balcony scene from *Romeo and Juliet* – 'But soft, what light through yonder window breaks? It is the East and Juliet is the sun'[37] – before dropping away radically to an understanding of memory as the ultimate form of awareness and a source of grieving. It seems Nick already had a highly attuned sense of the nature of loss and its inevitability.

Nick would become an inveterate letter writer (and then emailer) for the rest of his life. Together with his notebooks, journals and numerous inky drafts of his prose and lyrics, he would place increasing emphasis on the physical act of writing as much as the words themselves, a graphomania that found its most potent embodiment in 'Love Letter' (2001), a song he wrote during the early stages of his courtship with Susie Bick.[38]

It's for this reason, perhaps, that Nick is especially touched to hear of an extensive and effusive thirteen-page letter written about him by his first real girlfriend, Davina Davidson (née Sherman).[39] When he reads it he is amazed by 'the accuracy of Davina's memories, the textures, and the little things I'd forgot[ten] that were so true, like the way I would never take my shoes off even when I was inside the house'.

Nick had only just finished fourth form when their relationship began. Davina can still picture them meeting on an intense summer's day during the Christmas school holidays of 1973–74. Colin Cave's role as the Director of Adult Education in Melbourne continued to give Nick entrée into all kinds of courses and subjects. Davina found herself doing a ceramics class with an intense young man hunched over a series of clay figures that she remembers taking shape as a clown, a violinist and a vagabond. Nick was inclined to dismiss his sculptures as rubbish, but Davina thought them vivid, if a little grotesque. Not so their maker, with his long legs and dark hair and a single earing. So cool.

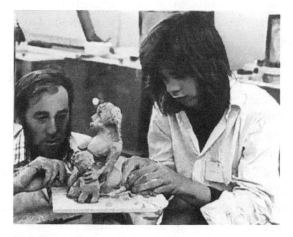

Nick Cave, sculpture course, c. 1975 *(photographer unknown)*

Davina fondly remembers the black clogs Nick liked to wear in summer, the sound of him when he stood to walk across a room.

Nick says that soon after he and Davina met, 'We went to the Myer Music Bowl for a date and had a kiss and a cuddle. As I was walking her home, she got all upset and said, "I can't be with you." I couldn't think what the problem was. Then I'm thinking it's because she's a lesbian. Then she says, "Cause I'm Jewish!" She had to stop going to the synagogue to be with me. She was living in Melbourne with Jewish foster parents at the time. It was a really big deal.'

Davina was only a year younger than Nick, but a year can mean a lot when you are just fifteen. She describes her sixteen-year-old boyfriend as a deeply serious and artistic young man, exceptionally mature and sure of himself. Within a week of their Myer Music Bowl date, Nick would show her a hardcover notebook full of short stories and poems he was working on. A week after that, Nick handwrote Davina a personalised tale based on the Book of Genesis story of Methuselah. Nick took advantage of what was then his beautifully cursive and flowing penmanship to make the gift all the more impressive. A few days after that, Davina came home from school and found a single red rose Nick had left for her.

As romantic gifts go, a rose from a teenage boy is a bit more conventional than a short story about the oldest human being to appear in the Bible. The grandfather of Noah and a connecting patriarch between the Christian and Jewish faiths, Methuselah was being used by Nick to write his way into romantic harmony with Davina, despite her family concerns over their differing faiths. Davina says, 'I have a very vague memory the short story was influenced by Hemingway's *The Old Man and the Sea*, perhaps in style. I do not remember it having a particularly outright Biblical slant, although there was a Biblical undertow. Nick was very good at that ... connections, interconnections, innuendoes.'[40]

'During the years we dated I remember clearly that Nick had a turbulent relationship with God. He was not at all "keen" on Jesus and was excessively sceptical about him being "the Son of God". He had an extensive criticism of the Church, that I remember clearly. But he was not reading the Bible much. If anything, *Lolita* was in his pocket, not the New or Old Testament.'[41]

Somewhere between the moment of his introduction to Leonard Cohen's *Songs of Love and Hate* and the news of his imminent departure from Wang, Nick had begun to write poetry. He was twelve years old when he started. His father's lecture on *Lolita* was welded into this unhappy transition in Nick's life and how he began to process it with writing. This was well advanced by the time Nick was sixteen and falling in love with Davina Davidson. She was enchanted by his talents as the first few weeks of their relationship blossomed. Nick could sculpt and draw and paint. Nick could write stories and poetry. Nick was a romantic with his roses. And she was about to find out that Nick had musical abilities too.

'Often he would write me poems and stories and draw me sketches,' Davina says. 'I saw them as being little parts of Nick that he gifted me.' She remembers the very first time she visited the Cave family home and going upstairs with Nick to his bedroom, where 'pretty much immediately he pushed into my hand a hardcover notebook with some of his writings … It was definitely a first to meet a boy that was happy to have you see his insides.' Digging out an old diary from 1974, Davina finds she has written these words: 'The figurines caught my eye, his writing has snatched my heart.'[42]

A Caulfield Grammar school report for Term 2 in 1974 contains a revealing list of complaints and praise from those less loved. An unnamed art teacher thinks Nick uses the classes as 'little more than an escape'. Various other teachers suggest that Nick's grades are below what he is capable of, or above what he deserves. Cave's English teacher goes into the details: 'Though he has not done all the set written work, Nikolas [sic] has achieved some very interesting results particularly at home. His attitude to the subject and the teacher is subject to moods brought into class. He'd make it easier for others if he withdrew into a book to allow me to help others who have not yet finished.' Below this grievance, the English teacher added a somewhat surprised note: 'NB Nikolas's [sic] poetry is due to be published in a school magazine and reflects a profound craftsman!!'[43]

Tim Cave saw the provocative side of his brother's language abilities. He recalls disputes with Nick in which 'he would say things and call you names where you weren't really sure what he was calling you. I remember us arguing one time and Nick saying something to me like, "You're pernicious." I had to check it in the dictionary. That was the kind of thing Nick would come out with all the time.'[44]

⸻

Nick and Davina lived only a few blocks apart and the habits of their romance quickly took shape. 'I used to pass her and her girlfriend on the way to school,' he says. 'They'd sit on the fence and titter as I walked by.' Come the end of each weekday, Davina would rush over to the Cave residence. 'I can still remember her clacking up the driveway in her Dr. Scholl's and her school uniform to meet me.'

While the bond with her Jewish foster parents was strained by the ongoing relationship with Nick, Davina found herself happily accepted, even adopted into the Cave family. Her memories of Nick's mother are domestic and warm: Dawn kneeling on a mat and weeding and planting in her garden, or simply sitting in the kitchen, working on a crossword puzzle in the daily newspaper.

Davina recalls Nick was supposed to mow the lawns, but it was a duty he was dragged to and tended to avoid.

Colin was often not home. As well as working in the city with Adult Education, in his spare time he was heavily involved with the Malvern Theatre Company as a director. Nick remembers his father being around more at the weekend, when Colin liked to sit outside 'in the backyard, under the apricot tree doing his crossword and looking at the birds in the aviary he built. Must be why I like birds so much.'

There was a small room beside the kitchen with an old upright black piano that Nick liked to play. Davina would sit there for hours with him. Nick sang songs such as Lou Reed's 'Perfect Day' – a tune Davina still thinks of as the proverbial 'our song' – and composed his own early works beside her. On Saturdays she would go with him to band practice, where Nick and his friends worked with mixed success on covers by David Bowie, Lou Reed, Bryan Ferry, Genesis, Queen. These were all favourites of Nick's back then, Davina says. She began to notice that although he was not the leader in any apparent way, Nick was becoming the centre of the band, exerting an influence that affected and drove everyone. One thing she recalls, absolutely, is 'Nick's desire to be famous'. A desire she dismissed, even with all her admiration for him, as a typical teenage fantasy. Looking back, she believes Nick knew he was indeed exceptional and was already working hard towards the destiny he had mapped out for himself.

Each member of the band had their quirks. Mick Harvey was thoughtful and quiet, Davina says. John Cocivera shy and a little vulnerable. Phill Calvert somewhat cocky and sure of himself. Tracy Pew, who was only hanging around, but soon to join the band, was wilder and different to the others. As an outsider observing them, Davina felt that each of the boys was so distinct in his personality that they hardly made any sense as a group of friends, let alone as a band that might stay together.

Mick Harvey, Roxy Music fan, 1975
(Ashley Mackevicius)

Davina and Nick would spend hours and hours in Nick's bedroom, chastely listening to music, she insists. Going to a concert by Queen was their most memorable live event. The young couple loved Freddie Mercury's singing, but what really fascinated Nick, Davina says, was Mercury's ability to play the piano and yet dominate the stage as a performer. Davina and Nick saw a lot of theatre, encouraged by Colin Cave's connections to that world. Melbourne productions of Samuel Beckett's *Waiting for Godot* and the musical *Hair*[45] were the shows that impressed them the most, until they saw Lindsay Kemp's fairy-tale version of *A Midsummer's Night's Dream*. Kemp had been an early mentor of Nick's hero, David Bowie, and not for the first time Nick would be hypnotised by the ambiguous sexual energy and other-worldly fluidity that such artists conjured.

Sundays were reserved for visiting art galleries. Davina remembers Nick being so obsessed with Brett Whiteley that they would have to search the city for his paintings, hunting out any place they might be shown. She remembers, too, Nick's love of Francis Bacon, an artist whose cold theatricality and biomorphic horror she could less relate to. There was a stream of others they discussed at length, Klimt, Schiele, Munch, Picasso and Degas among them. One of the few times they argued about art was over Jackson Pollock's *Blue Poles*, which, as noted, had recently been purchased for what seemed an astronomical sum ($1.3 million) by the Australian government for the new National Gallery in Canberra. It was one of those rare occasions when a work of art had become a front-page news item and part of common conversation. Davina just couldn't see the value in it. Eventually, Nick pulled out a huge book of Pollock paintings that he seemed to have permanently borrowed from the library. He went through them in detail, discussing the painter's life and how his work had developed. Davina thoroughly enjoyed the art lesson, but she was struck by how adamant Nick was about the boundary-pushing skill behind the work and its importance in the face of public ridicule. It was as if the ridicule drove him all the more strongly to understand and defend the work.

Davina would see even more intense intellectual debates happening between Nick and Colin at their kitchen table. Father and son never seemed to agree on anything. She felt that Nick admired his father to an extreme degree but had a habit of taking the opposite position to anything Colin said – sometimes purely for the sake of winding his father up. And yet there was a curious form of love and attentiveness thriving in the friction between them. Colin was an absolute classicist in his tastes, be it music, literature or art. Nick was all for the modernists, favouring the abstract and the avant-garde. Underlying this was what Davina calls 'Nick's love of loves, anarchy'.[46]

Nick's competing interests in order and disorder were only just beginning to emerge. Davina had already seen that Nick's favourite book, thanks to Colin's guidance, was *Lolita*. She can remember Nick reading it and rereading it at least three times over the two years they dated. Nick never seemed to let it go. He wasn't just enjoying it, he was studying it. *Tess of the D'Urbervilles*, *Crime and Punishment*, *Waiting for Godot*, *Othello*, *Macbeth*, *Long Day's Journey into Night*, *The Stranger* – they all came up in conversations between Nick and Davina, and more especially between Nick and Colin. Davina thinks Nick was always running his ideas by his father. They would dissect the characters and their plights 'down to minute details', she says. Colin was in his element in these discussions: informed, energised, commanding in his analyses. Davina felt Colin 'knew his stuff upside down and back to front'.[47] Her image of Colin and his son hunkered down in a match of wits over art and literature, with Colin pointing the way, echoes the frequent guru references that Nick makes in songs much later, notably the sinister yet attractive figure in 'Red Right Hand' and the God-like presence who has disappeared and taken order and meaning with him in 'We Call Upon the Author to Explain'.

When it came to music, the conversations between Nick and Colin moved from discussion and debate into openly fierce clashes. There was very little common ground. Colin thought of pop and rock music in the lowest of terms. Nick defended his heroes to the hilt. Davina found these arguments a little frightening, even 'unforgiving'.[48] But deep down she thought Nick did influence his father's perspective on the likes of David Bowie, Bryan Ferry and T-Rex, if only because Colin saw aspects of his son more clearly through Nick's love of their work. Colin was extremely proud of Nick – that was never in question. Nick, in turn, kept seeking his father's 'appreciation', Davina says, through the arguments they had.

'I am careful not to use the word "approval", for that I never saw,' Davina says. 'Nick trusted himself when it came to things of the mind and spirit. What do I mean by this? It's hard to explain. He knew what he knew and he didn't doubt his opinions, theories and choices. It's not that he was arrogant or self-assured. He wasn't overly confident, but he knew what he knew and I don't remember him needing anyone's stamp of approval. I also remember there was a charm to him. Nick was soft-spoken, polite, a gentleman through and through, especially around adults. But among his peers or once he got on stage, he was a whole other Nick, loud and untameable. It was an amazing mixture. After *Lolita* I think his next favourite book was the *Roget's Thesaurus*! He had a vocabulary from here to forever and his favourite word was "fuck".[49]

Double Trouble

MELBOURNE

1975–76

At Caulfield Grammar the Art House gang had long ago begun to conduct themselves as a separate entity from the student majority. Just before Nick and his friends were due to take their exams for their graduation in 1975, a lower-form student was cajoled into running into the Art House and shouting, 'Poofs!' as loudly as he could. Unfortunately for the student, Nick and the others caught him, leaned him over a table and threatened to 'pants' him, all the while muttering feverishly about how they had been 'waiting for the buttocks' of a juicy young lad with which to pleasure themselves. Eventually the boy was released, unharmed but terrified. The story spread like wildfire.

On their last day of school, traditionally a muck-up day, Phill Calvert says, 'A mock awards ceremony was held at the final assembly. I was given "The Handbag Award" for dressing too gay or something. I was later taunted for carrying it round at recess as part of the joke.' In response, the Art House gang 'hatched a plan to put a brick in it and when taunted I would let them have it with the bag. They thought a handbag wouldn't hurt ... Surprise!'[1]

The Art House gang in 1976, including Mick Harvey, seated left; Phill Calvert, bottom left; and Nick Cave, head of hair. Nick made the sign. The young women were student teachers *(Wayne Purcell, courtesy of Phill Calvert)*

By the end of high school, the group had improved markedly and their playing already hinted at the band that would evolve into The Boys Next Door. Later, Nick would reflect on the next five years of covers and experimentation as a time when the band were 'nothing more than the sum of our influences'. Each original song that emerged was just an attempt to be like something they admired. This would continue, he felt, until The Boys Next Door evolved into The Birthday Party. It would not be till the latter's *Prayers on Fire* that they would begin to find what Nick calls 'a voice of our own that was recognisable'. And yet Nick would return again and again to the Promethean theme of artistic theft as fundamental to everything he did.[2] Patching things together, stealing fragments and whole ideas, transforming them … it would be part of a lifelong creative approach.

The sum of Nick's formative influences was made obvious in the heartfelt origins of his first band. Them's 'Gloria', a rock 'n' roll chestnut, had entered their repertoire over the summer of 1976 after being given a new lease of life by Patti Smith on her startlingly poetic debut album, *Horses*. It was ironic that one of the heralds of the punk revolution to come – a supposed Year Zero for a new generation's artistic expression – should choose to open her recording career with a hoary old standard such as 'Gloria'. But Smith's trip would always be about transcendence, her ethos a return to Romantic Classicism (New York style) rather than politicised nihilism and anarchy (London calling). Her free-form poetics atop the persistent, galloping beat of 'Gloria' sent Nick back to Van Morrison's ferocious 1964 recording, which he much preferred. Both interpretations were irradiated with vocal attitude, a sense of each singer having swallowed the song whole and then let it burst like a fire from their chests. The gospel form that 'Gloria' insinuated – the spelled-out, call-and-response chant – evoked desire as a raw form of spiritual ecstasy. 'Gloria' may have appeared a clichéd cover choice, but it provoked a similar urge in Nick to improvise at the microphone while the band punched out the brutally simple rhythm-and-blues foundations. Though they would disown a live bootleg of them doing this song as mere juvenilia – and much else about their 1970s evolution besides – 'Gloria' was a copybook lesson in how a one-time classic need not fade into a nostalgic retread.

Alice Cooper's song 'I'm Eighteen' added more swagger to the band's set list, a metallic pop ode to feeling confused and indifferent at once. Cooper's bittersweet lyric received a vocal from Nick that took on a self-flagellating pride, most of all as he celebrated his own eighteenth year. Cooper is one of the great vocalists of rock 'n' roll and his singing is no easy thing to emulate, despite the hard, flashing swagger that made the song seem so loose and edgy. Nick chose to overwhelm 'I'm Eighteen' with autobiographical energy in order to compensate for any lack of vocal command. He'd just about scream the chorus at people. The Who's 'My Generation' was a cover in the same vein, another teenage soundtrack for prancing around your bedroom letting no-one in particular know that you have had enough. Nick, however, delivered this one with an element of sarcasm, as if it were a satire rather than an anthem. There was a precocious sense of being both inside and outside the music, a theatrical quality that could be underestimated when compared to the more direct performance heat Nick was generating. The band's interpretation of Screamin' Jay Hawkins' 'I Put a Spell on You' should have had more hoodoo than voodoo in the same sideshow magician vein, but it was treated very seriously: a spatially barren as well as bluesy, if amateurish, precursor to Nick's later interests on classic Bad Seeds album *The Firstborn Is Dead*.[3]

It is startling to recognise how much of what was to come was present in these teenage beginnings, including Nick's paradoxical approach to interpreting the songs on stage. Nick speaks of seeking out 'music I could get lost in'. Lost, but not oblivious. There was something similar to the way Colin – deaf in one ear since a childhood illness – would turn up Johann Sebastian Bach before dinner, refusing to come to the table, his daughter Julie says, until the music had passed through a series of peaks to its ultimate climax: 'He'd have the music blasting. "Wait for it," Dad would say, "wait for it. Here it comes, listen … now!"'[4]

'Dad was a conservative in his tastes, but a progressive in the sense that he loved art and experimentation,' says Nick. 'He didn't have much time for rock. And he loathed shock value for the sake of it.' Clashes were inevitable. 'We had to play all our music in the lounge room on our family gramophone. I took perverse pleasure in it.' Julie remembers endless rounds of 'us playing pool with The Doors just blasting all the time'. Colin would have recognised The Doors' version of a Brecht–Weill show tune, 'Alabama Song

(Whisky Bar)'. He may have hated shock value for the sake of it, but he loved drama with purpose – and so did his son.

Despite Davina's memories of affection and respect in the way Nick and his father Colin exchanged ideas, there was a counter-current of hurt developing and intensifying beneath their differences. Nick would always pay tribute to the influence of his father as essential to who he became. But in a remarkably candid documentary in 1997 called *The Good Son*, he'd hint at Colin's overbearing qualities and his father's tendency to define parenthood, and even love itself, as little more than another form of teaching. 'He was probably a great teacher but not perhaps the best father,' Nick says. Sitting beside a garden waterway as he talks, it's hard not to imagine it as a trickling echo of the Ovens River of his Wangaratta childhood. The flow of the water soundtracks his words and his boyhood reflections. He becomes distinctly emotional as he explains, 'When I stopped wanting to be a student of his, when I started having ideas of my own, then things became very complicated between me and my father. At some point I started saying, "Look at this," and he would dismiss things I brought to him. And that's when the trouble started.' Nick goes on to say, 'And then he died when I was nineteen [sic] and he never really saw me amount to anything.'[5]

Without school to bind him to the group, Brett Purcell lost interest in the weekend rehearsals and left in early 1976. Nick was glad. Purcell had only encouraged him to keep on being the vocalist 'because you don't have any other musical abilities'. 'He had always let me know what a poor singer I was,' Nick says. 'He told me I was dead wood when it came to the group achieving anything.' On a few occasions the pair came close to brawling. Purcell's opinions and schoolboy backhanders opened up wounds from Nick's days of being banished to the back rows of the cathedral choir in Wangaratta. Nick's experiences at Caulfield Grammar under music teacher Norman Kaye had done nothing to dispel this lack of confidence as a singer (if not a lack of enthusiastic posing whenever the band played a dance at Shelford Girls' Grammar). His early stint with the school choir was short-lived from the moment Nick was asked to open his mouth and sing a note. All Norman Kaye could do was wince.[6]

With Purcell gone, that mate of Nick's who'd been lurking around at band practices volunteered to replace him on the bass guitar. Unlike his more bourgeois friends, Tracy Pew was a suburban boy from Mount Waverley who had won a scholarship to study at Caulfield Grammar. He arrived in fourth form in 1973 as an outsider, much as Nick had been when he had landed there an unruly country boy. The two established an immediate rapport, partners in crime quite literally, their misdeeds heightening as they went from underage drinking sprees to acts of casual vandalism. Knowing that even their close friends might disapprove, they kept much of this destructive behaviour to themselves. Cave and Pew were tight indeed, but each was also a world unto himself – so much so that when Purcell left the band, no-one knew that Pew was learning the bass guitar, not even Nick. Thus far Pew had only distinguished himself in their music classes with cursory, almost sarcastically bad efforts on the clarinet, an instrument at which he was actually quite adept. Not only could Pew play rudimentary bass, his partnership with drummer Phill Calvert would develop into one of the best rhythm sections in Melbourne.

To perform with the band in public, however, Pew needed his own amplifier. He was with Cave one night when they spotted one in the window of a music shop. Pew simply smashed the glass and took what he needed. Nick was surprised, but also impressed that Pew could be so brazen. They had destroyed a few telephone booths together, but this was a step up in intensity. 'I was with him on another night when we walked past a bakery. Tracy was hungry, so he smashed the window and took some rolls to eat. I thought that was getting a little extreme.' Before school was over, Nick would join Tracy on joyrides in cars Tracy had stolen.

'I was a loudmouth smart-arse,' says Nick. 'Tracy was much more clever and in his way more subversive. There were things going on in Tracy no-one will ever understand. I think some terrible tragedy happened at home, where he saw the accidental death of his baby sibling.[7] On some level he was deeply disturbed – but the warmest, funniest guy in the world when he wasn't being witheringly sarcastic. He was a natural scholar who didn't go to classes. Pissed everybody off. Didn't attend any English Literature classes and got straight As. When he was told to get a haircut, he shaved his head and was suspended as a result. He wore a skullcap to school for a period of time, said he had converted to Judaism, and was eventually suspended again. He drew penises on every blank piece of paper he could find. Obsessively. Weirdly, I had a thing for drawing naked women at school that became quite a problem for me as well. Tracy eventually had to go to the school "psychiatrist" about it. The psychiatrist, who was sucking a pencil, asked Tracy what things reminded him of penises. Tracy said, "Balloons … and … pencils." He was suspended again. He was suspended quite often, actually.'

Despite her sense of the band's almost overwhelming differences as individuals, Davina began to realise that Nick and Tracy were actually the most alike in character. It was something that would vaguely bother her, as Nick would be different in her company, so much softer and more sensitive. Coincidentally, Tracy began dating a Jewish girl as well, bonding them together as a happy foursome. Tracy's intelligence and humour calmed any reservations that Davina had. He and Nick kept their wild world very carefully to themselves. Of course, the secrecy only made their boyish villainy all the more fun.

Considering their lack of focus on their studies, the band members surprised even themselves by getting reasonable passes for their Higher School Certificate. Mick Harvey notes he had 'done the bare minimum', and he didn't think the others made much more effort. Predictably, Nick did well in English. Pew shone in English, French and History, an outstanding student above all of them. At the start of 1976 the group had to face up to what they 'really' planned to do with the rest of their lives. Nick set off for art school at the Caulfield Institute of Technology (now part of Monash University) with ambitions to be a painter; Mick took up a position as a clerk in the tax office in order to postpone committing to a university degree;

Nick Cave entertains the Art House Gang, 1976 *(Wayne Purcell; courtesy of Phill Calvert)*. Nick: 'I just hate that photo but somehow it makes its way back out in public again.'

Phill started at teachers' college, before dropping out to become an apprentice hairdresser; Tracy got work doing graphic design and paste-up for advertisements for the Dendy Cinema chain, exploiting a natural aptitude for art and illustration.

Mick Harvey's plan was to earn money and get the band happening while taking what he told his father was 'just a gap year'. But as 1976 progressed, their reliance on playing covers was becoming wearying to him. Nick's voice, meanwhile, began to develop a pronounced Bryan Ferry quiver that saw less-informed detractors continue to denounce him as a Bowie imitator. It was a confused, if backhanded, compliment. Much like his first chameleon hero, Nick was willing to use anything and everything around him in order to grow. Perversely, Bowie was lifting some of his own look and gestures from Bryan Ferry too. Nick's feathered hairstyle and heavy use of mascara perpetuated the Bowie comparisons. Both Ferry and Bowie were actually putting a contemporary spin on what old-time crooner Frank Sinatra represented at his 1950s height: the existential romantic with enough detachment to put every nuance of a story across in song, an aural stylist painting himself into the picture with words, all the while creating an illusion of intimacy.[8] At a far more amateur level, Cave was likewise trying to become a better singer, rather than just belt out a tune with bravado. Rock 'n' roll was all about abandon, but Nick saw this could be controlled. His father's theatrical sensibilities were an influence on this.

Roxy Music's 'Love Is the Drug' had throbbed like a pulse out of radios everywhere over the past year. Bryan Ferry's new solo single, 'Let's Stick Together', confirmed him as the sex-addicted playboy king of art pop. It was a pose Nick rather liked the look of.[9] Eventually Nick's obsession with copying Bryan Ferry and suggestions from the band for even more covers to play caused a boil-over from Mick Harvey, and in late 1976 he left them in a huff over their lack of commitment towards developing original material. Mick had observed 'Nick's tendency to arrive at practice with lyrics and interesting ideas for songs. I could see the potential in that, in him, quite early.' Harvey felt that these ideas were worth taking further, rather than moving on to a new batch of covers by their favourite artist. 'I just didn't think that was the right way to go at all,' he says. 'I thought they [the band members] were just being lazy.'[10]

Dating Nick Cave's beginnings as a songwriter is a difficult task, not least because it is complicated by his teenage romances and a tendency to blur dates and details. Allusions in the British media to his first serious girlfriend being a radical lesbian and him not losing his virginity till he was nineteen are typical of Nick's capacity for half-truths with a twist of humour. In an extensive interview with English journalist Phil Sutcliffe, Cave admitted the first song he ever wrote 'was very much based on this Australian singer Stevie Wright's "Evie (Parts 1, 2 and 3)", an epic love song in three parts. I had a girlfriend in school I fancied called Julie, so I wrote "Julie (Parts 1, 2 and 3)" ... It was heavily derivative!'[11]

Nick confirms that as fact. 'It's true. The girl's name was Julie and she lived in Wangaratta and went to the high school while I was there. I always thought she was very beautiful – black hair and pale skin – but never spoke to her and she never spoke to anyone. In Melbourne (after Davina), I ran into her, as she was friends with a girl called Janine, who was the girlfriend of a guy called Howard, who was maybe twenty-four or so – much older than I was – who kind of adopted me. He had an Afro and wore Staggers and was, I thought at the time, extremely hip. He got me into the Alex Harvey Band, for example, and turned me on to smoking pot and we let him play tambourine in The Boys Next Door – in my Bowie phase – kabuki make-up and acne and dyed red hair – for a gig or two.

'Anyway, Julie was Janine's friend and I fell for her hard. She was much better-looking than I deserved at the time, but the three of them, Howard and Janine and Julie, were involved on some level with the Melbourne underground – which seemed to operate out of the Station Hotel in Greville Street, Prahran. We used to go there every Saturday afternoon and Julie would dress me up in drag – hot pants and clogs and Duffo[12] stuff, I guess – and we would hang out with the fags and the psychos and the Maori gangs, listening to Renée Geyer and The Angels and stuff like that. I was a complete babe in the woods and was so besotted with Julie that I let her do whatever she liked with me and so they had their young schoolboy they could play dress-ups with. Anyway, one day we had a date and Julie didn't turn up and I realised it was over and I was heartbroken and ran around to Howard's place and he tried to tell me not to worry and women come and go and all that sort of thing, but I was devastated. After that I dyed my hair black – which had as much to do with trying to become Julie as it did with seeing the cover of "These Foolish Things" by Bryan Ferry. Have dyed it ever since. It was through that period that I wrote "Julie (Parts 1, 2 and 3)", which when you think about it was pretty savvy for a sixteen-year-old – even then I understood the lure of the song and how if you wanted to win the girl all you had to do was to immortalise her.'

In the 2014 documentary *20,000 Days on Earth*, Nick remembers Julie in a very different way. For the sake of the cameras, he sits down with his real-life psychotherapist, Darian Leader[13], and openly discusses his first sexual experience in the darkness of Julie's bedroom. Though they would not consummate the act, there is an intensity to the intimacy, a strange merger or communication that clearly impressed itself on Nick. 'There was something about the shifting of her, she turned it back on me. I could see this face in the half-light, this white face. And that had quite a big effect on me.'[14]

This image of a luminous woman would be repeated throughout Nick's life: it was a mirroring he would toy with overtly in the video of 'Henry Lee' with PJ Harvey and in many photo sessions with his wife, Susie Bick. It's something echoed in both the brutal and romantic extremes of his song writing. Where is his luminous feminine side? How can he find it? Polly Borland's art photography (as much a collaboration as anything like a conventional portrait in a comically warped yet unsettling image like *Untitled*, aka 'Disco Nick', of Cave in a blue wig and dress) offers a fluid expression of this searching and mutable identity within. It might also explain the deeply rejected nature of some of Nick's former male collaborators, as well as the energy of his most virulent antagonists, who seem to respond less like friends and enemies and more like embittered lovers.

A few months after leaving the group, Mick Harvey saw them in a Battle of the Bands competition at Mount Waverley. 'And they were playing originals again!' he says with a laugh. Mick wasn't sure how much he had inadvertently inspired this redevelopment, and how much it came down to thoughtless teenage perversity on the part of the band. In any case, he rejoined – much to his and everyone else's relief; his temporary replacement, Ashley Mackevicius, bowed out to pursue a career in photography.[15]

Harvey was by now developing into an extremely strong rhythm guitarist, his sound indebted to Velvet Underground-era Lou Reed – if sharper and more sheared in character, terser and more mindful. His brief but important absence from the group had only further defined what Mick was now able to do within it.

Phill Calvert says, 'Mick had decided to get serious. He'd taken guitar lessons.'[16] Largely self-taught, Mick Harvey appeared to have made great strides in technique after going to the well-known jazz guitarist Bruce Clarke.[17] Mick is not so sure of any grand progression occurring at the time. 'It was only half a dozen lessons. Bruce taught me how to hold my pick properly. And how to play chords the right way. But I went back pretty quickly to the finger formation that was most comfortable for me,' he says, laughing. 'I still play the D major with the wrong finger.'[18]

Throughout these comings and goings, the band was learning about the power of subtractions as much as additions. Pew's arrival was the first revelation, a sudden anchoring of the sound and a tightening of the gang camaraderie that had threatened to unravel in the wake of graduating from school. Mick Harvey's departure and return clarified his sonic purpose, giving them a renewed cohesion and musical direction. Chris Coyne had stopped playing saxophone for them, though he promised to help out if needed.[19] No matter: Nick could play a little sax and add the odd blurt if necessary, and Tracy had years of practice on the clarinet to call on too, not that anyone was especially interested in that.

Nick was also a competent pianist, but it was a skill this guitar-dominated band didn't require. The line-up was firming, their sound more their own, even if a sped-up Roxy flavour was prevalent in everything from the grandiose edges of the music to the boys' passion for wearing eyeliner on stage. It was an image and sound that made them seem 'New Wave', even 'New Romantic', before such terms had even been coined.

Guitarist John Cocivera was a fine musician, but it was increasingly obvious his dense and ethereal playing style was ill-suited to the group's direction. Matters got worse, Nick says, when 'me and David "Dud" Green and Tracy dropped some acid around my place in Airdrie Road and John came around and we kind of coaxed him into joining in – he was pretty conservative in such matters – and it had a devastating effect on him. I think he kept having flashbacks for years, the poor guy. On the upside, that day I discovered the wonderful Carpenters on the test pattern on the TV – I sat there watching it for hours – and have loved the band in a special way ever since.'

Cocivera's father was desperate to get his son away from Nick, and so sent John on a long recuperative holiday to the United States. Cocivera returned in ghostly shape and with a love of disco and much else besides, instilled in the hard-partying nightclubs of Philadelphia. He jammed with Nick on his return, but his absence had made it obvious they no longer gelled. Cocivera's guitar came down like a funky jumbo jet over Nick's increasingly nervy and angular pop-rock songs. Nick had begun cultivating a more deliberate (as opposed to amateurish) garage-band edge, inspired by obsessively listening to The Stooges' *Raw Power* (1973) and a new 'punk' band from New York with whom Nick had become besotted, called the Ramones.

It was Cocivera's departure that caused the group's first real problems, pushing Mick Harvey out of his rhythmic comfort zone and back onto the frontlines playing lead. Many of their original songs had been developed with two guitars in mind, and the loss of Cocivera forced a retreat from these during late 1976 and a reintroduction of the covers. Harvey wanted more from, and for, the band. For him it was like recutting a jigsaw to make the pieces fit again. His guitar sound broadened to fill the space Cocivera had left, and his playing became even more driven, gaining what some fans described as 'a sinister, snarling'[20] quality by mid-1977, thanks in part to the fresh influence of The Stooges' guitarist James Williamson, whose jagged, expressive style Harvey was absorbing.[21] This would be the start of Harvey's adaptations around any musical obstacles that were put before him and the band, a facility for expansion or contraction that would mark him out in the longer run as a formidable instrumentalist and ruthlessly selfless song arranger. Phill Calvert noted it: Mick Harvey had a unique capacity to see the music in a material way that none of the others had. It was a real gift.

Though they had grown apart musically, Nick confesses to 'feeling sad' that Cocivera was gone for good. He had lost another friend and it reinforced an unsettling truth he had previously tried to ignore: 'I got the very strong feeling none of my friends' parents liked me very much. That I was not welcome in their homes. Mick would tell me later that most of the parents thought I was the ruination of their children's lives.'[22]

Coincidentally, the members of the band were all estranged from their fathers in different ways, and correspondingly close to their mothers. Mick Harvey's Church of England minister father moved his family around to various parish postings until they settled in Ashburton, near Caulfield North, in 1969. The Reverend Arthur Harvey's best friend had committed suicide back in the mid-1950s after an unsuccessful affair destroyed his marriage. It was something that added even more weight to the minister's already sober presence.[23] Mick observes that: 'Colin [Cave] was very similar to my dad – an intellectual with a potbelly and a bit of white in his beard who was also a bit unreachable. Both our families were made up of three sons and one daughter, of which Nick and I were both the third-born. Both our mothers are called Dawn. There were a lot of strange coincidences like that with Nick and me.'[24]

What Mick and Nick shared most of all was a stable and well-educated family background they could depend on, however much they chafed against its patriarchal order. Relations between Phill Calvert and his father were far more difficult. Robert Calvert – known as 'Captain Bob' to his friends – would at times forbid his son from attending rehearsals, and, on at least one occasion prevented Phill from turning up for a gig. Tracy Pew was the most sympathetic to this situation. Nick recalls Tracy tiring of the parental bullying and leaping into his car to go and get Phill. 'So Tracy drives his car right up Mr Calvert's driveway and takes out one side of the flowerbeds he has planted there beside it. Out comes Phill's dad ready for a fight. Tracy says he's here for his drummer! But then Phill sticks his face out the door looking pretty upset and shakes his head "no" to us from behind his dad's back. So, Tracy jumps back in the car and reverses. Takes out the flowerbed on the other side on the way out. To be fair to Phill's dad, he did let us practise in his shed for a while, so he wasn't all bad. He was a weight-lifter, Scottish [sic][25] ... I just remember that air of suppressed rage about him. He certainly never had a problem telling me to get off his property!'

Nick and Mick continued to live at home, while Tracy and Phill moved into a flat in Windsor. It was opposite the Redd Tulip factory in High Street, and near Prahran Tech. The sickly sweet

Nick Cave in his bedroom at his family home in Caulfield North, c. 1974
(Ashley Mackevicius / Collection: National Portrait Gallery)

smell of confectionary being manufactured hung heavy in the air. During band meetings at their flat, Nick was faintly reminded of the abattoir smells that flooded Wangaratta when he was a boy.

Phill Calvert says, 'Tracy was the only kid in our school era who came from a broken home. It's hard to understand now what a big deal that was. These days it's *The Brady Bunch* on fire out there, but back then it was not something widely accepted. You tried not to let people know. People didn't talk about it openly.' Tracy's mother, Nancy, admits it was not easy. Her husband, Richard, a businessman, moved out when Tracy was just fourteen and his sister, Fiona, was nine. Tracy was in the process of shifting to Caulfield Grammar after a difficult history at less salubrious schools. It seems Nancy, who worked as a financial adviser and would go on to study philosophy and sociology at Monash University once she retired, was unique among the disapproving parents of Caulfield Grammar in making Nick feel immediately at home in the Pew residence. Nick describes Nancy as 'a wonderfully bawdy, witty woman'. In his graphically inclined paintings, Tracy would depict his mother as a vamp wearing green eye shadow, something that still amuses her. Nancy and her husband were ill-matched, and a series of tragedies had only deepened the distance between them. 'Tracy did some very sensitive things sometimes,' Nancy says. During a particularly unpleasant and penultimate argument with Richard Pew over her serving of divorce papers in 1975, Nancy remembers, 'Tracy took Fiona away and told her to come and watch television with him.'[26]

Nancy considers how the boys have changed. 'Mick is a very serious fellow now he's a grown man, but when he was young he was a real giggler. I'd always be hearing him and Tracy giggling away over something,' she says. 'Mick, though, when he meets you, will shake your hand. That's just him. Nick's a hugger, very affectionate. You could have conversations with Nick more easily than you could with Mick. I didn't see as much of Phill, but he was always very polite, absolutely charming. I just love teenagers. They were all such lovely young men, really. And I will keep saying that about them till I am sixty!' says the woman riding a lively eighty-plus years.[27]

You can detect the quick humour her son Tracy inherited in such statements – and the pain that can suddenly emerge. Nancy gestures across her lounge room. She tells a story that explains a lot about what might have made Tracy the person he was. Episodes and glimpses that flow on to how she feels about his death.

'The little boy we lost, Gary, fell from that bench over there,' she says. 'Tracy was next to him washing his hands. Richard had turned around. Tracy was only three. Gary was only a baby. I was in the garden, just outside those glass doors. It was the loudest sound I had ever heard, as if he'd been thrown across the room. Gary had never had a seizure that we know of. But we don't really know what happened. Tracy saw it happen. He said to me, "Gary just closed his eyes and fell, Mum." Richard and I had another little boy later, stillborn. We hadn't named him but we didn't want to forget him when we buried him. Fiona said, "I'd like to call him Christopher, Mum." So that's what we called him. Gary and Christopher, we lost them. The sad thing is you don't think about them as much because you don't have the memories. I had twenty-one years of memories of Tracy, not counting the years he was overseas with the band, before he died. I always remember Tracy watching *The World According to Garp* on video when he first moved back home after The Birthday Party broke up. Tracy would get teary when he watched it. I always thought he was connecting it to Gary in some way.'[28]

153

Nick would call The Stooges' *Raw Power* 'the album that changed my life', claiming he bought it on the basis of seeing its cover image alone sometime during 1975. It is more likely he heard it at the house of Tracy's friend Chris Walsh, after Pew began singing its praises. A somewhat brooding figure, Walsh was a fan of underground comics and way ahead of the curve in collecting what was then obscure and imported vinyl by the likes of the New York Dolls, the Ramones and The Stooges. It was Walsh who had taught his Mount Waverley buddy Tracy Pew how to play bass by listening to those albums. Walsh would also initiate Nick into outlaw country music by the likes of Waylon Jennings and Merle Haggard, reawakening an old Wangaratta passion for Johnny Cash into the bargain.

Wherever and whenever Nick first heard *Raw Power*, there's no denying the impact of just seeing the album. Its cover depicted a lean, shirtless and golden-bodied Iggy Pop, with heavy mascara and black lipstick, clasping a microphone stand with full phallic intent. At a time when denim-clad, West Coast, easy-listening rock bands such as the Eagles were the dominant force on radio, an unplayed but nonetheless notorious Iggy Pop appeared as if he had surfed in on an alternate American wave of sulphur and electricity. The fact Bowie had mixed *Raw Power* did not escape young Nick's attention, nor did the extravagant rock magazine back-stories of Iggy Pop as the untameable wild child of the 1970s, caught in a spiral of heroin addiction and dumped in a lunatic asylum before Bowie rescued him after writing 'The Jean Genie' in his honour. Though his original *Raw Power* mix would be tampered with and supposedly improved later for its CD re-release, Bowie would maintain it had 'more wound-up ferocity and chaos and, in my humble opinion, is a hallmark roots sound for what was later to become punk'.[29] The fact that everybody from the Sex Pistols to Nirvana tuned in to that record in its vinyl format only justifies his point of view. The young band that would soon be known as The Boys Next Door, before finally evolving into The Birthday Party, were no different in following the *Raw Power* trajectory into legend.

Nick was cultivating what he would joke was an 'idiot savant' aspect to his personality. On the heels of Patti Smith's *Horses*, the Ramones had arrived in 1976 with their self-titled debut and a comic-book delinquent look that was all sneakers, torn stovepipe denim jeans, T-shirts and leather jackets. Their wraparound sunglasses masked eyes that peered moronically from beneath dark fringes while they slouched in front of a brick wall on the cover. Both *Horses* and *Ramones* signalled the rebirth of a New York music scene formerly symbolised by the underground taboos of The Velvet Underground. But if Patti Smith had come on like a rock 'n' roll Baudelaire, the Ramones – purporting to all be 'bruders' – promoted themselves as dumber than dumb. Their wall-of-noise approach was matched by a deceptively melodic and concise set of bent pop songs, including 'Beat on the Brat' and 'Blitzkrieg Bop', both of which The Boys Next Door would play. Drenched in high-speed musicianship and streetwise American humour, the *Ramones* album would echo in a thousand punk bands to come, not to mention a twisted animation series titled *Beavis and Butt-Head*. It was the smartest 'stoopid' music you could hear, a glorious marriage of sonics and image that suggested a 1970s version of The Monkees high on 'sniffin' glue'.[30]

It is hard to explain the significance of such releases in today's information age, when youth culture is so obviously saturated with imagery and choice. It takes a great leap of the imagination to envision a world in which there was no internet, no mobile phones, no Spotify, no easily accessible alternative media and no alternative radio – let alone options such as gaming, Instagram, YouTube, TikTok and Facebook. Youth culture was music culture and the choices within it were highly restricted. Records outside the Top 40 could only be understood on the basis of having been read about in relatively hard-to-get and erratically available magazines before they were ever actually heard. These singles and albums were only available in Australia via the post, ordered through record clubs where aberrant and eccentric offerings would be randomly, and briefly, advertised alongside standard fare like Boz Scaggs' *Silk Degrees* and Neil Diamond's *Hot August Night*.[31] It could take up to six weeks to receive a package, and the arrival of a record by what would seem like horseback delivery today would often prompt a devotional round of listening among those finally able to hear it. Everything was studied, from the album art and production credits to the record label and the lyrics. There was a sense of receiving news from what Nick calls 'some invisible front line where the real dramas of life and art were taking place'.

Not far away, another young group of people were responding to the same arcane signals and moving through the same subset of influences – and discovering The Stooges' catalogue at the same time. Among them was The Boys Next Door's future guitarist, Rowland S Howard, who was still attending Swinburne Community School.[32] Among his fellow pupils were the 'music geek' and future Au Go Go Records founder Bruce Milne and his younger, opinionated brother, Peter Milne, who was toying with what would become a significant interest in photography. A flame-haired girl with a nervy, poetic disposition called Bronwyn Adams had become part of their peer group. Adams would later join Crime and the City Solution and marry singer Simon Bonney, becoming better known as the violinist Bronwyn Bonney. She would also help Nick to edit his first novel, *And the Ass Saw the Angel*, in Hamburg in the mid-1980s.[33]

Rowland S Howard and friend Gina Riley, later of *Kath & Kim* fame,
aged sixteen, 1976 *(Peter Milne)*

The liberal and artistic teaching philosophies behind the
Swinburne educational institution added up to what was loosely
called 'a free school'. It had a very different culture from the
history-conscious and traditional Caulfield Grammar. Even so,
Bruce Milne hastens to point out that Swinburne Community
School 'was an odd mix' of children from stereotypically
bohemian and 'leftie' families and what he calls 'the sons and
daughters of sharpies and skinheads that none of the other schools
could tolerate'.[34] It was in this environment that the Milne
brothers, Bronwyn Adams and Rowland S Howard would bloom
like hothouse flowers. Each would have a lasting impact on Nick.
Most immediately, they were all zealous music fans, part of the
inner core of a scene that would gather around The Boys Next
Door and fuel them artistically.

'*Raw Power* was a very big deal for us,' says Bruce Milne. 'We were also into Bowie, Roxy Music, Sparks ... Then we discovered the New York Dolls and The Modern Lovers. Our gang of four or five thought we were the only ones in all of Australia who knew who these people were. We were friends largely because of music. I'd have the first Velvets album; Rowland would have *White Light/White Heat*. We'd make cassettes for each other and swap them. That was how things worked for everyone.

'Anyway, there was this Bad Film Festival at the Palais in late 1976. I think they had a screening of John Waters' *Pink Flamingos*. I went with Rowland. And we saw other people there who were like us. Other people who didn't have long hair, who were wearing ill-fitting suits and skinny ties. That was Nick, Mick and their gang. And there was Chris Walsh and his gang. It seemed like these three suburban groups in Melbourne all connected on that night.'[35]

Rowland S Howard cut a distinct figure, even amid all these strong personalities. There was a feeling, Nick says, 'that Rowland had somehow arrived fully formed on the scene'. At age sixteen he wore suits and presented himself as if he were a nineteenth-century poet in the iconoclastic vein of Arthur Rimbaud. Precociously, Rowland made an armband with the words 'Model of Youth' written across it. Another badge said 'OCT', celebrating the month of his birthday.[36] Though his parents were folkies, his own tastes were distinctly modern, including a passion for sci-fi literature. Nik Cohn's idiosyncratic take on the history of popular music, *Awopbopaloobop Alopbamboom*, would inspire him to start dabbling in rock journalism. With a set of rOtring pens perpetually poking from his jacket pocket, he was interested in the possibility of becoming a graphic artist. Rowland – or 'Rowlie', as his friends liked to call him – loved comics such as *The Spirit* and *The Shadow*.

For Rowland, the latest thing was always the most exciting thing, technologically and creatively. He learned saxophone largely because he liked the way Andy Mackay looked on the inside sleeve photo of Roxy Music's first album. 'When you look at film of them,' Rowland would remark, 'it was like they came from another planet, which is a pretty good criteria for a rock band.' Rowland then started to learn guitar, playing along obsessively to Roxy Music's Phil Manzanera and King Crimson's Robert Fripp. There was something about a guitar not sounding like a guitar that especially appealed to him. Syd Barrett's solo albums were another source of inspiration, surreal testaments from an artist falling apart at the end of the psychedelic era.

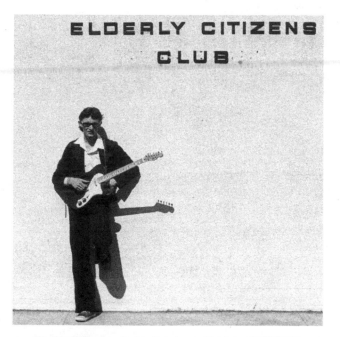

Rowland prepares for his first show with his band TATROC (Tootho & The Ring of Confidence), Prahran, 1976. *(Peter Milne)*

Bronwyn Bonney describes the young Rowland S Howard as 'very romantic. And he stayed a romantic all his life. And absolutely emotional. He was very unusual in that most people who are like Rowland – people who are clever and witty and cutting – are also a bit cold around the heart. Rowland was never like that. That is why he found it so hard to cope later. Even back then, it was a tough time to grow up in Melbourne because it was a very brutish culture in the suburbs. People who were ugly or different were left in no doubt about their failings as people, their failure to be normal.'[37]

Nick had begun developing a philosophy of the world in which 'ordinary' and 'extraordinary' people conflicted. It was a notion he had lifted from *Crime and Punishment*, and a delirious speech by Raskolnikov that captures his rollercoaster of ecstasies and guilt in the wake of committing murder. Though Dostoyevsky's novel actually satirises the notion of extraordinary people being given any licence to do as they please over and above the so-called ordinary, Raskolnikov's delusional insights excited Nick no end. A part of that excitement lay in the dreamlike force of Dostoyevsky's writing, and the feverish penetration of reality that Raskolnikov's speech invited. Combining this with his love affair with The Stooges' LSD-flavoured brutishness and singer Iggy Pop's heroin-coated crooning, Nick was leaving behind relatively innocent glam-rock ideas about being an 'alien' and confirming a much darker Romantic vision: the artist as criminal outsider. His raucous friendship with Tracy Pew was another hedonistic spur to this worldview. He and Tracy were not just going on joyrides now, they were crashing the stolen cars for fun.

'I was bowled over in my teens by the basic premise of *Crime and Punishment*,' Nick says with a trace of amusement.

'It was really the first bit of philosophy I could get my head around, and it probably inspired me to be an extraordinary arsehole all of my life.'

Davina Davidson saw this taking form in a rather schizoid way. 'On the one hand Nick was a rebel, completely unconventional, not the teeny tiniest bit mainstream,' she says, 'and yet it bothered him not a bit to go places with his parents all the time. Although I was more than happy to do things and go places with them as well, I was, for example, never interested in socialising with my own parents, and took it for granted that my attitude to my parents was normal teenage behaviour. I often wondered about it then. How Nick was so non-conformist in his thinking and yet completely comfortable in situations where he was required to "behave by the rules".'[38]

This was, in fact, a duality Nick would always manage, right through his wildest days to come.[39] But there was no doubting he and Davina were growing apart. She did not share in Nick's drug taking, which he kept mostly separate from her. Nick was making new friends at art school, while his latest interests in music were being defined in drinking sessions with Tracy Pew at Chris Walsh's house in Mount Waverley. Davina describes the circles she and Nick were moving in as having become 'mutually exclusive'. Towards the middle of 1976 they agreed – at Nick's behest – that they would be free to date other people. 'I was still very much in love with him, so deep down I was uninterested, and in the beginning I was both confused and sad, though I do remember making brave attempts at going out with other guys. They were all a little dull, not much fun, definitely not as colourful.'[40]

While Nick's relationship with Davina was disintegrating, the music scene reflected a parallel turbulence. Articles had begun to pop up in *RAM* (*Rock Australia Magazine*) about a band called Radio Birdman, which had won an event called the

Sydney Punk Band Thriller over Christmas of 1975. Bands such as The Stooges and MC5 were freely referenced. Intrigued, Mick Harvey ordered a copy of Radio Birdman's EP *Burn My Eye* through the mail. Stories of Radio Birdman banging their heads with VB cans for percussion and hauling sheets of corrugated iron from a building site to line the interior of their studio thrilled Nick. For all the hype preceding it, *Burn My Eye* was sonically underwhelming, but the band, the songs and the artwork all emanated an unmistakeably aggressive call-to-arms quality that would be vindicated by Radio Birdman in the live arena.

Even more exciting was the sudden and absolute arrival of The Saints with their first single, '(I'm) Stranded', in late 1976. It was a work produced, pressed and distributed by the band alone – that this was done from total isolation in Brisbane, Queensland, then Australia's most right-wing and menacingly policed state, made The Saints' artistic achievement all the more impressive. While even the dissident Birdman had created industry rumblings in Sydney via the press, The Saints had come out of nowhere. They were all that Nick and the others dreamed of being while listening to their Stooges and Ramones albums: an aggressively shimmering, buzzing blend of fury and intelligence that skittled everything in their path. '(I'm) Stranded' snarled out with such force it was acclaimed overseas in the influential UK music magazine *Sounds* in its 16 October 1976 issue as 'Single Of This Week And Every Week' in a quarter-page review. The following issue of *Sounds* had The Damned's 'New Rose' as its single of the week, a record widely credited these days as the first vinyl shot announcing the punk-rock revolution in the United Kingdom. Beneath praise for The Damned was a second review of ('I'm) Stranded', saying 'Still Single Of The Week And Any Other Week'. A postal address to order the single from Eternal Productions in Queensland was provided.[41] Other influential UK trade publications such as the *NME* and *Melody Maker* followed suit in their enthusiasm. These were unbelievable accolades for a band that had been stewing in a tiny cohort of about fifty police-harassed fans in Brisbane. 'They were a very strange group,' Nick said. 'It seemed to me they had arrived at this particular sound entirely independently ... I would say they inspired a movement.'

By November of that same year the Sex Pistols had released 'Anarchy in the UK', and the explosion of punk sounds across England had prompted the London branch of EMI to force its Australian office to sign up The Saints. *Countdown*, the nation's massively popular Sunday-night pop program, even screened a raw film clip of the group performing '(I'm) Stranded' in a deserted, seemingly trashed Brisbane terrace house. It was actually where the band lived and staged its own shows. Suddenly there was a heroic new act in Australia that was not following any overseas trends, that was even a step ahead of the action in London and New York. The Saints had kicked a door open and they shouldered through it like no-one could stop them.

Nick and Davina would break up once and for all while '(I'm) Stranded' burned a hole in Nick's mind. The genius of the song lay in the way it evoked everything from Australia's exiled heritage as a convict-settled nation, to youthful feelings of suburban alienation, to forcefully ending a relationship and sharing in the pain that such an act of severance involves. Davina Davidson recalls a deep tenderness from Nick as 'I struggled with my new independence'.[42]

'That summer,' she writes, 'I have a beautiful memory of joining Nick and his family at a beach house they rented somewhere. It was built on a hill with rooms going down the slope and stairs on the outside so that the bedrooms were like separate units, under the main living and kitchen area on the top floor. That big room was surreal, with all these stuffed-animal heads hung on the walls. Nick was not a beach person, so I don't remember actually going to the beach with him, just lovely memories of the family in that big living area and he and I in his room. In fact, we never went swimming together, and the only time we actually did go to the beach, I think Tracy was with us. I went in the water while Nick and Tracy were sitting on the rocks fully clothed. Nick didn't even take off his clogs. He just sat there watching from the sidelines.[43]

Zoo
Music Girl

MELBOURNE
1976-77

N ick Cave is emphatic. 'I loved going to art school. I didn't do a lot but I learned a lot. People there had a massive influence on me. Just the time spent in the pub, talking about art all the time and about what we would do. Meeting artists like Jenny Watson and Gareth Sansom and Tony Clark. I can't begin to tell you what this was like after being at Caulfield Grammar School.'

During his first year at the Caulfield Institute of Technology (CIT) in 1976, Nick earned A-level passes for both his essays and paintings. Fellow student and future *Women's Weekly* editor-in-chief Deborah Thomas recalls his work as being 'very Expressionist, very well painted. Nick was a good artist.' Thomas and her friends Kate Durham and Wendy Bannister were a year ahead. She would become a top model before venturing into journalism, Durham a famous jeweller, Bannister a leading stylist. 'The three of us took him under our wing,' Thomas says. 'The first time I clapped eyes on Nick he arrived at art school wearing one of those vintage Hawaiian shirts. He used to wear them all the time.' For the most part Nick was relatively studious and shy, Thomas says, 'a good middle-class private-school boy. I would say he was a very typical Melbourne boy, in that respect, from a well-to-do family but looking to break out and find something more exciting.'[1]

Gareth Sansom and Jenny Watson were both teaching at CIT, though neither had Nick in their classes. Tony Clark was lecturing at Prahran Art College and yet to emerge as one of Nick's most important mentors. Despite Nick's track record at high school, he retained a lingering respect for the profession of teaching, a by-product of his father's profession and philosophy that 'education never ends, it's life-long and it should always continue'.[2] A little distance from the formal restrictions of the classroom meant relations with Sansom and Watson, and later Clark, could develop freely. The notorious legend of Nick using people was also beginning to take shape, but it's the trope of learning from people and moving on that lies at its heart.[3]

Nick Cave, Caulfield Institute of Technology (CIT),
1977 *(Gareth Sansom)*

Nick's ongoing passion for the art of Brett Whiteley paralleled his interest in the music of David Bowie. Both artists were dramatic, even theatrical about the way they presented themselves, with a brazen, bowerbird approach to collecting influences and claiming them as their own. By the late 1970s, Whiteley was widely identified as Australia's most rock 'n' roll painter. A former habitué of the Chelsea Hotel in New York during the 1960s, he'd been a friend of Janis Joplin and Jimi Hendrix, and his notoriety as a heroin addict only added to his wild child image. Whiteley was an expressionist, influenced by everything from Japanese calligraphy to American Pop Art and British abstract art, and his shape-shifting obsession with landscapes and nudes was rooted in his extraordinary drawing abilities: free-flowing, hallucinogenic and erotic. His inclination towards figurative distortion and interest in macabre criminals such as the English serial killer John Christie reflected the influence of English artist Francis Bacon. But Whiteley was always a lotus-eater at heart, if nonetheless an artist corrupted and tormented by his hedonism. Bacon was not nearly so free or generously sensual, and more brutal by a country mile. Whiteley seduced; Bacon overpowered, even terrorised. Whiteley's constantly evolving willingness to take anything from anywhere greatly appealed to Nick, who was seeking out an accord between music and painting that might determine his own future. 'Brett Whiteley painted the way I wanted to paint, for sure,' says Nick. 'After I saw his work, the way I used space [in my paintings] changed overnight. He had the most beautiful line.'

Gareth Sansom recognised this early on. He describes Nick's paintings as 'kind of Brett Whiteley and Francis Bacon combined – all flesh, gesture and teeth – kind of cartoonish as well – talented but not very original. But he hardly attended and he failed for that rather than his paintings, if I remember correctly.'[4]

Jenny Watson is more enthusiastic. She recalls Nick presenting 'a fabulous picture of a figure wrapped in barbed wire' during his second year in 1977. 'It was a quintessential Nick Cave image,' she says, 'the suffering, the helplessness. I've heard he still paints. I hope that's true.'[5] The image arose from a reading of Flannery O'Connor's *Wise Blood*. Its central character, Hazel Motes, ends up binding himself with barbed wire and walking around with glass in his shoes after failing to extinguish the notions of Christ and divinity in his life that were instilled by his preacher father. This would be the last overtly serious work Nick Cave attempted at art school.

His interests in pornography as well as religious art were intensifying, though yet to converge. 'Then I saw this girl in third year's work and it just blew me away,' Nick says. 'She was a rampant hardcore dyke. She'd do these beautiful paintings that the teachers would like, and then over the top she would draw penises in black paints and completely deface them. They were the most violent pictures I've seen anyone produce. I don't even think she passed.'

Nick began exhibiting a similar desire to mock and confront that could border on the infantile. A teacher eventually told him that 'she couldn't relate to sleazy art and could no longer talk to me. I think this could run parallel to the way The Birthday Party developed, to a certain extent. Just the thrill that ran through me when I heard her say that, the joy of displeasing somebody, was such that she was responsible for the entire direction my painting went in from that day.'

This is one version of the story. But, depending on who Nick is speaking with, the retelling of his failure at art school can most definitely hint at his hurt and resentment as much as any rebellious pride. Sidney Nolan, Brett Whiteley, Nick Cave – this had been the dream pantheon he'd lined himself up in. It was never going to happen like he had imagined.

'I had huge artistic ambitions as a kid. I liked a lot of the tortured, gothic, religious stuff – Matthias Grünewald and Stefan

Lochner and the Spaniards – and I wanted to make paintings with that kind of power. There was something about just being in a room by yourself and making art that excited me. It's exciting to me still, this weird medium of applying paint to a canvas and the restrictions of a square, two-dimensional frame. It's not unlike the restrictions of a song, in a way.'[6]

'77. Nick's second year at Caulfield Tech. The year that Elvis Presley died. The Sex Pistols' Johnny Rotten defined the new mood, and it was not one of mourning: 'Elvis represented everything we're trying to react against. He was a fat, rich, sick reclusive rock star who was dead before he died. His gut was so big it cast a shadow over rock 'n' roll.'[7]

Punk was reaching its full, furious, singular bloom. The mainstream charts may have belonged to Boz Scaggs, Electric Light Orchestra, Fleetwood Mac and the Eagles – the four biggest-selling-album artists of the year in Australia and just about everywhere else – but they were creatures of the past, not the future. Hating these acts, erasing them from the scenery, was part of the new punk ethos. The arrival of *Saturday Night Fever* and disco hitting its peak in the very same year as punk's snarling breakthrough only reinforced a feeling that the old guard of rock 'n' roll were finished. Nick, however, harboured a sneaking affection for this old guard – especially Bob Dylan and Van Morrison, as well as younger classicists such as Bruce Springsteen. In a telling interview years later in West Berlin, the Dutch documentary maker Bram van Splunteren would ask Nick about the inherent pessimism in his music. Taking umbrage, Nick would advise him to go ask Springsteen where the positivity in his music comes from. 'Now that would be something to read.'[8]

Such tastes were not only deeply unfashionable in 1977, they were verboten. A purge was occurring and you had to be absolutely clear which side you were on. The Sex Pistols' triple whammy of 'Anarchy in the UK', 'God Save the Queen' and 'Pretty Vacant' made for a spectacular run of singles from November 1976 to July 1977. More than any other act they defined punk rock as a war on mainstream culture. In later years Nick would describe this era with a catchphrase that amused him: 'the time when we fought the big one'.

Once punk did the demolition work, the musical clock was reset again. Many likened it to the 1950s, when rock 'n' roll first arrived. Nick was absorbing the fresh noises and new ideas, an empowering sense that anything could – and should – happen. In this, Australia experienced the American and English scenes as they overlapped and competed for pre-eminence. There was great benefit in being caught between these colonising forces: between the Phil Spector–influenced, New York pop and the Eddie Cochran-ite, agit-prop rock that were respectively dominant in the self-titled debuts by Blondie and The Clash; in the energy evoked by Talking Heads' nervy, urban claustrophobia on 77, and by Ian Dury's ribald Cockney puns and music-hall street grotesques on *New Boots and Panties!!*; in what distinguished the Ramones' delinquent humour on their sophomore album, *Leave Home*, from the utterly primary detonation that was *Never Mind the Bollocks, Here's the Sex Pistols*. There were musical counterpoints everywhere from which to draw and hybridise new ideas.

For all its nihilistic affectations, punk actually played into the apocalyptic fantasies of youth and briefly empowered a generation to reboot rock 'n' roll in a multitude of ways. It was a savage fairytale brought to life. The DIY philosophy of punk not only encouraged extreme forms of enthused amateurism and garage-rock rawness, it also sparked an avant-garde counter-movement that dabbled in everything from frenetic musical deconstructions to a pioneering use of synthesisers and tape loops that implied a sonic landscape from tomorrow. An aesthetic of malice and erasure would soon mingle with frostily Romantic and strongly Germanic brands of futurism, respectively evoked by new UK bands such as Magazine and robotic pioneers like Kraftwerk. Anarchist philosophies opened quickly to absurdist playfulness and extreme forms of performance art that used the body itself as a site for radical protest and distortion. Independently pressed and distributed vinyl proliferated, if only on a highly localised cottage-industry level. The diffuse and scattering impact of this would not be felt again till the viral age of instantly downloadable music and imagery on the internet.

The music industry reeled in confusion as a young audience developed its own heroes, and its own culture, from the pamphleteering force of photocopied, stapled-together zines to the self-adapted, safety-pinned, second-hand jumbles of punk fashion. Distance imbued the Australian scene with a driving obsession about not being left behind, smashing open parochial feelings of inadequacy and the feebler tendencies to imitate. In a published essay on Cave, rock critic Robert Brokenmouth notes:

Australia was in a lost world between the past and the present; by the time the music papers and import records arrived in Australia with the latest trend they were three months out of date – we all knew it was history. This galvanised many bands ... to out-do what was happening overseas, because they knew they were always going to be three months behind. Positioned in the past, they strove mightily to be current. Musical history was something to be investigated in the present, a pattern which remains with many Australian 'old punks' to this day. This is another key to understanding The Boys Next Door and, ultimately, Nick.'[9]

Bruce Milne recalls the importance of the fantasy side of punk from an Australian perspective. He speaks of buying copies of the New York magazine *Rock Scene* as far back as 1974. It would become an extremely influential publication among the small coterie of musicians and fans who would dominate the rest of the decade in Melbourne. 'It showed lots of photos of the CBGB New York music scene in the mid-1970s, photos of Television, Patti Smith, the Ramones, Neon Boys,' says Milne. 'We had been seeing these photos of these people for almost two years before they ever put a record out, going back to 1975 in that magazine. So we were fanatical fans of the Ramones and Television before we ever even heard them. Just because they looked so cool! At a time when everything was singer-songwritery or metally glam, they had short hair and arty retro clothing, a whole look to them. And their names, too: Verlaine, Hell ... they just seemed perfect. When [Television's first single] "Little Johnny Jewel" finally came out in late '76 someone I knew had gotten a hold of it. I was so excited I got them to play it for me down the telephone line. I remember being shocked by how slow it was, like it was playing at the wrong speed or something. Until all those records came through here, everyone had had to imagine what the bands sounded like just by looking at photos of them. A lot of music got made that way. It was funny how often what people imagined was so close to being right.'[10]

The touchpaper in Melbourne was lit within the space of two months in early 1977: first in March with a tour by Radio Birdman; then in April with the arrival of The Saints. Nick, Mick, Tracy and Phill went to see both bands, pursuing every show they played across town. Initially, Radio Birdman blitzed them with a quasi-militaristic attack that owed as much to the hard-edged psychedelic radicalism of the MC5's *Kick Out the*

Jams (1969) as to their beloved Stooges or an American pop metal group like Blue Öyster Cult. Mick Harvey, in particular, was attracted to Birdman's lethally controlled, sonically dense musical attack, though he found the invoked audience salutes and mass chants of 'Yeah hup!' hard to swallow. Phill Calvert recalls himself and Nick in a less discriminating mood, 'right up the front, dancing wildly, drinking a pot [of beer] per song'.[11] After the show Nick and Tracy invited the band to a party. Tracy Pew was pulled over by police and booked for ferrying Radio Birdman's guitarist Deniz Tek and their singer, Rob Younger, on his blue Vespa motor scooter. Younger was riding pillion, Tek was right out front on the handlebars.

This camaraderie with the loyalty-obsessed Birdman would dissolve the moment The Saints hit town a few weeks later, and the heads of the aspiring young Melbourne group were immediately turned in another direction. By the time Radio Birdman came back in June for their 'Rock 'n' Roll Soldiers Tour', they were aware that relations with their new comrades had cooled.

A little competitive jealousy would always be enough to pour petrol on Nick's flame. Deniz Tek was a formidable figure in every way, and did not lack for a little attitude himself. Born in the United States, he'd seen The Stooges first-hand as a teenager in Detroit and had become a truly great guitarist, driving Radio Birdman to its sonic heights while also studying medicine for what would become a career as an ER doctor. He would later become a Navy flight surgeon with the US Marines, his 'Iceman' call-sign inspiring the character of the same name in the film *Top Gun*. If Tek was not a real person, you'd think him an unbelievable character in a corny novel. Need it be added that he was extraordinarily handsome? His classic dark looks were reminiscent of a cooler, more contained Tom Cruise.

Nicky Danger, as Nick was calling himself then, did an interview for the punk zine *Alive 'n' Pumping*, in which he gave his bile against Tek free rein. Asked what bands he liked or hated, Nick was pure punk disrespect. 'I think Deniz Tek is an arsehole and his brain is as big as a pea. Birdman rip off everyone like The Stooges, MC5, Doors, Bay City Rollers, etc. I guess Rob Younger is a good front man, though; I mean that seriously. The Pistols are okay.'

Within a year Nick would be up in Sydney with The Boys Next Door saying things such as 'I hate Radio Birdman'[12] on stage for no other reason than to take yet another gratuitous stab at that band's legendary status – this time on Birdman's home turf. It was a very Nick thing to do, and not the first or last time he would define himself with an unforgiving zest against others. It all went with punk rock's demolishing ethos of malice and disrespect, though it still must have been galling to be so obviously and quickly dropped, as well as slurred for no clear reason. To make matters worse, the 'other' great Australian act of the era, The Saints, had behaved boorishly in Sydney after Radio Birdman had welcomed the Brisbane band by organising live shows and accommodation.

The Saints' loose, gang-like image and unruly humour were always going to appeal to the likes of Nick Cave – right down to singer Chris Bailey's Irish background and the way he echoed the Ned Kelly fantasies of Nick's Wangaratta childhood. While Radio Birdman's intensity demanded a regimented, even cultish fandom that drowned itself in their maelstrom[13], The Saints' sprawling menace and innate lyricism celebrated a far more reckless and poetic individualism. Nick would later recall his excitement at seeing his favourite band: 'The Saints would come down to Melbourne and play these concerts which were the most alarming things you've ever seen, just such anti-rock kind of shows, where the singer wouldn't come on stage. When he did, he was this fat alcoholic. It was so misanthropic, it was unbelievable, and the whole band was like that. They were so loud!'[14]

Chris Bailey of The Saints makes a powerful impression on a young
Nick Cave, who is flanked by David 'Dud' Green (left) and Garry Gray
(right), 1977. *(Rennie Ellis)*

He cut out a rock-magazine photo that caught him standing front-of-stage in The Saints' audience, staring boyishly agog at a prone and still-singing Chris Bailey bathed in sweat and glory. It remained in his wallet for years, becoming crumpled and faded, till it finally disintegrated in his fingertips as he stood, disoriented and stoned, on a snowy street in West Berlin in the mid-1980s. By then many considered Nick the most dangerous and exciting rock star in the world. He was a right mess as well.

One night in 1977, Nick took a tab of acid. It was warm and the music was loud, the air thick with sound. Radio Birdman's 'TV Eye', Patti Smith's 'Horses', Richard Hell's 'Love Comes in Spurts', The Modern Lovers' 'Roadrunner', the New York Dolls' 'Personality Crisis' – the songs kept coming in waves. According to fellow partiers, a nineteen-year-old Nick tried to use his bare hands to pull a sink away from the bathroom wall. Everyone thought he was a maniac. But it was a very 'punk' thing to do.

Rowland S Howard stood in the hallway, listening to the music as it rolled out of the lounge room. He was seventeen and straight as a die; these were his pre-heroin days and he was not even drinking. Suddenly someone grabbed him by the suit lapels and pushed him hard up against the wall. A still rampaging Nick Cave stared into his face from about an inch away and blurted, 'Are you a punk or are you a poof?'

Rowland had seen Nick's band play a show at another friend's party just a few weeks before. He didn't think they were particularly good, but the singer had something. Nick was well aware of Rowland's presence on the scene. Rowland's teeth, his ears, his eyes: like some punk-rock Nosferatu in an op-shop suit, Rowland was an effete and pale-skinned poseur who was hard to miss. Nick was monkey-handsome by comparison, Rowland's feral opposite: taller, darker, more boyish and wild. Pinned to the wall, Rowland didn't answer. So Nick loomed into his face again and asked him a second time, 'Are you a punk or are you a poof?!'

Television's mighty signature track for *Marquee Moon* crashed over them as Nick released Rowland during a pause in the song. Then those duelling guitars started up again, a classic reprise. Nick staggered off into the party without waiting for a reply or saying another word. The music kept going, ascending and falling away till it broke completely on some imaginary shore above them all. Nick felt as if it were made of glittering particles that were coming apart in his ears. It was Rowland's favourite album that year and came to define his early sound as a guitarist.

'The next night I was at a gig and he [Nick] apologised profusely and gave me a little hand-drawn map of how to get to a party,' Rowland said. 'I went there and the same thing happened again. Tracy was there as well and I thought he was a complete psychopath.'[15]

It was in early August 1977 that a group calling themselves The Boys Next Door officially entered the fray. Up until then, Nick says, their sporadic appearances at school dances, friends' parties and backyard barbecues had been 'complete fiascos … Phill could drum okay but the rest of us were totally incompetent. I was a terrible singer.' The Reverend Arthur Harvey gave his son permission to stage a public event at the church hall in Ashburton where the freshly re-christened The Boys Next Door had been rehearsing during the previous few years. The event was advertised through the usual process of hand-distributed leaflets and word-of-mouth. The band may have been inexperienced professionally, but Phill Calvert recalls Mick Harvey's 'drive', along with weekly rehearsals that were now being taken very seriously indeed. Contrary to the reckless image Nick and Tracy Pew projected, the group was acquiring a strong work ethic and a certainty they had something worth pursuing.

The departure of both The Saints and Radio Birdman for the United Kingdom by the middle of 1977 left a vacuum that was immediately felt in the Australian underground music scene. For all their 'punk' qualities, Radio Birdman and The Saints were bands of adroit, forceful musicians fronted by deeply charismatic singers and marked by generation-defining guitar players. This was no everyday combination to pull together. Whether they knew it or not, The Boys Next Door had those base materials at hand. And while The Saints and Radio Birdman made their names from Brisbane and Sydney, Melbourne still lacked a punk band

Rowland S Howard, Nick Cave, Ollie Olsen, Megan Bannister, Anita Lane and Bronwyn Adams at Nauru House, Melbourne, 1977 *(Peter Milne)*

of national prominence. This seemed to confirm the annoying northern prejudice that Sydney was a city and Melbourne was just a town.

The church hall show at Ashburton was to be The Boys Next Door's first step towards putting themselves forward. It was aided and abetted by Tracy Pew's friend Chris Walsh, who had temporarily become their 'manager'. Walsh's own punk band, Reals, which featured guitarist (and future Melbourne electronic music guru) Ian 'Ollie' Olsen and singer Garry Gray (later infamous as the chainsaw-wielding vocalist for The Sacred Cowboys), would be the support act on the night. Reals specialised in trying to out-Stooge The Stooges. They failed, but they could still generate enough thudding, ominous aggression to get a punk crowd slamming.

Nick had come up with the new band name as 'a reaction against the names that were going around at the time', he says. 'The more vulgar names.'[16] Mick Harvey admits, 'We didn't know what we were [then], we'd been doing this kind of stuff which was a precursor to punk, to some degree, so when punk came along, we thought, Oh, that's what we must be, but of course it wasn't. We twisted what we were doing a bit.'[17] Harvey indicates it wasn't just a groovy mix of Roxy Music affectations, garage rock thrashing and Nick's half-baked reading of Alvin Toffler's sociological philosophies in *Future Shock*: 'We used to include "To Sir, With Love" in our set for a while, you know.'[18]

In naming the group The Boys Next Door and mocking the punk context around them, Nick was as conscious of their middle-class origins as any of their earliest critics. Yet even their roadie, Shane Middleton, remained cynical. 'They were a bunch of pussies,' he said. 'They're all private-school boys, a bit like Hugh Grant. Upper-middle-class, close to peerage, don't know the seamy side of life. In a popular movement, you adapt your looks and behaviour to fit in. That's what they all did.'[19]

Nick is more circumspect on how The Boys Next Door evolved: 'We weren't swept along by the whole punk thing, thinking, Oh, punk rock, everything is great, let's get everything, let's listen to everything ... We did listen to everything, but we were able to differentiate. The Pistols we thought were great, and the Ramones we thought were a great band, but The Damned were shit. And we didn't reject everything else wholesale when punk came along, so we were still listening to The Stooges, Alex Harvey, a lot of country music, blues music, other stuff. So there was all that kind of thing mixed together.'

Novelist Michel Faber recalls meeting the young band for an interview with the University of Melbourne's student magazine, *Farrago*. Faber describes Melbourne back then as 'a city whose centre was roughly a mile square. Surrounding this modest metropolis were endless acres of suburbia characterised by eucalyptus trees, milk bars, carpet emporiums, scout halls and local chapters of the Returned Servicemen's League. Music venues where anything more radical than Doobie Brothers covers, heavy rock or blues could feasibly be attempted were few. When Nick Cave ... refers to an audience of "Homesglen skinheads", he doesn't mean skinheads in the British sense. He means the denizens of a suburban wasteland of shopping centres and barbecues, the natural fans not of ska but of Suzi Quatro.'[20]

It was these denizens who had gathered at Ashburton Parish Hall for The Boys Next Door and The Reals. If their previous appearances as Concrete Vulture et cetera had been 'fiascos', this night would be a sign of times to come, turning into an all-in band-and-audience brawl. Nick told Faber that, on the night, 'All these skinheads – Homesglen skinheads – were screaming at us, "Punks!" and stuff like that. And it suddenly occurred to me that we *were* punks, because everyone said we were. So, I just sort of thought, "What do punks do? Will I fart, shit, gob, spit or whatever?" So I spat, and consequently got beaten to a pulp.'[21]

Julie Cave was in the audience and gives what appears to be the more reliable account. 'I was there at the fight,' she says. 'Nick had been singing and spitting all night, and the majority of it was landing on this one guy. And he kept directing his comments and all that spitting at this one guy, who was actually a fan of what the band were doing. He wasn't trying to cause trouble. I kept thinking, Nick, stop doing that to that poor guy. But Nick just kept at him. Then Nick asks for a drink and this guy passes him something like an ouzo and Coke; Nick takes a drink then pours the rest over him. That was the last straw … the guy grabbed him and all hell broke loose. Everyone was grabbing everyone else. I always thought a boy would never hit a woman, then I saw this girl getting cracked over the head with a bottle of beer. Some local skinheads were on Nick, and I jumped in and was screaming, "Leave my brother alone!" It was chaos. Chris [Walsh] had an indentation mark from getting elbowed so hard in the chin it stayed there for days after, this knitted-jumper elbow mark.'[22]

Due to noise complaints, the police were already on their way, arriving at the scene within minutes to close the evening down. Ashburton Parish Hall was no longer available for the band's shows.

The immediate interest The Boys Next Door generated says something about their charisma. The fact that their debut had ended in a mini riot ensured word-of-mouth notoriety in a small underground scene. Their second public performance, and their first ever professionally, was on the middle of the bill one week later, on 19 August 1977 at the 'Cheap Thrills New Wave Rock Show' at Swinburne College (later Swinburne University), put together by the ever-supportive Bruce Milne. Rowland S Howard

Tracy Pew and Nick Cave, Boys Next Door gig,
Swinburne College, 1977 *(Peter Milne)*

could only laugh about the way Nick Cave described it to him later. 'Nick told me it was the best night of his life. He'd played a gig, got drunk and got laid.'[23]

Milne had become a DJ at the college radio station, 3SW, and had already taken a crack at a fanzine called *Plastered Press*, singing the praises of the New York Dolls and The Modern Lovers to all who would listen. He was now co-producing a locally oriented fanzine entitled *Pulp,* in partnership with Brisbane's Clinton Walker, who would go on to become the Australian post-punk music scene's most important historian.

In the interest of pre-promotion for the Swinburne show, Milne had offered The Boys Next Door a free full-page ad in *Pulp*. Over pizzas at Topolino's in St Kilda, the band drafted a rough advertisement based on their zest for fantasy identities: 'Nicky Danger (vcls), Johnny America (Ld gtr), Phill Thump (dms), Mick Harvey (gtr) and Buddy Love (bs). These guys have been together for a while ...' As well as listing covers such as 'Andy Warhol', 'These Boots Are Made for Walkin'' and 'I Put a Spell on You', they alluded to originals entitled 'I'm So Ugly' and 'Thalidomide Babies (Have More Fun)', along with 'a Cliff Richard influence'. As the ad shows, The Boys Next Door were still coming out of their Nicky Danger phase.

With Milne based in Melbourne and Walker living in Brisbane, *Pulp* took a twin-cities approach. Brisbane's The Saints and The Leftovers, and Melbourne's The Boys Next Door and the yet-to-perform Young Charlatans would soon dominate the content. The masthead was designed by Rowland S Howard, with Clinton Walker writing a review in the February 1978 issue praising The Boys Next Door as 'the best practising rock 'n' roll group in Melbourne'. Though it was nothing more than a Xeroxed-and-stapled-together affair lasting four issues and fifteen months, *Pulp* was a surprisingly important building block in the social networks that would flourish between the Melbourne and

Brisbane music and art scenes over the next five years. It also sowed a few seeds of an alternative music press that flowered with the formation of editor Donald Robertson's free-spirited national rock magazine *Roadrunner* in Adelaide in 1979. The scene was so tiny in Australia that an individual's actions had seismic potential.

What Bruce Milne remembers most about The Boys Next Door at Swinburne was how 'the band were musically not very good. And Nick could not sing a note.' He laughs. 'But the band – and Nick – had some interesting pretensions, and I say that in a good way. They had a vision of what they were doing. And that vision did not look like they had just looked at some photos of the Sex Pistols. Which is how an awful lot of bands did look and sound. Nick was actually very shy off stage. He'd often come across ... you'd think he was ... "dumb" is not the right word, but you would not be aware of the intellect he has since revealed through his music and writing. Looking back, he was very good at presenting himself as a blank canvas and absorbing what was around him.'[24]

The set list for The Boys Next Door that night was: 'Blitzkrieg Bop' (Ramones), 'Ain't It Funny', 'I'm Eighteen' (Alice Cooper), 'Gloria' (Them), 'Masturbation Generation', 'Who Needs You?', 'I Put a Spell on You' (Screamin' Jay Hawkins), 'Commando' (Ramones), 'My Generation' (The Who), 'Big Future', 'These Boots Are Made for Walkin'' (Lee Hazlewood/Nancy Sinatra) and 'World Panic', with an encore of the garage-rock perennial 'Louie Louie' (Richard Berry/The Kingsmen) served up à la The Stooges. Mick Harvey is mildly affronted by Bruce Milne's description of them. 'Rowland used to say the same thing about seeing us. I don't think we were *that* bad. We could play okay. I thought we did all right.'[25] The songs played again serve as an early template for Nick Cave's future aesthetic: from the shock-rock romanticism of Alice Cooper and the cartoon aggression of the Ramones, through to the street-tough Irish rhythm and blues of Them and the stagey sexual

Nick Cave, Boys Next Door gig, Swinburne College, 1977
(Peter Milne)

voodoo of Screamin' Jay Hawkins. 'Ain't It Funny', 'Masturbation Generation', 'Big Future' and 'World Panic' were all band originals featuring Nick's earliest lyrical efforts, much of it surprisingly sociological and satirical, if not downright comedic. The exception was 'Who Needs You? (That Means You)', the first and last song penned entirely by Mick Harvey that the band – in any of its incarnations – would ever do, or for that matter would ever have offered to them by Mick. It was a bold move for a teenage group of this era to step out with a set that was even close to one-quarter originals, and to attempt to make the covers their own.

Rowland was there in the audience watching. Years later he would compare Nick's presence that evening with his stage control as a consummate performer in the mid-1990s with The Bad Seeds: 'They [The Boys Next Door] were just a garage band doing "Gloria" and I remember I was pretty unimpressed with them musically, but they did have real spark. And Nick was doing things with "Gloria" and injecting himself into the songs. He was always very good at improvising lyrically, which he doesn't do so much anymore, which is a real shame 'cause he rejected a lot more of the spontaneous elements of his performance. Not in terms of how he presents himself visually, but it's a little more stilted … His song writing is more formalised now.'[26]

A bootleg recording of the Swinburne show reveals a surprisingly confident young band, with an astounding degree of commitment from Nick as the vocalist. He blurs the lyrics for 'Gloria' with a confrontational spoken-word improvisation that references The Stooges' 'Loose' to evoke an on-stage sex act of prolonged and savage intensity. You had to wonder: where was so much erotic fury coming from? And who could possibly absorb it into a loving relationship?

Anita Lane was the kind of girl everybody noticed. Rowland provided Nick with an introduction to her about a week after The Boys Next Door's Swinburne performance.

'I met Anita at a party,' Nick says. 'Rowland was there too. I think he was always kinda in love with Anita. And she was this incredible force of nature. There was very loud music playing in this front room. And for some reason she started talking to me. You might not believe this, but I just assumed at that point in my life women weren't that interested in me. I had my talents, but women were definitely not one of them. Anyway, she started talking to me and I could not hear what she was saying; she was so beautiful I just kept nodding my head and saying, "Yeah," for hours. Then all of a sudden she leaned in close to me and said, "I think I'm falling in love with you." I just grabbed her. I took it that the floodgates were opened. And we danced off into the night. And at that point, on that night, we became completely connected.

'Tracy had a really nice girlfriend at the time too [Gina Riley, of *Kath & Kim* fame]. You have got to remember we had been to an all-boys school – we hadn't known that many girls in our lives. I remember early on driving with Tracy to get them both. Anita and Tracy's girlfriend were at a bus stop, waiting for us. Anita was wearing chocolate suede knee-high boots and a miniskirt. Tracy's girlfriend had on something like that too. And I looked at Tracy and said, "Fuck me, it doesn't get any better than this!"

'Anita and I both wanted to be painters. She had this very delicate line, very confident and sure, but very vulnerable and beautiful and without any artifice,' Nick says, tracing his finger through the air. 'Me, I was always trying to have that sensitive line. But the way I draw is not like that. It's bold and hard and it's ugly. Anita's always had something magical about it I didn't possess. Brett Whiteley had a beautiful sense of line like that in his paintings too. These days I can work some of that into a [handwritten] lyric or a doodle. But Anita had the raw talent to be a great artist. She'd do pastels that were extraordinary. She could do the cruellest caricatures, too. She was someone who never tried. There was something criminal about the whole thing, that there was so much talent in her. But there was also something that prevented her from applying herself to the task. I think it might all stem way back ...'

Nick stops and thinks about what he is going to say. He starts again. 'We were just different people. Maybe that's why we worked so well together. I remember one time she said to me, "If you were hit by a car, you'd reach for your pencil and try to write what it was like before you died." I don't think I was so much

Anita Lane, Seaview Ballroom (Crystal Ballroom), late 1970s *(Peter Milne)*

like that in the early days, actually, but I did develop a way of applying myself no matter what was going on. I think you need to feel it is a part of who you are, for sure. And I think Anita felt there were greater issues at stake than her creativity. It was very frustrating – because she was better than everybody else. And by that I mean more naturally gifted than almost anybody I ever met. She was incredibly interested in ideas and it was really, really exciting to be with her. And she was full of the same irreverence towards things too. After that first night we were inseparable. Until we got separated ...

'She influenced a lot of people, not just me. Everyone will tell you. Anita was an amazing person. Anita is an amazing person. I think it might be difficult for her now. And that it has been difficult for her for some time,' Nick says. 'Time has moved on. And she is still dealing with her demons ... It's quite difficult to talk about. I don't have any great love for what I was doing back then. But I couldn't stop doing it.'

The Boys Next Door's third show was supporting Keith Glass and The Living Legends (soon to become KGB or the Keith Glass Band) at the Tiger Room in Richmond on 14 September 1977. Glass was among those smitten at the start with The Boys Next Door, though his significance to the group would not be immediately obvious. Glass was 'cool' in the classic sense, and not the type of guy easily impressed by radical poses, punk or otherwise. A talented musician and songwriter, he had done everything from playing in a baroque 1960s acid-pop band to starring in the Sydney production of *Hair* – a role that made Glass the first man to ever appear fully nude on an Australian stage.[27] A passion for obscure rockabilly, country, blues and 1960s Australian garage-rock bands would inspire him to open

Melbourne's leading alternative music store in the early 1970s, Archie 'n' Jugheads. With a shift in location to Flinders Lane, the record shop changed its name to Missing Link in 1976 and became, he says, 'Punk Central'.

As soon as Glass saw The Boys Next Door, he liked the way 'the band was ... witty. They were doing the punk thing but they were trying to avoid the clichés. It's hard to see that now.' He immediately sensed 'an Elvis sorta thing about Nick that I loved'. At his invitation, they became KGB's regular support act at the Tiger Room. Glass jokes that 'within six months our [KGB's] residency was overrun by all these pogo-ing punks demanding we play faster. We decided to go perform somewhere else and let them have the place to themselves.'[28]

Deborah Thomas was there on the first evening at the Tiger Room. Nick was 'very entertaining and staggeringly drunk', she says. 'He'd only just told us he had a band and that they were going to play there ... We all went along thinking how shy he was and wondering how he would go. But it was like, wow, so much energy. They introduced this woman called "Vulva" on stage, a rather large girl, who started throwing mincemeat from the stage at everyone while he sang "These Boots Are Made for Walkin'". It was really quite a performance. Shy Nick.'[29]

Jenny Watson perceived 'showbiz' characteristics. 'He was and is a consummate performer, almost like a comedian. In those early Boys Next Door shows at the Tiger Room there would be red neon on stage flashing in time to the music. It was a show in the Las Vegas sense of a show. And that's what happens with success, especially mega-success, you become an entertainer.'[30]

Novelist Tobsha Learner became an early habitué of the Tiger Room and, later, the Crystal Ballroom, where The Boys Next Door would rule over their own private kingdom. 'Mr Cave always had an extremely conscious sense of the projection of his image,' she says. 'And it was very structured from the get-go. He was very self-conscious, very self-aware. The way he articulated himself, his look, his movements, it was very staged. I did think Rowland was the most beautiful man of them all back then – he looked ethereal in those days. But Nick had a narrative for himself, and that's what lifted him out of Melbourne and out of Australia so quickly. It separated him from almost everyone. You could see it.'

Learner describes the early Nick Cave on stage as 'God under a follow spot', and speaks of how all the women on the scene 'would be enthralled going to see Nick. You'd feel this core of sex and desire running straight from his movements right into you. He really was absolutely captivating. But he was very on, and very off.' She implies something tantamount to an ability to throw a switch at will. After a while Nick learned to exploit this to the maximum, sometimes brutally. 'He was the singer. He embodied the inaccessible,' Learner says, 'and with that he had that whiff of someone who was going to be great. You knew you were watching the runaway train pulling out of the station even then. Right at the very start.'[31]

Karen Marks had been fulfilling the role of manager for The Boys Next Door since the start of 1977. Marks was just a few years senior, but for the band that was enough to make her part of an older generation. She had already begun making a name for herself as a rock journalist. and was quite a presence on the scene. During the time she managed The Boys Next Door, Marks was dating the legendary musician Ross Wilson of Daddy Cool (who became a fan of The Boys Next Door)[32], then the equally regarded Greg Quill of Country Radio and Southern Cross. She was also share-housing with Greg Macainsh of Skyhooks fame, and Jenny Brown, one of the leading rock journalists of the era. 'It was just one of those houses,' Marks says, laughing.

What she remembers most clearly is Phill Calvert being the first to approach her about managing the band. 'Phill knew I had all these connections. He was quite open about it. That was fine. I was surprised, but I thought why not? Ross really encouraged me. You know, I was on a panel recently and someone got up to say how chauvinistic the punk scene was at the time, but I don't agree. The fact the boys came to me and wanted me to be their manager was pretty unusual. There were lots of girls around in bands playing like it was no big deal too. I remember it mostly as the opposite of chauvinistic. I look back and think there was me and Caroline Coon early on in the UK managing The Clash. Two women looking after what would turn out to be two of the most important bands to come out of that time.

'I have to say, Phil was the most together, the most professional and the most ambitious,' Marks says. 'It was him. Him and Mick Harvey made that band happen. In my opinion, without Mick Harvey musically there would not *be* a Nick Cave. I see Mick the same way as I see Lenny Kaye with Patti Smith. History would be a lot different without those underestimated relationships. It's something people don't always understand or see. But it's so important and it needs to be said.'[33]

After her night with Nick Cave, Anita Lane told her friends she'd just met the ugliest boy. This was by no means an insult. If anything, it was her idea of flattery. Nick, too, regarded himself as ugly. But not in the original or quirky way Anita Lane celebrated. Contrary to later perceptions of him as one of rock 'n' roll's ultimate portrait subjects, Nick was prone to taking slights with disproportionate resentment and would be uneasy with having his picture taken when not performing. Photographers such as Anton Corbijn and Polly Borland, a close friend of Nick, saw what a difficult subject he could be even at the height of his fame. 'People think Nick is very photogenic,' Borland says, 'but the truth is that he isn't. He doesn't like the way he looks and that can create a lot of problems. It took Nick years to trust me, to believe that I would get a good picture of him. He was so self-conscious, and he could be a really hard taskmaster about it. There were many times when I swore I would never photograph him again. I can still remember the day when I first put something in front of him that he liked. "You see, Nick, I can actually take a good photo."

'Really it's only in the last ten years that he has been able to relax in front of a camera. It just wasn't something he could do. And he was always difficult when he was on drugs. He never really felt or understood that he was beautiful. He is more handsome in the flesh. Unusual and handsome – it's hard to get that mixture. I don't think growing up that he liked himself or got much positive affirmation. He even describes himself as a freak. I liken Nick to Marilyn in *The Munsters* – because he is a freak: he grew up in this suburban, very normal family environment. Look at the rest of his family and look at him. Where does he come from?'[34]

Like Anita Lane, Polly Borland first met Nick in late 1977. Her boyfriend at the time was Pierre Voltaire (the stage name for Peter Sutcliffe, who was also known as Mr Pierre). Already evolving into the scene's court jester, Voltaire's humour had a vicious, irreverent edge that went with the era's confrontational punk attitude. Borland herself had only just returned from London at the height of the Sex Pistols explosion. Her hair was dyed shocking pink, her stockings lacerated. 'I have this thing about my weight, which has gone up and down all my life,' she says. 'I still remember when I first met Nick. Pierre said to him, "This is fat Polly." Nick has always been really kind and understanding of how I feel. As soon as Pierre said that, Nick said, "She's not fat." I know what people say about Nick, that he's a misogynist, things like that, but it's something he explores in his work. It's not how he is. Nick has always been very kind to me from the start, very sensitive. That's who he really is.'[35]

Nick's empathy for artistic outsiders would only grow keener. He admits, 'I've always been uncomfortable with the way I am – I'm still learning to be comfortable with certain aspects of what it's like to live and be a human being. The more well-known you become, the less possible it is to have a normal relationship with the normal world – not that I am complaining, I've got it pretty good. You can't imagine how isolated Michael Jackson must have been.'

Though he was speaking about the nature of fame as much as his own physicality, the two have a corollary in Nick's background. 'In school I was an anti-magnet for women,' he would say, only half-joking. It was after joining a band that things 'immediately changed in terms of my attractiveness'. When Anita Lane started dating him, Nick had already done what she describes as 'a lot of self-portraits at Caulfield Tech. They were very unflattering, Expressionistic paintings, figurative in style. He was a great painter. I still think he is. The art school teachers didn't like him very much at all.'[36]

By then Nick was well on the way to failing. Too lazy to stretch a fresh canvas over a frame, he'd slap a new painting over the top of an old one. For his major project at the end of second year in 1977, he submitted a picture of a circus strongman looking up a ballerina's dress. A dotted line connected the strong man's eyes to what Nick called 'the ballerina's fundaments'. To his teachers it was a bad joke, even a sign of contempt for the institution. Typically perverse, it echoed an event in Nick's family history: a badly behaved boy at Wangaratta High School who had been forced, as a disciplining action by Nick's father, to star in one of Colin Cave's student theatre productions. According to a school magazine article, the boy had 'totally upstaged all the other actors by very obviously bending down at the front of the stage and looking up the dresses of the girls who were fairies. He got a huge laugh.' Behind what Nick himself now calls 'a pretty stupid painting' it is possible to perceive another gesture: the resentful son constructing a work that helped ruin his future at art school and sent a covert message to his father.

Nick's relationship with Anita Lane, a Lolita come to life, must have given him one more edge in the frictions he actively sought with Colin Cave. Ned Kelly, *Crime and Punishment*, Brett Whiteley, The Stooges, the New York Dolls – Nick was building an artistic identity that grew out of an inherited and subterranean dialogue more felt than fully understood. Ironically, Poppa Frank Cave had been irritated and mystified by Colin's preferences for classical music over the popular songs and folk tunes he enjoyed. Poppa was also 'very materialistic', Dawn Cave says, and determined that his son should 'never preach or teach. He had wanted Colin to get into advertising.'[37] Colin would, of course, become vocationally obsessed with education after a brief flirtation with journalism. His struggle to go his own way despite Frank Cave's demands was one of the reasons for Colin's tolerance of his own son's wayward self-determination.

Anita Lane has stated that when she and Nick met, she was seventeen and he was nineteen. Within a few weeks of their first encounter Nick turned twenty; details of her birth date are not available, and estimates of her age vary, due in part to her baby-doll image and voice. Most people indicate Lane was sixteen, not seventeen as she claims. 'You haven't decided on anything at that age,' she says. 'You're all open and you want the world to show you everything, having rejected what your parents had planned for you. That was the springboard: rebelliousness. You just jump into the arms of whatever comes along and so we did ... I guess everyone came to life out of punk rock, all that feeling that was going round at that time. It was funny for us because we weren't poor, working class or upset. What were we? I don't know. I never cared what anyone was doing or what the fashion was. The tastes I had then happened to be in fashion, and that's probably the case with Nick too. We were accidentally in time.'[38]

Dawn Cave says that when Nick first brought Anita home, 'she was like a little doll in a yellow raincoat with black piping'.[39] Davina Davidson likewise remembers meeting Anita Lane in late 1977, just after Nick and Anita started dating. The three were walking through the streets of St Kilda together. 'Anita was wearing skin-tight black leggings, black long-sleeved shirt, dark eyeliner around her eyes and bright pink rubber boots on her feet. The effect was stunning,' Davina says. 'This was thirty-five years ago. Nobody dressed like this. It was art in every sense of the word.'[40]

Anita was the apple of her father's eye. He was a much older man who doted on his only daughter, driving her all over town. Her only brother, John, two years her senior, was similarly amenable to indulging his sister's needs. The product of a Steiner school education, Anita was a free spirit destined for an artistic life. Her mother, Pearl, was renowned for her intelligence and saucy wit. 'Pearlie was fun to be around, quite flamboyant,' says Dawn Cave.[41] Anita, unfortunately, clashed with her mother, whom she sometimes referred to as 'Dirty Pearl'. Pierre Voltaire describes Pearl Lane more flatly as 'a total bitch'.[42]

It is unusual to hear a conversation about Anita Lane in which her beauty and unusualness are not the leading subjects. Nick's two closest friends of the era – apart from Tracy Pew – Rowland S Howard and Pierre Voltaire, were enchanted. They were just the start of a long line of men to have been dazzled by Lane's promise and, in recalling her presence years later, strangely saddened by what became of it. Lane's most memorable attribute appears to have been her voice, high and tiny and whispered like a child's. It masked what Nick describes as 'Anita's ability to eviscerate people with a single comment'. He'd later write the Birthday Party song 'Zoo Music Girl' for her. Set to a jungle rhythm, it blurted out a sex-mad B-movie horror story celebrating the wild at heart.

Deborah Thomas says Anita had 'big eyes, and an innocent, beautiful face. She was the first of those girls to have a vaguely mystical air – not in a hippie sense, more off with the pixies. She was not an outgoing person in a group. You know, here I am thinking back to art school and she was there every day with Nick [though not attending CIT herself], and I can't think of one conversation she and I ever had. But she was young. A fifteen- or sixteen-year-old mixing with twenty-year-olds, which is a big gap now and back then was even more so.

'When she got with Nick, it was something introverted. They became a little unit, locked away and quite separate. I hate to describe it like this, but it was a little bit like Yoko Ono. He was certainly besotted by her. She had a Jane Birkin look, twisting her hair, those big eyes staring out from under a fringe, the short skirts, a slightly dishevelled air. There was a Nico thing going on with her as well, that look. I don't think his friends liked her very much at first. She took him away from them. She was besotted with Nick, too – in that handmaiden style. But there was obviously more to her than that. Nick was too intelligent and creative to have a long-running, intense relationship with someone who was vacuous. She was one of those girls who would have made sure she was surprising. She reminded me in a way of Rodin's muse, Rose Beuret. There was just something about her.'[43]

Boy
Hero

MELBOURNE
1977–78

On 30 November 1977 The Boys Next Door were graced with another blessing when members of Blondie turned up at Martini's in Carlton to see them play. Deborah Thomas struck up a conversation with the group and became lifelong friends with Blondie drummer Clem Burke, who, she says, 'still remembers the night he saw The Boys Next Door in Melbourne. He thought they were great. He loved the rawness, and thought they had really captured something. I think he always felt happy to watch how Nick developed from afar, and to know he'd been there at the start of something.'[1]

Blondie were touring the country thanks to the chart success of their chiming and seductive 'In the Flesh'. The song was originally a B-side, but it became a fluke hit in Australia after the pop-music program *Countdown* played it, supposedly by accident, instead of the single's intended A-side, 'X-Offender'. More likely this was the decision of *Countdown*'s host and talent coordinator, Ian 'Molly' Meldrum, who was on his way to becoming one of the most powerful figures in the Australian music industry. Quite apart from singer Deborah Harry's sultry, bleached-blonde-in-a-beret-and-little-black-dress glamour, the band oozed a New York vein of CBGB's nightclub decadence that had its roots in heroes such as The Velvet Underground. Blondie's Brisbane show had been called off due to illness, but word on the street in Melbourne was that an excess of high-quality heroin had stupefied half the band. Their music might have sounded like an update of pop acts such as The Shangri-Las and The Crystals, but Blondie evoked something far more knowing, a Ray-Banned vision and cathedral sound that was both sugary and dark.

After witnessing The Boys Next Door, Blondie told the host of Australia's number-one music program they were a very exciting young band. Meldrum had been in the audience with them and mostly underwhelmed by The Boys Next Door's original songs, despite the band's intensity on stage. Blondie's enthusiasm prompted him to write a brief but favourable note in his weekly newspaper music column anyway, tipping The Boys Next Door as a band to watch – and suggesting they consider recording their cover of 'These Boots Are Made for Walkin''.

Within weeks the band was approached backstage at the Tiger Room (which around this time changed its name to the Tiger Lounge) by Barrie Earl, who was stitching together what would become the country's first major punk label, Suicide Records. Earl was all over town, searching for groups that fitted the mould. Nick says, 'He was like your cartoon manager type: big turquoise Navajo jewellery, a cigar in his mouth. He comes straight into our change room like that at the Tiger Lounge and says, "Do you wanna make a record, boys?" Of course we did.'

Earl also convinced The Boys Next Door to let him manage the band. Any notion of a conflict of interest passed everyone by. Letting Karen Marks know her services were no longer required was never going to be something teenagers handled well. The Boys Next Door arrived at her home in a prankish mood, smoking thin cigars to signal their newly corrupt involvement with Barrie Earl and the Suicide label. She knew something was up as soon as she saw the way they were carrying on. Marks remembers Nick being 'the one who actually said I was sacked. He just sat there at my kitchen table eating Twisties while he told me. He always had that nineteen-year-old attitude – a punk attitude – it was an act, being sullen and grumpy and eating junk food. To me he was just this gangly, pimply boy with a drop-dead gorgeous girlfriend. Him and Anita were like salt and pepper shakers going everywhere together. As a couple they were like those early photos of the Rolling Stones you see with their stunning girlfriends. Anita and Nick were like that when they were out, dressed up and looking fabulous. But there was nothing much else going on. Anita gave me nothing in conversation. I never got a single ounce of personality from her. Nothing. It was all this attitude with both of them. The body language, oh God, like sulky teenagers, that was their whole demeanour sitting there in front of you. To be honest, I never liked Nick's music that much, except for the band's cover of "Boots". It wasn't my kind of thing. I was friends with JPY and Sherbet; I liked The Dingoes and The Sports. I just wanted to help, and we were all having fun. People make out like the punk thing was this big division from the scene before, but it was more like one big happy family. We were all going to the same venues and seeing the same bands, up and down Punt Road, all the same people turning up at three different gigs over the one evening. Back then I always thought Nick was a bit of a fake ... no ... not a fraud ... how can I explain it? I always thought he was *acting* at being. Do you know what I mean? He presented himself as this writer-poet. But some of the poetry, the lyrics, I used to think, Oh my God, please! A lot of it was plagiarised, too. It was just an image. But Nick really succeeded. Over time he has become that thing he was acting. He has grown into what he was trying to do. He really did it. Good on him. He's a true artist now.'[2]

The boys next door

Nick Cave, Mick Harvey, Phill Calvert and Tracy Pew at the Tiger Lounge, 1978 *(Phill Calvert)*. Phill had just bought himself a polaroid camera: 'I think I got Tracy to shoot me.'

'No sooner had we signed with him than Barrie calls us into his office,' Nick says. 'We all file in and he turns to us and says, "Just been on the phone from London, boys. Punk rock's out, power pop's in!" Then he holds up all these boards with drawings and pictures of clothes that we should wear instead of the way we were dressed. Tracy's outfit was supposed to be these animal-print, Lycra, tight-leather-trousers kinda thing. Tracy actually liked the trousers a lot – but we all said to ourselves, "We're making a mistake here." At least we said no to the clothes.'

Earl had only returned from the United States and England in 1977. He'd been taking notes on how punk was exploding. A former hairdresser and self-styled impresario, Earl modelled himself on Jake Rivera (alias Andrew Jakeman), the forceful manager of Elvis Costello (alias Declan MacManus) and one of the key figures behind Stiff Records in the United Kingdom. Punk's guiding spirits of purification and self-reinvention saw a lot of name changing, opportunism and corporate rebranding in pursuit of its reformation ethos. The walls of the music industry would not fall as the punk scene hoped, but spiv capitalism would thrive. Earl caught a whiff of these trade winds, and upon his return to Melbourne convinced Mushroom Records boss Michael Gudinski that an Australian version of Stiff – which had established a striking label identity thanks to the design work of Barney Bubbles (alias Colin Fulcher) and slogans such as 'If It Ain't Stiff, It Ain't Worth a Fuck' – should be developed locally.

The catch was that Gudinski had only just established Mushroom as a major independent label with the massive success of Skyhooks in the mid-1970s. He had virtually single-handedly put the idea of an Australian music business and an Australian sound on the map (with no small thanks to the vernacular song-writing genius of Greg Macainsh) and was understandably reluctant to dilute the already iconic Mushroom brand. Something of a piratical idealist, Gudinski nonetheless assisted Earl in establishing Suicide as a nominally separate entity with a production and distribution deal that went through a major record company, RCA. It was an odd arrangement that was perceived as Gudinski's way of having his cake and eating it too, investing limited resources while securing contract options for Mushroom on all the bands for recording and publishing over the next five years. Once the dust settled on the experiment, it effectively meant Mushroom could take its pick of the survivors. With a growl redolent of an ageing sabre-tooth tiger moving across the musical tundra, Gudinski says, 'All that punk shit was only just starting to happen here.' He recalls Barrie Earl 'trying to be an English type of producer–manager figure. He loved that. It was Barrie's way or the highway. That was not the most artist-friendly approach.'[3]

Even so, Earl moved quickly and effectively. Before 1977 was over he had signed The Boys Next Door and Spred (soon to start calling themselves Teenage Radio Stars), as well as JAB, X-Ray-Z and Negatives (formerly Reals) in Melbourne, Wasted Daze in Sydney and The Survivors in Brisbane. The Saints' penetration of the British Top 40 in August 1977 with their single 'This Perfect Day'[4], and their appearance on *Top of the Pops* in the same week as both the Sex Pistols and The Jam, gave many of these young Australian groups the feeling that international success was there to be seized. Even so, the local scene was soon divided between those who were aligned with Suicide and those who stood apart.

'We told Barrie that if he really wanted a punk band, there was this group in Sydney called The Filth that he should get,' Nick says, clearly enjoying the story. 'They were this crazy, violent, self-mutilating band. So Barrie flew up to Sydney to see them. When they met, all the singer did was keep running into a door and headbutting it, blood everywhere. They wouldn't sign anything. They abused him the whole time and threw a chair at him. Barrie had to let them go.'

Michael Gudinski calls Barrie Earl 'a born loser', but it is said with an odd grain of affection, even praise. 'He just didn't deal with people properly. But if you look back at who was on *Lethal Weapons* [the 1978 showcase compilation from the Suicide label] and what became of them – and most of the things Barrie did – he was really right on the money. Whatever Barrie did wrong, he would back people no-one else would. Unfortunately he was his own worst enemy – ahead of his time and never able to last the distance.'[5]

The truth is Gudinski and Earl were part of an Australian music business that punched above its weight to shrug off overseas cultural and corporate dominance. The characters left standing could be vicious or roguishly charming on the flip of a coin. Sometimes a tag-team of that order was required. Along with Mushroom Records, Gudinski ran the Premier Artists agency, which booked most of the prime venues in Melbourne and many others across the country: bands fitted in or were deprived of the oxygen to perform and expand their audience base.

Missing Link's Keith Glass saw the predicament in this way: 'Australian music could only ever be Mushroom music.'[6] Like his young protégé Bruce Milne, who was now working behind the counter of his record store in Flinders Lane, Glass embraced punk rock in countercultural rather than business terms. Without intending to set themselves up as such, Glass and Milne were seen as gurus for an anti-Suicide bloc in Melbourne. Milne did try to warn bands about the Suicide contracts and getting a lawyer to check them out before signing. No-one listened.

Karen Marks is surprisingly generous about Barrie Earl, whom she knew both professionally and personally due to the cottage-industry nature of the scene in Melbourne. 'I had a lot of time for Barrie. I knew he had been pissing in the boys' ears to sign to Suicide. Telling them, "I can make you a star." But I still think Barrie was terrific. He was used by Gudinski. Barrie was always known for having great ideas. He was really good at spotting trends. He was famous for it. None of it would have happened without him. And he spotted Nick and The Boys Next Door, didn't he?'[7]

In the meantime, Nick was having one lesson ground into him repeatedly: 'After Barrie tried to get us to change what we wore on stage, we were invited over to Gudinski's office a few days later. He had a whole spiel about how "one day, boys, I am going to make you all stars". I've heard that kind of thing with a lot of the older set over the years. "Look what I can do for you." That kinda thing; they all say stuff like that.'

Suicide Records immediately put The Boys Next Door into the studio with Greg Macainsh as a producer. As well as being Karen Marks's housemate, Macainsh was the one of the most successful pop-rock songwriters of the era, thanks to the Skyhooks phenomenon. It was quite a trajectory for The Boys Next Door: here they were, just coming out of their teens and having only played six professional shows, laying down a single for national release with a genuinely original and revered figure in the industry.

Nick's memories, however, are less enthusiastic. He thinks Greg Macainsh 'was obviously told to sort our music out and give it a pop edge. So, with my vocals I had to sing them, then double-track the vocals again manually to give them that pleasing edge. We didn't know what we were doing. We didn't have any experience to be able to say, "This is shit."'

'I wasn't appalled by the result,' Macainsh observes drolly. He was one of a handful of older musicians on the Melbourne scene who'd each been matched with a young Suicide band in a studio,

The Boys Next Door, 1978. Left to right: Tracy Pew, Phill Calvert, Nick Cave, Mick Harvey *(Ashley Mackevicius)*

with a view to compiling what would be the *Lethal Weapons* album. 'The idea was to give the record some varied flavours – and it was cheaper than using a big-name producer, too,' Macainsh says. 'Suicide did have a sign-'em-up-spit-'em-out-and-see-what-sticks approach. Barrie was a hustler, but he believed in the whole thing and no-one else had any idea at all about the punk thing happening in England. Certainly not Michael [Gudinski]. Barrie was the messenger for all that. He made it happen. And Michael went with Barrie on it. Michael made a lot of records like that back then, and they would not have been made any other way without him. That needs to be acknowledged.'[8]

Macainsh understood The Boys Next Door's disillusionment. 'Hearing yourself played back in the studio for the first time is always confronting and disappointing. The experience is like looking into a mirror and not liking what you see. I knew they had something to express. They knew it. But they didn't quite know *how* to express it. They could only listen to it and say, "That's not how we sound."' Macainsh underlines this when he says, 'The band was still purely an expression of an attitude.'

'I found Nick a difficult person. I couldn't connect with him. That's not a big issue. You don't need to be someone's best friend to work with them. But to me Nick was inside his own world. And that made things more difficult. Just a simple technical thing like the way you want the last word of each phrase to not tail off into noise; that need for a bit of intention behind what is sung – you want those lyrics to be heard. The great rock singers know how to push their voices through a wall of noise, both in the studio and live. Nick's voice ... had a deadness. It was quite round but it didn't have a leading edge. That's what I was pushing for. Obviously he has a learned a lot since those days.'

Macainsh adds that Phill Calvert was 'probably the best musician in the band'. Mick Harvey was 'an earnest chap'. Tracy had a Fender Coronado semi-acoustic bass that was a major problem for the recording, as it was prone to creating feedback, despite the deep tones Pew loved when he played it on stage. Macainsh eventually loaned Tracy his famous Fender L electric bass, which featured the torso of a nude woman painted on it. It was an instrument of greater precision and Tracy took a shine to it. He took a shine to a few other things as well. 'Tracy created some discussion, as there was something about him pinching hubcaps from vehicles in the studio car park. The studio owner was not happy.'[9]

Michael Shipley was the engineer on the recording sessions. Macainsh points out that Shipley had recently finished working with the Sex Pistols in the studio, so it was not a completely ham-fisted scenario. Shipley had also worked with Queen.[10] The sound is clean and sharp, and truer to the band's spirit than what would eventuate seven months later when The Boys Next Door began recording their debut album with a different producer. What Macainsh managed to do in the interim was help them capture a brash, driving cover of Lee Hazlewood's 'These Boots Are Made for Walkin" as well as two lively (if stock-standard New Wave) originals, 'Boy Hero' and 'Masturbation Generation'.

The latter was yet another dig by Nick at the punk tag everyone kept labelling them with. The song had grown out of a drunken sparring match with Reals singer Garry Gray, as to who could come up with the worst song title and do something creative with it. Nick suggested 'I'm So Ugly'[11], which Gray never used; Gray gave Nick 'Masturbation Generation'. The recorded version of 'Masturbation Generation' featured a spat-out pun mocking 'Suicide' as an option that even the most miserable of souls should give up on. It was classic Nick, biting the hand that feeds and behaving like an innocent when quizzed about the lyrical coincidence.

Nick's reading of 'Boots' drew from Nancy Sinatra's famous version in which she was told by songwriter and producer Lee Hazlewood to sing 'like a fourteen-year-old that fucks truckers'.[12] When it first became a hit in 1966, the song was often used as a soundtrack to news stories propagandising the war in Vietnam, adding to its aura of malice and giving it twisted punk appeal a decade later. Nick's vocal is overtly nastier than Nancy Sinatra's, the sound thrashier and trashier, with a pop edge still intact. It's a good interpretation, inverting the proto-feminist S&M strut of the original to proudly signal young male narcissism and lip-curling cruelty. The sleeve notes for *Lethal Weapons* brag it was 'deranged' rather than arranged by The Boys Next Door.

Live footage now available on YouTube[13] reveals a distinctly aggressive power-pop band playing originals like 'Secret Life' and 'Sex Crimes' at Swinburne College, songs they'd say they wished they had recorded instead. But who had the talent or resources, let alone the will, to catch that sound and put it out on vinyl?

Nick Cave at the photoshoot for the cover of *Brave Exhibitions*,
June 1978 *(Michel Lawrence)*

Maybe the band was right retrospectively, and their raw demos were better than the polished results with Macainsh. A new boutique label like Suicide – which was looking for a punk–pop crossover into the charts – was never going to release to radio songs with that rawness. In those early days of the punk era, not many people in the industry understood what it was all about, much less how to capture the energy on vinyl. Not even The Boys Next Door did, for that matter. Macainsh was quite right: the band had the attitude, but did it really have an identity?

When Nick took the recording of 'These Boots Are Made for Walkin'' home to his father, Colin laughed at it. Bach was in no danger of being swept aside by his son. The sting of that as much as anything else might explain why Nick had such a strong negative reaction to the whole experience. And even more to prove.

Gudinski, Earl and Macainsh were soon all in the hit-maker Molly Meldrum's ear, telling him to pay even more attention to The Boys Next Door. The band were becoming a Suicide *cause célèbre* and generating much interest, especially whenever they played live. At the 1977 New Year's Eve street party called 'Punk Gunk' – where Nick's father saw him perform – they were forced to ignore antagonism from their peers about them becoming 'sellouts'. All the hype and marketing that Barrie Earl was building around the coming *Lethal Weapons* compilation had prompted a word-of-mouth anti-Suicide slogan around the traps: 'Sign to Suicide, or suicide to sign?' Karen Marks says 'a lot of the bands began to feel embarrassed about being involved. It was really stupid.'[14] Nick's reaction was to give an especially wild performance at Punk Gunk, singing and rolling around in the gutter like a man possessed (much to Colin Cave's dismay). He took it right into the faces of everyone who was doubting them.

Three months later 'These Boots Are Made for Walking [sic]' was released, launching the Suicide label in March 1978. The Boys Next Door were able to stride in and play 'live' on Meldrum's *Countdown*, an unheard-of coup for a group of upstarts so fresh to the scene. It was somewhat anticlimactic to find they had to mime to a tape of their spiky interpretation of 'Boots', while an audience of twelve-year-old girls did their best to wave their hands in the air as instructed by the program's floor manager.

The band had wanted to launch themselves on the public with an original song, but here they were being chewed up and doing exactly as they were told. Nick had fantasised about being as risqué and dangerous as his latest favourites, the New York Dolls. Instead it felt like they were following in the footsteps of teenyboppers like the Bay City Rollers. The fact Blondie had digested some similar influences to The Boys Next Door and achieved something original and subversive was a reminder of other possibilities. Nick sat in his bedroom blasting the New York Dolls' 'Personality Crisis' over and over after returning from the *Countdown* performance. Its lyrics are about getting so caught up in popular culture you lose sight of whoever you thought you were. They also reference a then popular notion in psychology that focused on teenagers and how their roleplay in society advanced or damaged their ability to evolve into adults. '"Personality crisis", whatever happened to that term?' Nick asks, still flogging the song on his car stereo at high volume as he drives around St Kilda forty years later. 'It just disappeared into a whole bunch of other terms. But maybe it was more accurate.'

A sharp film clip by Chris Löfvén of The Boys Next Door performing 'These Boots Are Made for Walking' – not screened at the time – shows them on a white set decorated with cardboard cut-out hearts. Anita Lane had come up with the bold red-and-white set design. Nick stands on a heart that is uniquely pierced by a Cupid's arrow; Lane has hung another heart, half-broken, on the wall behind his head. The band members behave as if they were pumping out the song with all the terse and bright ferocity of old-school Australian rock 'n' roll favourites like The Easybeats. Suited up and tensely theatrical, Nick even looks like a mod–meets–glam–meets–punk evolution of The Easybeats' singer Stevie Wright, with a defiant, spread-leg singing posture that owes more than a little to The Saints' Chris Bailey as well. This bad–boy–for–love image confirmed Nick as an early presence; it's a convincingly stylised picture, and one that shows that The Boys Next Door had the goods – as the members of Blondie believed – to do things their way, if they could only stick to their guns.[15]

Nick's mind drifted back to Alex Harvey's remark that a rock 'n' roll guitar was more powerful than an AK–47. Yeah, he really needed more firepower.

With his blazing eyes, goatee beard and mane of grey hair, the painter Tony Clark looks the part of a Mephistopheles ready to roll. It is not hard to imagine his more youthful charisma decades earlier. In the summer months leading into 1978, Nick Cave fell under his sway as an inner circle established itself during late-night drinking sessions at Clark's tiny St Kilda flat.

Anita Lane provided the introductions. The artist was an early mentor to both her and Rowland S Howard, teaching them art history during their first year at Prahran Technical College in 1977. 'I was only a few years older than them, so it was not the normal teacher–student relationship,' Tony Clark emphasises. 'You know, it is only with the passing of the years that I have realised how special this particular group of people were and how incredibly lucky I was to meet them all.'[16]

Like Nick, Anita had a habit of bucking against hierarchies and rules. Clark remembers Lane trying to take advantage of their extracurricular friendship by refusing to submit her end-of-year essay. She seemed to be going out of her way to fail, and to provoke Clark into the bargain. 'Well, Nick was absolutely devoted to her at that point. So he went off to the library and wrote an essay on Egon Schiele for her so that she could pass,' Clark says, laughing.[17]

Both Lane and Howard would drop out before their second year got underway in early 1978, but they would stay close to Clark – as would Lane's best friend and fellow Prahran art student, Lisa Craswell, with whom Howard was infatuated. Where Lane was a punkish red-headed Pre-Raphaelite beauty with *Lolita* overtones, Craswell was her opposite, a dark-eyed brunette of equally stunning looks who assumed the mantle of black queen to Anita Lane's off-kilter and ethereal white.

As a group, these powerful individuals forged an informal salon that pushed Nick to reconsider all his ideas – none more so than Anita Lane. 'Nick told me how Anita had stayed at his [family] house,' says Howard, 'and, coming back to his room from a shower, she was reading his lyrics to "Joyride"[18] ... And he was mortified that she was laughing at them and saying, "This is stupid." He went out of his way to write to impress Anita [after that]; the band was becoming more than a joke and a hobby, and it hadn't been necessary for him to apply himself seriously before. Suddenly Nick was meeting people who expected more of him.'[19]

'Meeting Tony was like entering into an alternative art history course,' Nick says. 'The painters I was looking at, and Tony too, they all worked very hard. They did it every day, all day in their studios, working and painting. I learned a lot from that. It was something I held onto. It's not like rock musicians are known for working hard,' he says, laughing. 'That discipline and practice were definitely things I took note of.'

Despite having failed at CIT, Nick excelled in essay writing and art history. He and Clark could talk for hours. 'When I grew a moustache, Nick used to like to tease me and tell me I looked like August Strindberg,' Clark says.[20] As could sometimes be the case with Nick, this comment was three parts flattery and one part dagger to the ribs. Clark could take it. Clark's encounters with the nascent punk scene were confirming his passion for 'outsider art' and raw forms of expression that converged with his idiosyncratic interests in classical art. In this convergence Cave and Clark discovered a mutual interest.

Nick's favourite painting at the time was Matthias Grünewald's *The Crucifixion from the Isenheim Altar*. He was also a fan of the Spanish Renaissance, Baroque and Romantic periods: the dark mysticism of El Greco; the sensuous, confronting portraiture of Diego Velázquez; and Francisco Goya's nightmarish Black Paintings. These were very old-fashioned obsessions in a cultural environment leaning towards the early stages of a conceptual shift known as postmodernism. As with the music scene, there was the sense of a changing present at war with the weight of the past. But in this battle, Nick was well on the side of the traditionalists, and even a radical conservative. Apart from the works of Francis Bacon and Brett Whiteley, the closest Nick got to enthusing about anything contemporary was the Berlin and Viennese Expressionist movement of the early twentieth century.

'It's no accident Nick chose Egon Schiele to write about [for Anita Lane's essay],' Clark says. 'He was plunged into the revival of Expressionist art at the time. People were rejecting the art of the 1970s in favour of art from the 1920s and before. And Nick himself appealed to visual artists as well. Jenny Watson did those portraits of him and all of The Boys Next Door very early on [in 1977] because they were so strong visually.'[21] A budding, if aberrant, classicist like Nick Cave was bound to find a magus-like figure such as Tony Clark highly attractive – and helpful to his own development. Jenny Watson observed Clark at close quarters and the way he took a leading role. 'He had the same advantages I did,' she says, 'and that lay in him being just a little older and having a degree of remove that an art historical view can give you.'[22]

Born in Canberra to a diplomat father and educated in England, Clark had spent most of his adolescence in Italy during the 1960s. 'I grew up in the Fascist quarter of Rome, and that was a showcase for Fascist classicism. And some of that had an Expressionist element to it too; it wasn't just all polish, some of it was kind of Art Deco,' Clark says. 'All these unexpected elements that don't fit the stereotype of the classical world, I liked that. Particularly towards the end of the Roman Empire, you could see, right where I lived and walked the streets, how it just got rougher, [and] that's the kind of classicism I love the best – when it's really on its last legs and getting rougher and rougher, and [artists, sculptors and architects are] referring to their past artistic history in a very schematic way that is also very intense and expressive.'

Clark links this savage classicism to his own experiences witnessing the genesis of punk in London in the mid-1970s, before he returned to Australia in late 1976. After spending a few months living with the pop artist Martin Sharp in Sydney, he finally wandered down to Melbourne to take up his teaching post at Prahran in 1977. Everything was primed. Rowland S Howard would invite Clark to come along and see The Saints early that same year. 'They were really the beginning of something significant for everyone,' Clark says firmly. 'It was like a light went off in people's minds.' Though actually an accomplished jazz bass guitarist, Tony Clark decided to apply punk's DIY philosophy to making art, utilising canvas boards and painting materials that were considered the province of the rank amateur. While Nick was leaving art behind for music, Clark was heading in the opposite direction. They crossed paths at an ideal time for both.

'Events in Melbourne,' Clark says, 'gave me the confidence to really kick-start my painting. My angle at the time was that I was nostalgic for, and involved in, high culture – a lot more than most of my peers were – but I didn't want to do nice, refined things with it. I was trying to look for, or look at, if you like, Expressionist and outsider art as another side of classicism. At one stage I called it "St Kilda Classicism", which doesn't mean anything now, but at the time St Kilda was full of drug users and prostitutes and general deadbeats – so the meaning of "St Kilda Classicism" was referring to that classical world which I was familiar with because of where I had grown up in Rome – but putting that reference down in a way that was completely rough and almost kind of psychotic-looking, like very, very crude images of temples and very, very crude representations of the classical landscape. And Nick, it has to be said, was extremely supportive of all this stuff that I did and took a genuine interest in it.'[23]

According to Nick, 'Tony was never a loud or demonstrative person. But he knew about things we didn't know about. He was someone we listened to. Lisa Craswell, Anita and me, Rowland, maybe Genevieve [McGuckin] too … we were all hungry. I was hungry. I still am hungry. And Tony was always articulate and hugely intelligent and just really knew his stuff. The way he talked about particular painters and the originality of his viewpoint were such that even to this day those artists he introduced me to I still have a … special place for in my heart. Louis Wain is the obvious example. Alberto Savinio is another one. Tony would be like, "Sure, there's De Chirico, but have you seen what his brother does?" So I had Tony Clark showing me how there's great art, yes, but there's this other stuff out there that is equally as valid and exciting. I think his pictures are exciting too. All that was having a huge influence over the way I saw myself. But I don't think I knew how to work that out with what I was doing personally or in my music.'

In light of that comment, it's interesting to reflect on Tony Clark's updated term for his own aesthetic and what sprang from the time and place that formed him and Nick as artists: 'punk classicism'.

Nick's delinquent musical friendships with the likes of Pierre Voltaire and Tracy Pew seemed to carry on in some other parallel and, indeed, rougher world. Voltaire says he found the endless conversations on art 'a real snore'.[24] Neither he nor Pew was fond of visiting Clark's eyrie. The journalist Clinton Walker, who was very much a part of The Boys Next Door's hard-partying Tiger Lounge scene, thinks the art school and intellectual emphasis on their origins is way overrated. 'There was just as much naughty schoolboy and Billy Bunter to them as David Bowie's *Low*,' he says.[25]

This mischievous side emerged on at least one memorable occasion at Clark's home during a long conversation on the connections between the French composer Erik Satie and Brian Eno's ambient experiments. Tracy Pew was finding the discussion a little precious and he piped up that he heard a wonderful album of piano music recently that might interest them all. Knowing what Pew was like, Nick played the straight man and asked Tracy what this wonderful music was. Pew deadpanned, '*The Sting*.'[26]

The *Lethal Weapons* compilation was released in May 1978, recycling The Boys Next Door single 'These Boots Are Made for Walking', the B-side 'Boy Hero' and the as-yet-unreleased 'Masturbation Generation' as their representative tracks. The album cover featured blood oozing from the barrel of a revolver, a comic-book pastiche based on a Barrie Earl concept and realised by the graphic artist John CJ Taylor. It made for a striking package, with the record itself pressed on milk-white vinyl rather than the usual black. The music, however, was less developed than the promotional campaign, which featured slogans such as 'Progressive Pop for Modern People' and 'Revving Towards Tomorrow Today', as well as giveaway packets of 'Suicide' cinnamon-flavoured chewing gum bullets to match the gun imagery. Punk's anti-establishment stance always had a symbiotic relationship with the evolution of guerrilla marketing, but Earl had overdone it. This looked like a record company trying too hard, with the logo and gimmicks evoking an opportunistic budget label like K-Tel Australia rather than anything as cool as Stiff in the United Kingdom. Many of the bands reacted with shame, even outright antagonism. The fact Nick had fallen in with such sophisticated cultural company, thanks to his relationship with Anita Lane, only made everything about Suicide appear crasser to him.

'Boots' remained The Boys Next Door's best track on *Lethal Weapons* for two obvious reasons: it was better written than their originals, and it was delivered with a *Nuggets*-like presence that was hard to top.[27] Satirical as it may have been, 'Masturbation Generation' was basically a sub-Ramones singalong that was begging for attention. Being with Suicide compromised its rebellious stance, however much Nick tried to throw out a knowing lyrical wink that no-one owned him. Along with their intensifying live shows, Nick was reconsidering his relationship to the audience in ways that would have long-term implications, ultimately leading to the confrontational style of The Birthday Party. For now he kept himself busy making lists, such as one entitled 'things I am not happy with, within the boys next door'. One of the most heinous crimes was how much his band wanted to please its audience.[28]

'Boy Hero' was unique for being the first Nick Cave/Mick Harvey co-write. The song's proto–New Wave sound featured frenetic, buzzing Formula One racetrack guitar work from Harvey, and it again drew lyrically on Cave's desire for attention with the parallel story of a hero who drowns in his own acclaim. Reputedly based on a banal newspaper item about a swimming accident, the song could be read as a fable inspired by Nick's own hero, the increasingly coked-out David Bowie.[29] Sonically and lyrically, however, 'Boy Hero' was light years behind the Thin White Duke, who was well into his Berlin phase with conspirators such as Iggy Pop, Tony Visconti and Brian Eno, all of whom Nick would continue to study closely. From the start, Nick was tuning in to a mythology that could envelop him and take him forward. He seemed to be looking for stories he could attach himself to and somehow enter or absorb around him. Years later, Mick Harvey would remark on another aspect to 'Boy Hero': how it echoes the tale of a teenage Ned Kelly saving a boy from drowning, an interpretation that connects Nick's lyric to the Wangaratta mythology that shaped his boyhood dreams.[30]

All three songs on *Lethal Weapons* revealed an awareness of the gap between public display and what passed for self-revelation, with a knowing way of addressing, involving and accusing an audience during the interplay. For now, this look-at-me, don't-you-dare-look-at-me narcissism was flirtatiously adolescent, an aggressive pose bordering on camp. Nick's lyrics and performance nonetheless showed there was something going on with The Boys Next Door that set them apart from every other band showcased on *Lethal Weapons*. Nick told *Roadrunner* journalist Jillian Burt, 'A lot of the songs are about being a star and drowning under it. Real corny sort of stuff.' Then he summed them up more simply: 'The songs are kind of sad and tragic, but they're treated with a sort of sarcasm.'[31]

When *Lethal Weapons* was released, Nick did an interview with the *Sydney Mirror* in which he once again did his best to separate The Boys Next Door from the punk marketing around them. His refutations were starting to exhaust him: 'We're not talking about society,' he said. 'We have nothing to direct to the audience in the way of complaints – we are not really angry young men.'[32]

On *Lethal Weapons*, only Teenage Radio Stars (featuring Sean Kelly and James Freud) matched The Boys Next Door for star power, cloning their own Bowie-meets-T-Rex pop sound with a garage-pop sneer. JAB made pioneering use of Ash Wednesday's[33] synthesiser playing as well as the thin, dirty guitar work and Cockney accent of their English-born vocalist Bohdan X (Bohdan Kubiakowski). They sounded legitimately punk and a lot of fun too, if not particularly complex; their 'Blonde and Bombed' was almost a Calypso-Cockney rap song, as well as a hilarious celebration of X's desire for Deborah Thomas. Humour was close to the surface of what many Australian punk bands were developing as an ethos. The grey-faced anger of English punk could not be adopted entirely seriously in a sunny Australian context. If you didn't listen too closely to the Jim Morrison–lite lyrics, Chris Walsh's new band Negatives (with Garry Gray once again on vocals) nearly stole the show with a brooding, cinematic piece called 'Planet on the Prowl'. Negatives would bitterly disown it due to the imposition of Eric Gradman's production effects and ambient violin without their permission, but the awful truth was these were probably the song's best attributes. After slagging off Gradman and Macainsh all over town for their studio efforts, Walsh's gang and The Boys Next Door retreated to Walsh's house on a regular basis, stewing over his Stooges and Bowie albums and how their grand vision had been frustrated by fools.[34]

Label camaraderie was completely dissolving by the time Suicide sent all the bands out on regional and national package tours. Pierre Voltaire, who had initially joined Teenage Radio Stars as a bassist, quickly defected to JAB. He says that on the Suicide showcase nights, 'the focus of the audience was always on Nick. All the other bands were jealous of Boys Next Door because of Nick. Even then, though, he was fairly disdainful. He was an "art student", not a "rock star",' Voltaire adds in a haughty voice. 'That was the attitude. Nick was a big ponce … flamboyant and charismatic from the day he walked on stage. That side of him is one of the truest things about him, actually.'[35]

Playing on a triple bill with Teenage Radio Stars and X-Ray-Z, The Boys Next Door caused a minor sensation in Adelaide when they announced they were going to play 'Masturbation Generation' to a lunchtime crowd in Rundle Mall. Police on hand to supervise this punk event threatened to pull the plug, so Nick re-announced the song as 'Frustration Generation' and sang the original lyrics anyway. Afterwards, he and Tracy caused an even bigger stir by goose-stepping around the mall behind the backs of the police and giving Nazi salutes to them from a balcony. An aspiring young singer by the name of Dave Graney was delighted. The band's set, he said, was 'riveting' and 'fantastic', with Nick by turns scarecrow-like, strangely comic and 'exotic'. Graney would be excited enough by The Boys Next Door to hatch his own plans to head eastwards to Melbourne in search of a music career of his own. 'Adelaide wasn't large enough for someone to cultivate a mysterious, tubercular side to their character,' he says.[36]

Jillian Burt would similarly become one of Cave's biggest fans and most sensitive critics. In May she wrote a review for *Juke* magazine of a show that took place at the Highway Inn in Adelaide. In it she describes Nick as 'somewhere between the smouldering sensuality of Valentino and the brooding villainy of Vincent Price with a dash of Chaplineseque tragic/comic.'[37] Nick later protested that it was over the top; by then Rowland S Howard was at his side, archly lamenting, 'I wish people said great things like that about me.'[38]

In an interview with Burt for the newly launched, Adelaide-based national music magazine *Roadrunner*, Nick said, 'I get a real kick out of performing. I don't just dance around. Most of our songs are kind of tragic little songs and I try to put that across by breaking into tears and things like that. I've really got a fascination with the real corny kinds of performers like Barry Manilow, with the way he skips across the stage and does all these sort of really flamboyant gestures.'[39]

Rowland's high-school band The Obsessions had been supposed to perform with The Reals and The Boys Next Door back at their Swinburne College show in August 1977; instead, his group broke apart before playing a single gig. Mick Harvey was sceptical about Rowland's credentials for much more than getting noticed for his dress sense, his cutting opinions and his memorable ability to strike poses at parties. 'I didn't really feel like buying it on face value,' says Harvey. 'I think I pretty much told him that at some party once: "Well, it's about time you did something rather just talking the talk." I hadn't seen much evidence of him doing anything … I hadn't seen him play a note still. I was a little dubious of whether there was anything behind it. Or whether he was just a well-read dandy.'[40]

Rowland convened with a similarly self-possessed Ian 'Ollie' Olsen from Reals at a party that same August. The pair agreed to form a new band before the year was over. Ironically, this was the same party at which Nick and Anita had got together, a measure of how small the Melbourne scene was. In 1995, Rowland would describe Olsen as 'the most remarkable self-publicist. He had all these people convinced that he was a complete genius. He still does, to a certain extent.'[41]

A student of the Melbourne electronic composer Felix Werder, Olsen had an informed passion for Bartók, Wagner, Cage and Stockhausen, as well as an interest in the atmospheric and fractured approach of German rock bands such as Neu! and Can. The classical influences were not particularly obvious in his own music, but Olsen saw common ground in that 'they were all subversive and they were all hitting out in their own way'.[42] Already a formidable musician, he was particularly adept at mimicking the guitar work from *Marquee Moon*. Olsen even played a white Fender Jaguar identical to that of Tom Verlaine of Television. Rowland longed for an instrument just like it. His younger brother, Harry, says Rowland 'played a red Gibson Firebird copy because Phil Manzanera used to play one in Roxy Music. The early Eno albums were big hits in our house too; those droning guitars and sustained notes were an inspiration. Rowland had just bought this Blue Box effects pedal that became one of his signature sounds – it creates this extraordinary sustain. It came with a piece of literature that said it was designed to emulate a clarinet.'[43]

Howard and Olsen would select their musical cohorts carefully, first conscripting Jeffrey Wegener when he moved to Melbourne to partake of the booming live scene. A highly regarded Brisbane musician, Wegener had originally been offered the role of drummer for The Saints. Howard and Olsen were not to know this gentle, thoughtful man of self-deprecating intensity could undergo Jekyll-

Party in Keith and Helena Glass's backyard, South Yarra, 1977. Left to right: Gina 'Red Socks' Riley (face obscured), Tracy Pew, Ollie Olsen, Peter Milne, Anita Lane, Rowland S Howard, Nick Cave. *(David Pepperell)*

and-Hyde transformations after a few drinks. Wegener was about
to be name-checked as 'the Professor' in a brilliant new Saints song
called 'Know Your Product'. It was as good a reference as any young
musician could hope for, but the line actually exhorted everyone to
shoot Wegener, if only to save themselves from his wild side.

The three then travelled to Sydney by train to meet with bassist
Janine Hall and persuade her to come south and join them. Hall
was a few years older and a rising star with a few offers on the table
in Sydney, but the zeal and talent of her new young friends was
hard to resist. With Wegener and Hall in place, Young Charlatans
rehearsed hard, and were perceived as something of a supergroup
in Melbourne before they played a note. Howard would describe
the anticipation around them as 'ridiculous'. Mick Harvey recalls:
'Everyone was waiting for them to come together and there was an
inevitability it was going to be genius.'[44]

The fact is, it was. When Young Charlatans played their
first show in December 1977, The Boys Next Door were shaken
out of a prematurely self-satisfied torpor as a freshly recorded
Suicide act. Young Charlatans came out fully formed, presenting
a host of sophisticated songs with a driven, even possessed,
musical attack that worked off the interplay between Rowland S
Howard and Ollie Olsen as blazing guitarist-songwriters who
shared vocal duties.

Rowland's song 'Shivers' was merely one gem in a very
rich set – not even their best song, fans would argue. As with
any great young band, there was a feeling the amplifiers could
barely contain them. Up against the rushing, jagged scope of the
Young Charlatans, The Boys Next Door appeared limited, even
contrived. Nick's lyrics wilted by comparison with Howard's
sardonic and convincing love poetry and Olsen's jump-cut visions
of reality. What The Boys Next Door fought back with was the
honed intensity of a former schoolboy unit that had been playing
together for years.

Journalist Clinton Walker had only just arrived from Brisbane when all this started to happen. He claims that by early 1978, 'Young Charlatan[s] was the band The Boys Next Door wanted to be.'[45] As luck would have it, no sooner had Young Charlatans set Melbourne alight than their flame started to flicker and die. A whole new experimental scene enchanted by the synthesiser was developing around the squats and low-rent housing in the university suburb of North Fitzroy where Olsen lived. Howard was making serious strides with his guitar playing, but his deeply romantic songs – for all their wry asides – were increasingly at odds with Olsen's Burroughs-influenced cut-up approach to lyrics and his deepening passion for electronics. The seventeen-year-old Howard was also sick of the nineteen-year-old Olsen's controlling and petulant ways; Olsen had walked out on the group a few times. Manager Bruce Milne – still only twenty years old himself – was powerless to stop the disintegration of what, for barely six months, had been the hottest band in town. Even the volatile Jeffrey Wegener could only shake his head and say, on reflection, 'Fucking Ollie!'[46]

Mick Harvey would recall them being 'very important' and 'mind-boggling', noting the significant musical careers of each band member after Young Charlatans. 'Quite simply,' Harvey says, 'I don't see why that sort of thing should be forgotten just because there is no recorded product.'[47] Olsen would continue to cross swords with Nick as he established a hardcore reputation on the Australian electronic music scene, later forming Max Q with Michael Hutchence.[48] Wegener would distinguish himself as one of the key musicians of the post-punk era, playing drums for Ed Kuepper's Laughing Clowns and briefly joining The Birthday Party (who reputedly sacked him for being too much even for them, though this is disputed). Janine Hall would go on to play a crucial role in a reformed version of The Saints under Chris Bailey's rowdy leadership.

Apart from a barely listenable live tape and some demo recordings, the reputation of the unrecorded Young Charlatans would be sustained mainly in people's memories, part of a moment that was briefly and hectically theirs. The Boys Next Door were about to absorb this fast-burning mythology in the form of Rowland S Howard, who would transform not only Nick Cave's vision of song writing, but his band entirely.

By June 1978, The Boys Next Door were trapped in Allan Eaton Studio with producer Les Karski (of the British pub-funk band Supercharge), unhappily at work on their debut album. Mick Harvey would become even more depressed after playing a game of pool with Karski during which the producer denounced Roxy Music and The Velvet Underground and declared reggae his favourite music. It was hard to see where a meeting of minds might be achieved. Charged with giving The Boys Next Door a New Wave sound that matched the latest musical trends in the United Kingdom, Karski emphasised Phill Calvert's precise drumming and guest musician Andrew Duffield's keyboards, as well as his own backing vocal flourishes, pushing Cave even harder than Greg Macainsh had done to enunciate his vocals. In a 1983 interview with a fanzine called *The Offense*, Nick looked back on the recordings and said: 'I think my singing style at that particular period was totally repulsive.'[49]

Nick had big visions beforehand, as usual. He'd told the Sydney fanzine *Spurt!*, 'I never had much faith in punk rock at all.' The Berlin sound of David Bowie and Iggy Pop was now all-consuming in his ears. 'We're getting another member,' he said mysteriously, refusing to give a name at the time of interview. 'Synthesiser. He'll be playing a major role on the album. We'd like to use a lot of keyboards. My interest has always been synthetic music anyway.'[50]

Sadly, the struggles with Les Karski saw Duffield, the young synthesiser genius, used far more conventionally and finally sidelined. He felt jilted by Nick's fast-moving enthusiasm and convenient disenchantment with his abilities as Karski dominated the direction the recordings took. Duffield would get his artistic revenge, playing in Ollie Olsen's Whirlywirld before joining Models.[51] He would look back on working with difficult characters like Nick Cave and Ollie Olsen and regard them as 'visionaries' deeply informed by the influences and tensions that were shaping so many bands across the city: 'We were kind of drawn together by the punk movement, half of them from a new electronic music scene, half from this punk garage rock school, and an amateur kind of *soif de vivre* – a feeling of just going for it.'[52]

The Boys Next Door work in progress, dubbed *Brave Exhibitions*, would not emerge from the pressure cooker with Karski. RCA, with whom Mushroom had negotiated a distribution deal, were already losing faith in everyone associated with the Suicide label after *Lethal Weapons* had failed to make an impact commercially. They passed on *Brave Exhibitions*, describing it as 'not being technically satisfactory'. As Suicide unravelled and no-one could be found to release *Brave Exhibitions*, the album was caught in limbo. The more The Boys Next Door listened to what they had done – and what had been done to them – the unhappier they became. Corporate boots were the ones doing the walking – and it was all over them.

Howard had visited the band during the recording process. When he, Nick and Tracy were sent to fetch alcohol, Rowland was surprised when Tracy simply broke into the nearest car and he and Nick casually piled in. It seemed to be a primary-school teacher's vehicle, the back seat filled with children's drawings. Once they had the alcohol and were nearing the studio, Tracy suggested they crash the car for fun. Nick agreed and, while Rowland screamed for them to stop, Tracy accelerated into a telegraph pole, cutting his head open on the steering wheel when they hit it. 'We got out of the car and Tracy and Nick stood there pelting the car with bricks in a matter-of-fact fashion, as if this was expected of them,' Rowland said. They all then fled the scene and walked back to the studio with the alcohol, blood still streaming down Tracy's face. 'I didn't know them that well at that time,' Rowland added, 'and to me the idea of driving along with somebody, in a stolen car, saying, "Let's crash the car!" was just not in my sphere of social reference.'[53]

Photoshoot for the cover of *Brave Exhibitions*, June 1978. Left to right: Phill Calvert, Mick Harvey, Nick Cave, Tracy Pew. *(Michel Lawrence)*

Janet Austin had begun co-editing *Pulp* with Bruce Milne and Clinton Walker. She says that The Boys Next Door had a big advantage over most of the other bands on the scene because they'd been a tight-knit unit since their school days. 'They had that camaraderie that set them apart, particularly Nick and Tracy. I knew all of them before I had ever even seen them play. They were a highly visible group. I don't want to use the word "gang", but they had an identity even before they got up on a stage. They were tough – that's a good word. But they had this camp way of talking, mocking the whole punk thing in a way, as well as embracing it: "Thank you, ladies and gentleman, and the next song is …" Early on, they'd end their first set with a mock country instrumental as if we were at a country scone bake-off.'[54]

The band hung out late at Topolino's Pizzeria in St Kilda, where, Austin says, 'they got this idea for new stage names based on the pizza toppings. Nick was "Tropicana". Tracy was "With the Lot". He used to call himself "Buddy Love" too, from [the 1963 Jerry Lewis film] *The Nutty Professor*. For a while Tracy wouldn't answer to anyone unless you called him Buddy. Tracy used to say he looked like Karl Malden from *The Streets of San Francisco*. He did a drawing of himself looking like that. He did another great one of Nick, a caricature, it was all Adam's apple.'[55]

When Tracy got too drunk to play the bass and sing at the same time, Rowland would sometimes join the group on stage at the Tiger Lounge and help out with backing vocals. Even so, he still found Pew very difficult to relate to. On one of his first visits to the bassist's home, he discovered Pew reading Plato's *Republic* while all around him on the floor were beer cans and pornographic magazines. Nick thought Rowland harboured similar impressions about him. He told the makers of the documentary *Auutoluminescent*: 'Rowland had this perception of me being this inarticulate punk or something like that … He was impressed by the idiot savant aspect of my nature.' When Rowland finally visited Cave's home, he was 'disillusioned'. Nick's shelves were crammed with novels by Nabokov and Dostoyevsky. 'You read this stuff!' said Rowland, 'I thought you were for real!'[56]

Despite his friendship with Rowland, once it became clear Young Charlatans were falling to pieces, Nick began making overtures to Ollie Olsen about joining The Boys Next Door. Olsen was the superior musician back then, 'a pretty bloody good guitarist', says Mick Harvey. Even Howard later offered backhanded praise: 'Ollie was much more capable of doing a very passable Tom Verlaine imitation.'[57] Olsen's interest in synthesisers, the art-noise ethos of the New York 'No Wave' scene and a multitude of German musical acts from Kraftwerk to Amon Düül II only added to his avant-garde allure and the fantasies Nick was having for where The Boys Next Door might go.

Olsen's intense personality made him the prince of Fitzroy in much the same way as, just across the Yarra River, Nick's rock 'n' roll charisma had crowned him the prince of St Kilda. Bruce Milne shakes his head as he tries to describe just how powerful they were as figures on the Melbourne underground music scene. 'Nick was passively aggressive by comparison,' Milne says, laughing. 'Ollie was aggressively aggressive. Very strong, very dominating.'[58]

Mick Harvey confirms: 'There was this weird period where Nick courted Ollie to be our guitar player. But Ollie was just playing a game with Nick, just tricking him and laughing at him behind his back. They were very competitive back then, and there was a basic disrespect from Ollie. When he didn't end up joining us, that really pissed off Nick – there's a bit of bad blood there over whatever happened. When that fell through, the obvious and much better choice was Rowland anyway. And he was always much less likely to take over the lead vocals.'[59]

This history would be simplified once Rowland S Howard's entry into The Boys Next Door was announced in August 1978: it would even be seen as a seduction by Nick, a long game crafted in Machiavellian fashion to destroy the Young Charlatans. Rowland, however, was far from oblivious to his own merits and the new possibilities on offer. 'Nick really wanted to change what the band [The Boys Next Door] was and how it sounded, but he didn't know how to. So, getting me into the band was a shortcut.'[60] The guitarist explained, 'He [Nick] wanted to move away from poppish-rock music and towards something a lot more like his paintings. They were splattery and grotesque, and the music he was making at the time had nothing to do with that sort of thing.'[61]

As well as a host of fine songs such as 'Shivers' and 'A.K.A.' that The Boys Next Door could adopt as their own, Howard had half a dozen fresh pieces, including 'Guilt Parade', that he was working on. Phill Calvert laughs at what was an embarrassment of riches for the band. 'It was like all of a sudden we had fourteen new songs to choose from.'[62] Nick was pushed not only by the quantity of Rowland's output, but by the quality as well. Mick Harvey was adamant: 'Nick changed his style of song writing totally. Because Rowland's songs sounded so much more refined than his.'[63]

It would take a while for Rowland to establish himself in the band's pecking order – even with Nick in his corner. 'I was feeling my influences; Rimbaud, for example ... Tracy used to mock me mercilessly and I was generally considered pretentious.'[64] Pierre Voltaire remembers 'sitting in the Cave family's backyard on some swings and talking to Rowland. He told me, "I'm worried about Tracy, he's being mean to me."'[65]

Nick's relationship with Howard developed as the first of a handful of platonic love affairs in which a creative sidekick complemented his own vision. As if to emphasise how passionate this type of male bonding with Nick could be, Voltaire laments, 'Nick and I used to be best friends before Rowland came along and Nick fell in love with him. But we were all like that, really. Obsessed with an idea of ourselves and each other.'[66]

Peter Milne, Bruce Milne's younger brother, recalls the energy, week to week, as the band caught fire. 'They [The Boys Next Door] made great music and they had great songs, as much as they might try and disown that stuff now,' he says. 'Every time they played, it was like a gathering of the clan. It's where you went and your name would be on the door. Of course, being seventeen, the fact that you didn't have to pay the $4.50 cover charge was important. They'd come up with new songs, or reinvent old ones; there'd always be a development. I used to go see them rehearse as well, it was interesting to watch them work on new material. That's why I became a photographer, so I could become a fly on the wall and watch things go on. Mick Harvey was always working on the music, making it more interesting.'[67]

Nick's relationship with Mick Harvey operated on a cooler level and would continue to work that way. As Howard asserted his presence, Harvey appeared to become sidelined. Sometimes he was forced off guitar altogether and onto synthesiser or other keyboards. Ironically, it was Harvey who had helped in this process, working hard to integrate Rowland into the band. Both guitarists were heavily influenced by the clipped feedback screams and elegant, neo-psychedelic textures of Roxy Music's Phil Manzanera. The sonic similarities would further obscure Harvey's contributions as Howard took more of the improvising limelight live and their dual guitar interplay became difficult to unthread on record. 'I superseded Mick's position; all of a sudden I was the guitarist,' said Rowland. 'And that must have been hard on him, but his reaction was, "I don't care. I'm not looking for attention. I don't care if I get to play in the songs, if I don't play guitar; I don't care if someone sings the backing parts because I'm just happy for the group to be as good as it possibly can be." But of course he fucking cared.'[68]

With Suicide falling apart as quickly as it had come together, the Australian music industry flirtation with 'punk' appeared to have culminated in a spectacular disaster for all concerned. Sales of *Lethal Weapons* were poor, despite *Countdown* appearances by both The Boys Next Door and Teenage Radio Stars, peaking at around 7000 units. A minor tabloid controversy over the Suicide label's name failed to translate into substantial radio attention. The album received lukewarm reviews that added to the marketplace bruising it received, not to mention the cult disrespect. Neither the chewing-gum bullets that were given away with early copies of *Lethal Weapons* nor the 'collector's-edition' white vinyl had made much of a dent in the public interest. The masses sat at home, oblivious to the Australian New Wave's call to arms, content instead with the unstoppable *Saturday Night Fever* soundtrack and Meatloaf's *Bat Out of Hell*. If Nick later felt they had 'fought the big one' in an artistic revolution driven by punk rock, the truth is that in Australia they resoundingly lost the first battle in this culture war. Sadly, a listen back to *Lethal Weapons* today shows it to be a pretty good barometer of the times.

In an interview for *RAM*, Barrie Earl was scathing about the end of Suicide. He had a message for all the punks he'd worked with: 'The dream is over, the dream is over because of their [the bands'] attitudes of "fuck the world, fuck the establishment"; the industry is part of the establishment and that attitude never has and never will work in rock 'n' roll. What it boils down to is that those bands have not happened. If they had a hit single or a big following, they wouldn't be complaining! Affinity and strength lies in a band itself. I think they have made a lot of mistakes, they're fucked and so is their attitude! The last person a band ever blames is themselves … We've had more press for our bands than any Australian band since the sixties – no band is going to get better treatment. The guys had it dished up for them on a silver platter, they went from playing in their bedrooms, to identity and recognition throughout the whole industry!'[69]

After that tirade, journalist Miranda Brown was 'reminded of a spurned parent'.[70] It was a feeling Nick had a special knack for stirring.

One of the most important things The Boys Next Door gained from the Suicide debacle was a determination to control their own destiny. The other benefit was more basic, but just as significant: stepping outside their comfort zone, which they did while touring hard and playing live in Melbourne's outer suburbs as well as in Sydney and Adelaide, often to uninterested, if not downright antagonistic, audiences. Clinton Walker observes: 'Unlike Young Charlatans, The Boys Next Door did not arrive fully formed. They had to go out and play to become the entity they grew into. In 1977 they did, like, six shows. In 1978 they did 100. In 1979 I think it was closer to 200 ... That's what made The Boys Next Door and helped lay down the foundations for what became The Birthday Party. It's exactly what George Young [of The Easybeats and mentor to AC/DC] says, "You're not a real band till you've done 200 gigs." That gives you real strength. Working in the pubs makes you real tough real fast, if it doesn't destroy you.'[71]

The band was fortunate to gain another crucial supporter in the form of Stephen Cummings, singer for The Sports. An R&B pop band of considerable talent, The Sports were signed directly to Mushroom in Australia. When their *Fair Game* EP was named 'Record of the Week' in the *NME* back in early 1977, the group was quickly licensed to Stiff Records in the United Kingdom to record an entire album. This was theoretically a good match. Stiff had caught the crossover between joyfully tough English pub rock bands such as Dr Feelgood and Brinsley Schwarz and the punk-rock explosion, pushing artists such as Elvis Costello, Graham Parker and the Rumour, Nick Lowe, Wreckless Eric, Wilko Johnson, and Ian Dury and the Blockheads. The Sports had risen out of the ashes of The Pelaco Brothers in Melbourne and the 1950s-inclined, bohemian counterculture of the Carlton scene. Despite the Suicide label's fantasies of being just like Stiff, it was actually Mushroom itself and the Carlton scene from which it had grown that were a better match, at least in terms of a crossover musical heritage that involved pub rock, R&B sounds and punk attitude. Bands such as The Sports, Jo Jo Zep and the Falcons, and a young Paul Kelly walked the line between tradition and this punkier feel, roots rock 'n' roll with a smirk, a twist and a dose of lyrical intelligence that played well to the university crowds around Carlton throughout the 1970s. According to Stephen Cummings, 'At the time Australian writers and artists were examining our culture, and celebrating it. We weren't embarrassed by it.'[72]

By 1978, The Sports' single 'Who Listens to the Radio?' would be charting in the American Top 40. Tracy Pew and Phill Calvert could be seen in a video clip dancing along in the chorus. Cummings' pent-up, alarm-clock stage gestures channelled the best of a neurotic personality whose decisions would unfortunately be the undoing of his very fine band. By way of thanks a decade later, Nick Cave put pen to paper when Cummings was a solo artist: 'Stevie puts on quite a live show. His signature surrealist wit flashes between songs, reminding me of someone trying to repair a watch wearing boxing gloves!'[73]

The Sports took The Boys Next Door on the road with them whenever they could. They also offered them support slots at the Kingston Hotel in Richmond, where The Boys Next Door eventually got a gig of their own. Nick says, 'We had a residency [there] for about a month on Saturday afternoons ... where we played two short sets so that the owner could keep the bar open through the day. Live entertainment extended his licence. This bar was truly fucked up. A mix of white trash, derros and a handful of punks who would come along to see the band. It was great actually. I remember walking into the toilet to take a piss between sets and there were two guys in there – one had stabbed the other in the arse with a knife. The stabbed one was walking around with blood running out his trousers going, "He stabbed me in the bloody bum!" The manager sticks his head in the door and I'm like, "I think you've got a situation here." And he says, "Yeah, and you're supposed to be on stage now."'

Nick has what he calls 'another colourful story'. The Boys Next Door were supporting The Sports in Canberra in mid-1978. 'We were travelling in the gear truck. We were the support band, so we weren't living it large,' says Nick. 'There was no more room in the front, so me and Tracy were put in the back where all the equipment was piled up, along with an enormous amount of alcohol. Anyway, we started drinking. At some point we thought we needed a piss. We waited and waited for an opportunity, till finally we were on some country road. And right at the moment when we had lifted the roll-up door up fully and started to piss, the truck accelerated and overtook a car. We were like, "What the fuck!" But it was too late for us to stop. We had drunk a lot. Anyway, we finally finished and closed the door again. As it happened, it was a woman who was driving the car behind us, and as it happened, she was also the local policeman's wife.

'The next thing we knew we were being pulled over by the cops and hauled off to a country jail cell. They knew we had a gig that night in Canberra – and they kept us in the cells long enough to fuck it up for us. Anyway, a court case came out of it, where we had to return. The woman had made a statement that we "masturbated for seven miles" in front of her. They threw that out of court for obvious reasons. But we did miss the show,

Tracy Pew at the photoshoot for cover of *Brave Exhibitions*, June 1978 *(Michel Lawrence)*

so the cops did get to punish us in their own way. When we finally got to Canberra on the night itself, hours late, one of the guys in The Sports gave us this big lecture about how "if you ever want to make it in this business, don't ever do that again".

'It's these experiences that form you,' says Nick. 'I mean, we did vow never to masturbate for seven miles again, for a start. And after our history with Greg Macainsh and the problems we were still going through then with Les Karski, the other thing we vowed was to never hand over ourselves to a producer again, or to anybody telling us what to do. In future we'd only work in a collaborative way. It took us decades before we let someone come into the studio again … We figured we could do it better ourselves if we had the right help.'

The Suicide label would be officially wound up in December 1978. An embittered Barrie Earl turned to managing one-time Teenage Radio Stars member James Freud as the boy most likely to succeed. Earl had seen early potential in making Nick a pop star by zeroing in on the fact he appeared to cry on stage. A by-product of too much make-up and sweat, those crocodile tears were precisely what the label manager loved to exploit as a marketable gimmick. It was not to be. Pierre Voltaire was amused: 'Nick was just so difficult compared to James Freud, who did whatever he was told. Nick really frustrated Barrie.'[74]

Before the year had ended, every band on the Lethal Weapons compilation bar The Boys Next Door had broken up. This alone gives an indication of their will as a unit. Members of Teenage Radio Stars and JAB mutated into the group Models, named and formed by Pierre Voltaire, who soon departed to be replaced by Mark Ferrie. A nervy pop-rock band distinguished by Sean Kelly's nasal, barking snarl and Ash Wednesday's innovative synthesiser work, Models now had a killer rhythm section in place, with Johnny Crash on drums and Ferrie on bass. They were also being managed by one Karen Marks.

Models would give The Boys Next Door a run for their money on the live circuit during 1979, and arguably overtake them. Ollie Olsen disdained Models and The Boys Next Door as commercial pawns, and took up a more vanguard post with his pulsating new electronic act, Whirlywirld. He was helped in no small measure by Andrew Duffield's talent for synth soundscapes. When Marks and Wednesday went to live overseas (Wednesday would eventually join the German group Einstürzende Neubauten), Duffield quickly defected to Models. The stage was being set, as incestuous and competitive as it ever was. Three great bands were taking shape on the Melbourne scene, each seeking to establish their hegemony.

PART IV

GOD'S
HOTEL

Shivers

MELBOURNE
1978–79

B ad dreams. Ever since Nick had been sent away from
Wangaratta to attend boarding school in Melbourne his sleep
had become increasingly disturbed. Now, at the age of twenty
one, the restless nights could beset him for prolonged stretches.
There were more reasons than usual for another bout of insomnia
at his parents' house in the second week of 1979. On Wednesday,
10 January, after being awake for days, Nick had finally slept
through the morning, or at least experienced an unconscious state
that was as good a sleep as any he could have in the circumstances.
That afternoon he sat on the balcony outside his bedroom smoking
a wake-up cigarette, staring up into the branches of the huge
deodar cedar that dominated the front yard. 'I used to like sitting
on the balcony having a fag, so no one would know,' Nick says.
'Just sitting there … looking at my dear old tree.'

Downstairs, strangers were speaking to his mother in hushed
tones. Smoke curled through Nick's fingers while he felt the
vibrations coming from below.

'I remember it was summer,' Phill Calvert says. 'Nick only
lived three blocks away in Caulfield North. I caught a tram to his

place. I went through a little gate into the backyard and up to the back door. I could see Dawn and Julie through the window, and all these guys in suits. I went in and said, "Hi, Mrs Cave." Dawn said, "Oh, Phill, we've had some bad news. Colin has been killed in a car accident."

'You're twenty, twenty-one, you haven't got the presence of mind to respond. All I could say was, "Is Nick around?" I was just overwhelmed. You think you're a man when you're twenty-one? You're not. Dawn sent me upstairs. I found Nick in his room. The first thing he said to me was, "Let's get out of here. This is doing my head in."'[1]

There had been a marked acceleration of Nick's unruly behaviour in the years before Colin Cave's death. It now looks like someone heading towards a precipice. What that precipice turned out to be no-one could have predicted. It is, of course, easy to turn facts fatal once you cast a retrospective light over them. But it is this way of reading into events that is important to understanding what came later. Two simple but powerful questions emerge across all the years since: Did you forgive your father, Nick? Did you forgive yourself?

Nick had been wilder than ever during 1978. Given his attitude while attending CIT, he admits, 'I was outraged that I failed art school [in 1977]. I was mortified that these fuckin' professors could fail me.' It's not hard to see this as a reflection of the paternal conflict Nick was engaged in with his own teacher-father. His anger and recalcitrance, combined with the early success of The Boys Next Door, was like a double-shot of adrenaline.

Rowland continued to be stunned by his behaviour. 'Nick was a real tearaway,' he says, describing how Nick would climb out of a car Pew was driving and 'just hang there like a big black spider'[2] as they careened on down the sweeping curve of The Boulevard in Port Melbourne. 'We'd be on our way to a party in two cars that Tracy Pew had stolen,' confirms friend and fellow musician Greg Perano, 'and you'd look across and see Nick on the roof. He used to do it all the time.'[3]

One incident stands out. Pew, unfortunately, was not behind the wheel. Rowland and Nick had been drinking and taking Serepax. The pair hitched a ride with a fan after a Boys Next Door show at the Tiger Lounge. Nick did his usual trick, opening the car door at high speed and clambering out on top of the vehicle. For a joke, Rowland told the driver to hit the brakes, not really expecting him to do so. In one version of the story, Rowland admits the driver probably hit the brakes 'because he was so scared of us'. Nick came off instantly, rolling over the bonnet and skidding across the road on his back. 'I don't think he was wearing a shirt at the time,' Rowland said, 'or if he was, he wasn't afterwards.' It left a permanent scar down Nick Cave's back. More than fifteen years later, Howard would say, 'He's never forgiven me.' In telling this story, the guitarist emphasised, 'Nick enjoys taking risks. He probably wouldn't take a risk if he thought he'd wind up dead. Nick doesn't have some asinine "death wish", but a craving for more … It's as if real life just doesn't measure up, so he feels obliged to increase its sensory qualities.'[4]

As well as consuming alcohol, Serepax and Tuinal, Nick was snorting lines of speed (amphetamines) and drinking cough mixture cheaply obtained from chemists. According to Pierre Voltaire, who was fast turning into Nick's biggest drug buddy, 'That's when everyone was chugging "Tuggalugs" as we called it, Tussidex Forte; we would have bought them by the six pack if we could.'[5] The hallucinogenic qualities of Tussidex Forte, when imbibed by the bottle rather than the spoonful, were not yet sufficiently widely known to see the medication withdrawn as an over-the-counter purchase. Serepax and Tuinal required a prescription. In Nick's case, these were easy to come by. Both were antidepressants given to people suffering from sleeplessness and anxiety, but anyone able to feign tiredness and stress in front of a GP could access it. Females on the scene seemed to have an endless supply in their handbags. The magnifying effects of Serepax or Tuinal when combined with alcohol could be quite hypnotic, if not downright narcoleptic. They also took the edge off bad hangovers: the next day drifted along swimmingly.

St Kilda was ready-made for Nick's derangement of the senses, being populated by the kind of figures you might expect to see in Expressionist artworks. In her book *The George*, historian Gillian Upton describes the area in rich detail:

> With its street upon street of boarding houses, bed-sits and flats ... [the suburb had] attracted the displaced. Many of the unemployed, elderly, mentally ill and sole parents – people on the edge of 'normal' society – moved to St Kilda, adding to the already variegated population. They were joined by tens of thousands of refugees and migrants, particularly Jews, from post-war Europe ... The suburb's already seedy reputation grew as St Kilda drew more gangs, criminals, drug dealers and prostitutes. In a spiral of reputation and reality, people came from all over Melbourne in pursuit of these things until the very name of the suburb became synonymous with sex, violence and drugs.[6]

A pattern of rapid development and low-rent accommodation meant that by the late 1960s St Kilda had twice the population density of any other suburb in the city. Students from the newly opened CIT, Prahran Tech and the Victorian Colleges of the Arts frequented the bars, cake shops and takeaway food joints in the 1970s, along with daytime tourists to the seaside and nocturnal visitors curious to explore Melbourne's red-light district. Fitzroy Street was renowned for 'whoring and scoring'. The area's bacchanalian freakishness was confirmed at night by the flash-lit, leering smile of Mr Moon, the iconic open-mouthed gateway that devoured all-comers to Luna Park at the water's edge. Nick was absorbing images that would echo across songs as varied as 'The Moon Is in the Gutter' (1984) and his true-blue cover of The Seekers' 1965 hit 'The Carnival Is Over' (1986). Details that might seem exaggerated, surreal or self-consciously symbolic were real enough. If Wangaratta was the lost world of his innocence, St Kilda was the start of his journey into pandemonium.

The suburb's main drinking establishment, The George Hotel, more commonly known as the Seaview Hotel, had four different bars operating out of the same building. Its whitewashed Victorian architecture could not disguise a down-at-heel character, heightened by the raffish clientele inside. Each bar appealed to its own set of regulars, from chronic boozers and students downstairs, to Maoris and bikies at the aptly named 'Snakepit' (which sat below street level in vaporous hues cast from orange lampshades), to various attempts over the decades to establish a high-society function room upstairs. The latter aspiration had been overtaken by weddings and social events for the local Greek community on Saturday nights, with Sunday nights reserved for a long-running strip show, Arthur Luden's Getcha Gearoff. Despite its grand façade, The George's reputation for alcoholism, sleaze, violence, drug dealing and underage drinking was in no danger of rehabilitation. Prostitutes plied their trade in the rear alley, escorting customers upstairs to the hotel rooms where they lived. A nightwatchman would bring them toasted cheese sandwiches while they worked through the evening. The fact that one of the Seaview licensees was a retired policeman no doubt helped tolerance levels. Patrol cars were often sighted in the alley, reputedly loading their boots with free cartons of beer or being treated to other pleasures.

When Dolores San Miguel started booking bands into a small upstairs space at the Seaview she dubbed the Wintergarden Room in August 1978, its popularity soon made it clear she would need to use the larger function room beside it. The owners agreed 'the Greeks aren't drinking enough' and pushed them out to make way for bands like The Boys Next Door and their followers. The group sold out the venue to a New Year's Eve crowd of over a thousand people, a phenomenal feat for such an obscure act even given the end-of-year occasion. Before long, the burgeoning punk scene would take over every bar in the hotel – except the dreaded Snakepit – while a residue

Mick Harvey and Rowland S Howard, St Kilda Beach, 1977 *(Peter Milne)*

of hardcore drinkers sat like barnacles among an influx of the young, the weird and the beautiful.

So it was that an entire scene, which was to become known as the Crystal Ballroom, found itself a palatial home amid the squalor of St Kilda. San Miguel describes it as being 'a little bit like your grandparents giving you the keys to their mansion'.[7] This was to Melbourne what CBGBs was to New York and the Marquee Club was to London – with the added architectural glories of a wide marble staircase and entrance hall, an array of faded gilt mirrors, red velvet curtains around the main stage, and a sprung ballroom dance floor over which hung the Venetian crystal chandelier that gave the upstairs room, and eventually the entire venue, its most famous name. This mix of glamour, hedonism and desolation would give the Crystal Ballroom a lush, edgy atmosphere and a naturally theatrical ambience. Here the audience, as much as bands such as The Boys Next Door, Models, Whirlywirld and Primitive Calculators, were on show.

Crowds paraded between the Ballroom and, when it expanded, the Birdcage and Paradise Lounge bars on the ground floor. The stairwell was an informal stage in its own right, dominated by a stained-glass window that depicted Saint George slaying a dragon. Over the next decade, art and fashion as much as music would be affected by the ambience established at the venue. Creating a look became an obsessive pastime. This was where you became someone. Everybody looked into the faded gilt mirrors – at themselves and each other – before the venue became so packed they had to be taken down lest the mirrors fall and kill someone. According to San Miguel, 'The Boys Next Door always filled the place and Nick was the shaman.'[8]

A tour to Sydney in December 1978 had introduced The Boys Next Door to Crime and the City Solution, a dramatic young band fronted by a teenage runaway by the name of Simon Bonney. Crime and the City Solution's music was strangely epic in scope, combining the chills-and-warmth of John Cale-era Velvet Underground with splashes of free jazz saxophone. Bonney's lyrics and deep-voiced vocalising in 'Snow Child' and 'Here Comes the Dawn' gave the whole package a drowned poetic sensibility. Mick Harvey remembers 'Listless, Listless' and 'Platform' as songs that impressed The Boys Next Door the most. 'They had *some* kind of sound,' he says, searching for words to explain their impact. 'It was otherworldly. Especially with them being based in Sydney, where Radio Birdman and the Oxford Tavern scene and that whole Detroit sound were so dominant. Crime were totally different to that. It was partly due to all the idiosyncrasies of untrained musicians playing together. They couldn't sound the way they wanted to. And so they became something else.'[9]

Not yet seventeen, Simon Bonney was living in Kings Cross with a middle-aged woman and proving to be a talent of dazzling possibility. Rowland S Howard, Ollie Olsen, Simon Bonney – Nick was naturally drawn to them, and being pressed to show how good he could be by comparison. Radio Birdman and The Saints were self-combusting in Europe; these young unknowns were Nick's immediate peers, his competition at home.

On his return to Melbourne, Nick had seemed physically changed by the encounter with Crime and the City Solution, mimicking Bonney's flamenco-like, snaking gestures on stage: the burying of the head in a raised arm being a favourite, if melodramatic, offering directly copied from his latest infatuation. When Crime visited Melbourne at the Boys' invitation, Nick's debt to Simon Bonney's mesmerist-meets-bullfighter stagecraft became obvious. In years to come this would be viewed as a form of theft, as if anyone could copyright a pose.

Mick Harvey laughs at the pseudo-controversy around Nick stealing anything from Bonney. 'When I asked Simon about it, he told me he'd actually been copying Nick's moves!' Harvey explains that Bonney was freeze-framing particular stage gestures of Nick's that he liked. 'So Simon was copying Nick and performing in his own way, and Nick saw Simon and copied that. And around it went in a circle between them.'[10] A decade later, each would dance on stage before the film cameras in Wim Wenders' Berlin love letter, *Wings of Desire*. By then Rowland S Howard was Simon Bonney's gun-slinging guitar foil. Many thought Crime got the better of that cinematic duel, but it was Howard more than Cave or Bonney who people felt drawn to on the screen. Ironically, the mutual enchantment between Nick Cave and Simon Bonney was first visible in the video clip that was developed for The Boys Next Door's interpretation of Rowland S Howard's song 'Shivers'.

Rowland always insisted that he had written 'Shivers' while he was still at Swinburne Community School. If true, he would have been only sixteen or seventeen years old when the song first came to him. He may indeed have had a draft by the time he finished high school in 1976, but according to others in his circle, the song found its full emotional realisation in response to events of the following year.

The painter Jenny Watson identifies Lisa Craswell, of whom Rowland continued to be enamoured, as the prime inspiration for 'Shivers', with its references to the vanity of the beloved: 'He [Rowland] was dead right. There was something almost creepy about her vanity. This Edwardian Gothic dressing-up thing was happening. Lots of make-up, big earrings, everyone getting clothes from op shops, which just goes to show the old adage is true: you don't have to have money to have style. A lot of those looks have now gone into popular culture. You see it in Johnny Depp and [the film] *Alice in Wonderland*. But back then it was still very underground.'[11]

Fellow artist Megan Bannister[12], who was living with Ollie Olsen at the time, believes the final version of the song derived from a particular incident: 'Rowland had gone to see Lisa ... When he got there, this other guy was there. And he got really upset, and walked back to the house. But he punched a wall along the way. Rowland was absolutely devastated. He had cut up his knuckles. Where we lived was about three miles away. And he walked home. There was this verandah on the roof. Rowland had his guitar. We were all sitting on the roof. I think, from memory, he got it [the song] pretty much at that time ... You know sometimes you do something and it just works. Sometimes it's positively inspired. And I remember thinking, what a great pop song, because, more than anything, it was a great pop song.'[13]

Photographer Peter Milne arrived at the house only moments after Rowland had finished playing it to Olsen and Bannister. He remembers, 'There was this wonderful little stone bridge over the railway near where they lived, the Sandringham Line. Coincidently, somebody painted "The Boys Next Door" on it [later]; the graffiti was there for many, many years. Anyway, it was on that little stone bridge that Rowland, while walking home that day, punched his hand. He used to stub cigarettes out on himself, do all sorts of tragic, kind of Rimbaud, gestures of romantic love ... It only took him fifteen minutes to write, and from the word go it was supposed to be a joke. When Nick sang it, he sang it as if it was torn out of his soul; when Rowland sang it, it was a sardonic piss-take.'[14]

The 'other guy' Rowland had found in bed with Lisa Craswell was Tony Clark. Their relationship had begun as a student–teacher affair, and something of that air of secrecy and ambiguity clung to them as a couple, a seductive energy that pulled people further into their orbit. Rowland had read Goethe's semi-autobiographical novel *The Sorrows of Young Werther* before writing 'Shivers'. He would have recognised echoes of his own predicament in the eighteenth-century tale of a love triangle that forms between a volatile teenage artist, the young woman who befriends him, and her older lover. Like Goethe, Howard would spend the rest of his life disowning the emotional excess of his first major work. In the novel, the young man's unrequited feelings precipitate a decision to commit suicide, though he can barely shake off his own ennui to follow through on the act without requiring a semblance of his beloved's permission and complicity. 'Shivers' shares in the same emotional torpor with a greater degree of sarcasm. The carapace of cynicism sounds like thin bragging, which is why you feel the sentiments behind it even more.

An alert, impish presence, Genevieve McGuckin seems to conduct her conversation on two levels: the apparent, passionate one and another from which she evaluates you all the while she keeps engaging. It is an odd mix of closeness and distance, vulnerability and submerged judgement. She was not yet involved with Rowland S Howard, nor had she tried heroin, when she began a brief fling with Nick Cave towards the end of 1978 in Melbourne. McGuckin says she saw how 'Rowlie and Nick were very different people who shared a similar sensibility with books and films. Both found it difficult to exist in a world where it is deemed wrong to be sad. Rowlie found it very hard to accept that if you weren't happy, you should just shut up. Nick did too, but he was always more of a networker – he gathers people around him who are good for him, or who do his will,' she says, laughing. 'Rowland was a lot more insular in his nature, and just more sensitive. Other people's problems tended to become his. He tended to overestimate his own failings too.'[15]

When the affair between Cave and McGuckin began, it was, typically, 'at a party somewhere'. As the two of them left, Phill Calvert stopped Nick and asked him, 'What about Neat [Anita Lane]?' Nick shrugged him off. McGuckin asked who Calvert was talking about, to which Nick came back with the memorably offhand line 'She's someone who makes clothes for me.'

The connection between McGuckin and Cave would only last a few weeks. What stands out most in McGuckin's memory is arriving at another party: 'I saw this extraordinarily beautiful girl with a blue teardrop painted on her face, dressed in a man's silver-grey suit. That was Anita. And all these girls who also looked amazing were gathered around her like ladies in waiting, looking daggers at me. That's when I thought, "Oh no, what the hell have I got myself into here?"'

Anita Lane and Genevieve McGuckin at the photoshoot for the cover of *Brave Exhibitions*, 1978 *(Michel Lawrence)*

'But that's how I got with Rowlie, through Nick. Rowlie was always there – he was Nick's friend, he always made sure I was fine when we were out together, he was fantastically caring, a fount of information about all kinds of things, always making a running commentary on what was going on around us, he was funny ...' McGuckin pauses. 'I think I left Nick because of Nick. We lasted, like, a few minutes. He was just too much trouble. And there was obviously unfinished business between him and Anita. Nick is so charming, he is very easy to like at first, but there is so much hurt, so much fucked-up-ness. Anyway, we had stopped being involved, and I was somewhere with Rowlie where he was standing on a stool on this table and I was holding on and I just looked up at him and I realised: Oh my god, he's the one, I'm in love with him, it's him.'[16]

Such incestuous behaviour only tightened the connections between everyone once Anita and Nick got back together and all was forgiven or forgotten. Mick Harvey was already with Katy Beale[17], a young painter of aristocratic bearing with a nervy, private manner that matched his own inclinations towards separateness from the madding crowd. Tracy Pew was still dating Gina Riley, who was funny and sexy and smart, much to Pew's taste, with a bit of sassy attitude to match. Bronwyn Bonney says, 'Gina Riley was great. She was the only well-adjusted one out of all of us, the only person who liked herself, who wasn't at war with herself.'[18]

As for Phill Calvert, he really was the boy next door: blond, handsome, amenable, a heterosexual hairdresser with a line of admiring and beautiful women longing after him as the ideal boyfriend. He was, of course, in a committed relationship and just too good to be true. Quite apart from the personality clashes that were developing, it is easy to see how someone as straightforward and well liked as Calvert aroused the jealousy of such self-annihilating – and less conventionally handsome – romantics as Nick Cave and Rowland S Howard. Though Nick and Rowland would always comment that Phill had a habit of saying the most annoying things, Calvert's dogged sense of loyalty to the group would only magnify their frustration. The more he did – from getting Karen Marks to be their first manager, to beginning part-time work behind the counter at Missing Link in 1978 and building stronger connections with Keith Glass – the less thanks he would get. The fact they were all well aware of Calvert's difficulties with his overbearing father makes Nick and Rowland's treatment of him seem even more cruel. It is interesting to consider how much this low-level propensity for schoolboy bullying within The Boys Next Door would animate the sadomasochistic heart of The Birthday Party, driving its violent aesthetic and finally destroying that band from within. For now, though, the gang was all here and ready for action. And Nick had plenty to give.

When Mick Harvey, Genevieve McGuckin and Rowland S Howard were living in a flat on The Esplanade in St Kilda, Mick woke up one night and saw Nick in his room with blood all over his hand. Pierre Voltaire was there too, as was his girlfriend at the time. People had been drinking. Mick went back to sleep, already bored with the goings on. Again. Rowland was drunk and asleep in bed with Genevieve when he woke to see a policeman standing over him shining a torch in his face. They pulled him from the bed, then dropped him on his back again. Not this one, they said. Mick Harvey says the situation was very confused, with people coming and going. 'It was quite heavy by the end, police with guns in their holsters like they were ready to use them.'

A lavish red chair with gold trim had sat in the large glass window of an apartment block nearby. Everybody had noticed it, mocked its prominence to the point of it becoming a landmark.

Loaded up with alcohol and speed, Nick, Pierre and his girlfriend decided to pay Mick, Genevieve and Rowland a late-night visit. As they passed the throne-like chair, Pierre vaguely remembers them breaking into the rear of a tradesman's parked car, pulling out all the tools and 'at some point us dancing around in the street with a saw'.[19]

Pierre's girlfriend then hurled a brick through the apartment's large plate-glass window to get the chair, finishing the job off with a stolen hammer. In an effort to dissuade her, Nick climbed in after her, cutting his right hand on the glass. Eventually all three took off with the chair, getting as far as their friends' apartment block just a few doors along. The chair was so big it was impossible to manoeuvre into the building, let alone up the stairs. With sirens ringing out, they managed to raise it up and dump it over the back fence before fleeing. Unfortunately they'd left a trail of broken glass and, more crucially, blood behind them.

When the police arrived, Nick was caught, quite literally, red-handed. He took the blame, covering for Pierre's girlfriend, who was also a close friend of Anita. Nick was arrested that night, then released the following morning to his family. While at the station organising his son's bail, Colin Cave offered to pay for the damages in an attempt to stave off prosecution.

A few days later, on Friday, 5 January 1979, in his role as Director for the Council for Adult Education, Nick's father set off for the classical music song camp in Harrietville, near Wangaratta. It was not the best of times to be going anywhere. Nick was called back to St Kilda East police station for further enquiries on Sunday, 7 January. Colin was by then driving back to Melbourne from Harrietville and not contactable. Worried, Dawn decided to accompany her son to the station. While they were seated in the interview room, she was asked to step outside. Nick's sister, Julie, and their cousin were there with what Dawn describes as 'this awful news'.[20]

Colin Cave had been killed in a car crash, inexplicably detouring along a dirt road just outside of Wangaratta. She was told Adrian Twitt had formally identified the body of his friend. Upon hearing this news, Dawn was understandably stunned. Nick came out of the interview room to find out what was happening. In an adjoining area two officers were discussing the rape and murder of a prostitute as if it were a workaday joke. Dawn could not hear the conversation, or she has blotted it out, but she remembers the laughter. All she could think, she says, was, 'How can people be laughing? How can anyone in the world be laughing now?'[21]

Nick began to shout at the police, to no avail. He had previously mocked one of them for their spelling after they had written down his occupation as 'muskian' on a charge sheet. The two officers continued their conversation about the dead prostitute without regard for Dawn Cave or the news the family was dealing with. Nick's first impulse was to protect his mother – but look at where he had put her. Look at what he had done. Look at the choices his father had made, too. It was all wrong.

The death of Nick's father would be mentioned time and again in interviews and biographies as central to the artist Nick became, and to many of his songs and thematic obsessions. But there is another side to the tragedy that is rarely remarked on: the grief Dawn Cave felt for the loss of her husband.

Nick seems to shake with energy when he says, 'I was really very, very worried about my mother, and that was my primary concern and reaction, how devastated she seemed. And the inability I felt in being able to look after her – that was more the problem. Me not having a clue. Not having a clue how to approach something that was so serious. I was twenty-one years old and I was monumentally ill-equipped to deal with my mother's pain. It was so overwhelming I never even looked at it from my own point of view. I never looked at it from how I might feel for years.'

On the day Phill Calvert helped Nick escape from the funeral and cremation arrangements being made at home in Caulfield North, the drummer recalls, 'We bought some beers and went back to my place. Nick was upset, obviously; he was angry too. He said a lot of things. I can't tell you what we talked about. This is all around the time Nick had been busted for some stupid, petty thing. His dad had got Nick out when he was arrested. I know plenty of people where the dad dies and there's unfinished business. That's how it was with Nick,' Calvert says of the time. 'Then we talked about band stuff, plans. It's funny, I don't even relate the death of Nick's dad to when we started recording, I don't think I even thought about it or made any connection then. We just kicked on. It didn't seem to stop the band at any stage.'[22]

Soon after Phill's visit, Nick disappeared for two days, completely isolating himself at the home of a female friend. According to Mick Harvey, no-one saw him during this patch of time.

Nick says he barely remembers his father's funeral. It would appear the whole thing is blotted out. In the wake of Colin Cave's death and the need to complete the recordings for what would be *Door, Door*, Nick still had to go to court. He was given a good-behaviour bond thanks to his father's earlier intervention and character references. Friends would claim Nick was sorry he could never explain to his father that he had done the chivalrous thing and taken the blame for someone else. Why that regret should then express itself in such an intense rage is harder to say.

Dolores San Miguel says, 'Nick was always an angry young man but after his father died it was like he became ten times angrier.' News of Colin Cave's death spread quickly through the community that gathered at the Crystal Ballroom. Though she was in her late twenties and already a mother as well as a happening venue promoter, Dolores admits, 'I always felt somewhat intimidated by Nick and some of his friends. Apparently I was not alone. This night I was standing at the bottom of the Ballroom staircase as Nick, and some band members and friends, were leaning over the banister above. I expressed my condolences to Nick, even though I felt uncomfortable and somewhat embarrassed. Nick's reaction stunned me. "Thanks, but I really don't care at all. He deserved to die."

'And that was that,' Dolores says. 'He was obviously feeling pain and hurt, but he was a punk and had to keep that mask on – perhaps he wanted to shock me. I knew he meant none of what he said, but, still, I was flabbergasted at the time. In later days and months, I really started to sense the emotion, sadness and bewilderment Nick was feeling.'[23]

Just ten days after Nick's father was killed, The Boys Next Door entered Richmond Recorders with a brilliant young sound engineer named Tony Cohen.

The journey back into the studio had been protracted and confusing. In the hope of recouping their investment, Mushroom decided at the close of 1978 to press ahead and release *Brave Exhibitions*. It was almost six months since the original June recordings had become caught up in record-company wrangling while Suicide expired as a label. The idea of finally throwing *Brave Exhibitions* into the marketplace was a plan The Boys Next Door argued strongly against. Mick Harvey says, 'We were young and changing so fast we didn't know where we were or how we wanted to sound, really. Something we had done two months ago seemed old hat to us. Six months later and it was three times old hat.'[24]

Rowland Howard's arrival had intensified the restless and radical shifts in direction The Boys Next Door were going through. 'There was always an anger directed at the band,' Rowland observed, 'but after I joined, it was more blatant; people suddenly regarded us as art-house dilettantes. People who used to like the band hated the band after I joined. They'd call out for "Boy Hero" and we wouldn't do it, and they'd come up to us afterwards and say, "You think you're just fucking great, don't you? We're your fans and you can't fucking do it!" They were just incensed, because Australian rock bands used to play what the audience wanted them to.'[25] Rowland recalled, with some amusement, 'After I joined the band, even though we were still under contract … nobody from Mushroom ever came to see us again, which was … nice.'[26]

At a blistering show for the 3RRR-FM Christmas party on 12 December 1978, The Boys Next Door had been welcomed to the stage like conquering heroes as 'the band that survived Suicide!' In the broadcast, you can feel the group hitting an early, thrilling peak, poised between the power-pop of their immediate past and a fiery expansion driven by the sonic energy and melodic richness of Howard's guitar work and song writing.[27] Provocative as ever, Nick dedicated the freshly minted, Boys-own 'Shivers' to Mushroom's boss: 'Are you listening, Michael Gudinski?'

Finally, the band and the record company came to a compromise regarding *Brave Exhibitions*. Mushroom would finance cheap studio time at night to record a handful of fresh tracks in the New Year. In return, The Boys Next Door would salvage the best of the material from their sessions with Les Karski. The group decided these older songs would constitute side one of a 'new' album; side two would be reserved for work to be recorded with Tony Cohen. In this way their rapid evolution as a quintet with Rowland S Howard could be delineated to give a more representative picture of the band as it now was – on what would become their debut album, *Door, Door*.

The rejected songs from the Karski session were 'Secret Life', 'Sex Crimes', 'Conversations', 'Earthling in the Orient' and 'Spoilt Music'. There was also an improvised duet, with Rowland (not yet officially in the band at the time of recording) bashing away on piano and Nick singing semi-coherently. They'd wanted to horrify Karski and it had worked.

The fact that five of Nick's songs were shunted to make way for Rowland's compositions says something about the strength of the guitarist's material. Live, things had gone the same way, with Nick and Rowland's songs equally divided in the band's set, in between covers such as Lou Reed's 'Caroline Says (II)', Iggy Pop's 'China Girl' and the New York Dolls' 'Personality Crisis'.

Already a phenomenally experienced engineer for his age, the nineteen-year-old Tony Cohen was 'still a hippie' when he met The Boys Next Door. He was nonetheless the great studio collaborator of whom Nick Cave and Mick Harvey had been dreaming. Being the same age, he could understand their frustrations with how things were supposed to be done when recording – and the tame results they had achieved as a result. The relationship he forged with Nick and Mick would be one of the most important influences on their sound for the next two decades.

'TC', as he was sometimes referred to, had 'grown up playing drums in garage bands. As I got older, I had this fascination for tape recorders.' He was still at school when his training began at Armstrong Studios with the jazz producer and owner Bill Armstrong and an expatriate Englishman, Roger Savage, who had worked on early demos for The Rolling Stones and would go on to have a major career in film soundtracks. 'I was that young, I think I bought lollies with my first pay packet,' Cohen told me decades later.

He soon became the unlikely protégé of *Countdown*'s Molly Meldrum, who had learned his own trade in London 'watching the White Album get made. The Beatles all loved Molly because he was such a party animal,' Cohen said. Meldrum invited TC to assist him on hit records such as Supernaut's 'I Like It Both Ways' (1976) and The Ferrets' 'Don't Fall in Love' (1977).

'Molly did take me under his wing, but it was more because I was a pretty young boy than because of any talent,' said Cohen. 'I was far too inexperienced to be doing albums like Supernaut and The Ferrets. Being a good Catholic boy, I didn't even know what a poof was. But Molly never put it on you; he knew who was straight and who wasn't. He was a shitload of fun. My main job was to pour Molly his Scotch and Cokes. Once they kicked in, he'd be playing Elton John at 1000 decibels, shouting at us all about this sound and that he was wanting. They didn't have studio-engineering schools like they do now. It's not like you ever saw ads for an apprenticeship or a course to do it in the newspaper. I didn't even know the job existed when I started. I didn't even know it had a name. Molly used to come into the studio with this seven-foot high Maori drag queen. She lifted up her dress once to show us. That was my education,' he said, laughing.[28]

One of the most important studio lessons Meldrum taught Cohen involved the virtues of volume: 'Basically, when you're mixing, if a guitar solo comes in and sounds nice, to turn it up stronger. Don't be subtle. That way the guitar or vocals will jump out at you later. See, in the studio you are hearing perfect sound, but on a car radio or at home on a stereo those same things can sound flat. The contrasts need to be stronger than you think. Mixing is the tricky part of it. Things can sound good, but to get some depth to it, some things need to be in your face and others back. And that's a lot harder to do well than most people understand. Mixing is actually where most people fuck up, even when they have made a good recording.'[29]

It would take a while for Cohen to harness this understanding of volume and depth to the increasingly adventurous needs of The Boys Next Door and Nick's later incarnations, but he and the band would serve their apprenticeship in the studio together. By January 1979 the group were desperate to capture their sound, and happy to provoke people along the way after being pushed around so much over the previous twelve months. When Cohen first walked into Richmond Recorders on the night they were booked, he found a grand piano filled with pieces of metal and paper clips. The band was half-expecting the arrival of a far more senior engineer who would have the inevitable meltdown. After his experiences with Meldrum, Cohen was not one to be fazed. He looked at the abused instrument and said, 'Ah, that should sound interesting,' and immediately started to set up mikes inside it. Nick Cave says he and Mick Harvey looked at each other and said, 'He'll do.'

'There were things Tony didn't know about as an engineer,' Harvey says. 'But that was good for us. We needed each other. Even just as characters who didn't want all these boring old guys around us telling us what to do. We realised Tony was a guy who could help us control our own destiny.'[30]

'For the sake of variety' on *Door, Door*, Cohen suggested that 'it might be a good idea if Rowland performed a few of his own songs'. That idea was put down immediately, Cohen said. 'Nick wouldn't have a bar of it. "I'm the singer!"'[31] In the immediate aftermath of his father's death, it is hardly surprising Nick might have been feeling vulnerable. It should also be noted that Howard's deadpan nasal vocals were an acquired taste, his distinct, slung-out phrasing yet to fully develop. A single voice would also help ensure coherence across the extended and disparate recording process. The more obvious approach was to use Rowland's songs with Nick on lead vocals, mirroring what was mostly happening in their live performances anyway. Rowland decided to bide his time. In the long term, however, the guitarist's ambitions would become a source of deep-rooted tensions with Nick.

Phill Calvert shakes his head. 'It was never, ever gonna be Rowland's band. It was never, ever gonna be Nick singing Rowland's songs. It wasn't Jagger and Richards. And Rowland was not going to be allowed to sing a song of his on every record. He believed he was going to do that. But it was never, ever going to work out that way.'[32] Rowland's brother Harry Howard indicates this was not quite the deal that was struck when Nick invited Rowland to first join The Boys Next Door. There had been 'a promise' Rowland would sing some of his own songs, but this understanding quickly fell away.[33]

On *Door, Door* it was Nick, though, who suffered from the comparisons with a preternaturally ascendant Rowland S Howard. What became Nick's side of the album as a songwriter opened with 'The Nightwatchman', followed by 'Brave Exhibitions', 'Friends of My World', 'The Voice', 'Roman Roman' and 'Somebody's Watching'. These were all a year or more old and shaped under Karski's sterile, if crisp, regime. 'The Nightwatchman', 'Brave Exhibitions', 'The Voice' and 'Somebody's Watching' emerged as conventional New Wave pop songs, full of self-conscious preening. Their obsession with being watched could be interpreted as political – the woo-hoo theme of the time due to the advent of video technology and counter-culture surveillance paranoia – but even a cursory look at Cave's lyrics revealed a fundamental, if perverse, pleasure in being observed. Nick's diaries at the time overflow with little more than gig dates and grooming notes on what clothes and hair dye he needed. A throwaway pun in 'Somebody's Watching' says it all: Nick compares himself to Da Vinci's *Mona Lisa*.

Despite a negative self-image, or perhaps because of it, Nick was cultivating a peacock aggression that his gifts for sarcasm only enhanced. Melbourne was still a deeply conservative place in the late 1970s and it was possible to cause a commotion on the street with only the slightest deviations from normality. Nick revelled in a formative persona that not only caused people to stop and look but also frightened them. He was barely getting started on how far that could go, both on and off stage.

With police-siren synth lines courtesy of Andrew Duffield and Nick's vocal histrionics, 'Friends of My World' is positively grandiose in defining a maverick image and making those public and personal connections felt. Nick constructs a criminal fantasy for the Tiger Lounge crowd to revel in, with himself at the centre. He's the star of the story he tells. It's his world. What gave this narcissism real power was the stage itself, where a well-drilled band accentuated Nick's tensely romantic delivery and flashy gift for mockery. Anita Lane had begun styling Nick from the start of their relationship and he was looking sharper than ever. Shock-haired and suited up, he often sported a bowtie and polka-dot vest for good measure, appearing as master of ceremonies with a *Cabaret*-inspired Kit Kat Club edge that harked back to his obsession with Roxy Music's Bryan Ferry.

Rowland Howard always insisted that The Boys Next Door had a finely tuned pop sensibility. The show-stopping intensity of 'Somebody's Watching' live, with its fearless use of Beach Boys–style backing vocals, confirms this perception, however gun-shy the band were about being perceived as just another pop group. There certainly weren't many acts coming out of the local punk scene making sophisticated use of vocal harmonies and viciously camp showmanship. Nick's emphatic singing style drew on repeated listenings to what became known as 'the Berlin Quartet' – Bowie's *Low* and *Heroes* and Iggy Pop's *The Idiot* and *Lust For Life* – which had all come out in 1977 and were, Clinton Walker says, 'totally part of the air around Melbourne wherever you went'.[34] Given his aspirations to be a Sinatra of darkness in the same futuristic league as Bowie, Pop and Ferry, Nick was going to find appearing like yesterday's power-pop man on *Door, Door* very hard to swallow when the reviews came in. What really made him and the Boys sneer at Karski's production was that it put all the focus on their professional shine and none on their artistic shadow.

'Roman, Roman' was the throwaway anomaly in Nick's suite of songs, a hyperactive punk polka eulogising the renowned film director who'd fled the United States after being charged with the rape of a thirteen-year-old girl in 1977. This was Nick flexing his *Lolita* obsession, as well as a schoolboy humour in lyrics that would not be out of place in *Viz* magazine[35], even if the polka tune showed a surprising conceptual wit given Polanski's Polish background. Playing it live with the band, Nick freely adapted the chorus into an on-stage declaration of love, changing Polanski's first name for 'Rowland, Rowland'.

On the album version of 'Somebody's Watching', Nick buried the word 'Mona' with a groan and emphasised 'Lisa' with a sexual gasp. Rowland was obviously not the only one to have noticed Lisa Craswell moving through their midst. It's unlikely Nick wrote the line for her, but he was becoming adept at retooling a reference to any moment that suited him. Be it for Craswell, Howard or the entire Tiger Lounge scene, Nick was nothing if not charming when he chose to be, drawing in everyone and everything around him.

Side two was Rowland S Howard's turn to display his wares. 'After a Fashion' opened with a blatant Richard Lloyd–Television guitar sound. Phill Calvert admits, 'When Rowland started playing it we all looked at each other and thought, "Can we do this?"'[36] The influence of *Marquee Moon* on Rowland's playing may have been obvious, but it was addictive to hear and highly confident. Tony Cohen's engineering work also gave the music a presence that was lacking on side one. 'After a Fashion' would become a staple of the band's set, with Michael Gudinski of Mushroom keen to make it the first single off the album. 'I Mistake Myself' was the most startling of Rowland's new songs, an awkward, brooding contemplation of the nature of identity, suspended over Tracy Pew's stealthy bass line. It made Nick's lyrics seem decidedly shallow. Philosophically, the album was a battle between side one's 'How do I look?' and side two's 'Who am I?'

One was more energetic and fun (Nick), but the other cut much deeper (Rowland). 'I Mistake Myself' was the most English-sounding track on the record, and would not have been out of place on an early album by The Cure. Howard was bringing an even greater pop sensibility to the band, but his perspective had atmospheric and existential qualities that felt very contemporary. The Boys Next Door gained new poise in the process. The band began to look like a serious proposition, and Nick's star would shine all the stronger as a result of Rowland's song-writing sophistication.

The lack of fresh material from Nick was odd in comparison to Howard's rush of blood. Rowland was progressing and producing at a rate of knots; Nick seemed to have stopped altogether. Never previously unproductive, Nick would excuse himself by saying, 'I went through a dry spell.' Come early 1979, the wind had been taken out of Nick Cave's sails for very understandable reasons. Apart from the sudden death of his father, a number of other factors were in play: Anita Lane's noted distaste for Nick's 'stupid' lyrics; the highbrow influence of Tony Clark's salon; the battering of Nick's vocal confidence at the hands of Macainsh and Karski as producers; and, finally, Rowland's vividly superior swathe of songs. All of this caused a withdrawal by Nick as he reassessed what he was capable of, both as a writer and, just as importantly, as a singer.

Early photo session in Nick's bedroom just after Rowland S Howard
joined The Boys Next Door, 1978 *(Peter Milne)*

For the new sessions with Tony Cohen, Nick had only
one worthwhile contribution, the off-kilter fairground swirl of
'Dive Position' – an erotic lament inspired by his passionate, if
already stormy, relationship with Anita. The song's dissonant
organ-grinder construction was a naïve hint of the dark circus
Nick would later bring to fruition in 'The Carny', while its
connections between grief and sexual comfort – with a sly
lyrical reference to The Doors' 'Touch Me' – suggested it was a
very new song for Nick, and a radical advance on anything he
had written before. The use of abstract and fragmented imagery
to camouflage, as well as broaden, his intimate concerns would
be an important strategy in the future. Strangely, the song
was written a few months before Nick's father was killed, not
afterwards, as the lyrics might imply. It's hard to know who is
crying for what in the song, only that an immersion into pleasure

is needed to exorcise uncertainty and pain, and that this pain can even heighten ecstasy as Nick cries out to be touched again. Horror and desire are never far from one another, a tension that would stay with Nick for a long time.

The last track on the album was to become Nick Cave's first transcendent moment as a recording artist. Yet when he was interviewed for the 2011 memorial documentary *Autoluminescent: Rowland S Howard*, Nick admitted to regrets over his decision to sing 'Shivers'. 'I was never able to do that song justice, especially back then. Rowland must have been squirming,' he said, laughing, 'every time I sang it … I wish he had sung that, actually. I wish he had sung that when we recorded that because it was his. It was his song. He should have sung that.'[37]

Howard came to despise Nick's 'hammy and overblown'[38] reading. In Young Charlatans, and again when he was a solo artist, the guitarist's vocal put a caustic spin on the words. Cave's interpretation withdraws Howard's stinging disdain, although the guitarist's flattened voice tended to give everything that same droll edge. Demos recorded for a never-undertaken Young Charlatans album reveal that Howard was just as capable of taking his own snarl to camp extremes, but he gets it right, too. Howard's best interpretations make it clear that 'Shivers' is a fuck-you song: a revenge fantasy that says, 'I could kill myself for you, but you are not worth it' – and notes how amusing it is even to have considered such dramas. Nick croons 'Shivers' in a way that is singularly haunted and grand and right on the edge. Oddly, it is this same excess of passion – an almost marble sheen to Nick's quavering baritone – that brings the song closer to the theme of death, even if it obscures the snarling energy Howard felt it required.[39] Ollie Olsen would find it strange that what became the definitive punk song of the era was in fact a ballad. But he would also pinpoint something very precise: 'It captures that whole St Kilda thing. Historically, that's where the song lives.'[40]

Pierre Voltaire disputes Howard's assertions as to how it should have been delivered. 'Rowland only decided the song was meant to be ironic after, you know. I don't think that was necessarily how it was when he first wrote it.'[41] Rowland's former Young Charlatans bandmate Jeffrey Wegener continued to describe 'Shivers' over thirty years later as 'absolutely romantic'.[42] Bruce Milne says, 'Listening back to it, I realised "Shivers" is very directly an attempt at writing a song in a Roxy Music style – it has that whole ennui, Roxy kinda vibe. You can imagine Bryan Ferry in a suit singing it. But Rowland was not really comfortable with doing that sort of thing. Nick had that self-confidence, the sense of movement on a stage, the charisma to pull it off.'[43]

Mick Harvey doesn't accept anyone's recriminations – or regrets. 'When it comes to the singing of "Shivers", Rowland should have been more vocal about it at the time. I think he is right about Nick's singing of the song, but he is turning around and saying it with the benefit of hindsight. He let it happen, so he is culpable too. I was sitting there as a passive observer and I could hear how Nick was singing it. Which was not tongue-in-cheek. But where were those criticisms of Nick at the time when, perhaps, they were needed? You do have to be careful where and when you choose to criticise a singer; you can't be on their case all the time because it will create fractures. Nick now thinks he over-emoted? When did he stop over-emoting!' Harvey laughs. 'Being overblown is a part of Nick's historical practice. The thing is, I think most singers do over-emote. A part of what is great about Nick is his vocal performance, and the way he pushes it hard into an area where you have to deal with him. There's a purpose behind what he is doing.'[44] Clinton Walker believes that Rowland had 'already peaked as a songwriter. At that stage he was way ahead of Nick. Nick and Mick, of course, would overtake him.'[45]

'Shivers' would emerge as the anthem of the Crystal Ballroom generation, a sob-soaked love ballad from what sounds like the hallowed halls of St Kilda's punk-rock mausoleum. The song defined Nick as the Romantic hero of the era and a star in the making. 'It was something so total, and it was loved by everybody,' Nick said, 'and it talked to everybody like a great song is supposed to do. But, on the other hand, you write that, you can hang your fucking guitar up and do something else, it's so accomplished.'[46]

Rowland would see this very differently. He'd find himself harnessing, and eventually suppressing, his talents in order to write only songs that Nick could sing. Within a few years he'd admit to forgetting how to write anything that came from inside him. His guitar would have to do that soul work for him. And he'd make it cry and scream.

Though *Door, Door* would carry a dedication of gratitude to 'our mentor, Barry [sic] Earl', the reality was they were completely without management by the time of the January recordings.[47] For all their popularity at the Ballroom, The Boys Next Door were caught in a record deal they didn't like with a company they had not originally signed to, and had been buffeted from one studio to the next without much ability to assert their own direction. The decision to self-produce side two of *Door, Door* with Tony Cohen's engineering assistance was a step towards autonomy, but, as Mick Harvey says, 'we were still tripping over our own feet. We didn't really know what we were doing in the studio.'[48]

Keith Glass had always liked The Boys Next Door, but now he was starting to perceive greatness in the band. 'I remember going to see them one of the first times Rowland played with them,' he says. 'It was a fairly dramatic improvement and change in direction. But it wasn't all Rowland. They'd got him in so the rest of them could grow musically.'[49]

The Suicide label had taken a short-term and gimmicky attitude; Mushroom, according to Glass, 'had no idea'. 'The band were turning into the biggest drawing act in the city and no-one knew what to do with them.' He couldn't stand it. Having just returned from a visit to London in late January, Glass was convinced The Boys Next Door needed to get to England as soon as possible. His record store, Missing Link, was booming; Phill Calvert was keeping him in the know about the band's plight. 'So I made an offer to manage The Boys Next Door, with an eye to eventually recording them as well.'[50] He also promised to have them in London before another twelve months went by.

Glass's plan was manna from heaven. Though they'd slowly come to regard each other with suspicion and even contempt, Mick Harvey admits, 'Keith was "cool". He had this aura about him that is hard to put a finger on. He was probably only in his late twenties when we met him, but he'd done so much compared to us. He had a business, a record shop, and he was going to start a record label of his own. He seemed to know everyone worth knowing in the music industry, and a lot about music too. He always used to say to us that one of our biggest advantages was that we had a really strong rhythm section, that a lot of punk bands didn't have a strong rhythm section. He said it's what makes you convincing. And he was right. With a great rhythm section, even if your ideas aren't strong, you have a strong platform from which they can spring and develop.'[51]

The Missing Link record store owner began his management tenure by expanding the band's musical palette considerably. Glass introduced The Boys Next Door to the obscene agit-prop folk collages of The Fugs and to Captain Beefheart's surreal rock-blues-jazz abrasions, along with obscurely comic, thuggish and horny rockabilly songs. Glass rolls his eyes and says, 'The Bowie thing was so prevalent then among all the young bands. If you think Bowie is the lynchpin of modern music, you're in serious trouble.'[52]

Nick and Rowland were meanwhile immersing themselves in Dadaist art and literature, and this, combined with a passion for radically new young bands such as The Pop Group and Pere Ubu, tilted them towards weirdly primitive funk and garage jazz sounds that splintered what they were doing musically. Glass's 'little record-playing sessions' emphasised a renewing physicality and aggression to match the intellectualised and fey deconstructions that were taking root. A strong sense of musical history was being developed that was counter to the obsessions with art theory, fragmentation and futurist progress. Mick Harvey says, 'We took all these different directions. We were very impressionable at that time. A new record would come along and Nick would write three songs like it. But they are all kind of accidental developments anyway. As much as Nick and Rowland were overly influenced by Pere Ubu and The Pop Group, it was nonetheless a kind of freeing up in the way you could approach things.'[53]

Nick was thoroughly into The Pop Group's first single, 'She Is Beyond Good and Evil', a bass-shaking 12-inch vinyl release that used its dub-production sound like a weapon. But he would describe their second single, 'We Are All Prostitutes', as 'the great Pop Group song'. A deeply political act who combined free jazz and funk influences with a ferocious punk sensibility, The Pop Group would be credited by *The Guardian* with 'almost single-handedly' jolting the era into its post-punk phase. 'We Are All Prostitutes' stepped up their assault on consumerism as a disease of complicity. Songwriter and singer Mark Stewart was into revolutionary ideals, ideologically and aesthetically. Nick was taken in by the anger, if not the politics. 'It had everything that I think rock 'n' roll should have,' he said. 'It was violent, paranoid music for a kind of violent, paranoid time. I've been listening to a lot, actually, recently, and it just gets me in exactly the same way. Even talking about it.'[54]

Ironically, Nick had nursed a distrust of the punk phenomenon, dating from the day Elvis Presley died and Johnny Rotten declared his joy. Both he and Rowland were conscious of punk becoming a genre rather than a philosophy, a packaging that ensured its limits rather than its possibilities. The evidence of that was made explicit to them when Sid Vicious, the Sex Pistols' iconic former bassist, was found dead from a heroin overdose at the Chelsea Hotel in New York on 2 February 1979. He had allegedly committed suicide after murdering his girlfriend, Nancy Spungen, the previous October in a death pact gone wrong. This murky, inept story played into a ghoulishly moronic reduction of punk's formerly subversive edges. By then cast as 'a leading punk in Melbourne', Nick Cave was contacted by both *The Truth* newspaper and the *Willesee at 7* news show to offer his comments on the death of Sid Vicious. He wisely refused the opportunity to be identified as a grieving spokesperson for the so-called 'Blank Generation'. Soon afterwards, Nick told *Roadrunner*, 'The people who don't know anything about young music still consider us punk.'[55]

Mick Harvey states: 'There were a lot of groups around. The initial excitement of '77 had kind of given way to a mixture of pragmatism and delusion, and a cynicism about movements. So many groups had their own vision by 1979. Instead of being derivative, they really found their feet, their own voice. But they seemed to have a common purpose, which was to present something original.'[56]

Of much greater interest to Nick than the death of Sid Vicious that February was the painter John Nixon's newly opened Arts Projects, an exhibition and performance space in a rundown office building at 566 Lonsdale Street, Melbourne. Together with Tony Clark and others, Nixon encouraged a passion for muzak and the tape recorder in performance pieces and installations at his gallery. Clark and Nixon came up with exhibition projects such as *Invisible Music*, which 'denied to any piece of music injected into the public domain any autonomy or authorship'.[57] They also developed what they called an anti-music opera entitled *Towards New Horizons*. Their manifesto favoured minimal and 'roomy' sounds, to use a favoured buzzword, emphasising amateur and random creations from a non-studio environment. The outcomes were surprisingly ambient and tuneful, akin to crudely realised Brian Eno compositions. Clark would take Nick down to Arts Projects of a weekday afternoon, where Nick was fascinated by the idea of random music by non-musicians. In some cases this was completely self-generated once the cassette player and synth technology had been switched on and programmed. Suitably impressed, Nick began to practise synthesiser himself.

Lyrically, Nick was feeding off similarly radical influences at work on the Melbourne poetry scene. On his gallery crawls he picked up random copies of *Born to Concrete*, a literary magazine dedicated to 'concrete' poetry (later known as 'visual' or 'shape' poetry). The movement had originated in Brazil in the 1960s and had an enduring impact on the more avant-garde corners of the Melbourne writing world. Exploiting typography, visual puns, word games, collage and repetition, it appealed to the artist in Nick as much as the poet-lyricist. The emphasis on the written word as a physical entity supported the absurdist and futurist doctrines he and Rowland were exploring, and appealed to their innate graphic-art interests.

Increasing competition with Ollie Olsen's Whirlywirld and the burgeoning North Fitzroy 'Little Bands' scene on the other side of the Yarra River underlined the need to absorb such new possibilities. Sometimes dubbed 'the North Fitzroy Beat', the Little Bands were floating, anarchist-inspired aggregations that performed rapid-fire, fifteen-minute sets (or less) under names such as Thrush and the Cunts, The JP Sartre Band, Oroton Bags and Too Fat to Fit Through the Door. Even Whirlywirld, who were based next door to the shopfront warehouse where all these acts germinated and disappeared again, were considered refined and careerist by comparison with these built-to-self-destruct acts.

One Little Band, however, emerged with a more dedicated agenda: Primitive Calculators, who practised relentlessly with their drum machines and synthesisers. Clinton Walker reckons 'seeing them live was the first time I ever saw a band use a drum machine'.[58] Ardent communists, they had been the prime movers behind the whole Little Band concept, sharing their instruments and warehouse so that what were often pretty chaotic performances could take place. Despite the anti-professional ethos, two major groups would evolve out of the creative debris: Hunters & Collectors and Dead Can Dance.

Primitive Calculators regarded the Crystal Ballroom gang in St Kilda as bourgeois lightweights. To them, The Boys Next Door were about as musically radical as Duran Duran. Ironically, Richard Lowenstein's filmic tribute to the Little Bands era, *Dogs in Space*, leaned on The Boys Next Door glamour via the true-life narrative of another quasi–Little Band act called the Ears, who had a foot in both the St Kilda and North Fitzroy camps. In the film, Michael Hutchence's character is based on the Ears singer Sam Sejavka, who in turn was channelling a young Nick Cave at the time in his own performances.

As for Primitive Calculators, they conceived of themselves as a nasty electronic 'boogie band', according to central figure Stuart Grant, dedicated to 'setting people free of the capitalist yoke' and 'trying to find a note to make people shit their pants'.[59] Live, this meant they could be devastatingly intense or dominant to the point of repugnance. Soon enough their nihilist musical revolution would see them consume themselves in heroin and speed use, wiping out whatever promise Primitive Calculators might have allowed for themselves. Perhaps they were not so different from their bourgeois enemies after all.

Nick may have felt some kinship with the raging Dadaist imperatives that drove the Little Bands scene in North Fitzroy, but he was made well aware 'that we [The Boys Next Door] were not welcome there'. Even so, the activity and friction fuelled the energy of both scenes and further inspired the direction The Boys Next Door were headed in.

Nick had formed a muck-around band called Little Cuties with Vicki Bonet. This was the same woman Deborah Thomas had seen throwing mincemeat from the stage during The Boys Next Door's debut performance of 'These Boots Are Made for Walking' at the Tiger Lounge. Pierre Voltaire says, 'Vicki was quite overweight. She dressed like Divine. She had a doctor who prescribed her Duromine, which was pure amphetamine, in vitamin-sized bottles, the most phenomenal speed. She'd share them with us.' In Little Cuties, Pierre says, 'Vicki sang, Nick played organ, Rowland played bass, Gen [McGuckin] guitar, Mick drums, and I played guitar. We did [Kraftwerk's] "Hall of Mirrors" and "The Model", but they were like AC/DC versions, and then we did a really soft version of an AC/DC song, I can't remember what. We collapsed the speakers at a rehearsal studio in North Melbourne we were so drunk and playing so loud. We were just enjoying the freedom of instruments we didn't know how to play. We crashed the sound system at a party. We crashed the sound system at the Crystal Ballroom. It was great. It was really just this altruistic thing of doing for the love of each other and to thank Vicki for all the pizzas she bought us.'[60]

Door, Door would not appear till the end of May 1979. Dave Graney describes the relationship between the album and The

Boys Next Door's live shows as 'really schizophrenic, they'd changed so much live since recording it'.[61] By then the band was exploring more abstract and experimental territory in new songs such as Nick's 'A Catholic Skin' (Nick was Anglican, but no matter, it sounded good) and Rowland's 'Death by Drowning'. Jim Thirlwell, later to start making his reputation overseas as a brutalist composer under pseudonyms including Clint Ruin and Foetus, thought 'Door, Door did not capture just how good they [The Boys Next Door] really were. They had already stamped their own identity on their sound. They were extremely charismatic and exciting. You didn't get that, it was not even close. Not even 50 per cent.'[62]

Asked to help devise an advertisement that might promote the album, Nick and Rowland came back with the slogan 'Drunk on the Pope's Blood'. This was not quite the tagline Mushroom were looking for. As Howard said, 'They thought we were completely insane. We thought it was really funny. It didn't occur to us that anybody would be offended by it, 'cause the only people who read the rock press ... well, I guess Catholics read the rock press too.'[63] Pope's Blood was actually pink gin, a cocktail mixed at the Ballroom.

It would not be long before Nick began what would become his standard process of destroying anything in his history that he felt did not warrant further investigation. In a 1982 edition of *Rolling Stone Australia*, he looked back on 1979 as if from an eyrie on a faraway past. 'We were adolescents and very late developers. There was a period where we were confused and had a lot of problems and we put out an album like *Door, Door* which is a product of all those things. I mean, it was a complete wet dream that record. I hate it. It reeks of a band trying to be musically intelligent and write clever, witty lyrics. It's a complete wank.'[64]

The album sold dismally, only 2000 copies. Nick told fanzine *The Offense*, 'It was obvious we were a flop. A big flop.'[65] Many years on, he laughs about that and says, 'Michael Gudinski was disappointed we didn't sound like Plastic Bertrand and that no-one on the record had a song like "Ça Plane Pour Moi" [aka 'Jet Boy Jet Girl'].'

Tony Cohen was less dismissive of *Door, Door.* 'You know, even though the guys say it is not a great record, we were learning. It changed my life, man. Just the total disrespect they showed for how things should be done in the studio. Overnight I went from a hippie to a punk because of it. They changed too. We all did as time moved on. It was a constant thing,' he said. You could still see the enthusiastic boy in Cohen as he spoke about those early days: the long, lank dark hair, by then streaked with grey, and a teenage hunched quality, as if the boy he'd once been was suddenly time-warped forward into the body of an older man. '*Door, Door* was the beginning,' Cohen said, with what seemed like a note of ominous idealism. 'And I still like those songs. I think we did pretty good overall. I mean, we did "Shivers", for a fucking start.'[66]

Viewing *Door, Door* through the lens of The Birthday Party's later achievements, the English critic Barney Hoskyns later described it as 'a spite marriage of the Ramones and XTC'.[67] Clinton Walker would reflect that 'it was one half of a good record', that half being 'Rowland's side'. Reviews were positive at the time in Australia, but the fact none of those reviews arrived in the mainstream music press till December 1979, more than six months after the album's release, indicates how insignificant The Boys Next Door were to the local industry. In *Rolling Stone Australia*, Toby Creswell pinpointed a few obvious references: David Bowie, Roxy Music and Ultravox. That last comparison horrified the group, who always conceived of themselves as standing apart from the punk mob and felt they were already pushing into avant-garde territory – only to be now cast in with Ultravox and the latest pop fad, New Romanticism.

The most telling insight into *Door, Door* came from Andrew McMillan in *RAM*. He saw the record as highly promising, if hamstrung by what he called 'the English sound of '77'. He linked this to Nick's vocals and made a surprising comparison with Jim Cairns, the idealistic anti-Vietnam campaigner, left-wing economist and former Labor Party deputy prime minister of the Whitlam era. McMillan likened Nick's singing in 1979 to Cairns' iconic resignation speech in 1975, hearing in each case the sound of man who 'believed in himself' so much you could hear him bleed'.[68]

The cover art for *Door, Door* was drawn from an obscure 1934 Expressionist play called *The Hangman*. Nick borrowed the image from a book owned by the girl who had smashed the glass to get the red chair on the night he was arrested. The play is based on a 1933 novel of the same name by the Nobel Prize–winning Swedish author Pär Lagerkvist. A deeply anti-totalitarian work, it combines visionary and philosophical passages that merge Lagerkvist's trademark black humour into a stream of haunting loneliness. Lagerkvist influenced Camus, encouraging the notion that rebellion could be a creative act in itself, a necessary path to take against overwhelming despair and meaninglessness. Certainly, Nick's self-belief helped him to rebel against the harrowing set of circumstances he'd just come through. As Anita Lane later observed, 'Nick's got this incredible drive that's got him through everything. He's a workaholic. When we were younger I thought it was something he'd grow out of and get over. He really wanted to impress his father and wanted him to think he was clever. His father would just laugh at him, he wouldn't take any notice. When his father died I wondered what was going to happen to Nick's drive, but it just got stronger.'[69]

Flight
from
Death

MELBOURNE

1979

The crowds flooding into the Ballroom meant big money. Within six months of opening its doors to Melbourne's underground music scene, the hotel's managers told Dolores San Miguel she would no longer be needed. The Boys Next Door and Whirlywirld played a farewell show for her on 13 January 1979, five days after the death of Colin Cave. Recordings for *Door, Door* filled out the rest of the month. On 3 February The Boys Next Door joined with The Sports to relaunch the venue under Laurie Richards, an innovative booking promoter who had been running the Tiger Lounge with an ear to Keith Glass's sage advice. San Miguel was a little surprised by the speed with which she could be dispensed. After successfully launching a series of smaller rooms around the city she would be invited back in March the following year to help manage Ballroom bookings again: a marriage of her taste and connections with hard-hearted business, though of course it's never that simple.

It was Laurie Richards who officially renamed the venue the Crystal Ballroom; Richards who brought in closed-circuit televisions so people downstairs could watch what was happening in the main room above; Richards who invited the postmodern pop artists Philip Brophy and Maria Kozic to paint a mural in the newly opened lounge area. In every way he enhanced the voyeurism and spectacle, escalating the mood and expanding the venue's possibilities. 'But you wouldn't imagine Laurie was a mover and shaker,' Mick Harvey says. 'He just saw the numbers and followed his nose. Dolores knew what needed to get booked, and the venue had that feel, some sensitivity to what was going on there.'[1]

Artist Jenny Watson agrees: 'It was a wonderful vision Dolores had.' Despite her ousting, the Crystal Ballroom continued to feed off San Miguel's original vision for the rest of the year, following her lead on acts such as Crime and the City Solution, the Ears (who would inspire the 1986 Richard Lowenstein film *Dogs in Space*)[2], and, upon her return, a promising Brisbane band called The Go-Betweens. Bronwyn Bonney says: 'The air was charged, like some weird alchemy was going on – rare qualities gathered, concentrated and combined in one bunch of people who seemed all sparkling with brilliance. Like a little treasure trove of gems – so beautifully cut, so eye-catching, and giving off a lovely prismatic light. That was how the Ballroom felt to me.'[3] Off to the sides, Bonney admits, shadows were looming: 'There was a lot of damage in there too, a lot of mental fragility, an undercurrent of nihilism that got stronger as the initial energy wore off. And there was a cliquey, snobbish in-crowd thing socially. And in time there was a horrible epidemic of addiction. But that was later.'[4]

Cultural critic Ashley Crawford was just becoming immersed in the scene. Compressing the next five years of the Ballroom into what feels like one dazzling evening, Crawford describes how 'a smattering of artists who would become substantial if not major figures in the Melbourne, national and, at times, even international art world made up a good percentage of the audience. John Nixon, then dating Watson, would attempt to outdo Tony Clark in melancholy black. Clark would stand to the rear, arms crossed in regal bearing as though passing judgement over some Grecian legal ritual, a perpetual scowl imprinted on his visage. [Painter] Howard Arkley, with spotted tie, would sport the only facial hair in the room. The venue would be filled with younger art students, a veritable who's who of new talent, including Brett Colquhoun, Jon Cattapan, Greg Ades, Stephen Bush, Vivienne Shark LeWitt, Nick Seymour, Maria Kozic, Peter Tyndall, John Matthew, Megan Bannister, Peter Walsh, Stephen Eastaugh and Andrew Browne, along with playwright Tobsha Learner, photographer Polly Borland, writer Stephanie Holt and filmmakers-to-be Richard Lowenstein and John Hillcoat; it was, in effect, a breeding ground for a new generation.'[5]

When speaking of The Boys Next Door and the circles that moved around them, Bruce Milne smiles uneasily. Speed and booze were enough for him; mixing cough syrup with alcohol had never appealed, and when people began shooting up, Milne says, 'I started to back off. Everyone in that gang was always looking for a new kind of kick.'[6] How much Nick Cave might be blamed for those kicks is hard to say. 'Nick definitely started the Faulkner craze,' Pierre Voltaire says sarcastically. 'The old novel-in-the-back-pocket trick, we all tried that.'[7]

According to Rowland S Howard, 'Nick tried heroin some time in 1979.'[8] Anecdotally this date can be narrowed down to between early January and *Door, Door*'s release in May. 'Nick always drank and took speed a lot,' Howard said. 'He'd tried heroin a few times before introducing it to me through a friend who was a part-time user. Heroin came at the right time for me, and for an extended period of time I was able to take it on a daily basis, leading inevitably to a habit. The effects of speed and alcohol can be devastating in concentrated amounts, but since heroin lets you keep going and makes you feel good without apparent side-effects [sic], it's easy to keep taking it if the supply is there.'[9]

Any suggestion that Nick took heroin to anaesthetise his grief is something he disputes strongly. 'I was already on my way. It was going to happen,' Nick says. 'Certainly within the crowd I operated in, heroin was the drug of choice. It was cheap and it was effective and it was freely available. At that point it felt like something I wanted to dedicate myself to. And there was a seismic shift in my whole life. Funnily enough, I thought

Mick Harvey and Nick Cave at the Crystal Ballroom, late 1970s
(Peter Milne)

everybody shot up, I just assumed with people I moved around in that was the case. But that wasn't the case.'

Nick can still remember the first time he tried it. 'I was standing on the corner where the National Theatre is, at the crossroads ... Pierre rocked up with his ... girlfriend and said, "We've just been down to Fitzroy Street and bought some heroin. You wanna take it?" I said, "Fuck, yeah." I chopped it out on the fire hydrant right there and then on the street. Of course it didn't do anything. It doesn't do anything for a while. You have to be quite dedicated to be a junkie, really. Anyway, we did that and then we found Genevieve [McGuckin] and Lisa [Craswell] and went and got another $50 bag. For me it seemed to be the logical step.

'Some weeks later, we were at a friend's house. These bikers were there. We had bought some smack. Anyway, we stopped in the lounge room to find somewhere to start chopping it out. This biker looks at us and says, "What the fuck are you doing? Come over here." And he got his syringe out and' – Nick makes a stabbing gesture into his arm – 'BANG. Something happened in that moment. Everything changed, at the time I thought for the better, I'm not so sure now ...

'The thing about it is, it for me was a way to separate myself from what else was going on around me. And that's what happens for sure with heroin. Alcohol initially makes you more gregarious. It integrates you into society. Heroin separates you, and on some level that was really attractive.'

Anne Tsoulis was an aspiring filmmaker working on the door at the Ballroom. As the girlfriend of Garry Gray of Negatives (née Reals), she had watched The Boys Next Door go from debuting rowdily at Ashburton Hall to dominating the Tiger

Lounge, before bursting onto the Crystal Ballroom stage and stretching their tentacles across the country, all in barely more than a year. Tsoulis was not impressed. 'Nick knew he was a star at nineteen. He'd visit our flat and he'd always come with an entourage; it drove me crazy. He'd make the same type of entry at the Ballroom: Nick, followed by Rowland, followed by admirers, followed by the girls,' she says. 'I have memories of walking over Nick Cave and his mob passed out on my loungeroom floor as I'd be scrabbling over them to get to the door to work – that's when I was living with Garry Gray. Garry used to make me hide my Joni Mitchell and Tim Buckley and Carole King albums before they came over. It was all so self-conscious, and it was Nick that set that elitist bullshit. Too many drugs were going down and, really, Nick was at the centre of it all, because if you didn't take heroin you weren't cool like Nick – a very sad fact, and why I've never been a fan.'[10]

The flow of heroin into the Crystal Ballroom increased rapidly as 1979 progressed. Bruce Milne says, 'It seemed to happen overnight and suddenly it was everywhere.'[11] Legend has it that a spoon was permanently hidden in the last cubicle of the women's toilets to facilitate cooking up the drug. The nature of heroin married itself to the venue's atmosphere to confirm a submerged and otherworldly intensity. Everything was blossoming and getting darker. Ashley Crawford writes extravagantly of how the Ballroom's entrance was 'via a gamut of passed-out drunks, semi-conscious junkies, syringes piercing skin, a slick swamp of vomit, and a littering of Victoria Bitter cans. This was the St Kilda of the damned, long before polished floorboards and café latte. This was still the St Kilda of [painter] Albert Tucker's visions of *Good and Evil*, prostitutes loitering in the dim light of tram stops, a world of the living dead. At the time Tucker still lived around the corner and could often be spied stalking the streets, glowering at all around him.'[12]

It's not uncommon for heroin users in the early stages of addiction to experience visionary side effects, or what are described as waking dreams. Going 'on the nod' can involve the illusion of things continuing after one has unplugged from the world; returning to consciousness can have a slipstream effect, your dream extending into reality before dissipating. It is possible that initiations into heroin had social, and even cultural, equivalents to these 'waking dreams' at the Crystal Ballroom when so many people began experimenting with it at around the same time. Disorders such as insomnia are the flipside to this during withdrawal from the drug, when users are locked out of sleep and any sweetness it may have once offered. For Nick, the lockout would become a way of life. He'd turn to his father's literary light, Vladimir Nabokov, for insight into the problem, if not quite consolation. 'I call insomnia my third life. Waking life, sleeping life, and the in-between life. Nabokov talks about insomnia and always wished he had a third side to roll on to,' he says. Nick may have learned to live and work with his insomnia in the longer run, but in these early days he was only just beginning to 'wake up and crawl the walls'.

The insights of William Burroughs, one of the most articulate modern writers on addiction, have special resonance for such drug-fuelled highs and lows among the crowds entering the Ballroom. In a 1965 conversation with *The Paris Review*, the *Junky* author discusses the nature of morphine and heroin as painkillers, and their inherent tendency to disable and anaesthetise creative activities and dreaming. And he describes the phenomenon of 'heroin dreams', a kind of afterburn image or effect that involves hallucinations in day-to-day life. But, as Burroughs rightly points out, this is merely an interim state before heavy addiction sets in and the capacity for all dreaming – conscious and unconscious – is for the most part extinguished, and one becomes truly stoned.[13]

Nick was paying a lot of attention to the heroin-warmed, dreamlike spaces he was starting to move through, even if hindsight imbues his vision with a curious documentary flatness many years later. 'The prostitutes used to work what was loosely called the Devil's Triangle – Fitzroy Street, Acland Street and Barkly Street,' he says. 'Running through the centre of the triangle was Grey Street, where most of the hooker cruising action was. There were motels along Carlisle Street that rented by the hour, or just quick car jobbies. It wasn't organised like the Cross – no neon, no glamour, no tourists – just hookers and junkies and wasted youth and businessmen getting into trouble, fish-and-chip shops selling dim sims – which we lived on – pawn shops where I would hock my rings and studio equipment later, over and over again, to get money to score – the best ones were in Prahran. When I started, it was pre-AIDS, so there wasn't even a needle exchange. On the corner of Grey Street and Fitzroy Street was the strip bar with a giant sign that said "This Is The Show" – capitals HUGE, so it said 'TITS'. Fitzroy Street is where smack was dealt, in particular the St Kilda Cafe, a fish-and-chip shop that eventually drilled holes in the spoons so the junkies couldn't use them to shoot up in the toilet out back or, indeed, steal them.'

Greg Perano, who would go on to co-found Hunters & Collectors, describes the St Kilda Cafe as 'not that big, and a little claustrophobic. It was a classic fifties cafe gone to seed, not unlike the one that Iggy [Pop] and Tom [Waits] meet at in the Jim Jarmusch film *Coffee and Cigarettes* [2003]. It had those high-backed chairs up against each other and tables with Formica surfaces. A view of the street didn't come into the equation. You didn't stay long. Most people were in and out for the "special" sugar with their take-away coffee.

'I didn't partake myself,' Perano emphasises, 'as my first experience was a near-death one which put me off the stuff for life, but it did not seem a big deal at the time. The people who owned the place were pretty heavy but they treated us well. They would always give you a coffee or a snack if you were broke. I guess it was a good way to keep in with the clients. The local street girls were always in there as well. They were all good to us, really. At that time, if you were Mr or Mrs Suburban Straight Citizen, you did not really fit into St Kilda. The underworld has always seemed to treat eccentrics with a little respect. No-one from the Ballroom was ever going to muscle in on the drug scene in St Kilda! They were great days. Those suburbs are always at their best when they have gone to seed and the bohemians move in.'[14]

Bronwyn Bonney says, 'I have many memories but they are fused into a swirl – that high speed reel of endless drunken music and parties and intense self-regard of coolness and of belonging, and the glittery social bubble that was filled with so much chaotic youthful burnout and the mental pain of those very artistic, very fucked-up, very brilliant kids. It's not a coherent linear unfolding of moments for me in my memory. It's more immersive. It is like a blender. Being inside a blender of the times and the people and the sounds and the smells. It was the cross-pollination of ideas. All very open and comradely at the beginning. I was only very young when it started. I was only fifteen. Younger than everyone else there at the very start, which were not so many. But it grew big very fast. And other young kids appeared. It happened at breakneck speed before the drug plague wrecked everyone.'[15]

Greg Perano is sceptical of hyped-up portrayals that depict the Ballroom as a fantasy palace for heroin, with a young Nick Cave reigning over the transformation like a rock 'n' roll Lucifer on the rise. 'I think the only reason the Ballroom crowd loved heroin was because it eased the boredom between the exciting moments. The Ballroom itself was never filled with people nodding off. They tended to do it at home during the day.'[16] Genevieve McGuckin saw the seeds of happiness. 'Nick, Rowlie and Pierre being like a little gang in their own right, all tall and dark and handsome and funny.'[17]

Pierre Voltaire's memories initially match Greg Perano's analysis of the early days. 'Nick and me and Rowland was becoming a drug thing. We weren't using that much, or so often, it was an after-gig sort of thing, after you got a couple of dollars, you'd go down to Fitzroy Street and score, then go back to Rowland's flat or something. And it just snowballed from there. We'd just hang around drinking cider in the afternoons – because none of us liked beer – and shooting dope.

'You'd give the guy who made hamburgers at the St Kilda Cafe fifty dollars and he'd give you a tinfoil of heroin. There'd be all these urban myths about tourists and old ladies getting them by mistake. Maybe we thought we were punk rock and able to handle it, I don't know. The first time we sniffed it and stayed up all night, it was euphoric, blissful, it was really very different to what I thought it would be. I think that was with Nick and Anita, the next night Rowland and Genevieve were with us. It was all innocent – like a flirtation. We were sniffing, not injecting. That was for months and months. Then it became this thing we did every night. You'd wake up next day in the afternoon, read the paper, go down to Fitzroy Street, wearing a suit if it wasn't too hot, and start all over again, drink, party, shag ... The heroin went from being a nightcap and moved up the food chain. Snorting is slow. Shooting up blew our heads off. We got a lot more high. This is before AIDS; it was hard to get fresh needles, we'd have to use old blunt ones that we sharpened on the sides of matchboxes and shared with each other. That's why Hep C is so widespread now. Anyway, people started having their own private drug time. They'd turn up at gigs already stoned. It just became a bigger part of the scene. You'd have to admit that it was glamorous for a while.'[18]

It must have seemed that way when Tom Waits, who was touring off the back of *Blue Valentine*, appeared at the St Kilda Cafe one night in early May 1979. Only thirty years old himself, Waits was at the peak of his game artistically. He was also in the middle of what seemed a stalled career commercially, as well as majorly damaged by his recent break-up with singer Rickie Lee Jones. 'He was sitting in the cafe by himself waiting and we sat down with him,' says Greg Perano. 'We were not really big fans at the time, but he was an interesting character. I think it was Nick, Pierre Voltaire, Rowland, Genevieve, and me and my girlfriend Vanessa. You know why everyone went there. Tom had obviously been given the word by someone. What I remember of the Tom Waits encounter was a group of brash young folk exchanging witticisms with a very intelligent eccentric. I think Tom Waits looked for those seedy little places in every city because it is where he would find the real characters. He was quite interested in the post-punk crowd there, but he seemed like he could hold his own with anyone. Rowland and Nick liked to challenge people back then, so they were probably quite cynical about someone like Tom Waits, although that would all change. At that time the only music that existed for us was music that we saw as challenging what had gone before. That meant Pere Ubu, The Pop Group, The Fall, Suicide, The Cramps, Can, The Raincoats, The Contortions, The Slits ... all that period. Of course, people began to listen to Tom when he released *Swordfishtrombones* [1983] and *Rain Dogs* [1985], but I still think *Blue Valentine* [1979] is one of his best.'[19]

Tracy Pew was the one who educated Nick's ear to the charms of Tom Waits, and to *Blue Valentine* in particular, which the bassist adored. Waits' booze-hound version of 'Somewhere', a ballad of star-crossed lovers and their beautiful but futile dreams of ever making an escape from their circumstances in *West Side Story*, would be played at Pew's funeral in November 1986.[20]

Blue Valentine is a record Nick still likes to listen to every now and then. When he hears it, it is like Tracy is back in the room. 'Yeah,' Nick says. 'I still miss him.'

Paul Goldman had been following The Boys Next Door around since seeing them at the Tiger Lounge. He was a film student at Swinburne Institute of Technology, and for a television assignment requiring a shoot inside a studio he decided to approach Nick with the offer of directing a video for the band. In the pre-MTV age, this was not as obvious a move as it might now seem. The form was new and few people regarded it seriously. Goldman filmed 'After a Fashion' and 'Shivers' in a single day, with Evan English assisting him on lighting.

Goldman's clip for 'After a Fashion' was done on an all-white set and has now been 'either lost or destroyed', he says.[21] He'd spent most of the day working on it. His video for 'Shivers', shot in just two hours, survived, and remains one of the most iconic in Australian music history. It opens with a close-up of the 21-year-old Nick Cave as he reaches out of the darkness to grip a microphone and sing of suicide, style and a heart on its knees. A wan Rowland S Howard emerges in the background, looking on as if wounded, playing his slow-chiming guitar. Both he and Nick are wearing buttoned-to-the-neck frock coats like nineteenth-century artists. A rosy-cheeked, hesitant Tracy Pew appears beside Rowland, then Mick Harvey, barely discernible in the middle distance, and, briefly and more dramatically, Phill Calvert on drums. It's a clip for The Boys Next Door – but the focus is almost exclusively on Nick, and he gives a tour de force performance, creating odd, angular poses with his arms and hands, a one-man procession of romantic hieroglyphs and bullfighter semaphores.

The debt to the stage moves of Simon Bonney was apparent to fans. Bonney had just shifted base to Melbourne and was making waves as he set about reforming Crime and the City Solution in that city. He liked marching through the streets of St Kilda wearing a long, dark naval jacket, as befits a poet ready for a storm. 'Pierre Voltaire, who was like the knave of the scene,' says Bronwyn Bonney, 'nicknamed Simon "Tess".'[22] Like Mick Harvey, Rowland S Howard was sanguine about any copycat crimes: 'Both Simon and Nick saw things in each other that they wanted to be.'[23]

It was an observation that might have equally reflected the relationship between Rowland and Nick. One of Rowland's favourite books growing up was Alain-Fournier's *Le Grand Meaulnes*. A classic French coming-of-age tale, the book had helped inspire F Scott Fitzgerald to write *The Great Gatsby* (another Rowland favourite) and was similarly constructed, with a passive narrator observing and fatally absorbing the life of his friend, the novel's dynamic yet tragic hero. In a similar way, there's an unmistakeably wounded quality to Rowland as he stands in the background, observing Nick sing what had once been among the most personal of his songs in the film clip for 'Shivers'.[24] It's as if a gate was being slowly shut on Rowland S Howard with 'Shivers' and he knew he could only ever look on sadly at was happening around him, his dream having been absorbed into someone else's adventure. He was a critical part of that adventure, of course, but destined to be a creature living in its aftermath, struggling to come out from under a larger mythology.

Watching 'Shivers' still entertains Paul Goldman, who says, 'The reason Nick gets himself tied up in knots in that clip is because he insisted on having a mirror on the camera so he could see himself. So throughout he is actually watching himself, the great narcissist that he is.'[25]

Nick was also inspired by the album cover art for David Bowie's *Heroes* and Iggy Pop's *The Idiot*. He had spent many long hours dwelling on these images as he listened to the music in his bedroom. Both Bowie and Pop based their strange photo-portrait poses on the early-twentieth-century German artist Erich Heckel's painting *Roquairol*. Nick recognised this visual language immediately. Intensely conscious of his own Expressionist influences, he wanted to physically announce himself as a rock 'n' roll Egon Schiele. Ever since becoming an art student, Nick had been intrigued by Schiele's obsessive self-portraiture and disconcerting paintings of the human figure, many of them pubescent youths the artist had seduced before being driven out of his mother's hometown for his scandalous behaviour. Schiele demanded his models strike uncomfortable or extreme postures so that what he believed to be the body's essential qualities of sex and death were revealed. 'The picture must radiate light,' Schiele philosophised. 'The bodies have their own light which they consume to live: they burn, they are not lit from outside.'[26] Schiele's attraction to bodies that were physically contorted and in erotic torment had a corollary with martyrdom, of course, though they also came to be seen as premonitions of the Holocaust. It's no wonder this appealed to Nick more than ever in 1979, however temporary and self-conscious the manifestations may have been in shaping his stage moves. Thirty years later, the film clip for 'Shivers' would feed into academic analyses of Nick's early performing style, aligning it with gay identity and queer dance philosophy.[27] If all that seems strained, the fact remains that Nick was well aware of the Expressionist history behind the gestures he was making and the image he was creating. Hence that mirror to get it exactly right. Goldman may have been directing, but it was Nick who was certain of the role he wanted to play.

Nick was also familiar with the manner in which Schiele had died at the age of twenty-eight, during the Spanish influenza plague that swept Europe in 1918. The artist could only communicate with his last models, and eventually his loved ones, through a mirror placed in the doorway between two rooms. What was played out in Nick Cave's mirror in 1979 was another conversation, another dance with death. Perhaps Nick caught a glimpse of his father – if not in the mirror that day, then through a conversation the song's recording had first allowed him to have with a self-obsessed, forever out-of-reach object of love. Rowland might have intuited some of this as he watched Nick becoming a star right in front of him on the day that 'Shivers' was filmed. After all, Egon Schiele was his favourite painter too.

Rowland's close friend Bronwyn Bonney tells of how 'Nick had the right formula: very charismatic + not mentally ill + had family support + work ethic + personal creative vision + sense of chosenness + right place right time. Everyone else lacked two or three of those ingredients. Nick also has the ability to glamour [sic] people, to dazzle or hypnotise them. He is a natural tantric, he has sexual magnetism without consciously fostering it, and that gives him a lot of personal power. He can both give – and take away – many people in his orbit's sense of their own self-worth. He is also ruthless enough to prioritise his own work above all else, which is important to big success, unless you have a spouse or manager to do it for you. And he feels very invested in his own primacy and importance, without it being hollow or dumbly delusional. Yes, Rowland was always going to be sad – because he lacked a few key ingredients. Nick is innately very gifted, but he also marshals the talent around him so that it becomes his. Having talent by itself is nothing, even if it is an immense talent. That is why Anita is an obscurity. And many others from that talent-studded dysfunctional scene. Nick was not the most talented – but his other gifts were more crucial. It is also the times and the place that determine who is lost as it depends on the cultural values around the person too. What is deemed important can vary a lot. Every zeitgeist has its own particular heroes and dogs and baddies. People are partly angry at Nick because they envy him. He works like a demon. He deserves his success.'[28]

Just prior to the release of *Door, Door* in May 1979, Nick had complained to Jillian Burt of *Roadrunner* that 'Gudinski still considers us a punk rock group ... He doesn't think any of our material is single quality. In England there are singles that come out every week that will obviously never be on radio – and I'm not even sure that the bands consider that they would be on the radio – but they're still interesting and prestigious singles, which is mainly what we're concerned with.'[29]

Beautiful as 'Shivers' was, Gudinski and Mushroom felt it would never get airplay as a radio single because it mentioned suicide. The subject matter was not only sensitive, it brought up their recent punk label's disastrous collapse. Courting controversy with Barrie Earl had only confirmed how conservative the Australian market was, especially with spiky young acts like The Boys Next Door. It was very different in the UK, where the influence of the *NME* and a unique figure like BBC Radio 1 DJ John Peel meant that bizarre and avant-garde songs could find themselves in the national spotlight – and even lauded. Reading the *NME* provided ample evidence to Nick that the music scene in Britain was much wilder and more open to new things.

The Boys Next Door's live audience was substantial and devoted in inner-city Melbourne, but they were playing to the same crowds and their music was becoming more experimental. Their thinking across 1979 would become even more closely attuned to the British zeitgeist, where singles were less an expression of radio-friendly hopes than grenades thrown to announce a radical identity.

Nick told the journalist John Stapleton of his desire to get to London: 'We've gone about as far as we can here. We want to move on, to progress.'[30] Conversations between Keith Glass and The Boys Next Door confirmed their desperation to get out of Melbourne, and a hunger to make their mark overseas. Glass already knew exactly where they were looking. After all, through his store, Missing Link, he was the one supplying them with all those new singles and artistic statements they worshipped.

In order to finance the band's trip to the United Kingdom, Glass established a regime of hard gigging and stringent saving that rationed the band to five dollars each after a show's takings. Alcohol was usually free on the night, while fans were eager to supply them with everything from food and drink to sex and drugs. Alternative income came through a patchwork of unemployment benefits and part-time jobs. Over the previous few years Nick had done everything from manning a cigarette stand to serving as a sales assistant at Denim Den in Elsternwick. At the latter, he'd attempted to have sex in the alleyway with an equally enthusiastic customer, a story that greatly amused Pierre Voltaire. 'Nick ended up having an orgasm before he could do anything,' he laughs. 'I remember him being quite upset about that.'[31]

Nick was the only member of the band still living comfortably at home in 1979. Mick Harvey continued sharing an apartment on the St Kilda Esplanade with Rowland and Genevieve, from where it was a mere five-minute walk around the corner and up Fitzroy Street to the Crystal Ballroom. Tracy was now living round the corner in an apartment of his own. Phill admits to being a little confused about where he was living as 'people tended to move every six months', but for a good while he says he held court in Richmond with the band's roadie, Shane Middleton, and Beau Lazenby. 'I lived upstairs so I never knew what they were doing down below. It was like having my own little place.'[32]

In his diary notes for March 1979, Nick makes a number of references to visiting Beau or heading back to her place after practice. Though Nick was still seeing Anita, his connection with Beau Lazenby seems to date from early that year. Lazenby would later become the mother of Nick's eldest son, Jethro, in 1991. In 1979 she was known for attending gigs in her pyjamas, as well as carrying a teddy bear. But there was a real wildness to her. Recollections from The Boys Next Door era on *Nick Cave Fixes*, 'a Bad Seeds tribute blog', describe Beau Lazenby wearing a singlet with 'I Hate Men' written in her own blood. *Nick Cave Fixes* host Morgan Wolfe, another Crystal Ballroom habitué, makes a sardonic observation: 'Nicky's ego would have demanded that he conquer her.'[33]

In his somewhat sketchy diary notes for May 1979, Nick has an early lyric for what will become 'The Hair Shirt' drafted out, with the preliminary title 'The Hair Vest (Ode to an Oaf)'. There's another song idea entitled 'Haunted House' that has very little to it, other than a repeated mock-horror reference to an attic. Nick says that the band are in the process of learning a Rowland S Howard song called 'Running Goat' – inspired by a game Rowland used to play with his brother Harry when they were children. Nick is paying off the purchase of a new synthesiser and putting in a little practice on the instrument for use with Little Cuties. He documents films he sees at the cinema and on TV that have made an impression on him: *The Deerhunter, Padre Padrone, Jane Eyre* ... Other entries are filled with ill-matched support dates The Boys Next Door are playing with acts such as Jo Jo Zep and the Falcons, The Radiators, Jimmy and the Boys, and Split Enz. Because of their Roxy-obsessed, mascara-lashed early days, The Boys Next Door had been matched incongruously with the carnival-esque prog-rock power pop of the Enz, if only on the basis of appearances. Phill Calvert smiles and says, 'We liked them, they liked us, there just wasn't enough pancake to go around.'[34]

In an interview in Adelaide's *Sunday Mail* that same month, Nick Cave claimed, 'I never had any lyrics to most of the songs until a few months ago. I used to just have a few lines and then growl and make noises all the time.'[35]

From that comment, it is easy to tell that the songs for the *Hee Haw* EP were already taking shape – or, more precisely, unshape. In the meantime, Nick was pushing himself physically and psychologically in the same anticlockwise direction. The joker in him was only just beginning to cut loose. Everyone around him was in for a wild ride.

Nick and Tracy would often join Mick, Rowland and Genevieve at their apartment, and along with Anita Lane and Pierre Voltaire they would head off together for the evening's adventures. They made quite a scene moving along Fitzroy Street in a pack towards the Ballroom. People would literally stop and stare.

Voltaire's father had died when he was eleven. For all his withering humour, he was well attuned to the pain Nick was going through, and the aggressive masks one might wear to protect oneself. Tea and sympathy were never going to be part of the grief and recovery process so far as Voltaire was concerned. 'Nick never talked much about his dad,' he says. 'Dawn was always around, and she was lovely. Nick would come stay with me and shag girls and do drugs, then he would go home and get his mum to cook and do the washing for him. I figured he didn't do that much at home when Dawn was away one time and we had an Eat the Fridge Party. There was a dishwasher. I'd never seen one before, actually. Nick did not even know how to turn it on.'[36]

'It was always a mystery why Nick stayed at home,' says Voltaire. 'None of us could understand, because we all got out as soon as we could. I was fourteen when I left home. Rowland was sixteen. You could get the dole; rent was cheap. I mean, it was kinda weird he never moved out. He is still really close to his mum for someone who is not gay!'[37]

After the Ballroom closed at night, Nick and his friends would head down to the St Kilda Cafe to score heroin if they had enough money. Maybe Janet Austin or Vicki Bonet would be having a party. Alternatively, they would while away an hour at Topolino's, devouring cheap pizza or a favoured late-night snack of ice cream and rockmelon – 'something sweet and something nutritious', as Greg Perano puts it.[38] A heroin sweet tooth was driving those cravings, and it was healthier than eating sugar straight out of the cafe's bowls, which Pierre admits they also tried from time to time.

Keith Glass claims he never saw drugs being taken. This may well have involved turning a blind eye. As managers go, a hippie anarchist like Glass fitted right in with The Boys Next Door's increasingly twisted ethos. 'Nick was always a comedian. I saw him as a humorous, Dadaist sort of dude. Everyone was on the same wavelength humour-wise – mostly,' Glass says with a shrug. 'Phill was the odd man out in that department. Not cool. But such a great drummer; I was always puzzled musically why they got rid of him later. But there wasn't that much mental cruelty going on then. It was more fun.'[39]

A tour of Tasmania was typical of the problems Glass had to negotiate. On the flight to Hobart, Nick gathered all the food scraps from everyone's plates. 'He built this kind of meat sculpture,' says Glass, 'and plonked it down in front of me to show they were dissatisfied with me about something or other. I thought it was hilarious.'[40] The shows went well, but after the last performance Nick and Rowland headed off to a party with a local. Nick insisted he could drive the girl's car. Drunk and unlicensed, he proved so frightening behind the wheel that Howard asked to be let out. The guitarist promptly staggered back to the band's hotel and fell asleep. When Nick could not be found the next day, it emerged he had been arrested after driving the wrong way down a one-way street and crashing into a parked police car. Nick had initially fled the scene and hid behind some garbage bins. Mick Harvey says, 'From the way Nick described it to me, the police walked by him in the dark and said quite loudly, "Oh, I can't see him here." Then they just stood and waited while Nick came out from where he was hidden so they could grab him: "Aha, gotcha!"' Harvey smiles. 'When Nick was drinking he would get very naughty, very cheeky, very funny. I used to enjoy him drinking.'[41]

Miraculously, Glass was able to bail Nick out, cover the cost of the damages to the police car and avoid a prosecution that would have caused serious problems, given Nick's good-behaviour bond back in Melbourne. The prospect of charges involving interstate paperwork had meant the Tasmanian police did not take their enquiries far and were simply happy to see the back of the singer and his driving skills.

Nick's run-ins with the law did not make him any quieter in Melbourne. He had developed a habit of taking off his clothes at parties, an act usually inspired by plenty of drinking and taking speed. Nick would still hang out sometimes with Ollie Olsen, their friendship running hot and cold and having its own weirdly competitive symbiosis: 'I don't know why I took my clothes off. But Ollie started calling me "Nick the stripper". The phrase stayed in my mind.'

Melbourne punk singer, musician and stirrer Ron Rude enjoyed watching them become real presences on the scene. He first remembers meeting Olsen one morning in Hawthorn at the peak of the Young Charlatans hype. 'It's like 11 am and Ollie looked dressed to play Madison Square Garden. He was immaculate and handsome with an otherworldly voice and a hint of conceit. A thin white duke in a pink suit with a sneer.' He describes Rowland Howard as 'Ollie's fellow Martian, with pointy ears to boot, glaring vampiric eyes, and black shoes so shiny you could use them as a make-up mirror.' As a pair, they made quite an impression on him. 'I'd never seen anything like this.'[42]

As for the young Nick Cave, Rude can see how the idiot savant impression may have stuck to him at the time. 'In the early days, when folks knew Nick only as that loud, crazy drunk at parties screaming hog calls à la "Suey [sic]"[43] with Tracy, it wasn't apparent that he would become a successful singer, songwriter, piano and guitar player, novelist and screenplay writer, all at an international level ... I presume that Nick knew of hog-calling from his youth. I wonder now whether Nick's upbringing in rural places that have a hint of that weirdness precipitated his ongoing fascination with the American Deep South? My ex-wife said to me that when she read *And the Ass Saw the Angel* the landscape and people reminded her of the various Victorian country towns that she had lived in. Back in those days, Nick definitely sought out grim comic movies about the Deep South like *Wise Blood* [1979], but I don't know exactly where he got the hog-calling from ... It might have been from TV's *Green Acres*? I knew I'd seen it somewhere, because when he and Tracy were doing their drunken hog calls at parties, I recognised it as that.'[44]

Given Nick's attention-seeking spirit, it's hardly surprising he was becoming a fan of Ron Rude, who continuously struggled to get his music career off the ground despite being something of an established cult figure. Rude's act often involved stirring up abusive slanging matches with his audience, which could bring his shows to a hilarious, if grinding, halt. He was as much a performance artist and village idiot as musician. To get Eon FM[45] to play his singles, Rude went on a hunger strike in the window of Missing Link, Keith Glass's store. Phill Calvert says, 'Helena [Keith Glass's wife and business partner] was getting him Maccas after hours.'[46] When the hunger strike failed, Rude went into the lobby of Eon FM with a bucket of water and threatened to place his head inside it and drown himself. It may have been ridiculous, but Rude had enough intensity to make it seem within the realms of possibility. After that he chained himself to Molly Meldrum's fence, much to the horror of the *Countdown* host. The Boys Next Door took a big shine to him and invited Rude to play as their support act. 'Ron used to do this song I liked called "I'm the Best Orgasm You Will Have on a Saturday Night". Great title!' says Nick.[47]

To speak only of the rages of punk and the artiness of post-punk is to lose sight of a subversive stream of humour that distinguished the era and brought together many kindred spirits. Rude was just one of many anarchist spirits mining comedy and confrontation as a vein of energy in the punk era. Phill Calvert says, 'I remember funny things like being in a van on the way to somewhere and Nick singing "Take It to the Limit" by the Eagles. He also liked "I Can't Smile Without You" by Barry Manilow – I think it was more for the super-cheesy [film] clip that went with it. Shit like that would crack us all up. We were funny. Nick was funny … He had this line he always used when cadging a fag: "I'll shower you in cigarettes when we hit the big time." I wonder if he ever will?'[48]

Nick was far from being the only comedian in the band. Despite Tracy Pew's air of freewheeling criminality, and a capacity to intimidate that excess drinking and the wrong circumstance could uncork, he was generally considered extremely loveable and downright hilarious by his friends. In an intensely image-conscious band, Pew would get purposely bad haircuts and turn up to shows wearing his pyjamas or brightly coloured polyester suits that were deeply unfashionable rather than coolly ironic. The more pretentious Rowland and Nick got, the more inclined Pew was to play the buffoon. At times he could push it to breaking point with everyone. Nick laughs.

'He used to introduce his girlfriend as his cock holster, just to wind people up.'

Pew's bass playing was yet to find the stripped-back and menacing, sensual depths around which The Birthday Party would be built. But no-one ever underestimated the power and versatility of Phill and Tracy as a rhythm section, anchoring and propelling Nick, Rowland and Mick's increasingly abstract and jagged musical creations in The Boys Next Door. Rowland was never really sure where he stood with the bassist and tended to keep his distance; Nick had rather the opposite blessing. 'Tracy could always cut me down to size ... if I was getting carried away with myself. He was always funny. It's something I miss, actually. I don't think I ever found that with anyone ever again. He always kept my feet on the ground.'[49]

Melbourne underground cartoonist Fred Negro drew an amusing strip called 'One Nite after the Ballroom' that nonetheless captures how pretentious things could get. Negro depicts a party in Acland Street where everybody is having a great time dancing to the Rolling Stones' *Exile on Main Street*. Nick and Rowland turn up, with Nick scratching the Stones record on purpose before throwing it off the turntable and replacing it with Brian Eno's ambient masterpiece *Music for Airports*. Nick dramatically declares it to be 'the future of music' and everyone nods dutifully, sinking to the floor to contemplate what was on offer. Negro, however, tires of this after a few minutes and puts on Kiss's 'Rock and Roll All Nite', loudly declaring it to be 'the future of this party!' After which he and Nick dissolve into what he calls 'the most pathetic bitch slap fight in the history of St Kilda'. Fred Negro can laugh. He still dines out on the tale as people clamour to hear of 'the night I punched Nick Cave in the head'.[50]

Though yet to record *Hee Haw*, Nick envisaged it as 'far less clinical … The way we'll do these ones is just a real spontaneous sorta thing. With each song I've been writing, the lyrics are becoming more and more meaningless. The main reason for that is I don't think anybody ever really draws anything from lyrics anyway. Only that they like them. I don't think lyrics ever affect people in any way or affect their lives.'[51]

Howard was thinking similarly: 'In my old songs there used to be common images like mirrors and broken glass, but I've grown out of that,' he told *Roadrunner*. 'A song, as I see it, should be like a dream that you can hardly remember and they spark off something in the back of your mind, a series of half-familiar images.'[52]

Creatively, Nick and Rowland were right on each other's wavelength. 'We were definitely into the same sorts of things,' Nick observed. 'You know, left-field literature, the Dadaists. He [Rowland] himself was a huge Duchamp guy, much more than I was, actually. Alfred Jarry. This had a big influence over what he did for a long time and over what I did for a shorter while.'[53]

In 1979, Alfred Jarry was the philosopher king of Nick's universe. The French writer would exert a big influence on him for the next two years. Jarry's play *Ubu Roi* had caused a riot when it was first staged in Paris in 1896, opening with the word 'Merdre!' – the French word for 'shit', *merde*, with an extra 'r' added. The main character was based on a schoolboy caricature of a physics teacher, raw materials with which Nick could very much identify. In the play, Pere Ubu appears as a revolting old man nagged by his wife into attempting to become the king of Poland – effectively the king of nothing at all. A satire of greed and power, *Ubu Roi* developed as a bombastic yet sinister Punch and Judy parody of *Macbeth*. It took an audience through foul-mouthed scenes that featured an orgy, de-braining and shit-eating, adopting an aggressive absurdist stance the likes of which had not been seen on stage before. The characters wore distorting masks, with the corpulent and squeaky-voiced Pere Ubu distinguished by a large counter-clockwise spiral – more classically the sign of a spiritual quest when it flowed clockwise – marking his 'gidouille', or belly, into which everything was taken and, of course, excreted. Eventually, Pere Ubu shoves his conscience down the toilet as well. That always made Nick laugh.

Jarry's work preceded the Theatre of the Absurd and influenced writers including Eugène Ionesco and Samuel Beckett, even paving the way for a whacked-out vein of twentieth-century humour that ran from the Marx Brothers through to Monty Python and Spike Milligan. Ubu Roi was such a *succès de scandale* it was said to have consumed Jarry himself. He began to imitate the Pere Ubu character and speak in a strange little voice, helped along by an excess of alcohol and absinthe that finished him off at age thirty-two. The poet William Butler Yeats, who was at the riotous opening night of the play, is reputed to have turned aghast to another audience member and said, 'What more is possible? After us, the Savage God.' A savage god in whom Nick found a few angry and sardonic prayers creatively answered.

One of his and Rowland's most revered musical contemporaries, the American group Pere Ubu, had taken their name from the play. This only fuelled Nick and Rowland's craze for all things Jarry. Pere Ubu had come bursting out of Cleveland, Ohio, with a sound that suggested an absurdist garage blues band penetrated by distended surf rock sounds and freaked-out, metallic folk influences that seemed to have drifted in from an industrial no-man's land. Their albums *Modern Dance* and *Dub Housing* stood outside of any musical movements apparent at the time, and would be studied by Nick and Rowland like holy texts. Pere Ubu's sonic influence on *Hee Haw* is unmistakeable, from the jerking and breaking melodic structures and wild musical tangents to Nick's vocals, which took on a yelping, epileptic quality directly indebted to vocalist David Thomas's bird-meets-dog tonal affectations, not to mention the Pere Ubu singer's capacity to balance childlike enthusiasm with apocalyptic lamentations.

Although the avant-garde shell of The Boys Next Door's *Hee Haw* EP would be critically acclaimed (at least by those it did not mystify or repel), there is a case to argue that it was actually more derivative than the exuberant pop-punk of *Door, Door*. Mick Harvey would come to see *Hee Haw* as a critical step in the evolution of the band. Even so, Harvey was bothered at the time by how steamrolled The Boys Next Door's sound had been by the Pere Ubu obsession. Nick's goals were not intentionally imitative, but were as rudely driven and surreally profound as the philosophies of Alfred Jarry, his new French master. 'It is conventional to call "monster" any blending of dissonant elements,' Jarry wrote. 'I call "monster" every original inexhaustible beauty.' Nick lapped up that stuff. Jarry's confrontational attitude to bourgeois aesthetics – 'The work of art is a stuffed crocodile' – was also much to Nick's own taste. *Ubu Roi*'s juxtapositions of surreal violence, Shakespearian plot and character elements, and crude street-level humour pushed Nick further to break down walls – between high and low art, as well between the performer and the audience – in order to create something that had a similar bite.

Nick had also started reading the cultural anthropologist Ernest Becker's Pulitzer Prize–winning work, *The Denial of Death*. Published in 1973, it posited an anxiety about death as central to human identity and our social constructions, from religion through to art. The book describes how we build heroic narratives to ease our mortal fears and seek out consoling illusions of meaning and immortality. Becker's work built on the work of Freud and his former right-hand man, Otto Rank, as well as European philosophy; one of the epigraphs was from Spinoza: 'Not to laugh, not to lament, not to curse, but to understand.'

Nick would pass through all those feelings, and the proverbial five stages of grief, in the most human and messy ways most people do after a traumatic loss. But Becker's thesis that our consciousness and creativity give us an awareness of being that is unique and godlike, yet equally frustrated by our awareness of death – and with it, the nature of our bodies at their most basic, and even repugnant – struck Nick as deeply true. Becker's statement that we are 'gods with anuses' would stay with him.[54] He only had to look around him at the Crystal Ballroom to see that mix of glamour and horror playing out as a human grotesque. Beauty was transient. Decay and change were inevitable.

'You probably don't need to wade through the book to get an idea of what Becker is talking about,' Nick says. 'There's this academic, you see him in shorts and tie-dye T-shirts raving about Becker in lectures and stuff. Sheldon Solomon. TMT. Terror Management Theory. Google him. Really interesting. There is also a great documentary that used to be on YouTube that explains it all. It's called *Flight from Death: The Quest for Immortality.* The title says it all.'

The production for *Hee Haw* is credited to The Boys Next Door and Keith Glass. Glass certainly boosted everyone's confidence and encouraged the path they were on, but it was mainly engineer Tony Cohen who helped the band get the sounds they wanted or imagined. The band worked through July and August, at a pace that became feverish, entering the studio on midnight-to-dawn shifts after playing gigs. The first crucial decision they made was to record in a live situation rather than compartmentalise each instrument separately in a pristine but sterile isolated taping process. Though this meant sacrificing stereo fidelity, it brought a new level of dynamism to the performance of the songs. Together with Cohen, Nick Cave and Mick Harvey would develop this live approach into an ongoing practice they would perfect in Berlin in the mid-eighties at Hansa Studios.

TC had to puzzle out how to take advantage of The Boys Next Door's momentum as a performing unit – and still bring space and depth to their studio sound. On *Hee Haw*, he and the group attempted this with distinct pauses in both the individual playing and the song structures, and toying with overdubbed dissonant aural textures to enhance the contrasting patches of moodiness and mania.

The whole process built on Nick and Rowland's interest in an aesthetic that tilted towards the burlesque, admitting plenty of randomness and playfulness into their creative process. Nick loved the unsettled, wise-cracking energy that this stimulated in the new songs they were creating. Their approach was influenced by Nick's interest in Jarry's anarchistic humour, and Rowland's love of Marcel Duchamp's 'ready-mades', which he'd been pushing Nick to take note of. Duchamp's ready-mades consisted of found objects – such as a bicycle wheel, a comb, a snow shovel or, most famously, a urinal – that were then transformed into artworks through the simple act of being signed, given a witty title and placed in a gallery. Wasn't it possible to do the same kind of thing musically, Rowland suggested, puncturing the expected with the unexpected, the refined with rough and ready, the high with the low?

There was nothing particularly intellectual about Cohen's approach in realising those goals, however. He was pure sonic enthusiasm, aural genius. After the *Hee Haw* recordings he would state: 'The total disrespect for how things were supposed to be done was just fantastic.'[55] Excited by his new friends, the one-time hippie had cut his hair and 'started wearing shoes'. For the backing vocals on 'The Hair Shirt', Cohen recorded Nick singing through a telephone line. Alfred Jarry himself could have been yelling down the line. 'It was this squeaky, horrible voice. If you turned it up it would absolutely blow your head off. We were trying out all kinds of shit like that on *Hee Haw*,' says Cohen. 'Now if you want to exaggerate something you can dial it up with Pro Tools. But there's just something fun about putting people in concrete corridors or stairwells to get a sound that can't be got any other way.'[56]

Even the mixing of the songs was a source of entertainment for all concerned. 'It was all very analogue. In those days you didn't have computers to do it for you,' Cohen says, hammering his point home. 'I think Nick still uses tape now.[57] It just sounds better. We'd have all hands on deck; we'd all have our channels that we were each controlling. And we'd have to try and get through mixing a whole song without anyone making a mistake. But it was great. Everybody was making a performance of the mix.'[58]

The opening track on *Hee Haw*, 'A Catholic Skin', begins with the epic, swelling shimmer of Rowland S Howard's guitar, then breaks into a jerking, off-kilter song marked by Nick's newly hysterical vocal style – half-shouted and shrieked – before jumping into falsetto and being sheathed in echo effects, with Howard's high-fretted, scraping guitar behind it. Nick repeats what sounds like a nonsensical question about sin and describes being Anglican as akin to being spiritually filleted. The energy of his vocals and the lyrics invite an absurdist sense of being possessed, or a notion that Nick has somehow been born into the wrong religious body. The blunt force of the music's rhythm has a slapstick quality, a comic and violent awkwardness that would become a Boys Next Door trademark.

Rowland's song 'The Red Clock' follows, mechanistic-sounding and sci-fi paranoid, with the guitarist singing along in his droogy style as if pursued like an outlaw through the relentless tick-tocks of time.[59] 'Faint Heart' is another Nick Cave composition, and the EP's most extreme decomposition, as an apparently simple and fast-paced rock 'n' roll song about Nick's ghostly sense of self. It breaks down into studio voices and random sounds, a pounded poltergeist piano, with a lyric about loneliness and darkness at its anarchic centre. Nick chants of death and a need to pray with your truest feelings. 'Faint Heart' then reprises its conventional form before the song ends, as if the recording tape has been scorched off by Howard's guitar noise. What a strange amalgam it is – perhaps an effort by Nick to communicate with his dead father? Phill Calvert says 'dub freakout stuff by white guys' affected the song recording. 'We'd been listing to the album *Y* by The Pop Group a lot. No-one knew how to make those sounds in the studio with delays and tape stuff like the reggae guys use, so that was probably our attempt.'[60]

It is followed by another Rowland song, the lugubrious 'Death by Drowning', with Nick singing as if caught inside the soundtrack to an imaginary film adaptation of Albert Camus' novel *The Fall*. Rowland had collaged the lyrics together from phrases he'd found in a French–English grammar book to create something apparently meaningless and yet ominous, his own little satire of Existential literary style. It probably drowns itself – and marks the beginning of Rowland trying to accommodate Nick as a singer by creating a decentred lyrical base that had little to do with Rowland personally.

Nick's song 'The Hair Shirt' closes the EP with what is the only undisputed triumph of the entire recording. 'The Hair Shirt' was a lighter pop-rock preview of The Birthday Party beast to come, but for an obsessively repeated lyric about the colour of a corpse and an act of murder. Waves of guilt and, queerly, waves of triumph wash through it. Nick was getting better and better at this kind of negative duality.

Tracy Pew remained unconvinced about the artier direction the band was taking on *Hee Haw*, but he was such an adaptable, sinuous bass player he was able to work with everyone and give these jarring, self-conscious songs added meat. His clarinet playing on 'Death by Drowning' had more of a midday-movie, Arabia feel than anything a free jazz musician such as Pharoah Sanders might foment, but this only added to the alienating brashness and quirky humour that ran through the music.

Calvert had been going through a fanatical stint of playing along to James Brown albums at home, one of the reasons *Hee Haw* has a strangely funky, swinging dynamic that would continue into Birthday Party days. On 'The Hair Shirt', that early groove is self-evident. English groups of the moment such as The Pop Group and Gang of Four were similarly discovering this danceable direction with scarifying edges and chopping, aggressive rhythms. In terms of where things were heading musically, The Boys Next Door were right on the money.

Even so, *Hee Haw* can come off as annoying listening, a capricious outburst of energy and ideas from young wannabes. In a live setting the story was very different, with songs from the record taking on a surprising power, furiously expanding the band's palette. Keith Glass is still very fond of the EP, and took a highly strategic view of its possibilities while the band were recording. '*Hee Haw* was totally experimental,' he says. 'I saw it as a Captain Beefheart kinda thing, and I half-suspected Gudinski would hate it, which he did, and that it would help get them off the Mushroom label. Which is exactly what happened.'[61]

Nick and Tracy's taste for practical jokes was another factor in their ultimate departure from Mushroom. Glass recalls Tracy getting down on his hands and knees behind Gudinski while Nick approached him from the front at a Mushroom record launch. With a hearty, 'How are you going, Mike?', Cave pushed Gudinski backwards, sending him tumbling over Pew. Nick and Tracy thought this was hilarious. Gudinski did his best to laugh it off. Glass says, 'Gudinski almost broke his fucking neck.' It would be the first in a string of pranks that Nick Cave calls 'a kind of band tradition where we assault Gudinski whenever we run into him'.

Already their manager, Keith Glass could now sign the increasingly loutish band to his formative Missing Link label, giving them carte blanche to record and release music in whatever form they wished. Ollie Olsen's Whirlywirld was about to release their first single through his label, and Glass would soon sign The Laughing Clowns and The Go-Betweens to make albums too. He scored an unlikely hit that year by licensing an obscure single, a cover of 'Money' by The Flying Lizards, which surprised everyone by going to number one in the Top 40 charts. As if to cement his kudos, Glass visited the United States to negotiate releasing the entire back catalogue of the resolutely anonymous, quasi-anthropological avant-garde rock band The Residents, as well as the American hardcore punk protest music of Dead Kennedys. It was in this company on Missing Link that The Boys Next Door felt they were at finally at home.

Initially there was some tension between Mick Harvey's talents as an aspiring musical arranger and budding producer, and where Rowland Howard was taking the group as an innovative instrumentalist. To portray Harvey as the deacon of order and Howard as an angel of chaos is simplistic, but the archetypes suggest something of how the pair played off one another – and finally converged behind Nick in their vision. 'I actually entered into the studio process pretty slowly,' Mick Harvey says. 'Rowland had a much stronger understanding of sound than I did. It wasn't till 1981 that I started to be much more hands-on.'[62]

Rowland told a slightly different story. 'See, when I joined the band, Nick had ideas and stuff but they were fairly unmusical ideas. I remember talking to Mick Harvey when I was still in

Young Charlatans and he used to laugh about how some things I played on guitar were musically incorrect. So I think in a way I gave weight to Nick and his ideas and so when he'd say, "Let's do this," and Mick would say, "You can't do that," and I'd say, "So fuckin' what, that's irrelevant, the rules are what we make them, not what somebody else says." Also I showed Nick different ways of being able to write songs. Like, you could write songs with one chord or with one riff going all the way through them, which became a Birthday Party trademark. So I guess I gave Nick a crash course in doing things differently to the way he had been doing them.'[63]

'Through a mixture of ignorance and blind self-confidence I just did things 'cause I thought they sounded good,' Rowland said, 'and Nick would really encourage me to do things, like making ridiculous noises. I remember at one stage that every song Nick wrote for ages he would say, "And when it gets to this part I want you to make a really horrible noise; it has to be completely different from any horrible noise you've made in any of the other songs." So I used to rack my brains thinking of how I was going to make a noise singular to that song and not just the same as I'd done before.'[64]

Despite a deep competitiveness with Whirlywirld and Primitive Calculators, The Boys Next Door increasingly shared in the same aggressive attitudes to experimentation. The fractured warehouse surf sounds of Pere Ubu – and the squalling, brawling New York jazz punk of James Chance and the Contortions – worked as a visceral counterbalance to the more cerebral influences Nick was absorbing through John Nixon's Arts Projects and the poppier, even consciously kitsch synthesiser and imaginary film soundtracks emanating from the Clifton Hill Community Music Centre, which were likewise on the receiving end of Primitive Calculators' class-war hatred.[65] The Pop Group's ferocious blend of dub reggae production and free jazz punk continued to be an

Nick Cave and Mick Harvey, The Boys Next Door, Crystal Ballroom,
1979 *(courtesy of Phill Calvert)*

influence on The Boys Next Door. Out of this rapid realignment
of influences, Rowland increasingly believed the experimental
direction Nick was searching for could be achieved without
the use of synthesisers or taped effects. 'I think the beauty of
electric guitars is you can defeat their original purpose to a huge
extent ... they're incredibly live and you can get a lot of sounds
out of hitting them,' he said.[66]

Nick and Rowland's history with Ollie Olsen, meanwhile,
gave them more personal reasons to topple his avant-garde throne.
People could talk about the influences of Kraftwerk, Marxism or
French theories of structuralism and postmodern quotations all
they liked: this was also about who was going to be top dog on
the scene. 'The big difference between what we did and a band
like Whirlywird was that we'd progress quickly from one thing
to another, but it was a very natural, organic shift,' said Howard.
'Whereas Whirlywird would go, "Okay, now we're this."'[67]

Mick Harvey explains: 'As much as Nick says Rowland appeared fully formed – and Rowland's attitude certainly did – Rowland hadn't arrived fully formed musically. In the early days his playing had that trebly sound, that Television influence, the spindly riffs and strummy guitar. The signature things he started developing in 1979 were quite different to what he did at first. Because Rowland was put in the position of being the guitar player and not the singer, he started developing an invasive style of guitar playing that was like being a lead singer. By the time he got to the end of that with The Birthday Party he had sacrificed what he set out to do for himself. But that was his choice. He was the one who had put himself in the position of being frustrated.

'I can still remember when Nick had just written "The Hair Shirt". He'd written it on piano, it went round and round and round,' Harvey says of what he considers to have been an un-evolved work. 'Originally it had a "What Shall We Do with a Drunken Sailor" rhythm. It would have been developed from there by the band. We had this gig at the Kingston Hotel in Richmond. And Rowland hits a vibrato pedal through an amp, and it went into feedback and just took off. It was really fantastic. We'd been playing it live like that and had enough experience in that process to bring that into the recording.'[68]

Tracy Pew likewise noted, 'The songs are becoming more and more band compositions. Nick's offerings are getting less and less substantial. He doesn't bother composing them or arranging them.'[69] In the same interview with Clinton Walker, Nick agrees with Pew's observations, emphasising the open and organic process the band was developing. 'It's much easier, I think, to feel out an arrangement, as opposed to doing it beforehand,' Nick says. But no sooner is Pew openly identifying the outline of 'The Hair Shirt' as 'a sort of bastardised version of "What Shall We Do with a Drunken Sailor?"' than Nick cuts him off and reasserts his creative authority: 'I had the tune, and an idea of how the tune should be played, and the words, and the vocal melody.'[70]

Nick would have grown up listening to a Burl Ives album at the Cave family home. The answer to the sea shanty question 'What Shall We Do with a Drunken Sailor?' is him needing to drink the hair of the dog that has bitten him. It's interesting how Nick adapts this drinking song to his own purposes in 'The Hair Shirt'. Among heroin users, it's known that the better the quality of the drugs being injected, the more likely you are to itch due to the release of histamines into the body. Some addicts grow to enjoy the itch as a sign of first-class heroin; most cannot stand it. Nick had been bitten, all right, and 'The Hair Shirt' was an early creative response. In medieval religious history a 'cilice' or 'hair shirt' was made of coarse animal hair and worn close to the skin like a singlet. Its purpose was to cause great discomfort as punishment for one's sins. In more extreme cases, twigs and even wire were used, intensifying a mortification of the flesh redolent of the Crucifixion, with the express aim of helping a wearer move closer to God through constant penitence. In Molière's comic play *Tartuffe* (or *The Imposter*), however, the hypocritical and manipulative title character wears his hair shirt inside-out. Tartuffe's penance is witnessed by everyone, but never actually felt. Theatre audiences roared with amusement. Nick had seen an old German silent film version of the play not long after the death of his father.

Nick's best songs would evolve as highly personal explorations that took in wide-ranging influences and paradoxical associations like these. As he said upon the release of *Hee Haw*, which wouldn't occur until near Christmas 1979, 'A lot more of our own … obsessions, I suppose, are coming out.'[71] Nick was discovering a form he could write in, where all was revealed and everything was still a secret.

Crime
and
Punishment

MELBOURNE

1979–80

*H*ee *Haw* redefined Nick's vision for The Boys Next Door. 'When you're younger you tend to write more seriously. That's the way it worked with us,' he said at the time. By then a serious comedian, he spoke of trying 'as hard as I can to be as wicked and funny as possible with my lyrics', while taking pride along with the band in 'putting a certain amount of tension and unease in our music and doing it in quite original ways … I'd really hate our music to lose the potential for an audience to let itself go, but at the same time I would hate the music to be just that. I'd like to maintain the primal type of reaction to our music but at the same time I'd like them to get more out of it.'

Once again Nick disowned their polished beginnings. '*Door, Door* was controlled, tame, stilted, organised and heavily structured. This is a lot freer musically, more spontaneous, more chaotic, a lot more interesting. I'm very excited about it, very proud of it. It's far more adventurous; the band as a whole is becoming a lot looser. There is a lot more basic experimentation and improvisation, both on stage and on record.'[1]

Rowland Howard was similarly acidic about the band's start – '*Door, Door* was the last dregs of our Roxy phase' – while his enthusiasm for *Hee Haw* matched Cave's and proved to be more enduring. Tracy Pew secretly preferred *Door, Door*. At least it had songs you could sing along and drink to. He would be a lot happier once a more brutal aesthetic had forged them into The Birthday Party in the United Kingdom. Then he'd look back on their 'wank' days as The Boys Next Door and say, 'We became a pack of snivelling poofs.'[2] He was reacting to English critics who mistakenly associated the group with the New Romantic pop movement during their first year in London. Nick agreed with Tracy's revisionist judgement, confessing to *NME* journalist Barney Hoskyns in the same interview, 'I used to wear frilly shirts and pig tails before all that shit [the New Romantics].' Then he added, as his conversation closer on the subject of those one-time wimps The Boys Next Door, 'We made the unpardonable error of playing to the thinkers rather than the drinkers.'[3]

Cave would spend much of the coming decade demolishing past efforts in the wake of his latest creation, wiping the slate clean to exist in a perpetual Year Zero. By the time Howard started to question this constant push towards historical demolition and a life of pure exile, the guitarist would be well on his way to becoming a casualty rather than an ally. Nick had a way of not so much ending relationships as steadily grinding them down. Rowland carried the wound for a very long time. He would always feel Nick owed him something that was never paid back in full.

But fifteen years after *Hee Haw* galvanised their partnership in the studio with The Boys Next Door, Rowland S Howard could look back on happier days with Nick and say, 'When we made that record we were just trying as hard as we could to make a really adventurous record. After what we considered the humiliation of *Door, Door*, which is like the tamest thing possible, we just reacted very violently against that record in the most extreme direction away from that ... [*Hee Haw* is] like a psychedelic record. A Texas psychedelic record. Very naïve but very enthusiastic. I think it's really good personally.'[4] Rowland would also admit to just how much he and Nick were obsessed with Pere Ubu's *Dub Housing* and The Pop Group's *Y* at the time of making *Hee Haw*. 'You could hear the David Thomas influence in Nick's vocals on things like "[The] Hair Shirt". I think Nick tends to write off that period of the band because he finds it difficult to listen to himself being so blatantly influenced by somebody else. But it doesn't mean the whole thing has less value.'[5]

Nick's immediate lauding and then long-term disavowal of *Hee Haw* signal his preternatural awareness of the need to edit his canon from very early on. How much anger and chance drove him along that path, and exactly when Nick began asserting himself as the author of his own destiny, is hard to determine. Listening to the 2008 track 'We Call Upon the Author', you hear Nick attacking not only an absent God and his departed father for the loss of meaning in the universe, but mocking anyone who would demand similar explanations from him. He may as well have been shouting, 'I can't hear you!'

'I remember the [*Hee Haw*] sessions and the stuff we took to England, as well as *Prayers* [*on Fire*], as when we were the most creative and interesting as a working unit together,' Phill Calvert says. 'Everyone had input and all ideas were tried and tolerated in the interest of seeing how things would turn out. There was no friction between Nick and Rowland at this stage and stuff just flowed. We also worked incredibly fast – and mostly all night as well. I always thought Nick and Rowland's songs were incredibly complementary during this time.'[6]

It was Mick Harvey who was able to see the whole thing with equanimity after everyone's agendas dissolved and both The Boys Next Door and The Birthday Party were history. 'All of the late seventies was like our apprenticeship,' he says. '*Hee Haw* is definitely us dabbling with things and working out what to do with all that. "The Hair Shirt" is the most successful example. On *Hee Haw* it was the final track, the punctuation mark where we could say, "We've pulled it off here."'[7]

By then part of The Boys Next Door's inner circle, filmmaker Paul Goldman was often in the studio watching the band at work. He and Evan English's next project after 'Shivers' was meant to be a video for 'The Hair Shirt'. They collaborated with Nick on his idea to 'build a set that looked like *The Cabinet of Dr Caligari*'. New German Cinema was all the rage in Melbourne – directors such as Wim Wenders, Werner Herzog and Rainer Werner Fassbinder were making their mark – and with them came an interest in 1920s Weimar-era forebears such as Fritz Lang and FW Murnau. Nick was hooked on the noir-ish nightmare qualities of the old silent films. It took him, along with Goldman and English, almost a week to construct the set he envisaged for 'The Hair Shirt'. The band then stood and played amid a jigsaw townscape, with its claustrophobically tilted planes and distorted perspectives, while Goldman moved the camera around, he laughs, 'at insane speed'.

Hee Haw's experimental mood had infected the filmmakers, but the clip was too manic by half, and virtually unwatchable. Goldman had been suspended for breaching the copyright of Swinburne film school after releasing 'Shivers' for television broadcast. Despite that institutional rap across the knuckles, and the failure of 'The Hair Shirt' as a visual exercise, he and English

were on their way with Nick.[8] John Hillcoat, then an aspiring
editor and director at Swinburne and another future Cave
collaborator, describes how Goldman and English 'made everyone
see it was possible to get a film clip on national television with
"Shivers" and that you could do things outside of the accepted
industry fashion. It was very exciting to all of us.'[9]

Inspired by this community, Nick, Mick and Tracy
attempted to make a short film of their own. Based on The Doors'
'Unknown Soldier', it was meant to take place at a deserted beach,
but not even Nick could take his Jim Morrison fantasies that
seriously. The three of them gave up the project for an afternoon
drinking session. Even so, Nick and Mick's burgeoning interest
in filmmaking and film music was not about to abate.

The band was evolving rapidly. Jenny Watson's portraits
of the group during their Tiger Lounge days – an individually
framed set of what looked like Polaroid snaps done in gouache –
now seemed a far-sighted gesture barely two years on from their
teenage beginnings. At Nick's suggestion, Watson produced a
painting for him to use at the Crystal Ballroom during a 1979
performance of a song called 'Let's Talk About Art'. Watson titled
her work *An Original Oil Painting (Black and White) (For Nick Cave)*
and set the words in type across the canvas. Nick held the flag-
like, Mondrian-ish painting high above his head, threatening to
destroy it while he chanted and shrieked the song in a furious
manner that suggested art was in fact the last thing anyone here
wanted to talk about.

Despite the sophistication of the audience, Nick was well
aware of a deep anti-intellectual streak in Australia that could
masquerade as an abhorrence of pretension. The strange thing
about his performance was that Nick did not make it clear if he
was attacking this anti-intellectual streak or the pretensions of
those people in front of him, who very much wanted to have
that art conversation. Watson was renowned among the crowd,

The Boys Next Door at the Crystal Ballroom, performing 'Let's Talk
about Art'. Nick Cave holds Jenny Watson's painting *An Original
Oil Painting (Black and White) (for Nick Cave)*, 1979.
(John Nixon, courtesy of Anna Schwartz Gallery)

not just as a teacher and mentor to many of them, but also as
an artist on the cusp of international recognition, with gallery
shows opening in Berlin and London. The nervous tension in
the room as Nick manhandled the picture was palpable. No-
one was really sure what he intended to do with it, or what
he was saying. Nick would grow fond of leaving his riddles
unanswered, or of letting people live with what was only half
the picture until a day came when they saw the other side. On
the night in question he simply threw the painting from the
stage at the end of the song. It survived the hard landing and
skidded on into art history.

A host of young fashion designers were also taking notes at the live shows, drawn to the band's increasingly striking look, much of it put together by Anita Lane (with Lisa Craswell and Genevieve McGuckin contributing their own Gothic and impishly post-punk influences). Composed of many former audience members from these flamboyant Boys Next Door performances, the Fashion Design Council would launch itself at the Crystal Ballroom in 1983 as the defining guild for cutting-edge Australian fashion in the 1980s. Designer Alannah Hill mainly remembers Nick Cave striking poses in The Birdcage bar, sniggering and 'flicking wads of paper dunked in beer at me'. There's a suggestion that all he and The Boys Next Door stood for was a bullying form of cool that people were only too happy to be liberated from once the group left town. 'I thought they were dickheads,' she says.[10]

Phill Calvert insists that 'Nick had plenty of style before he met Anita'[11], but there's no doubting her originality in designing shirts made of everything from Christmas decorations to sleeping pills sewn into plastic pouches and attached to the material. Jenny Watson believes 'Anita basically set the scene for how people wanted to look. How people wanted to dress. And that included anti-glamour too. When all the girls started wearing little dresses and high heels like her, she turned up at the Crystal Ballroom wearing old school shoes and men's second-hand pants. She was … the sort of girl who could have done anything. Anything. I used to say to Anita, "What are you going to do for yourself?" That question of what women were going to do for themselves was a very big question in the culture. I think it's always very hard for women to be assertive and say, "I'm the genius." And I just think being in love with any of those guys in that band was a full-time job. She's a chanteuse, Anita. I love the records she ended up making with Mick Harvey.'[12]

'Anita was more than just a "muse",' Tony Clark agrees. 'She was like an image adviser to Nick, a collaborator. Anita was very funny, too; she had this oblique and interesting take on things. She understood kitsch, the power of dagginess. They all did. It was something distinctively Australian about them. Anita and Lisa Craswell both had this incredible feel for op-shop stuff – they were great stylists, and just effortless with it too. Effortless. There wasn't the pretentiousness of the European dandy in the aesthetics of what they created, but they were still contributing to the overall intensity of what was being projected. They were all steeped in these shitty children's TV shows too, the whole gang. It was really interesting. Instead of being embarrassed or running away from cultural phenomena that were debatable, they were very good at being able to use [them]. The English don't have that feel for the daggy that Australians have. English punk was more ruthless, in my experience. The scene here had a lot of sentimentality, not just violence. And it had a sense of comedy. Anita had that, Nick had it – it's one reason why they made such a great couple. Nick's got funny bones, as they say. I don't think the European understanding of his work has ever really got the comedic element that was there from the start and running through everything he did. Anita was able to tune in to that. Nick and Anita shared a language.'[13]

At this point, The Boys Next Door's squirting and writhing funhouse sound was exploding inside the pressure cooker of influences. Nothing about them was fixed, and it was in the live arena – rather than on record – that they rushed forth and thrilled an audience. The musical fracturing, song variety and intense delivery were capped by a haughty, sardonic presence that centred on Nick and Rowland as the city's definitive *poètes maudits*.

The Boys Next Door at the Tiger Lounge, 1979 *(Peter Milne)*

Bronwyn Bonney sums up their gravitational pull in this way: 'Our friends originally banded together under the punk-rock banner, but it was never about Mohawks and safety pins and working-class angst. The ideal was more genius-poet than tower-block delinquent. It was romantic, literate, aesthetic, all-dressed-up but raggedy too, subversive and inspired, hedonistic and out-on-a-bender.'[14]

Simon Bonney of Crime and the City Solution and Ollie Olsen of Whirlywirld could only look on as their mighty bands stalled while The Boys Next Door accelerated past them. Nick took an even more commanding stance on the scene. According to Rowland, there was a simple formula for what was going on: 'One of the reasons we progressed quickly is that we worked a lot.'[15] The Boys Next Door were playing three times a week, sometimes performing two sets a night, as well as continuing to record in the studio on midnight-to-dawn shifts, thanks to Keith Glass's largesse, all while assorted members also experimented in side projects.

Most of the other bands on the scene performed sporadically at most. Models were the only other group who were playing as often and showing similar determination.

The Boys Next Door encouraged a performance-art element to their shows by selecting opening acts such as Ron Rude and the multimedia artist Marcus Bergner, who had supplied the weirdly pagan and coded illustrations for the cover of *Hee Haw*. As part of the artwork for *Hee Haw*, Bergner, who was close to Rowland, drew a face with five sets of legs attached, each with a band member's name. Phill Calvert's legs are the only ones headed in the opposite direction. It suggests Calvert was a marked man from early on and that Rowland was already working on his demise.

A rowdy spirit of experimentation filtered into every decision, every move Nick was making in this company. On stage he sometimes played blurting sax like his latest, violently confrontational hero from the No Wave music scene in New York, James Chance. During a song called 'Safe House', Nick even strapped on an accordion to make a terrible, wheezing racket. Pew would ask, 'Where is the grinderman?' before they started playing the song. It was partly a dig at Nick turning them all into monkeys, if not 'poofs'. Tracy had that kind of thing down to an art, getting under Nick's skin in the same way he could rile the others: by using a barbed half-truth inside a joke. A lot of people would find it hard to tell if Tracy was being funny or on the verge of threatening them. Nick would absorb this humour into his own repartee, much as he absorbed everything else that came his way. But it always seemed as if Tracy had the edge on Nick. Always warm and a little melancholy in his recollections of Tracy Pew, Nick says, 'Like Anita, he did have an ability to eviscerate you with a single comment, sometimes just a single word. I'd be all dressed up to go on stage in a purple suit, thinking I looked pretty cool, and just as we were about to go on Tracy'd say, "Knock 'em dead, Willy Wonka."'

In the middle of recording *Hee Haw*, the band had spent a day crammed into Phill Calvert's bedroom, where they used their loyal roadie and sound mixer Steven 'Groper' Colgan's 4-track recorder to put down a host of other musical ideas and new songs, including Rowland's 'Scatterbrain'. Despite antagonism from Primitive Calculators and the Little Band scene towards The Boys Next Door, Groper was a key figure in facilitating these nights. He could quietly bring his equipment, experience and skills to The Boys Next Door, adding another edge to their live sound, just as Tony Cohen did in the studio.

In November The Boys Next Door combined with their erstwhile competitors Models to release a giveaway 7-inch single at the Crystal Ballroom, sharing a side each, respectively dedicated to 'Scatterbrain' and 'Early Morning Brain' – and the art of the modern hangover song. It arrived in a picture sleeve with the words 'A genuine relic from "the show"' typed across it. Nick was becoming so postmodern that even his sarcasm was ironic, posted in quotation marks to let you 'know'. 'Scatterbrain' would appear on a rare Missing Link cassette compilation known as *From the Archives* that same year.

Under the name Torn Ox Bodies, a rough anagram of The Boys Next Door, the band also recorded 'Show Me a Sign', an old punk tune of theirs with a bit of Saints attitude that Nick felt had real value. Surprisingly, they also did a cover of an Ollie Olsen song called 'Enemy of the State'. Caught in a cheap studio with two Italian brothers who were heavy-metal freaks in charge of the production, Nick and Rowland decided to turn a bad day to their advantage and wreak a little revenge on their annoying frenemy. Olsen's anarchist anthem was rendered as a laughably paranoid barricades melodrama, a dumb-ass *1984* theme. It was a measure of the band's prankster aesthetic, as well as of Nick's political ambivalence – and perhaps even gave a hint of his reactionary streak. Nick had always been inclined to vandalistic impulses with Tracy, and with Rowland's encouragement these were finding another form artistically.

Harry Howard saw a more playful side to it all. He recalls that when he was around ten years of age, he and his older brother 'just sat around making howling, weeping noises for twenty minutes. I do relate that to Rowland's guitar playing sometimes, that he had a sense of noise as opposed to what is thought of as music. And how he incorporated noise into music. So we would be rolling around laughing at the most absurd noises we could make, howling with exuberance.'[16]

In that same free spirit, Rowland, Mick and Phill went off to form a studio band of their own, with Keith Glass joining them on guitar. This unit played on 'Samurai Star', a single by the singer-songwriter Peter Lillie. An archetypal figure in the Carlton renaissance, Lillie wove a New Wave pop sound into something that was uniquely Melbourne-flavoured. Lillie was practically a wall fixture at the Crystal Ballroom. He was also struggling with a raging heroin habit, which had brought Nick and Rowland into his wisecracking poetic orbit. As part of R&B cult legends The Pelaco Brothers in the early 1970s, and again as a solo artist at the close of the decade, Lillie continued to exhibit a wry lyrical grasp of local culture. It plugged him into a milieu that embraced everyone from The Captain Matchbox Whoopee Band and Dave Warner's From the Suburbs to Mental as Anything and even Men at Work. Though less recognised than those names, Lillie was at the forefront of a sly new vernacular in Australian rock 'n' roll. Greg Macainsh of Skyhooks was the most famed exponent of this consciousness in Melbourne and, indeed, nationally at the time.

Across the Yarra River in Carlton, the figure who would ultimately prove to be Nick Cave's greatest competitor for the crown of Australia's rock 'n' roll poet laureate, one Paul Kelly, was being forged in a radically different furnace to that of the internationalist St Kilda scene. Nick was not a fan of that music, but he would take from the likes of Lillie and the entire Carlton scene – not least via his connections with Keith Glass and Stephen Cummings (another Pelaco Brothers alumnus) – an appreciation for its rapier lyrical thrust and colloquial assertiveness, not to mention its offbeat sense of humour with a sometimes knowing, druggy twist.

Bands in Carlton had discovered a joy in being Australian that was a million miles from any inflated chauvinism. While Lillie, Cummings and others were trying to uncover and articulate a fresh and more immediate sense of home, Nick was doing his best to hide or bury it in something abstract and mythical. Originality came from somewhere else – it seemed like the opposite of home to him, and yet everything he wrote was dogged by home's shadow.

Nick would ultimately translate his troubled identity fable into a faux-grotesque Deep South language that he'd picked up from reading William Faulkner and Flannery O'Connor novels. Birthday Party songs such as 'Deep in the Woods' and the Bad Seeds album *The Firstborn Is Dead*, not to mention his first novel, *And the Ass Saw the Angel*, are saturated in that shift. But his immersion in fantastically violent and mythic slices of Americana across the 1980s does not lessen the impact of those local artists defining themselves so vividly and originally in Carlton, often out of the same blues and roots music influences Nick would also adapt and melt himself into.

Eventually Nick would fight to have his Australian heritage acknowledged. It would prove to be a long journey back home for him. His 2007 induction into the ARIA Hall of Fame would mark the start of that rekindled hunger to be recognised for his true origins. It was perhaps a case of beginning to see himself again in a way he'd somehow become separated from. By then, he and Paul Kelly had emerged as the pre-eminent songwriters of their generation.

In mid-1979, Nick's Duromine-and-pizza-driven Little Cuties project had come to a grinding, noisy and anarchic halt. There were only so many PA systems left in Melbourne to blow up. Later in the year Nick persuaded The Boys Next Door (minus Tracy, who preferred to stand at the bar and drink) to form a backing band for Ron Rude. Nick dubbed them The Fucking Homos and assigned himself the task of playing loud, amateurish organ lines while Rude sought to transpose the sound and vision of Berlin-era Bowie onto songs about his life in outer-suburban Melbourne. Never far away from Rude's striving towards grandeur were the faint cackle and melancholy kitsch of a satirist such as Barry Humphries. On his more paranoid days Rude wondered why a band as good as The Boys Next Door indulged him. According to Rude, The Fucking Homos 'all swapped instruments to play ones they couldn't really play. Maybe that was why they did it?'

Rude says that Nick was the 'absolute stand-out figure' on the local scene: 'Punk rock was etched into his features. He was tall, and looked like a cross between Bryan Ferry, Chuck Berry, Genghis Khan and a drunken puppet from Pluto. He wore a white suit, like Bryan Ferry, flicked his leg up behind him like Chuck Berry, and had a wail like a banshee from hell. That wail is produced by inhaling against a Shure SM58 microphone, the standard rock microphone. If you imagine you are sucking the proverbial chrome off a doorknob, in other words, suck as hard as you can, then the diaphragm in the mike kinda implodes, producing the mother of all satanic screams. Possibly Nick Cave invented this, though I suspect he may have been informed by Lux Interior of The Cramps ... Correct me if I'm wrong.'[17]

It would take longer, however, before Rude understood how the dual energies of Howard and Cave were combining to forge something truly great. Rude writes: 'The BND with Rowland was a metamorphosis from a punk pop outfit to a noisenik post-punk horror show... [and it] was already fully formed by the time they arrived in England [later] as The Birthday Party. It's uncanny that it was so fast you could regard it as an overnight transformation, yet it was also so gradual that none of us locals here noticed. Who drove that evolution? Was it Rowland? Was Rowland like the monolith from *2001: A Space Odyssey* that by some strange power inspired the "cavemen" [no pun intended, but it sure reads as one] so that they would discover fire? You have to be fair to Nick, as well as Mick, Tracy and Phill. They were all up for some rapid evolution. Rowland told me that Nick once said to him, at rehearsal, "Last week you came up with a horrid, grating, otherworldly sound. Come up with an even more horrid, grating otherworldly sound that's different to that first one!" The drive toward intense originality was there.'[18]

Paul Goldman is unrestrained about Rowland's influence. 'I think he emboldened Nick,' Goldman says. 'But Nick is a consumer of anything and everything. He is the only person I have ever seen where everything – everything – is grist to his mill. Look at what happened to Phill Calvert, who was a very good drummer. His greatest crime was that he was a very sweet guy. He was a very faithful servant to that band and they treated him like a servant too in the end. They were very unkind. Keith Glass would end up getting an enormous caning as well. But the facts speak for themselves. No other band of their generation would spend so much time in the studio being so indulged, and Keith Glass supported that. He understood he was dealing with a ferocious talent that needed to be fed. He understood he was involved with a monster that needed to be indulged. Keith loved that band. And he was dedicated to letting them record and play and be as troublesome as they wanted. Can anyone imagine Nick was a sweet angelic boy? He wasn't. Rowland wasn't. Mick wasn't. Tracy wasn't. By the time they got to *Hee Haw* that band was shape-shifting so fast. Fucking hell, who else was gonna let them into the studio? They were just consuming ideas and people around them. It's not surprising they ended up consuming each other.'[19]

Nick and Rowland formed something of a Three Stooges act with Ron Rude on the few occasions they played with him. Rude remembers how they responded to crowd antagonism when they were on stage with him, Rowland sarcastically saying, 'Wait till you hear the next one,' and Nick chipping in with, 'It's even better.' Rude felt a little attacked from the front and the rear, but he took it on the chin and was delighted to have such a great band behind him. He'd always be a little upset that they never recorded with him later that year, despite promises made by Nick. Instead the band would take off for London and Rude would have to form another group and make his own way forward. Looking back at The Boys Next Door and their frenzy of activity at the time, at what eventually became of Nick, he is, however, only generous in his memories: 'All the less successful artists, the under-realised artists, the failed artists and the would-be artists who mope around under his enormous shadow, jealous of his success, wondering why they didn't get the same breaks, should reflect on whether they had anywhere near the degree of persistence, focus and determination as Nick Cave.'[20]

In her memoir *The After Life*, the poet and novelist Kathleen Stewart recalls being nineteen years old when she encountered Nick Cave. Two years had passed since the end of a previous relationship that had pushed her to attempt suicide, after which she'd been hospitalised for two months while being treated for depression. Six months later her father had killed himself.

When she met Nick at a gig in Sydney, the attractive energies between them were immediate and intense. 'We fell madly in love,' Stewart says. 'He carried me down to Melbourne a few nights later, sitting on his lap in the back of an off-white station wagon, driving down the Hume all night squeezed in with the rest of the band.'[21]

Stewart's poetic writing style is not served well by extracting her reminiscences from their larger, flooding context. Behind the youthful feeling, a genuine intensity is nonetheless palpable as the relationship accelerates:

> Nick tells me he loves me and he takes me to live with him in Melbourne. We sleep wrapped in each other breathing each other's breath. I am too frightened to make love with him in case he finds out there is something wrong with me or the way I do it or both. I am too frightened to tell him this. I am too frightened by the idea of what happened before happening again. I lie awake one night and I have a premonition. He will be unfaithful to me and I will not survive myself. I tell myself if I stay with him I will become silence. I will never fulfil myself to somehow find the truth and write it down.

Stewart continues in words that have the energy of being torn from a diary at the time:

> He has a girlfriend, who he expects to be happy that he has found me now. She smiles vaguely and follows us around. I find her hairs wound into my clothes. She is everywhere. He says it is okay with her. Why then does she come one night and lie beside our bed and cry? I cannot take it. One night when he is out I pack my small bag and leave. He is wretched, I later learn. He combs the city for me. I sit up

all night in bars and then all the next day in parks. I go to
an art gallery and sit, and then I board the night train back
to Sydney. I do not leave him an explanation. It is better
like this. I do not imagine his hurt and confusion. He is
better with her. I am saving my life.[22]

Trying to keep Anita Lane and Kathleen Stewart apart was a
nightmare for Nick's friends. Phill Calvert describes Stewart as
'a lovely person, great eyes, but she was a packet of trouble back
then'.[23] Her arrival in Melbourne, he says, 'caused a big ruckus'.
Drugs added to the complications of the love triangle, pulling
everyone into the emotional dramas around them.

Writing again from the present day, Stewart more calmly
reflects that, 'When Nick and I first met ... we both had dead-
white skin and blue–black dyed hair. His father, whose name [like
Stewart's father] was also Colin, had died a few months before.
Now that Nick is the same age my father reached, now that his
hair has receded into a pronounced M-line and he has grown a
moustache and likes to glower in photographs, I realise he looks
exactly like my father slimmed down.'[24]

Nick would pay belated tribute to Stewart in what became
a Birthday Party track called 'Kathy's Kisses'. The lyrics have
a creepy, insidious energy as her kisses become animate things
left on his floor that he must sweep away with the dust. Nick
becomes more manic as he repeats this haiku-like verse over and
over. The end result is so overtly sexual, as the exaggeratedly
sleazy saxophone lines being played by Nick himself suggest, that
it is laughable. The lustful voodoo of Screamin' Jay Hawkins
from the closing moments of 'I Put a Spell on You' is an obvious
inspiration for Nick's singing style. And yet despite the hint of
self-aware comedy, the song still sounds like an addiction of its
own peculiar and desperate kind. The entire scenario has the
shifting mood of a David Lynch film moment where you are

amused, turned on and disturbed all at once. Calvert thought the song cheap and ungracious, and told Nick so. His comments were not appreciated. The words are reproduced in Nick Cave's *The Complete Lyrics, 1978–2007*, but there's a sung couplet that is not included in the official print version. In those unpublished lines Nick refers repeatedly to the nature of Stewart's mouth as the song veers from wanting to escape the mythical Kathy's kisses to a wild and infinite need.

'Nick said, when I drily mentioned that song, that there were other Kathys he'd been involved with over the years. I give him poetic licence,' she says.[25]

He and Kathleen Stewart would meet a lot over the years in Melbourne, Sydney and London, though only as friends. But the relationship would be rekindled almost a decade later in Berlin, where he would once more play Henry Miller to her Anaïs Nin. All it took was a phone call out of the blue from Nick to reignite things and entice her to Berlin. Listening to Nick sing Tim Rose's 'Long Time Man' on *Your Funeral … My Trial* in 1986 would have been enough to give her strange chills.

The Boys Next Door spent a good deal of late 1979 and early 1980 going in and out of the studio thanks to Missing Link. In total they were involved in at least four major sessions at Richmond Recorders after completing *Hee Haw*. Tony Cohen said, 'Richmond Recorders was actually a pretty shitty studio but it was renowned [as] a great place to score drugs. You'd see traffic arrive like pizza delivery all the time, day and night. All the bands knew about it; that's why a certain type of band liked recording there.'

Speed was Cohen's drug of choice. It helped pull him through the long overnight recording hours – usually from midnight till 8 am. It was not uncommon to find a previously bug-eyed Cohen asleep under the mixing console after being worn down by a particularly gruelling series of late-night recording sessions. This practice of his was known to one and all as 'checking the wiring'. Phill Calvert says, 'Tony always had an answer or an idea to top anything we were coming up with, and he had the ability to get it onto the tape.' He describes one example of Cohen's wildly lateral approach during the *Hee Haw* sessions. It involved the engineer 'attaching a PZM mic to the glass of the control room and then getting Nick to sing at it from the other side'.[26]

Drugs are a nebulous influence on any artistic enterprise, but it's possible to hear the amphetamine corollaries in *Hee Haw*'s jumpy, driven attitudes and tendency to unhinge itself with relish. Not to mention fracturing heroin withdrawals. Another shift in The Boys Next Door's sound came with Keith Glass's purchase of Howard's dream instrument, a white 1966 Fender Jaguar guitar.[27] Howard had seen it hanging high in a shop, but the attendant refused to countenance hauling it down from the wall unless a sale was in the offing. Glass intervened and bought it for Rowland on the spot, with a deal to dock his gigging wages on a weekly basis to recover the cost. It was a barter the manager knew he would never make the guitarist follow through on. Glass was investing in something bigger. He was also settling into a paternal role for the band that was becoming quite intense.

Rowland had frequently invited his father, Jock, to come to see The Boys Next Door. Jock never showed much interest. The guitarist would be wounded early on when his father responded to yet another request from Rowland by asking his son, 'Why?' Jock explained he had already seen them perform once at the Tiger Lounge. True to his word, Jock would not see Rowland play again on a stage until his son's life was almost over. It's natural anyone dealing with this level of parental indifference, let alone a figure as hypersensitive as Rowland S Howard, might then gravitate towards the likes of Keith Glass. Nick was similarly susceptible to a kinship he'd felt more in the form of a competition, and then lost altogether that January with Colin Cave's car crash, and Phill Calvert's and Tracy Pew's experiences of violence and separation had alienated them from their respectively dominating and detached fathers. Even the emotionally reticent Mick Harvey was drawn in by Glass's energy. There was no-one the band trusted more that year, and for a brief moment the relationships were deeply felt indeed. The plain fact of it is The Boys Next Door were still just boys, and Glass was a man on whom they could depend.

The band had already worked hard through the recording of *Hee Haw* EP. Howard's playing, and more importantly his sonic palette, had advanced considerably with his new Fender Jaguar, and the group responded in kind. Glass was so excited by the outcomes – and by the energy flowing between their intense gigging and studio schedules – that he pushed The Boys Next Door to make even more demos. He saw how the recording process was opening up the band, and he actively sought to influence them further. 'I played them all this country music,' Glass said. 'Nick always liked Johnny Cash, the George Jones thing and the death-song thing; Gene Vincent's "Cat Man". When I was a kid it was the scariest song I'd ever heard. "What the fuck's a 'cat man'?" They grabbed that, they were grabbing things from anywhere and utilising them to their own purposes.'

As well as arranging interstate tours, including to Sydney and Adelaide, Glass got the band playing more regularly in the outer suburbs of Melbourne, where they continued to encounter uninterested audiences. It was a sobering experience. People would cheer when they finished their set at nightclubs, glad it was over. They returned to their fan base suitably chastened and toughened, and all the more restless to expand. 'From St Kilda to Carlton, though, they were the kings, the most popular, highest-drawing live band in the city,' Glass says. 'No-one could hold a candle to them on their home turf, not even Models, who were outwardly more successful.'[28]

Even so, the suburban shows made The Boys Next Door even more conscious of preaching only to the converted. This feeling was confirmed when they were invited to play bottom of the bill below Cold Chisel, The Angels and Flowers as part of a massive event at Festival Hall on 25 November 1979. The line-up cherry picked the most promising and commercially happening new generation of bands in the country. Unfortunately, when it came to The Boys Next Door, with the freakier treats of *Hee Haw* not yet released, the organisers were still responding to the relatively poppy promise of *Door, Door*. During the opening moments of their very first song at Festival Hall, a new one called 'The Friend Catcher', Nick says, something happened to Rowland's amp, pulling the band up to a halt. The audience thought this pretentious overture of sonic humming was the band's arty idea of a punk song. Nick laughs and says he could hear this slow rumble building until The Boys Next Door realised the entire hall of 10,000 people were booing at them. He answered the antagonistic crowd by smiling and striding over to the microphone to ask, 'Do you hate us as much as we hate you?'

From then on the booing never stopped. Glass was strangely impressed. 'Look, I've seen bad responses to bands. It happens to everybody and it had happened to The Boys Next Door before. But I'd never really seen a band booed so totally and so aggressively from start to finish like that. The crowd just hated them. Nick didn't seem to care at all. In fact, I think he got off on it.'[29]

Following their response to the debacle at Suicide, the creative battles over *Door, Door* and their departure from Mushroom, there was something contemptuous to the manner in which The Boys Next Door reintroduced themselves to the music industry with such an aggressively contrary EP as *Hee Haw*. 'Do you hate us as much as we hate you?' could have been their mantra.

If *Door, Door* was a flop commercially, *Hee Haw* really was career suicide. The album prompted industry consternation and horror as the kind of release only rock critics could possibly love. Nick told *Rolling Stone*, 'We let mistakes lie. We thought that added character.'[30] In *Roadrunner* he went further: 'Our records are never final statements. Other groups put out albums that are so definitive that they betray themselves, whereas we're really open-ended.'[31]

Missing Link only pressed a first run of 500 copies. Keith Glass was a dreamer, but he wasn't a fool. There was no rush to press more. Due to a printing error, the labels on each side were around the wrong way. The music seemed so off-the-wall it took a while for many listeners to notice. Fans rationalised it as another one of Nick and Rowland's Dadaist jokes.

A new band was being born, a band that acted as a law unto itself. Overseas groups such as Pere Ubu, The Pop Group and The Fall had arrived with the force of deconstructive genius, suggesting that the most unconventional of vocalists, the most uncomfortable of rhythms, the ugliest and most amateurish of sounds could build another musical world. These were the bands The Boys Next Door regarded as their true peers. *Hee Haw* was all about that push and strain for an international style, precipitating an increasingly confrontational attitude from Nick towards audiences who failed to respond to such ambitions. The die was cast: fans had to come with them. The Boys Next Door would not work to please anyone. Sitting in his bedroom at home, Nick no doubt crossed that concern off his list of band weaknesses. Things were improving.

And Nick's confidence as a singer was building. Michael Hutchence, for one, was blown away by Nick Cave's presence on stage. He was then the singer for an unknown band from the northern beaches of Sydney. Like The Boys Next Door, INXS had formed as a schoolboy unit, making their official debut at exactly the same time, August 1977. Unlike The Boys Next Door, INXS did not immediately gain attention and a recording contract. By late 1979, however, they were poised to make their first single at last. Always hungry to take in what was happening, Hutchence made a point of frequenting the Crystal Ballroom whenever he visited Melbourne. Though they did not know each other, he and Cave shared a mutual passion for sixties group The Loved Ones, whose front man, Gerry Humphrys, was the last word in coiled dynamism on Australian stages. Even on record, Humphrys' emphatically theatrical and sexual baritone was a thing to behold. Both Hutchence and Cave took a lot from Humphrys' bluesy, expressive way of possessing a song and twisting a lyric into a limbo between seduction and menace. It might even be said Hutchence and Cave became a little trapped in the former and latter territories. Both were destined to wish for a touch of what the other had when they finally became friends in London decades later, though in Michael Hutchence's mind Nick would always be the bigger talent.

'In the good old, bad old days, when Australia was way ahead of the rest of the world in music, the Boys were in front of everybody,' Hutchence observed. 'I remember seeing them in Melbourne's Crystal Ballroom, which was sorta like CBGBs or The Marquee. The stage was the size of a couch and there was Nick shaking it up. Johnny Rotten was a clown compared to what he was doing, he was so wild! And the music! I'd never experienced anything like it!!!! This sort of haunting, knife-stuck-between-your-ribs music. It was like highbrow meets lowbrow in a beautiful nightmare, but a nightmare where you go, "Oh

I'm scared! But actually could I have that again!!!" He was a big influence on me. Whaddya mean it doesn't show?!'[32]

Dolores San Miguel understands the comparison entirely, though many would at the time see Michael Hutchence and Nick Cave as more like opposites in their careers and their presence. It's perhaps easier now to appreciate them as the greatest front men of their era in Australian music. Dolores certainly remembers that from the very start with Nick, vividly describing the experience of him walking on stage with The Boys Next Door at the Crystal Ballroom as 'like a cold blast of air that makes your heart jump'.[33]

If *Hee Haw* was deemed an adventurous misstep, it nonetheless opened the doors to a stubbornly idiosyncratic run of singles that freed the band from their provincial horizons. 'Happy Birthday', 'Mr Clarinet' and 'The Friend Catcher' were recorded in Melbourne, with Tony Cohen again engineering. All were features of The Boys Next Door's live set in late 1979, though the latter two songs would not be released till they were making themselves known as The Birthday Party in England in 1980. 'I think they capture a part of the band that we moved away from,' said Rowland. 'It was a transitional phase. They were funky, but at the same time it's very light and nimble. It's not at all heavy or plodding. The songs are really short and concise even though we were experimenting in the confines of basically pop music.'[34]

Keith Glass was given a production credit on *Hee Haw* and these ensuing singles, but on later re-releases of the material his name would be deleted, an action he describes as 'churlish and petty, but a measure of what they could be like once you got on the wrong side of them. You were just written out of the story.'

Glass still exudes a mix of frustration and pride regarding his associations with a band he says wiped him out in more ways than one. There's an air of triumph as he recounts how he announced to leading industry figures in Australia in 1979 that The Boys Next Door were on their way to the United Kingdom and destined to be regarded in the same breath as The Easybeats. 'People thought that was a bit strong and they laughed at me, but time has proven me right. Weirdly, all the people in the industry that I was trying to get interested in The Boys Next Door were actually all five years younger than me. In spite of the falling-out we had, I don't regret a thing. The Birthday Party's success, Nick's success as a solo artist – it vindicates everything I tried to tell people back then. I actually don't have any problems with Nick anyway; the last time I saw him was in 1988 and he needed money and I gave him $5000 and he took it and went away. It's Mick who always complains and keeps on complaining – about money I never had and money that never existed. But that's who Mick is and that's what Mick does: he whinges.'[35]

Nick Cave with The Boys Next Door, Crystal Ballroom, 1979
(courtesy of Phill Calvert)

Mick Harvey admits Glass did get them to England exactly as he had promised. Though not in anything like the conditions they may have hoped for. 'It's really hard to describe this air about Keith. He can be very convincing.' Stated in the present tense over thirty years later, there is an immediacy to Harvey's words that is a sign of how persuasive and charismatic Glass could be.

It was only with Mick Harvey holding the wheel as manager during the 1980s – a role that would be forced upon him by circumstance – that the band's course began to sail straight. Not that the unruly crews Harvey was given in the form of The Birthday Party, and then The Bad Seeds, ever gave him much of a hand when it came to stability. Let alone having Nick as the nominal ship's captain, a drug-spun Ahab running amok on stage and off.

Nick Cave takes a less conciliatory view of his old manager, though he can admit that it was never easy. 'It's true Keith helped us out a lot at first. And he did introduce us to a lot of cool music He says he never ripped us off, I know, but ...' Nick takes a long breath and starts to laugh.

The story has got so old, the people involved can almost remember how it was when they first liked each other. Until they remember why their relationships ended. Is it any wonder that spiral on the belly of Alfred Jarry's Ubu Roi character became such a potent symbol for the band and everything they stirred up around them?

Over August and September 1979, The Boys Next Door had returned to the studio to record 'Hats on Wrong', 'Guilt Parade', 'Riddle House' and 'Happy Birthday'. 'Guilt Parade' was a driving and dramatic pop-rock song, but it lacked the swing and intense presence of 'The Hair Shirt'. Rowland's words are typically oblique, though there's an implied scenario of drug taking. The lyrics of 'Guilt Parade' also sound like faint imagistic precursors to Nick's later and better song 'The Friend Catcher'. 'Riddle House' had a herky-jerky rhythm that could prove wearing, another of Rowland's self-consciously off-centre musical contributions.

'Hats on Wrong' highlighted Nick's similar taste for absurdist boofhead scenarios and the band's interest in what might be described as 'drongo jazz', treading the line between an avant-garde style and the purposely ridiculous. It was 'Happy Birthday' that marshalled the nervy, clattering music, the cryptic lyrics and the increasingly dark humour into a hysterical balance. As 'Happy Birthday' draws to a close, what sound like clap sticks give off a harsh, spacey rhythm. They are in fact handclaps that Tony Cohen has jacked up the treble on, then soaked in reverb to create a cold metallic edge that sounds at once Aboriginal and industrial. The song was another breakthrough for the band. 'It was really unusual,' says Mick Harvey, 'because Nick and Rowland wrote the lyrics for "Happy Birthday" together, and I did the music. It was the first time that had happened with Nick and Rowland, and it would be the last time too.'[36]

The guitarist and singer had indeed got so tight that even Nick's penmanship appeared to be merging with Rowland's. Critic and biographer Robert Brokenmouth claims that 'during this period Nick stopped using his favoured narrow-nibbed rOtring Rapidograph pen and took up a blotchy "dip into ink" fountain pen. Nick wasn't intending tidy copperplate or polite calligraphy, quite the opposite.'[37] Bruce Milne noticed it too at the time – and reflected on it again after Howard died at the end of 2009. 'When I see Nick's writing it often reminds me of Rowland's: that handwriting that is like early Andy Warhol mixed with Gerald Scarfe and Ralph Steadman. A Jack the Ripper style that looks like an intelligent person who is a bit psycho.'[38]

It was in this 'psycho' hand that Nick scrawled the lyrics all over the front cover of 'Happy Birthday'. The song would be released as a giveaway single at the Crystal Ballroom on 16 February 1980, just two weeks before the band's planned departure for the United Kingdom. Howard would remember people openly scoffing when he told them they were going to London. 'Their attitude was, you can't honestly expect anyone over there would be interested in you!'[39] Clinton Walker in *RAM* described the 'Happy Birthday' single which was backed on the flipside with 'Riddle House' – as 'The Boys' parting gesture to their Australian fans ... a culminative statement – thrusting, splintered music of irony, melodrama and the absurd.'[40] The song demonstrates a malevolent, if still rowdy, sense of humour – and something of the old private-schoolboy nastiness for which the group were already known. Once more there's a Punch and Judy feel to this, a slapstick quality to the delivery. And with that a strengthening sense in 'Happy Birthday' of the performative quality in Nick's writing, of a song not delivered straight, but presented as a story from an unstable and unreliable narrator.

The lyrics are a twisted account of a boy's eleventh birthday party. They list an array of gifts, from a punch in the belly to a samurai sword. To free things up, Howard had originally encouraged Nick to improvise on the words he had written, but Nick's guiding consciousness inevitably pushed the lyric back towards a narrative form despite the seemingly dislocated images he stacked together. Tracy Pew possessed a samurai sword at home on his bedroom wall. This and other details imply the song is actually an account of the band members' various birthday gifts, coalescing around a nightmare of what should be – but are clearly *not* – many happy returns. Nick sings obsessively of a chair that is his own special surprise: a chair that can count. Then he barks to eleven crazily like a dog parodying intelligence and desiring to please. The red chair Nick helped to steal was obviously playing on his mind. At twenty-two, he was exactly twice the age of the protagonist of 'Happy Birthday', who is half-delighted and half-horrified by the special throne he receives. Nick's bark gives the song a demented, if comical, edge, further intensifying a mood of unease and bullying. Maurice Sendak's children's book *Where the Wild Things Are* springs to mind as a parallel and partially inspiring entity, with its covert message of a boy's anger and loneliness released by an otherworldly parade of anarchic caricatures. Rowland would look back at 'Happy Birthday' and many other songs he and Nick wrote in their youth – of which 'Shivers' was the benchmark – and quietly observe, 'Of course, humour is a form of defence.'[41]

As for the red chair that had caused them all so much trouble, the story was always that 'Pierre's girlfriend' had smashed the window that night. Ask Pierre, Mick Harvey, Genevieve McGuckin or Nick Cave who that mysterious girlfriend was and no one wants to give an answer. Rowland never did while he was alive. It's such a petty crime you'd think it mattered little, but of course the repercussions and timing were enormous in Nick's life and in many ways determined the direction he would take.

Inevitably you start to run through the names of the women who were close to Nick at the time, wondering who it was. But something in the details never quite rings true. What kind of young woman would smash the window of a tradesman's vehicle and then the larger plate-glass window of an apartment block and have the strength to carry a large, heavy lounge chair the distance she, Pierre and Nick managed before raising it and throwing it over a fence? It sounds more like the kind of thing Tracy Pew would do, someone who already had form when it came to smashing windows and taking what he liked, when he liked. By the time the police arrived, Nick would have realised that another such conviction might well have meant prison time for his friend. If that's true, the sacrifice was a measure of how much Nick loved Tracy. And it gives new meaning to the song 'Happy Birthday', with its list of childish gifts and the suffering they symbolised, and to the origins of what would become The Birthday Party.

As the countdown to leave grew closer, the band continued working with Tony Cohen at Richmond Recorders. Over January and February 1980 they recorded Nick's latest songs, 'Mr Clarinet' and 'The Friend Catcher', as well as Rowland's 'Waving My Arms' and an update of Gene Vincent and the Blue Caps' 'Cat Man'. Though the band was keen to develop originals, Mick Harvey says the cover was done at Nick's particular insistence. 'Cat Man' followed Van Morrison's 'Gloria' as another influential song that set Nick thinking about aural tattoos of desire, where each letter of a word becomes an anthemic thrust into the audience. Lyrically and, more importantly, vocally, Nick was interested in the way a single word could break down and mutate while retaining traces of its meaning or intention in nothing but sound. He continued to handwrite his lyrics in a demonically inky style; a shift back to working on a typewriter in the mid-1980s would intensify an almost chemical interest in words as compounds as he punched out each key. Nick finally consummated the ideal of an erotically charged, letter-by-letter chant in his song 'Loverman' (1994): 'L is for LOVE, baby / O is for OH yes I do / V is for VIRTUE, so I ain't gonna hurt you / E is for EVEN if you want me to …'[42]

The Boys Next Door played two nights in a row at Hearts in Carlton immediately before they were due to fly out to London. After the second show they spent the rest of the evening in the studio with Tony Cohen, mixing 'Mr Clarinet'. Down to their very last hours in Australia, all their energy was poured into the music. They had never stopped. If anything, the band's creativity and work ethic had intensified.[43] After completing 'Mr Clarinet', the band drove home in the dawn and packed hurriedly.

Missing Link had paid for a bus to take everyone to the airport, but only Tracy Pew boarded it with a group of close friends and fans. 'It was a sweet idea,' says Phill Calvert, but the rest of the band members opted to travel with their families.[44] While his mother was driving the car to the airport, Nick looked out the window to see a sign at the turn-off indicating where the highway continued on to Sunbury, the site for Australia's definitive musical festival of the early to mid-1970s. Sunbury had crowned everything from the crunching high-volume boogie of pub rock to the last idiosyncratic gasps of the Carlton sound in the glam-pop form of Skyhooks. The Boys Next Door had never fitted into these competing streams of brutish suburban hedonism and questing cultural identity. His band looked out into the world instead, searching for a sound and an audience to call their own. Now they were going to find out if there was an audience overseas waiting for them.

Defunct as a music festival, the very word 'Sunbury' evoked how quickly many local heroes faded, an irony that did not escape Nick. Heavy rains and Deep Purple's lavish performance fee had sent the iconic festival bust in 1975, though not before AC/DC had joined their road crew in a legendary stage brawl with the overseas visitors, whose indulgences had prevented them from performing afterwards. AC/DC's attitude yielded its own international rewards in the long run. Something about their yahoo toughness and humour excited Nick in much the same way The Saints had. You had to be ready to take the fight to anyone.[45]

At Tullamarine Airport people were crying in small mobs at the terminal as girlfriends, family and fans said their goodbyes to

The Boys Next Door. Someone gave the band red carnations to pin to their lapels as they passed through the departure gate. It made them look like ratty high-school debutants: Nick and Tracy were barely twenty-two years old, Mick and Phill still twenty-one, Rowland just twenty and so birdlike you'd think he had fallen from a nest.

Keith and Helena Glass felt as if they were throwing their own children into the void. They'd spent every dollar they had to get the band onto the plane. It would cost the couple even more dearly than they imagined. For now, they felt so sick they could barely speak. Phill Calvert writes, 'Helena Glass told me that she and Keith cried on the way back from the airport thinking, "What have we done to those poor kids?" It was the best thing that ever happened to any of us ... We would never have got on that plane at that point in time, in music ... There wouldn't be the Nick Cave that we know today, if it wasn't for Keith. Thank you, Keith Glass.'[46]

At a stopover in Perth, Western Australia, the band were told the coffin of AC/DC's singer, Bon Scott, had just passed through the terminal on its way to being cremated in Fremantle. Scott's death from 'acute alcohol poisoning' was understood to have occurred when he choked on his own vomit while passed out in the back of a friend's car during a sub-zero London winter's night. The return of this fallen warrior's body was of immense concern to the whole nation, but Scott's family insisted on keeping it a private affair. His gravesite would nonetheless become the most visited in all of Australia. 'It felt kinda strange for us,' Mick Harvey says. 'Not that we ever compared ourselves to AC/DC. We were just a bunch of shit-kickers compared to where they were at by then. But it was a funny connection, crossing paths like that. February twenty-ninth it was; I'll never forget it. A leap year, a leap day.'[47]

Something about this moment, the build-up to the trip and the endlessness of the flight prompted the band to consider

The Boys Next Door at Tullamarine Airport with Missing Link founder
and band manager Keith Glass, 29 February 1980
(Helena Glass; courtesy of Phill Calvert)

Wearing red carnations, the band head for the departure gate at
Melbourne, en route to London, 29 February 1980.
(Helena Glass; courtesy of Phill Calvert)

changing their name. It was an opportunity to become something new – 'to draw a line the sand', as Mick Harvey puts it. They'd toyed with calling themselves The Birthday Party at a gig before they left. But the idea had remained vague. Nick initially preferred The Friend Catchers, a phrase Anita had used to describe and title one of Nick's most impressionistic new songs. Though there was no such phrase in the lyric, Anita had a way of seeing into what Nick was doing and capturing it in a finger snap, sometimes acerbically – in this case a lyric about heroin use. It didn't sound quite right to the others as a band name, though. Later, Rowland, Mick and Nick would each claim they had been the first to seriously promote the idea of calling themselves The Birthday Party. The reference to 'Happy Birthday' is obvious, and the Harold Pinter overtones immediate. 'We were quite obsessed with a film of it [Pinter's play *The Birthday Party*], a Billy Friedkin thing that was on late TV all the time,' says Mick Harvey. 'It has this great opening sound with a tracking shot, the sound of tearing paper.'[48]

The film adaptation of Pinter's play *The Birthday Party* (1968) depicts a one-time piano player who appears to be hiding out at an English seaside boarding house after an unnamed crime or shameful act. Caught up in an increasingly sinister atmosphere, he is forced to partake in a birthday he keeps trying to explain is not his. This sustained and sadistic joke ends with him being taken away from the boarding house by two characters who may be gangsters preparing to execute him and whose actions are veiled in the mundane intentions of a few lads who've invited him to 'go out for a while' and continue the celebrations. Both the play and the film, for which Pinter also wrote the script, ooze with the writer's themes of guilt and retribution, not to mention director William Friedkin's flair for supernatural intensities.

These energies were very easy to relate to for a piano-playing lad on the lam like Nick Cave. As if to seal the deal, the gangsters in the film reminded Nick of the cops who'd arrested him for stealing that chair not so long ago in St Kilda.

Mick Harvey says he and Rowland talked with Nick on the plane about their new name and what The Birthday Party symbolised for them: 'No band that we were aware of had given themselves a name that inferred that they were an event in themselves. We kinda liked that. It's always had that aspect to me.'[49]

'Happy Birthday' would become the earliest of Nick Cave's songs to gain a place in *The Complete Lyrics*. Everything written prior to it is dispensed with as unworthy juvenilia. The song remains a case study for Nick's nascent mash-up of literary references with autobiographical hints. This may explain why he was oddly evasive when talking about it later: Nick would tend to avoid emphasising the significance of the Pinter play or film when discussing how the band name was invented. But if not directly inspired by it, 'Happy Birthday' was thematically close enough to Pinter's work to warrant Nick and Rowland referring to the song as 'The Birthday Party' when they first wrote it.

Later, Nick preferred to speak of scrambled associations he had made with *Crime and Punishment*, and a wake scene from the novel, which he had misremembered as a birthday party. This was a very unlikely mistake, given Nick's multiple readings of the book. Like so many of his habitual twists in telling a story, it's the truth wrapped inside a lie.

Mick Harvey remembers Nick becoming 'totally obsessed by *Crime and Punishment* again' in 1979. Nick had been rereading Dostoyevsky's novel slavishly, seeking meaning, if not quite consolation, in its pages. It does not take a psychology degree to equate Raskolnikov's murderous acts, ensuing guilt and compulsive need to confess with Nick's own existential predicaments in relation to his father's death and the nature of his creative acts in public. This contrary motion would see Nick burst forth violently as a songwriter and a performer, only to retreat in denial or confusion – not to mention a good deal of haughty resentment – depending on how he was being received.

A close examination of the long build-up to the relevant scene in *Crime and Punishment* shows how complex Nick's biographically laced literary associations could be. It begins with Raskolnikov befriending a drunken public servant in a bar by the name of Marmeladov, whose name not uncoincidentally echoes the word 'marmalade'. Despite Marmeladov's filthy, even repulsive, appearance, he retains his middle-class pride and an unsettling theatricality with it. 'But there was something very strange in him; there was a light in his eyes as though of intense feeling – perhaps there were even thought and intelligence, but at the same time there was a gleam of something like madness.'[50] The gleam of something like madness ... it's a description that could fit Nick at his performing height, or even, for that matter, the extremes of his father's vocational zeal.

For all his self-recrimination, Marmeladov is happy to let his wife and daughter sacrifice themselves to his drunken compulsions. Raskolnikov helps him home and, in a fit of pity, leaves money behind for the family. His mindset takes a misanthropic spin afterwards as the encounter regenerates his contempt for all human weakness, especially his own. Marmeladov confirms a belief in Raskolnikov that he must renounce his compassionate nature to become a higher man, superior to the common and the weak, and justified, therefore, in doing anything he wishes, including committing a murder to advance his own interests and live freely. After the trauma of a violent crime that was supposed to release him into this mastery, Raskolnikov comes across Marmeladov again, who has fallen down drunk in the street and been crushed beneath a horse-drawn carriage. Raskolnikov sees to it that the dying man is taken home. In these persistent gestures of compassion there are hints of redemption for both men, but the darker, greater truth is that Marmeladov is first a warning and then a premonition for Raskolnikov. Good and bad are twinned together; Jekyll and Hyde are never separated. The funeral feast for Marmeladov is, accordingly, a grotesque affair, a Last Supper in reverse. Marmeladov serves as a Christ-figure who dies not to save Raskolnikov from his sins, but to unmask his delusional belief in a brutal and transcendent will: a will that is caught up in compulsions that will prove Raskolnikov's undoing. Nick had locked on to Raskolnikov's 'superior man' philosophy before his father's death to justify his own inflamed pride and rebellious ambitions; afterwards, he saw things with different, but perhaps even darker, eyes. Raskolnikov was more like Marmeladov than he ever imagined. Nick was likewise still his father's son.

Any suggestion that such story elements in *Crime and Punishment* could end with Nick confusing the wake with a birthday party only reveals how attuned he was to the driving forces behind what was happening to him. In the long run, the title of a solo album, *Your Funeral ... My Trial* (1986), would make such double-edged associations explicit. Nick nonetheless claims, 'I really wasn't that conscious of how much it was influencing me at the time.' If that's even half-true, his unconscious must have been on fire. As Nick would often assert over the years: 'My father read the murder scene in *Crime and Punishment* to me when I was young. He told me to study it as a great piece of writing. Which I did do.' This study would continue to infiltrate everything from Birthday Party songs such as 'Deep in the Woods' to Nick Cave and The Bad Seeds' 'The Mercy Seat'.

There's another level to all this that is broadly true for Nick and his formative interests as a lyricist. It involves what can only be described as the aural intensity of *Crime and Punishment*, an ongoing sense of being able to hear Raskolnikov's voice, the fevered workings of his mind and those of his antagonists as they rise up from the page. Dostoyevsky sustained this burning orchestral intimacy across most of his work – a sense of being

overcome by the permeating force of others, and by what may
have been one and the same thing, the ferocious nature of his
own consciousness, as embodied in his vivid characters and their
capacity for a nihilism and evil well beyond his own Christian
morality. Dostoyevsky hears and feels the voices of the many.
At times this can be so intense it becomes a conflagration of
everything and everyone around the great Russian author as he
writes the people and the times into his work.

When asked if 'Mr Clarinet' or later songs like 'Sonny's
Burning' and 'Gun' were about people he knew, Nick would be
evasive. But Rowland was happy to say the songs were, almost
literally, 'his friends'. Nick jested they were his 'little bedfellows',
to which Rowland added 'friends who live in his closet'.[51] The
songs, their characters and the real people they were based on
were no longer divisible.

So much of Nick's art had sprung from the communal
wildness of the Crystal Ballroom scene in Melbourne, and the
tumult of his own life story all the way from Wangaratta to the
present moment of leaving. What could London possibly add to
that? How might things change for him again? Nick says he was
not feeling the least bit blue when he hugged his mother farewell
and kissed Anita Lane goodbye at the airport in Melbourne. The
town – indeed, the whole country – had become a dungeon. He'd
formed a gang around him and was making his escape, off at last
to storm another world and make it recognise him. 'Everything
I held precious in music, except for The Saints, seemed to be
across the water and waiting for me somehow. I had an idea it was
gonna be paradise.'

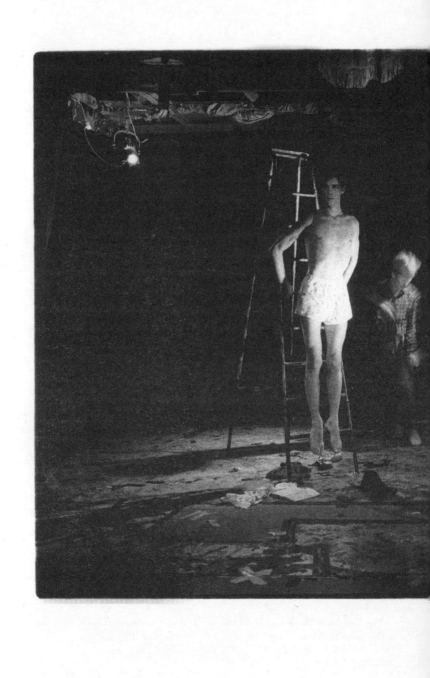

The Boys Next Door returned from London after a year away, reincarnated as The Birthday Party, here preparing to film the video for 'Nick the Stripper' at a rubbish dump. Cover try for *Prayers on Fire*, 1981. *(Peter Milne)*

The
Singer
and the
Song

I'm in a conversation inside a car inside a song. I say we're inside a song – as much as a car or a conversation – because the lyrics to 'Higgs Boson Blues' seem to define what Nick Cave and I are passing through as we cruise on up a highway north of Sydney towards a show with his band, The Bad Seeds, in the coastal steel town of Newcastle.

In the song, Nick Cave fantasises about taking a car journey to Geneva, where scientists anticipate an experiment that will isolate the Higgs boson or 'God particle' that is the subatomic building block of all matter. A litany of historical and pop-cultural images are mashed together into the archetypal 'hero's journey', in this case a road trip through a universe being steadily emptied of all spiritual illusions.

Right now, I feel strange echoes of the same dark road that he sings about, half-inviting, half-swallowing us, of all those 'tableaus of spiritual collapse' – as Nick has previously described 'Higgs Boson Blues' to me – fleeting past the corners of our eyes in new ways on this oppressively warm afternoon.

It's about a year and a half since Nick and Susie's fifteen-year-old son Arthur died. Nick's made the documentary *One More Time with Feeling* about the recording of his album *Skeleton Tree* in the wake of that tragedy. Now he is beginning to accept dealing with the media again, and I am invited along with photographer Bleddyn Butcher on the ride north to help in this process. As usual, it's another Australian summer tour for The Bad Seeds: in the last four decades Nick has rarely missed a chance to be with his mother, Dawn, on the anniversary of Colin Cave's death. He really is the good son.

For all his recent talk of no longer writing narrative lyrics, the truth is Nick Cave is still telling us stories in songs such as 'Higgs Boson Blues' and eerie stunners such as 'Magneto'. They're just more expressionistic, subconscious, dreamier and deeper, maybe, than before. It's certainly interesting to hear Cave admit, 'I can't write a song that I can't see.'

He nonetheless insists, 'I haven't much time for overtly narrative songs these days. It has felt hugely restrictive for some time. The idea that we live life in a straight line, like a story, seems to me to be increasingly absurd and more than anything a kind of intellectual convenience. I feel that the events in our lives are like a series of bells being struck and the vibrations spread outwards, affecting everything, our present and our futures, of course, but our past as well. Everything is changing and vibrating and in flux.

'So, to apply that to song writing, [in] a song like "I Need You", off *Skeleton Tree*, time and space all seem to be rushing and colliding into a kind of big bang of despair. There is a pure heart, but all around it is chaos.'

As it so happens, Newcastle is my hometown and the first place I ever saw the much-hyped Birthday Party, who'd only just changed their name from The Boys Next Door and returned from England in late 1980. I hated them, Nick most of all, whom I regarded as a poseur and someone who held the audience in contempt. It was clear none of the band wanted to be in Newcastle at an RSL, playing to a half-empty room. Musically, they were hedged between the power pop of *Door, Door*, the Jarry-esque experimentalism of the *Hee Haw* album and a pale vein of primitivism yet to open up with their *Prayers on Fire* recording. It's likely Newcastle was just a warm-up show, testing out the old and the new and deciding what they would do next.

Out of anger as much as anything else, I wrote one of the first rock journalism articles I ever had published for a great new underground arts magazine called *The Virgin Press*. I was very much under the sarcastic sway of *NME* writers such as Julie Burchill and Tony Parsons, and the destroy-to-create ethos still resonating out of punk. My review included a sneering line that was pulled out and used as a headline: 'Screaming Tom Waits and the Cacophony Kids'. I didn't tell Nick about that review when we met, and I always worried it might crop up in some obscure Google search by him one day. It's just not the kind of thing you tell someone when you're about to start writing their biography.

Barely a year or so later, in early 1982, I saw The Birthday Party in full bloom at a venue called the San Miguel Inn in Sydney, and found myself terrified by the tension in the room. There was a crackling sense of violence in the air, actual as well as artistic. I did my best not to catch anyone's eye as I moved about, seeking out a safe corner and then staying there. A young band called Hunters & Collectors were the support act, playing epic rock songs pierced by clanging industrial percussion on gas cylinders. They were like some heavyweight boxer flooring us with metallic punches that came slamming in from across a vast landscape. In the media, Nick had warned everyone, 'Hunters and Collectors will blow us off stage.' It seemed he might have been right about that. But then came The Birthday Party.

The only word that defines how they were that night is 'demonic'. Leaving the San Miguel Inn, I questioned the morality of the band's right to exist, but not their power. And they were only at the midpoint of their reincarnation. Bleddyn Butcher tells me it was around this time that the editor of the *NME* began to argue against giving the band publicity in the United Kingdom because they were 'evil'.[1] There's quite a funny interview with Bobby Gillespie of Primal Scream, in which he reminisces about seeing The Birthday Party. 'I'm not going to say "scary",' he says, then laughs and continues, 'but … ' The rest is left to your imagination.[2]

I genuinely felt as if I had entered into the music of the Inferno. And, yes, an evil heat wafted off their performance and into my body like nothing I'd experienced before. As I look back on that night, filmmaker Paul Goldman's comment about The Boys Next Door consuming everything around them to become The Birthday Party, and then consuming themselves in double-quick and ferocious time, seems especially apt.

Much later, in Wangaratta, I sat in the park beneath the giant tree that Nick and Bryan Wellington and Eddie Baumgarten had climbed. The tree beneath which Nick had sat and talked with Anne Baumgarten about what was inspiring him. The wind shook its mighty trunk; I stayed there a long while and felt its trembling inside me. It was as if something had called me there.

I came to know Wangaratta well. It echoed my own childhood in Newcastle, an edge-world where the residential tailed off into the semi-industrial. I knew the dream Nick had of himself like I knew my own dream.

There were other coincidences along the way, things I would rightly or wrongly read as having mystic significance. Nick driving me to the airport after a visit to Melbourne to interview him, sensing the difficulties I was in and the negative impact the book was having on me. 'You have to be careful of what you write, you know,' he told me. He arched his eyebrows a little, but he wasn't joking. 'Sometimes the things you create can make things happen. I've seen it with people. Seen it in my own work too.' And that recurring scene of us inside vehicles going somewhere and nowhere, passing through one limbo state after another, before or after a show usually. Sharing eternity for an hour or two. Up to this ride together to Newcastle, by which point I have atomised myself and lost all control of the biography and my life – though anything I have suffered seems like nothing next to Nick's losses.

Growing up in Wangaratta, the rapid evolution of The Boys Next Door: it was only the start. Nick was going on a long journey. Right through the heart of darkness and back out the other side. Ahead of him were London, Berlin and São Paulo, then Britain again. Ahead of him were full-blown heroin addiction and a mighty artistic career.

Picturing my biography of Nick Cave, I saw each era as having its own colours and textures. The Birthday Party period in London was akin to a photocopied leaflet or an inky copy of the *NME*, all grainy and dotted, a Rorschach test of blood spatter across a primary canvas. Berlin and Nick Cave's solo career were a deeper red and heavier blue, Expressionist cabaret, David Lynchian dream-nightmare. Brazil was hangover yellows in strong sunlight, night-sweats, cooling shadows in a church. And so on.

As I battled to complete my biography, people were not surprised by my struggles: *He's still alive. He does so much. How can you reach an end?* But keeping up with Nick's linear progress was never the biggest problem, though it has certainly been a challenge. It's the depth, how far down into Nick's work you can go, that causes you to get lost in rabbit holes, chasing artistic influences, secret connections and cross-references that never seem to end. As I told Mick Harvey once, each of Nick's songs is like a Russian doll, inside which there is another thing, and another and another, being revealed. Mick replied in a tone that suggested not only the depth, but an almost eerie capacity for the words to reach out beyond the moment they were created: 'Oh yes,' he said, 'I've had that experience with Nick's songs many times over the years.'[3]

On our road trip to Newcastle, Nick tells me that 'the notion of an idea within a song is very important to me. That a song has a greater meaning than its parts – its words and melody. But the idea is a tricky thing to catch, as it recedes as you approach it. So these days I tend to write words around an idea, kind of ring-fence it with words, because the idea disappears when you acknowledge it. It is very important for me to be able to access the idea when I play live – to fall deep into the song. It took me a long time to understand that the greater meaning of the song was not the words themselves, but lived behind the words or inside the words. I think my audience helped me understand this.'

The idea of something receding from you as you approach it and try to define it makes a lot of sense to me. I'd irritably tell people who wondered how I would end my biography that I was going to finish like *2001: A Space Odyssey* – with a hundred-page hallucinogenic trip about Nick being reborn as he slips through a black hole and re-enters the cosmos. People did not take to this idea, or even follow what the hell I was talking about, but to me it wasn't a bad concept.

After all, one of the strongest impressions I'd gained from my relationship with Nick was how hard he had worked to become a decent human being, if not exactly an ordinary one. Three or four times over the eight years that we corresponded he emailed me a copy of Philip Larkin's poem 'The Mower', a depiction of minor suburban trauma that ends by invoking kindness as a way to help us make it through our daily lives. I figured Nick was sending this message to himself as much as me, but it was interesting to see how much the poem meant to him. It was like a mantra.

Between leaving Wangaratta, and then losing his father, something had happened to him that had bent him out of shape. After The Boys Next Door, some intensely dark and brutal, as well as wildly humorous, music with The Birthday Party was on its way. It would be followed by a cinematic expansion of everything Nick had begun, with his next great band, The Bad Seeds. It certainly wasn't for nothing that he launched his solo career with 'Avalanche', a Leonard Cohen song about a hunchback. But along with the miscreant darkness and violence, the most marvellous and beautiful things emerged. As well as a rich array of finely drawn, almost literary characters who hark back time and again to Wangaratta and Melbourne and every place he has inhabited.

As the landscape rushes past us and we approach Newcastle in the late afternoon, Nick admits to me, 'I've worn my characters like armour. They protected me and allowed me to write about certain preoccupations without feeling implicated. The truth of the matter is there is much of me in the characters I have invented, as morally suspect as some of them are!' he says with a laugh.

Ages ago Nick told me, 'I have always been more of a style over content man.' So I wonder now if too much of a carapace has developed. A favourite poet of his, Frederick Seidel, mixes style with savagery. Can something like that set hard if you're not careful, and entrap you? In much the same way as he warned me a few years back about the emanations that can come from one's work? The softness in Nick's writing has always been there, but somehow it is stronger now. Is he breaking things open?

'It is not unusual to want to protect yourself,' he replies. 'We all have our identities that shield us from the world. [With Arthur's death] my shell was ripped off, suddenly and without warning, and I was basically a shivering slug and there were a lot of big, black birds in the sky. It still feels like that, really, on a daily basis. But to answer your question, I don't see style in poetry as a lack of courage or honesty, or that it is something you hide behind or that in some way gets in the way of basic truths. Some of the most moving and tender thoughts are contained within a stylistic savagery. Look at Seidel's poems. Look at *Lolita*. In regard to my stuff, a certain savagery is necessary because it makes the opposite more affecting. But ultimately it is the softer and more tender gesture that I am concerned with, and it is the ability to survive in sometimes extremely brutal landscapes that makes it all the more heroic and valuable.'

We arrive in Newcastle and any conversation of depth has to cease. Nick needs to prepare for the concert. The venue is a large amphitheatre in what feels like a fairly soulless and concrete entertainment complex. It jogs my memory, as it was in these same grounds that the Newcastle Show used to take place when I was a kid, one of those hybrid annual events that was part agricultural exhibition, part fairground entertainment, part freak display, with all the rides and carnies so harsh and shining in the artificial light.

I figure I'll take a walk around, through this very suburb I was raised in, where I used to cut through the stormwater drains and sing David Bowie's 'Heroes' to myself and imagine I was some kind of dolphin swimming my way into another world. There's not much for Nick and me to say now, other than that form of goodbye that promises another day without guaranteeing it will be there: 'See you later.'

So I walk through my home town, with Nick's words ringing in my head, about how the events in our lives are like a series of bells being struck, with the vibrations endlessly spreading outwards, affecting everything – our present, our futures, our past. Everything changing and vibrating and in flux. One emotion ringing in my mind above them all, as much a question as a calling note in the air: tenderness.

ACKNOWLEDGEMENTS

Biographies are built on worlds. The world of your subject, yes – in this case, one Nick Cave. But also the overlapping worlds of many others as they unite and part again on their journeys: how they influence one another, the way they combine to affect the culture they operate in, and the inheritance they leave behind and how that resonates in the lives of those who follow, sometimes for generations. I've always viewed this project as a social biography, with Nick at the centre of a kaleidoscope of stories. I hope there is some value in that as a picture of Nick's youth – and as a history of the places and times he moved through to become who he is today.

Writing a biography can be a fraught enterprise, as I have learned. One of the great ironies of the task is that life gets in the way. But here I am, indebted, likewise, to a kaleidoscope of people and stories. It is first of all important to thank Nick Cave himself for his cooperation and trust across almost a decade of communication, as well as the generous access he gave me to his family, especially his mother, Dawn, and his elder brother Tim, and younger sister, Julie (elder brother Peter preferred not to take part).

As I write these words, the morning news tells me that Nick has just posted on his website The Red Hand Files that his mother has passed away at the age of ninety-one. Sad news. I would have liked Dawn to see *Boy on Fire: The Young Nick Cave*. Not that she needed anything more to affirm her justifiable and inextinguishable love and pride in her youngest son. One of my fondest memories is of sitting at the kitchen table in Dawn's home after Nick and I had fetched a takeaway Thai meal for afternoon lunch, debating with some hilarity 'the New Atheism' of Richard Dawkins and the films of Clint Eastwood. For the record, I was the only one at the table pro-God, if only for the sake of art and architecture, rituals and archetypes. Dawn navigated a middle ground with a nod to the poetry of TS Eliot; Nick relished batting everything down with arguments so hyper-rational an element of comedy was inevitable. God got a mixed review, The Gospel According to Clint more regard.

Certain people make a mark on you when developing a biography. Certain moments too. Dawn Cave was definitely one of those people. Others who helped me immensely were Bleddyn Butcher, Mick Harvey and Phill Calvert. All three have been generous and precise in ways I hope I have honoured. The contributions of some people can be as emotionally meaningful as they are materially useful: even just a few words or an encouraging kindness can be small keys that open doors to how you might continue. To be honest, almost everyone I spoke to was like this in one way or another. One of the things that most impressed me about Nick's life was how many incredibly talented, sensitive and brilliant people he had connected with. If our friends – and, for that matter, our enemies – are the measure of us, then Nick has done well.

As *Boy on Fire* is a portrait of the artist as a young man, this is not where I can thank all those who have assisted in my research into the later stages and landscapes of Nick's life and career. Perhaps one day I will get the chance to do so. In the meantime, for their own unique and heartfelt contributions, I must thank Edward Clayton Jones, Harry Howard, Bronwyn Bonney, Polly Borland, John Hillcoat, Ross Waterman, Hugo Race, Genevieve McGuckin, Dave Graney, Clare Moore, Ron Rude, Ken Gormly and Caitlin Crauford. I also must thank Nick's management team, principally Rachel Willis and Suzi Goodrich, and Brian Message at

ATC Management, as well as Ton Maessen, the Bad Seeds' brilliant tour manager, and all the members of The Bad Seeds themselves, not to mention Rowland S Howard and Tracy Pew from The Boys Next Door and The Birthday Party, whose voices are here even if they are not.

HarperCollins Australia have been fantastic to work with, most of all my publisher, Catherine Milne, senior editor Scott Forbes, and copy editor Claire de Medici. In every way possible, they have brought sympathy and rigour to my project, and an energy that has helped carry me through, making this book into something better than I could ever have hoped for. Thanks also to proofreaders Julian Welch, who has improved my ability to spell 'dog' in Latin and find the Yarra River, and Madeleine James. A special thanks to Gary Seeger for tracking down lyrics permissions, and to Mute Song for their assistance.

My biography has had a long, even epic gestation. I'd like to thank people involved at earlier stages, including Jenny Darling, Fiona Hazard, Bernadette Foley and Matthew Kelly. We started together; we parted ways. The book became something else. But your contributions are appreciated.

The first part of my introduction, 'The Journalist and The Singer', was adapted from my essay in the literary journal *Meanjin* entitled 'Nick Cave: Man or Myth?'. Portions of the epilogue, 'The Singer and The Song', are drawn from my interview with Nick Cave that appeared in different forms in *The Guardian UK* and *Neighbourhood Paper*. I am also indebted to the *Sydney Review of Books* for publishing an earlier draft of my chapter on Wangaratta, 'Down by the River'.

I was fortunate to be a co-winner of the 2014 Peter Blazey Fellowship, awarded annually to writers in the non-fiction fields of biography, autobiography and life writing to further a work in progress, which helped me advance this project.

I am extremely grateful to Davina Davidson for permission

to quote from her letter outlining her teenage relationship with Nick, and to Kathleen Stewart for likewise granting permission to use material from her memoir, *The After Life*, detailing her later relationship with Nick. In both cases I appreciate the trust they put in me.

It would be remiss of me not to note a special debt to the writers who mapped out and laid down the roads I was able to travel on, principally Nick's previous biographers Robert Brokenmouth and Ian Johnston. Their works are referenced, but that feels a little inadequate – your excellent books gave me an east and west from which to orient myself in my attempt to find yet another Nick Cave story. Clinton Walker, the great oral historian and sociologist of Australian contemporary music, also deserves a special mention for preserving so much of what so few bothered to take care of. Music historian Ian McFarlane's vital preservation of our cultural heritage and his important in-depth interviews with figures like Rowland S Howard have been likewise significant. Mat Snow, Jillian Burt, Barney Hoskyns and many other journalists, great Australian rock magazines like *RAM* and *Roadrunner*, and dedicated fanzine makers and obsessed bloggers have all been invaluable to my work, too. Danijela Miletic's Facebook page 'Nick Cave, Wanted Man', Melynda Von Wayward's website *Punk Journey* (www.punkjourney.com), and the exceptional *From the Archives* (www.fromthearchives.org), and *Outta Black & Into the Ether* (rowland-s-howard.com) were particularly useful resources and distracting rabbit holes!

Janine Barrand, Director of the Australian Performing Arts Collection at The Arts Centre Melbourne has also been of great assistance, allowing access to the archives from Nick Cave: The Exhibition. Murray Bennett, with his superb collection of live recordings from The Boys Next Door and The Birthday Party, bent my ear with his sonic rarities. Andrew and Lynne Trute, devoted fans and collectors of Nick Cave memorabilia, were generous with their knowledge and good humour.

Photographers Ashley Mackevicius, Peter Milne and Michel Lawrence have helped me shape a visual narrative. My thanks also to Manuela Furci, Director of the Rennie Ellis Photographic Archive, and John Nixon, represented by Anna Schwartz of Anna Schwartz Gallery, for their images. Additional photos came from varied sources, not all of them easy to track. Phill Calvert, Keith Glass, David Pepperell, Bryan Wellington, Anne Shannon and Corin Johnson kindly provided photos from their collections.

Thanks, too, to Margaret Brickhill and Adrian Twitt; Ken Goodger, the Dean at Holy Trinity Cathedral; and Felicity Williams, Kim Gregg, Kris Penney and everyone, past and present, at the Centre for Continuing Education in Wangaratta. Anne Shannon's memories, along with those of Bryan Wellington, were vital to bringing Wangaratta and Nick's time there to life. Great people and a great town.

I'd also like to express my gratitude to John Corker, my lawyer ('I guess I must be your agent too now') for making this book happen when the whole project seemed lost – and more importantly for being my friend.

On a more personal level, I want to thank those close to me who have offered their love, friendship and support over the years, most especially Samantha Hutchison, Robert Miller, Michele Elliot, Dominic Lefebvre, Rika Wedlock, Beau Sevastos, Marcelle Lunam, John Stewart, Lucia Elliott, Virginia Fay, Aden Young, Lo Carmen, Beth Dyce, Russell Cheek, Jonathan Samway, Nerissa Kavanagh, Jarrad Ainsworth, Rosanna Barbero, Michael Wee, Andrea Healy, Trent McGinn, Carolyn Constantine, Nicole Lobegeiger and Matthew da Silva. I sincerely hope I haven't forgotten anyone. It's been a long haul and it's Friday night now, so forgive me.

In closing, I want to thank my brother and sisters, and my

mother and father (RIP), who always had my back and believed in me. Life is long, as the saying goes, and the path here has not always been so straight or obvious. I have dedicated this book to my children – and to the dreams that we share and are all part of in some way. I hope some of my gratitude comes through in the way I have conveyed the stories told to me. I return again with final thanks to Nick Cave and Susie Bick, and to the affirmations of beauty and kindness we make each time we create something worth living for.

ENDNOTES

Prologue: The Journalist and the Singer

1   Nick would repeat this phrase about being 'more of a writer' in
    various interviews at the time without fully believing it. Much later, in
    his 1996 essay 'The Flesh Made Word', he would look back on writing
    And the Ass Saw the Angel and regard its mix of Biblical language,
    Deep South vernacular and rampant obscenity as manifestations of
    artistic breakdown and creative blockage. If it wasn't already obvious
    from the book itself, Nick reflects in the essay on Euchrid as a kind of
    negative Jesus figure. Though the novel is densely overwritten, it offers
    a genuine yearning for redemption in the author's quest for a new
    language. The message would seem to be that Nick is trapped inside
    himself, or trapped inside a pain he is still finding the right words for.
    Loneliness is the major theme.

2   Strangely, Nick's disgust with rock 'n' roll reflected his father's classical
    tastes and disdain for popular forms. Nick would rebel against the
    influence and return to music as his true heartbeat.

3   Nick Cave, 'Readings from His Forthcoming Novel: *And the Ass Saw the
    Angel*', Mandolin Cinema, Sydney, 23 and 24 March 1988. Along with
    guest artists who embarrassed themselves trying to mock and upstage
    Nick, the event featured a special screening of John Huston's adaptation
    of Flannery O'Connor's novel *Wise Blood*. The film and the book both
    greatly influenced Nick at the time.

4   Mark Mordue, 'Let Love In', *Juice Magazine*, Sydney, April 1994.

5   There are many levels to this: the secret messaging that occurred
    in paintings back then, as well as our later understanding of the
    unconscious and what we project of ourselves onto others. For artists in
    the time of Da Vinci and Michelangelo, there was a conviction that all of
    God's secrets reside within us, and thus the mysteries and magnificence
    of Creation can be revealed if we look truly and deeply enough, finding
    in this our larger unity.

6   As well as in 'Red Right Hand' and the name of the Red Hand
    Files mailing list, the line is quoted in 'Song of Joy', where the killer

references Milton by writing the phrase 'his red right hand' on the walls in the victim's blood. 'Mutiny in Heaven', one of the very last Birthday Party songs, uses the narrative of *Paradise Lost* as a covert metaphor for the story of The Boys Next Door and The Birthday Party, as well as painting a fetishistic picture of heroin addiction and alluding to Nick's exile from his boyhood hometown of Wangaratta.

PART I: THE RIDER

Such Is Life

1   Nick Cave, Dawn Cave and Bleddyn Butcher were each interviewed independently by the author about the day of the ARIA Hall of Fame induction and events surrounding it.

2   Nick's off-hand reference to the seventh circle of hell comes from Dante's *Inferno*, with which he is well familiar. Dante reserves the seventh circle for those who have committed crimes of violence: against people and property, themselves and God.

3   AAP, 'Nick Cave, reluctantly famous', *The Age*, 23 October 2007. Also '"Arias bore me" – Nick Cave', *The Daily Telegraph*, 23 October 2007. Nick also discussed how he was feeling in a conversation with the author. Kebabs seem to be his favoured pre-awards snack.

4   Mick Harvey, interview with the author, Melbourne, 11 February 2010.

5   Nick Cave, 'Notes' (hardcover notebook), dated 1996–1997, Nick Cave: The Exhibition, The Arts Centre, Melbourne, Box H000653, File 2006.019.040.

6   Murray River was a favourite pseudonym Michael Hutchence used when booking hotel rooms.

7   Nick Cave, 'Notes' (hardcover notebook), dated 1996–1997, Nick Cave: The Exhibition, The Arts Centre, Melbourne, Box H000653, File 2006.019.040.

8   William Faulkner created an imaginary place called Yoknapatawpha County based on Lafeyette County, Mississippi, where he was raised. Almost all his novels would be set in this fabled version of his past, requiring Faulkner to create a 'map' of the landscape he rewrote, remembered and transformed. It helped Nick to see how he might unify his songs alongside the world he was developing for *And the Ass Saw the Angel*.

9   Bleddyn Butcher, interview with the author, Sydney, 5 May 2010.

10 Bleddyn Butcher, interview with the author, Sydney, 8 September 2012. Nick ploughed through a safety barrier and knocked down a Sussex Safer Roads Partnerships camera in 2010. He told the UK *Sun*,

'I became a local hero. I took out the camera along the sea front with my Jag. I was the toast of Brighton for about five days. Little Goths came and prayed at the scene and wrote, "Nick Cave was here."' – see www.nme.com/news/music/nick-cave-25-1252104, accessed 6 September 2020. Nick was not entirely joking. Graffiti had appeared on the sorry-looking camera pole: 'Nick Cave wuz ere Xmas 2010'. To avoid prosecution, Nick was offered a driver training course. He references these lessons in his song 'Mermaids'.

11 Dawn Cave, interview with the author, Melbourne, 27 March 2010.

12 Nick Cave: The Exhibition, The Arts Centre Gallery, Melbourne, 10 November 2007 – 6 April 2008 (then Adelaide, Brisbane and finally Canberra in 2010; now preserved in The Arts Centre's permanent archives). Curated by Janine Barrand in partnership with Nick Cave, it would form the basis for Stranger Than Kindness: The Nick Cave Exhibition, developed by Christina Back and Nick Cave for the Royal Danish Library in Copenhagen, originally set for 23 March – 3 October 2020 before COVID-19 delayed the opening till 8 June 2020. It was accompanied by a lavish hardback catalogue, *Stranger Than Kindness* (Canongate, Edinburgh, 2020).

13 Viviane Carneiro, interview with the author, London, 4 June 2010.

14 Interview with Nick Cave and Shane MacGowan, *MTV* Europe, 1993, available at www.youtube.com/watch?v=rhOvwLkXPuniD

15 'Sonny's Burning'. Lyrics by Nick Cave. Published by Mute Song Limited. All Rights Reserved. International Copyright Secured. Reproduced by kind permission.

16 Cormac McCarthy, *The Road*, 2007. TS Eliot, 'The Hollow Men', 1925. Bleddyn and Nick's conversation about *The Road*, apocalyptic futures, the nature of fatherhood and the search for spiritual consolation in art would help set Nick on a path towards writing the soundtrack, with Warren Ellis, for a 2010 film version of *The Road*, directed by Nick's friend and cinematic collaborator John Hillcoat. The story's intense focus on the relationship between a father and a son, and how one dies while the other must go on, naturally had an impact on Nick Cave.

17 Simon Hattenstone, 'Old Nick', *The Guardian*, 23 February 2008, available at www.guardian.co.uk/music/2008/feb/23/popandrock. features, accessed 4 June 2012.

18 Dawn Cave, interview with the author, Melbourne, 27 March 2010.

19 Nick's Shakespearian song references go beyond the direct influence of his teacher father, his own literary interests, or the construction of any romantic mythology. The Elizabethan villain-hero was usually stained

by a crime of some cosmic order, and capable of great as well as terrible deeds. In this regard, Nick seemed to believe he was fulfilling something predestined in his relationship with his father.

20 Seriously ill due to diabetes and with not much longer to live, the ageing Johnny Cash would record a powerfully redemptive, anti– capital punishment reading of 'The Mercy Seat'. He would also accept Nick's idea for their duet: the old Hank Williams number 'I'm So Lonesome I Could Cry'. They also had a crack at the old folk song 'Cindy, Cindy'. When Cash entered the studio, he was almost blind and unable to deal with the stairs on his own. He called out, 'Are you there, Nick? Are you there?' Nick had to help him down the stairs and give him time to sit down and let his eyes adjust. 'I was thinking, fucking hell, how is this guy going to sing anything?' But Cash changed with the singing of the song, Nick says, became something majestic. Ironically, Nick had been terrified of duetting with his hero and singing well enough to warrant the honour. After their first take, producer Rick Rubin asked for another. Nick said to Rubin, 'I was flat, right?' Rubin laughed. 'No, Johnny was.' June Carter told Nick, 'Get back in there with Johnny and sing those harmonies.' When Nick tells the story there is a deep reverence to it. 'Once Johnny started singing it was like the illness just fell away. It was incredible. I know some people were critical of Rick Rubin for bleeding the guy dry at the end of his life. But that's totally wrong. It wasn't like that at all. He was energising Johnny. It was a beautiful thing.'

21 A script outline was initiated at the request of John Hillcoat, with whom Nick had written the script for the movie *The Proposition*. The pair would research the project in depth, including doing interviews with door-to-door cosmetics salesmen. Hillcoat was interested in developing a 'kitchen-sink drama' that harked back to the gritty social realism of British movies of the 1950s. When the project failed to evolve, Nick was able to retool the research and outline into his novel *The Death of Bunny Munro* (Text Publishing, Melbourne, 2009). He frequently described the story as a hybrid of the Gospel of St Mark and radical feminist Valerie Solanas's *Scum Manifesto*. By then, Nick had taken the material to a more hallucinogenic level. Even after the novel appeared, he hoped to see it developed into a television miniseries with Ray Winstone, but the project ran aground on issues of taste as well as vision. The video for 'Jubilee Street' gives an idea of how it might have turned out visually.

22 Phil Sutcliffe, 'Nick Cave: Raw and Uncut 2', in Mat Snow, *Nick Cave: Sinner Saint: The True Confessions*, Plexus, London, 2011, p. 231. Nick's original text is lost, but the gist of the message was repeated, as jokes so often are, in interview with the author.

23 Stephen Dalton, 'The Light in the Cave', *The Age*, 19 September 2004, available at www.theage.com.au/articles/2004/09/17/1095320941733. html#, accessed 4 June 2012.

24 Robert Brokenmouth, *Nick Cave: The Birthday Party and Other Epic Adventures*, Omnibus Press, London, 1996, p. 64.

25 Nick Cave, 'We Call Upon the Author to Explain', *Dig!!! Lazarus, Dig!!!*, Mute Records, 2008.

26 Nick's relationship with Beau Lazenby dated back to The Boys Next Door era and an off-and-on affair that saw them spend time together in Melbourne when Nick Cave and The Bad Seeds toured in 1990. He'd admit to 'eternal regret' over not having much to do with Jethro when younger, and working hard to make up for lost time. Most of the father–son relationship healing would take place after Nick freed himself from his heroin addiction, when Jethro was entering his teens. His eldest son's path would prove especially difficult, as he lived in Melbourne, where Nick is an iconic figure. As Jethro said, 'It didn't start off great, having all this shit with my dad and being in his shadow.' (Hermione Eyre, 'Models and Rockers: Jethro Cave and Leah Weller', *ES Magazine, London Evening Standard*, 12 November 2009, www.standard.co.uk/ lifestyle/models-and-rockers-jethro-cave-and-leah-weller-6729475. html, accessed 7 September 2020.)

27 PJ Harvey appears to document her relationship with Nick Cave and her problems with him in 'The Garden' on *Is This Desire*. A close listen suggests Harvey is referencing the Birthday Party song 'Mutiny in Heaven' and sending Nick a haunting correction on the story of Adam and Eve.

28 'Mad, bad and dangerous to know' was the phrase Lady Caroline Lamb used to describe the Romantic poet Lord Byron. Some literary historians say Lamb was really describing herself. A married woman, she rejected his early advances with these famous words, then succumbed to Byron's increased ardour, immersing herself in a passionate affair. Lovers of the time commonly exchanged a lock of hair; Lady Caroline Lamb sent him a clipping of her pubic hair. Unfortunately, Byron was already struggling to end their relationship. His demonic social reputation and self-mythologising poems such as *Childe Harold's Pilgrimage* (1812–18), were only enhanced by Lamb's pioneering Gothic novel *Glenarvon* (1816). The book featured a thinly veiled and highly negative portrait of her ex-lover that, ironically, helped foment the grand Byronic archetype: solitary, brooding, cunning, rakish, self-destructive and mysterious. The German writer Goethe became a big fan of the novel. Nick would delve deeply into both Goethe and Byron. It's worth recalling that, as well as being the

great Romantic archetype, Byron was also a very witty and humorous lyricist, delighting in puns and wordplay across a mock-epic such as *Don Juan*.

29 Ed St John, press release, 2007 ARIA Hall of Fame, 28 October 2007.

30 Nick's father, Colin Cave, was one of Australia's leading scholars of Ned Kelly. See Colin F Cave, 'Introduction', *Ned Kelly: Man and Myth*, Cassell Australia, Melbourne, 1968.

31 'Such is life' are purported to be the last words of the Australian outlaw Ned Kelly before he was hanged on 11 November 1880. Peter Carey would write a Booker Prize–winning novel based on his life and exploits, *True History of the Kelly Gang*. As if to fulfil a generational prophecy dating back to the family history in Wangaratta, Nick Cave's son Earl would grow up to play Ned's younger brother, Dan Kelly, in the 2020 film translation of the book directed by Justin Kurzel.

32 AAP, 'Cave enters ARIA Hall of Fame on his own terms', *The Age*, 29 October 2007, available at www.theage.com.au/entertainment/cave-enters-aria-hall-of-fame-on-his-own-terms-20071029-ge65yv.html, accessed 19 September 2020.

33 Conflicts between Phill Calvert and Nick and Rowland Howard led to the drummer being ousted from The Birthday Party in 1982. Mick Harvey moved on to playing the drums. In the press, Rowland was disparaging of Phill's ability to come up with beats that suited the music, but the real reasons boiled down to their personality conflicts. He admits that being sacked from The Birthday Party was something he found very hard to deal with: 'We'd been together since we started high school.' Tracy Pew maintained their friendship, sending him postcards. Phill joined The Psychedelic Furs, but he was not comfortable in such a mainstream band. After leaving The Psychedelic Furs in 1984, he returned to Australia and formed Blue Ruin, a key Australian band of the 1980s. In later years he moved into production and started his own record label, Behind the Beat, supporting young and independent artists, as well as working again with Mick Harvey.

King and Country

1 'Colin Francis Cave', Inquisition, Wangaratta, Case No. F.360, Reference 790809, 21 May 1979.

2 Mary Brown, 'Introduction – the 60s', *Centre History*, The Centre for Continuing Education, Wangaratta, c. 2010, p. 5.

3 ibid.

4 Author interview with Chris Morris, Wangaratta, 25 March 2010.

5   Mary Brown, 'Introduction – the 60s', *Centre History*, The Centre for
    Continuing Education, Wangaratta, c. 2010, p. 7. Colin's stained red
    hands likely inspired Nick's song 'Red Right Hand'.

6   Nick's reflections on boating with Colin Cave at Lake Mulwala hint at
    the depth of meaning behind an album like *The Boatman's Call*, an overt
    reference to Jesus and his Apostles, and a covert allusion to the influence
    of his father Colin's life and death upon him.

7   Behind the scenes, Colin Cave held even grander visions, including
    the establishment of the state's first regional university in Wangaratta,
    for which The Centre might be a foundation stone. The competing
    regional town of Geelong would steal away this dream with the advent
    of Deakin University in 1978.

8   In his definitive biography of Ned Kelly, the author and historian Ian
    Jones credits Colin Cave's symposium with 'prompting quantum leaps
    in my studies'. (Ian Jones, 'Preface to the First Edition', *Ned Kelly: A
    Short Life,* Hachette Australia, Sydney, 2008, p. viii.) The imprimatur
    of Manning Clark for the Ned Kelly symposium is another interesting
    element. Clark's poetic writing style and focus on tragic individuals as a
    way of understanding the course of Australian history were obviously an
    influence on Colin Cave.

9   Colin F Cave, 'Introduction', *Ned Kelly: Man and Myth*, Cassell Australia,
    Melbourne, 1968, p. 8.

10 Tim Cave, interview with the author, Melbourne, 20 November 2010.

11 Colin F Cave, 'Introduction', *Ned Kelly: Man and Myth,* Cassell Australia,
    Melbourne, 1968, pp. 9–10.

12 Nick Cave would repeat the story of his father reading various literary
    passages to him, and how he saw his father transformed into a larger
    being in the process. It is almost certain that Ned Kelly's *Jerilderie
    Letter*, a rambling, often hilarious proto-republican document written
    as a justification for Kelly's outlaw actions, was one of the causes
    of Colin Cave's transformations. The novelist Peter Carey would
    note how 'all the time there is this original voice – uneducated but
    intelligent, funny and then angry, and with a line of Irish invective
    that would have made Paul Keating envious. His language came in a
    great, furious rush.' (Robert McCrum, 'Reawakening Ned Kelly', *The
    Guardian / The Observer*, United Kingdom, 7 January 2001.) Sidney
    Nolan's paintings were also influenced by Kelly's *Jerilderie Letter* and
    what the artist saw as 'their blend of poetry and political engagement'.
    (A New Home for Ned Kelly – The Ned Kelly Series, National
    Gallery of Australia, https://nga.gov.au/nolan)

13 The presence of Joe Byrne's body can be found in other songs by Nick
    Cave. The most significant is 'Dead Joe', his 1982 Christmas car-crash

song (co-written with Anita Lane), with bizarrely personal resonances that connect it to Colin Cave's accident. Nick's later decision to read the work as poetry in 1992, however drolly, indicates how important that song was to him. This reading is available at www.youtube.com/watch?v=ljdUNyaKsck (accessed 20 September 2020). The 1880 picture of Joe Byrne's burnt and bullet-riddled body strung up against a wall – reputedly Australia's first-ever press photograph – was used in a series of historical photographs at the beginning of *The Proposition*.

14 'Somebody's Watching', The Boys Next Door, *Door, Door,* Mushroom Records, April 1979.

15 This description would stay with Nick, as noted in the documentary *20,000 Days on Earth*, directed by Iain Forsyth and Jane Pollard, Pulse Films, London, 2014. Dawn Cave remembers her husband coming home from the evening thrilled by his son's performance. 'He told me, "Nick's a phenomenon!"' (Dawn Cave, interview with the author, Melbourne, 24 October 2010.)

16 'Colin Francis Cave', Inquisition, Wangaratta, Case No. F.360, Reference 790809, 21 May 1979.

17 ibid.

18 ibid.

19 Adrian Twitt, interview with the author, Wangaratta, 25 March 2010.

PART II: THE GOOD SON

Man in the Moon

1 *The Wimmera Mail-Times*, 'News', 20 June 2008, p. 1.

2 Sculptors and stonemasons created the first wave of these icons in the early to mid-twentieth century, usually paying tribute to Australian Federation, Anzac soldiers, pioneers, explorers and major events. The craft involved often reflected the migrant history of Australia – in Rusconi's case, his Swiss–Italian background and a wonderful skill with marble and bronze. Inspired by 'Bullocky Bill', the 1857 poem about a loyal dog that guards a drover's tuckerbox (a cattle herder's lunchbox), Rusconi's monument was intimate and quirky, and would appear in a plethora of poems and songs. It helped memorialise an Australian folk symbol whose echoes reverberate all the way through to the Louis de Bernières novel *Red Dog* (2001) and the Kriv Stenders 2011 film of the same name. An offbeat obsession with roadside icons of a more regional nature – usually of a spectacularly oversized variety – would proliferate in the late twentieth century: the Big Banana (Coffs Harbour), the Big Pineapple (Nambour), the Big Merino (Goulburn), etc. Gestures of Australian nationalism had by then devolved into a

kitsch folk art celebrating local produce, industry, quirks of history and shopping opportunities, in a manner that was increasingly epic in scale and absurdly minor in subject matter. Andy Warhol may have approved, though it is doubtful the creators would have heard of him. An attempt by adventure television pioneers The Leyland Brothers to create a small-scale 'monumental' Ayers Rock/Uluru out of a large hill of red-painted concrete failed as a tourist attraction.

3   *The Wimmera Mail-Times*, 'News', 23 June 2008, p. 2.

4   Dawn Cave, interview with the author, Melbourne, 27 March 2010.

5   Steve Packer, 'Story of a Nag from a Warracknabeal Wag', *The Age*, 18 December 2004, p. 18.

6   In a 2013 television interview with Angela Bishop, Cave was asked again about his statue plans and playfully insisted it was all still a possibility. When Bishop told him The Bee Gees' Barry Gibb was getting one in Redcliff, his old hometown, Cave paused, then asked, 'How big?' Bishop replied, 'Oh huge, life size.' Nick told her, 'I'm going way bigger than life size. I'm talking about like The Big Pineapple or something.' (Bish's Biz – Entertainment News with Angel Bishop', *Ten News*, Channel 10, 28 February 2013, www.youtube.com/watch?v=LQVzAAQJvss, accessed 20 September 2020.)

7   Corin Johnson, interview with the author, phone, 1 June 2011. In 2018 a group of citizens from Warracknabeal calling themselves The Cave Foundation attempted a crowdfunding campaign in support of Corin Johnson's bronze statue, seeking $250,000 to make the statue a reality. Their campaign petered out at just $4210. It's a little heartbreaking to see the goodwill and dreams of the town in a video for this appeal. What began half in jest has become something of a lifeline that they don't plan to give up on. Johnson happily supported their effort and explained the unusual challenges in creating his sculpture in the same video (Nick Cave Statue, Chuffed, campaign completed 15 September 2018, https://chuffed.org/project/nick-cave-statue, accessed 17 August 2020). At a viewing of Johnson's first attempt at a maquette for a statue, Nick had observed, 'You've made me far too muscley … I've got a body like a chick.' Johnson says, 'So I remodelled the torso to make him more skinny and feminine.' (Corin Johnson, email correspondence with the author, 5 July 2011.)

8   Anonymous, interview with the author, Wangaratta, 26 March 2010.

9   Steve Packer, 'Story of a Nag from a Warracknabeal Wag', *The Age*, 18 December 2004, p. 18. Cave's exaggerations connect him to an Australian storytelling tradition rooted in Gothic atmospheres (and sometimes laced with a peculiar strain of black humour). It's a quality detectable in everything from Henry Lawson's iconic short story 'The

Drover's Wife', through to the hallucinogenic fringes of Patrick White's and Peter Carey's novels. Songs by Australian bands such as The Triffids and The Moodists would evoke similarly disturbed states of mind on taking the road to nowhere, a kind of six-cylinder dreaming to match the suicidal melancholy of the nation's informal national anthem, 'Waltzing Matilda' (interpreted on record by Tom Waits and The Pogues, among others). Ted Kotcheff's landmark film *Wake in Fright* (1971) – based on Kenneth Cook's 1961 novel of the same name – serves this up in the archetypal Australian tale of a man becoming lost in a landscape that feels like a bad dream. Ironically enough, the central character, John Grant, is a middle-class teacher posted against his will to an outback town. Colin Cave may well have sympathised with Grant's employment predicament, though not with his loss of self-command; his son Nick was certainly inspired by the film's sweaty evocation of a nightmare unfolding in infinite and overpowering sunlight – a vision he would adapt to his own purposes in the script for *The Proposition*.

10 Dawn Cave, interview with the author, Melbourne, 21 November 2010.

11 ibid.

12 Frank Cave also ventured into making early mini-documentaries for cinema screenings that focused on travel in Australia and ended with his mellifluous voiceover, 'Things go better with Shell.'

13 Frank Landvoigt was born on 26 November 1898. He changed his name to Frank Jason Cave by deed poll on 8 July 1940. 'Jason' was a middle name he'd been using since the war for no other reason than that he liked the sound of it.

14 Dawn Cave, interview with the author, Melbourne, 21 November 2010.

15 The precise cause of death for Mary Jane Treadwell is not known.

16 Dawn Cave, interview with the author, Melbourne, 27 March 2010.

17 Stories of blind Edward Treadwell may have added to Nick's fascination for John Milton and his epic masterwork *Paradise Lost*, created after the seventeenth-century English poet had gone blind. Nick's memories of singing with an almost blind Johnny Cash likewise have an intensity to them that goes beyond meeting a hero. Nick's lyrical obsession with stars may be part of this: we see their light long after they have blackened and died.

18 Julie and Dawn Cave, interview with author, Melbourne, 23 November 2010.

19 ibid.

20 Nick Cave to journalist Jessamy Calkin in 1981: 'I want to write songs that are so sad, the kind of sad where you take someone's finger and break it in three places.' (Ian Johnston, *Bad Seed: The Biography of Nick*

Cave, Abacus, London, 1995, p. 91.) Jessamy Calkin told me the same story in London during an interview on 29 June 2010. She explained that it was part of an overheard conversation between Nick and Lydia Lunch: 'I never forgot it.'

21 Dawn Cave, interview with the author, Melbourne, 23 March 2010. Nick got his mother to play violin on a cover of the Phil Rosenthal song 'Muddy Water' on his album *Kicking Against the Pricks*, Mute Records, 1986. Johnny Cash had done a memorable interpretation of 'Muddy Water' in 1979. It had stayed with Nick, stirring up boyhood connections to watching *The Johnny Cash Show* on television and the Ovens River in Wangaratta.

22 Dawn Cave, interview with the author, Melbourne, 23 March 2010.

23 *Rope* was written by the British playwright Patrick Hamilton in 1929. Based on the Leopold and Loeb murder case earlier in the decade, it features a corpse hidden inside a chest, on which a meal is then served at a party. Alfred Hitchcock would make a famous film adaptation starring Jimmy Stewart in 1948. A version of the play would also be included in the *Shell Presents* series made for ABC TV in 1959, highlighting the theme of two friends killing someone for fun.

24 Dawn Cave, interview with the author, Melbourne, 27 March 2010.

25 ibid.

Down by the River

1 Mary Brown, 'Introduction – The 60s', *Centre History*, The Centre for Continuing Education, Wangaratta, c. 2010, p. 1.

2 *Holy Trinity Cathedral Wangaratta – A Short History and Guide*, published by Friends of the Holy Trinity Cathedral, Wangaratta, 2004.

3 Colin Cave's satirical poem appeared in the *Wangaratta Chronicle*, credited as 'A Reader Writes …' Photocopy supplied by Dawn Cave; 1967 given as likely year of publication. The subject matter of a slaughterhouse and its stench, and the verse it inspired, might be seen as a precursor to Nick Cave's 2004 song 'Abattoir Blues'. The mixture of disgust, revenge and humour in the words also suggests a tone of voice passed on from father to son.

4 'Red Right Hand'. Lyrics by Nick Cave. Published by Mute Song Limited. All Rights Reserved. International Copyright Secured. Reproduced by kind permission.

5 Bryan Wellington, interview with the author, phone, 16 November 2011.

6 Mrs Baumgarten also relished singing 'Popeye the Sailor Man' at the Mothers' Union, which her daughter Anne says Dawn Cave was also a

member of. 'It had special status in class-conscious Wangaratta.' (Anne Shannon [née Baumgarten], correspondence with the author, email, 23 August 2020.)

7 Myxomatosis was a viral disease artificially introduced into Australia in the 1950s to help control the rabbit plague. Rabbits had been first introduced into the country by a wealthy grazier in 1859, but within a few decades were running rampant in their millions, competing with livestock for feed and damaging the environment. In many places not a single blade of grass was left on the ground. A Brazilian virologist by the name of Aragao suggested myxomatosis as a solution in the early twentieth century. Scepticism and unease about it delayed action. By the 1950s desperation over the rabbit plague led to the introduction of myxomatosis, which was spread by mosquitoes and rabbit fleas. Its effects include swelling of the head and face, discharges, lethargy and slowing of movement, and what is called 'sleepy eyes', as well as blindness in many rabbits. Over time the rabbits have become immune to its effects.

8 Anne Shannon (née Baumgarten), interview with author, phone, 8 March 2012.

9 In the unreleased song 'Give Us a Kiss', caught during the recording of *Push the Sky Away* for the *20,000 Days on Earth* documentary, it is possible to see one of the most tender singing performances of Nick's career, evoking his boyhood dreaming places of Wangaratta and the sweet-sad yearnings of a first great love. The lyrics echo the map of the town that Nick's paints almost word for word in 'Red Right Hand'.

10 Leonard Cohen's *Songs of Love and Hate* was a surprisingly successful album for the singer in Australia, reaching number eight on the national album charts in 1971. Its complex and poetic content, dealing in courtly love, suicide and addiction – along with Paul Buckmaster's bleak orchestrations and Cohen's strangely confident assertion of his raspy storyteller's voice (always an acquired taste) – almost sank him as an artist of interest in the United States. Nick would enjoy discovering that the recording sessions for it began on the same date as his thirteenth birthday.

11 Discussing 'Avalanche', Nick would say, 'This song seemed like a true kind of confessional song. It just seemed to be so open and kind of honest in some way. Whether it is or not, I don't really know. It just had that effect on me and really changed the way I looked at things.' Leonard Cohen would be impressed: 'I guess you could say Nick Cave butchered my song "Avalanche", and if that's the case, let there be more butchers like that.' (Christof Graf, Cohenpedia, http://blog. leonardcohen.de/?p=14090)

12 Chris Morris, interview with the author, Wangaratta, 25 March 2010.

13 Adrian Twitt, interview with the author, Wangaratta, 25 March 2010.

14 ibid.

15 Bryan Wellington, interview with the author, 16 November 2011.

16 'Man in the Moon'. Lyrics by Nick Cave. Published by Mute Song Limited. All Rights Reserved. International Copyright Secured. Reproduced by kind permission.

17 Anne Shannon (née Baumgarten), correspondence with the author, email, 23 August 2020.

18 Nick Cave, 'Introduction', *The Gospel According to Mark*, Pocket Canons, Canongate Books, Edinburgh, 2010. Reproduced with the kind permission of Canongate Books Ltd.

19 Anne Shannon (née Baumgarten), correspondence with the author, email, 23 August 2020.

20 A less dismissive autobiographical account can be found in the song 'Do You Love Me? Pt 2' on *Let Love In*. One of the most dreamlike and shadowy in Nick Cave's repertoire, it gives seductive as well as sinister voice to a child molester at work. When I expressed a general unease around the subject in an informal car conversation with Nick, he was adamant about the need to explore this issue rather than sweep it under the carpet because it is just too difficult and dark to deal with.

21 Bryan Wellington, interview with the author, phone, 16 November 2011. Hendrix died on 18 September 1970, four days before Nick's birthday. Thereafter as a teenager, Nick would celebrate and mourn his hero on that day each year, listening to songs like 'Hey Joe', 'Stone Free', 'Little Wing' and 'The Wind Cries Mary'.

22 Dawn Cave, interview with the author, Melbourne, 21 November 2010.

23 Julie and Dawn Cave, interview with author, Melbourne, 21 October 2010.

PART III: SONNY'S BURNING

The Word

1 Robert Brokenmouth, *Nick Cave: The Birthday Party and Other Epic Adventures*, Omnibus Press, London, 1996, p. 11.

2 Mick Harvey, interview with the author, Sydney, 17 January 2012.

3 Bryan Wellington, interview with the author, phone, 20 January 2012.

4 ibid.

5 Bryan Wellington, interview with the author, phone, 16 November 2011.

6   Anne Shannon (née Baumgarten), correspondence with the author, email, 23 August 2020.

7   Bryan Wellington, interview with the author, phone, 20 January 2012. Note: Bryan Wellington would pass away in 2013. He was tremendously helpful about Nick's early years and their shared life in Wangaratta, granting a number of interviews and offering highly sensitive, searching insights into events that may have shaped various songs by Nick. When my essay 'Down by the River' was first published in *Sydney Review of Books* on 29 January 2019, it was dedicated to Bryan's memory. One area that Bryan hotly contested was Nick's story of jumping off the railway bridge over the Ovens River. Bryan felt this was not only an exaggeration or a myth: 'It's a dangerous lie. Someone could kill themselves trying to imitate it. I don't believe he did it, and certainly not more than once.'

8   Nick Cave, 'The Flesh Made Word', BBC Radio 3 Religious Services, London, 1996; the story can also be heard on *The Secret Life of the Love Song / The Flesh Made Word: Two Lectures by Nick Cave*, King Mob Spoken Word CD, 2000.

9   Nick Cave can be seen with his twin sons, Arthur and Earl, in the documentary *20,000 Days on Earth* (2014), eating pizza with them as the soundtrack to *Scarface* blares out from the television over their laughter. This particular conversation took place with Nick in Brighton in 2010.

10 It's likely the crime novel was by the British author Gerald Kersh. Kersh was a pulp writer with real literary flair at his best. Some of Kersh's seedy moralising influence can be felt in Nick Cave's second novel, *The Death of Bunny Munro* (Text Publishing, Melbourne, 2009).

11 This fascination would reach its height with Nick Cave and The Bad Seeds' *Murder Ballads* (1996). Nick would find reviews of it limited, even annoying, because they focused invariably on the violence documented in the songs. He had thought 'the album was really about language'.

12 Dawn Cave, interview with the author, phone, 18 May 2015.

13 Tim Cave, interview with the author, Melbourne, 20 November 2010.

14 El Greco's stormy and menacing *View of Toledo* likely served Nick as a visual premonition for the song 'Tupelo'.

15 Boys Next Door photo session in Nick Cave's bedroom, 1979. Photo by Peter Milne. See p. 269.

16 Nick misremembers this detail. It is actually in an earlier photo from 1976 by his friend Ashley Mackevicius that Nick's etching of Adolf Hitler appears on the wall. See p. 151.

17 In 2009 Nick would dedicate the Nick Cave and The Bad Seeds set at Glastonbury 'to the late, great … Farah Fawcett'. News of her death had been swamped by Michael Jackson's overdose.

18 The song came out as 'I Love You … Nor Do I'. Lane had come up with the idea of doing a purely English-language version. Working as her producer, Mick Harvey thought the idea impossible, citing ambiguities in language that did not translate from French into English. It was a strangely effective and autobiographical release, and very Anita Lane.

19 William 'Haystacks' Calhoun was famous for being the biggest wrestler there was, reputedly weighing in at 'over 800 pounds at six-and-a-half feet in height', or so Jack Little, the MC on *World Championship Wrestling*, liked to bark on TV. Calhoun's technique for defeating opponents largely revolved around manoeuvring them into a position where he could fall on them, a move Nick Cave recalls enthusiastically as 'the Big Splash!'. Calhoun dressed in overalls and wore a beard, a look that evoked a combination of Southern backwoods hick and giant baby. Mario Milano was Italian, and of more classical proportions.

20 Ian Johnston, *Bad Seed: The Biography of Nick Cave*, Abacus, London, 1996, p. 30.

21 'Class Acts', *Good Weekend*, *Sydney Morning Herald*, 14 November 2009, p. 32.

22 Mick Harvey, interview with the author, phone, 27 August 2020.

23 Mick Harvey, interview with author, Melbourne, 5 April 2012.

24 Anne Shannon (née Baumgarten), interview with the author, phone, 8 March 2012.

25 A reference to Norman Lindsay's 1918 classic Australian children's book *The Magic Pudding*. It is a mix of rhyming stories in sea shanty form, anthropomorphic characters and illustrations. Lindsay was later renowned for his outré obsession with sketching and painting nudes.

26 Mick Harvey, email correspondence, 21 August 2020.

27 West, Bruce and Laing were a blues rock supergroup of the early 1970s who formed from the ashes of the supergroup Cream.

28 Hawkwind's heavy psychedelic futurism would be a keystone to understanding Nick Cave's 21st-century vision for Grinderman.

29 Julie and Dawn Cave, interview with the author, Melbourne, 21 October 2010.

30 David Bowie, *The Ziggy Stardust Companion*, www.5years.com/quotes.htm, accessed 19 August 2020.

31 ibid.

32 A SAHB concert was broadcast live late at night in Australia on Channel 9 during the early to mid-1970s, thrilling Nick Cave and his schoolmates.

33 It's of note that Alex Harvey's Glaswegian background and the gravelly, committed quality of his vocals were a defining model for a generation of gritty Australian singers, among them the Scottish immigrants Bon Scott of AC/DC and Jimmy Barnes of Cold Chisel. Mick Harvey thinks Skyhooks, Australia's biggest band of the mid-1970s, built their whole image around the example of SAHB. By 1974 Nick was beginning to track down rock magazines, devouring their features on Harvey, who had become known for his saying, 'A Stratocaster is more powerful than an AK-47.'

34 Anne Shannon (née Baumgarten), correspondence with the author, email, 23 August 2020.

35 Anne Shannon (née Baumgarten), interview with author, phone, 8 March 2012.

36 ibid.

37 William Shakespeare, *Romeo and Juliet*, Act 2, Scene 2, lines 2–3.

38 Nick's fascination with epistolary relationships continues right up to the present day in his online correspondence with fans via The Red Hand Files.

39 Davina Davidson, correspondence with the author, email, 6 January 2011.

40 Davina Davidson, correspondence with the author, email, 28 January 2012.

41 Davina Davidson, correspondence with author, email, 28 June 2012.

42 Davina Davidson, correspondence with the author, email, 28 January 2012.

43 'Nicholas Edward Cave', Term 2, Year 10 report, Caulfield Grammar School, 1974. Courtesy of Dawn Cave.

44 Tim Cave, interview with the author, Melbourne, 20 November 2010.

45 *Hair* was banned in Queensland and New Zealand, and Victoria's conservative premier Henry Bolte was encouraged to send the vice squad along to theatre previews to police any outbreaks of indecency or obscenity. Producer Harry M. Miller and a brilliant young director, 24-year-old Jim Sharman, must have been delighted by all the attention and free publicity.

46 Davina Davidson, correspondence with the author, email, 6 January 2011.

47 ibid.

48 ibid.

49 ibid.

ENDNOTES

Double Trouble

1 Phill Calvert, correspondence with the author, 15 June 2020.

2 Nick Cave's reflections on the nature of influence and plagiarism were dealt with uniquely in a fan correspondence on The Red Hand Files; see www.theredhandfiles.com/originality-hard-to-obtain, accessed 21 August 2020.

3 Nick first heard 'I Put a Spell on You' via a gutsy Creedence Clearwater Revival version. The song was never a joke to him. It's possible to see *The Firstborn Is Dead* as an album seeded in his youth by Creedence Clearwater Revival and The Doors as much as it connected, when he was an adult, with John Lee Hooker's spooky intensity. Nick was never at ease with it being seen as a blues album so much as an 'idea of the blues' transplanted into the European Cold War context that defined West Berlin as a frontier town.

4 Dawn and Julie Cave, interview with the author, Melbourne, 21 November 2010.

5 *The Good Son*, VPRO Dutch Television, 1997, www.youtube.com/watch?v=xaJQwsLw5bg (accessed 21 August 2020). Nick's comment about being nineteen at the time of his father's death, not twenty-one as he actually was, is often repeated by him in interviews.

6 Norman Kaye would become a highly respected Australian actor thanks to his roles in Paul Cox–directed films *Lonely Hearts* (1982) and *Man of Flowers* (1983). His abilities as a piano player and organist would also see him write a number of film scores, available on the retrospective Move Records CD *The Remarkable Norman Kaye* (2007).

7 See p. 153, interview with Nancy Pew, Melbourne, 18 November 2010.

8 Sinatra had toured Australia in July of 1974, describing the male journalists as 'parasites' and the female journalists as 'broads and hookers' at a press conference. His abuse precipitated a targeted national strike against him and his entourage by various unions, in sympathy with the outraged journalists' union. This immobilised and isolated Sinatra in Melbourne, where he was denied everything from hotel room service to a flight out of the city. Though the matter was eventually resolved, it was comical evidence that Ol' Blue Eyes had lost none of his spite, despite the smooth vocal tones and sharp suits.

9 Mick Harvey wryly describes the artwork for Nick Cave and The Bad Seeds' *Kicking Against the Pricks* as 'Nick wanting to look like Bryan Ferry on those solo albums of his'. (Mick Harvey, interview with the author, phone, 27 July 2020.)

10 Mick Harvey, interview with the author, 10 February 2010.

11 Phil Sutcliffe, 'Nick Cave: Raw and Uncut 2', in Mat Snow (ed.), *Nick Cave – Sinner Saint: The True Confessions*, Plexus Publishing, London, 2011.

12 Jeff Duff, sometimes referred to as 'Duffo', was the lead singer of the early 1970s band Kush and has enjoyed an equally eccentric solo career. Blessed with a deep tenor voice, Duff could sing like Sinatra but came on like David Bowie, albeit in a warmer cabaret vein. 'I always dress as if I am performing on a stage, even if I am just going out to do the shopping,' he once told me after popping by my house for an interview in a three-piece white suit with a matching cane and fedora. Duff would befriend Nick Cave and Anita Lane in their early days in London and, concerned for their well-being, bring them croissants at their 'terrible' squat. Seemingly ageless, he remains a fluid combination of Quentin Crisp, Count Dracula and Peter Pan.

13 Nick Cave's choice of Darian Leader as a psychotherapist is a fascinating one. Leader's book *The New Black: Depression, Mourning and Melancholia (2008)* challenged the idea of depression as a purely negative state that needs to be immediately fixed through prescription drugs. Leader is interested in the way mourning and melancholia (his preferred terms to depression) can cause us to lose our form, or sense of identity, as well as the ways in which society rejects any long-term relationship with mourning as inappropriate and negative. He moves towards a concept of creativity through mourning, in which the arts and culture are the best means to communicate with a damaged selfhood and reshape oneself. There is an apparent rejection of the well-rounded individual as little more than a fantasy.

14 *20,000 Days on Earth*, directed by Iain Forsyth and Jane Pollard, Pulse Films, London, 2014.

15 Ashley Mackevicius's schoolboy portrait of Nick Cave (see p. 151) is now in the collection of the National Portrait Gallery in Canberra. In taking up photography, he'd been influenced by Tracy Pew, who'd been more heavily involved in it at the time. It was his friendship with Tracy that created the bond with Nick.

16 Phill Calvert, interview with the author, Sydney, 26 June 2012.

17 Bruce Clarke taught many notable Australian guitarists, among them Robert Goodge (I'm Talking), Andrew Pendlebury (The Sports) and Anne McCue. Clarke himself was greatly influenced by the swing-era guitarist John Collins, who worked with Nat King Cole. Collins was renowned for rarely soloing and staying focused on rhythm playing. It was a distinct quality that Clarke absorbed and passed on to his students. The likes of Frank Sinatra, Dizzy Gillespie, Stan Getz and Collins himself would invite Clarke to join them on their Australian tours.

A well-regarded orchestra arranger for radio during the 1950s and 1960s, Clarke also made pioneering use of the Moog synthesiser.

18 Mick Harvey, interview with the author, phone, 27 July 2020.

19 True to his word, Chris Coyne would return to play sax on The Boys Next Door album *Door, Door*. He'd also play live with The Captain Matchbox Whoopee Band, work with Paul Kelly on his album *Gossip* (1986), and record with Phill Calvert's post–Birthday Party band in Australia, Blue Ruin, playing sax on their debut album, *Such Sweet Thunder* (1986).

20 Robert Brokenmouth, *Nick Cave: The Birthday Party and Other Epic Adventures*, Omnibus Press, London, 1996, p. 2.

21 Former Smiths guitarist Johnny Marr would describe James Williamson's playing style as 'both demonic and intellectual, almost how you would imagine Darth Vader to sound if he was in a band'. (Will Hodgkinson and Alex Petridis, 'The World Was Not Ready for Iggy and The Stooges', *The Guardian*, 11 March 2010, available at www.guardian.co.uk/music/2010/mar/11/iggy-and-the-stooges-raw-power) Marr is reputed to have been inspired to play a Fender Jaguar after seeing Rowland S Howard with The Birthday Party. You can hear this influence in the glacial start to The Smiths' 'How Soon Is Now'.

22 Phill Calvert says Nick's concerns about his bad reputation with parents were well founded. Phill's father did not like Nick or, for that matter, any of the band. He told his son, 'I wish I had never sent you to school where you met those bums; it ruined your life!' (Phill Calvert, correspondence with the author, 15 June 2020.)

23 Mick Harvey would revisit this event for his song 'The Ballad of Jay Givens' on his album *Sketches from the Book of the Dead* (2011).

24 Mick Harvey, interview with the author, Sydney, 17 January 2012.

25 Nick's memory is incorrect here: Phill Calvert's father was English.

26 Nancy Pew, interview with the author, Melbourne, 18 November 2010.

27 ibid.

28 ibid. There's no denying the shadows at work in the band's formative identity. To overstate them becomes deterministic and even shallow. But every one of us has a share in Tolstoy's opening wisdom from *Anna Karenina*: 'Happy families are all alike; every unhappy family is unhappy in its own way.' If one were to extend this perception beyond their individual backgrounds to the band itself as an extended family drama, it's true to say Nick, Mick, Tracy and Phill were bonded by a history of personal pain as much as by any wild yearnings for pleasure and release. The arrival of guitarist Rowland S Howard, and the death of Colin Cave in a car crash, would intensify this alchemy,

as the title to a much later Birthday Party compilation video and
record release signposts: *Sometimes Pleasureheads Must Burn.*

29 David Bowie and Mick Rock, *Moonage Daydream: The Life and Times of Ziggy Stardust*, Hardie Grant Books, Sydney, 2005, p. 61.

30 Dee Dee Ramone's song 'Now I Wanna Sniff Some Glue' inspired the name of one of the most famous zines (self-published, usually photocopied fan magazines) of the British punk era. Mark Perry's *Sniffin' Glue* was launched in July 1976 with fifty copies. Perry would soon have 15,000 readers with ink stains on their fingers embracing a DIY aesthetic.

31 One in four Australian homes would reputedly own a copy of *Hot August Night* by 1975.

32 Nick and his friends referred to arts-oriented Swinburne as a 'free school'. It was part of an alternative and community school movement within the government sector in the 1970s.

33 Bronwyn Bonney (née Adams) paints a picture of working hard with Nick on the manuscript. She would not appreciate his tendency in interviews to portray the novel's development as lacking in any substantial editorial guidance. Nick would later apologise personally, but he failed to give her any credit at the time (Bronwyn Bonney, interview with the author, Sydney, 28 March 2011). Nick's general comments also suggested minimal input from Black Spring Press publisher Simon Pettifar, who had originally suggested the writing of a novel.

34 Bruce Milne, interview with the author, Melbourne, 26 February 2010.

35 ibid.

36 After Rowland S Howard died, he would be remembered by Mick Harvey in the song 'October Boy'.

37 Bronwyn Bonney (née Adams), interview with the author, Sydney, 28 March 2011.

38 Davina Davidson, email correspondence with the author, 6 January 2011.

39 Mick Harvey amusingly recalls Nick's capacity for 'swearing badly in front of people, in front of someone's family, then saying, "Oh, excuse me," very politely. It was water off a duck's back.' (Interview with the author, phone, 27 July 2020.)

40 Davina Davidson, email correspondence with the author, 6 January 2011.

41 Clinton Heylin, *Babylon's Burning: From Punk to Grunge*, Penguin, London, 2008, p. 52.

42 Davina Davidson, email correspondence with the author, 6 January 2011.

43 ibid.

Zoo Music Girl

1   Deborah Thomas, interview with the author, phone, 8 March 2012.

2   Mary Brown, 'Introduction – the 60s', *Centre History*, The Centre for Continuing Education, Wangaratta. n.d., p. 5.

3   It's interesting to consider this as a misapprehension or limiting of love itself, inculcated by Colin Cave's lessons. Nick would be critical of his father's tendency to define parenting as teaching alone, but it may be that the habit flowed on in the form of relationships that were dropped by Nick once the learning was over.

4   Gareth Sansom, interview with the author, email, 1 June 2012.

5   Jenny Watson, interview with the author, Brisbane, 17 March 2010. Within a year of meeting Nick Cave at art school, the young teacher and artist would be so impressed by a performance of The Boys Next Door at the Tiger Lounge that she'd do pencil and paper portraits of them all in 1977. Her friend and fellow artist Howard Arkley would also do a portrait of Nick Cave in 1999, using synthetic polymers on canvas.

6   John Wray, 'I Am the Real Nick Cave', *New York Times*, 1 July 2014.

7   Max Bell, 'What If Elvis Had Never Been Born?', *The Independent*, 4 July 2004, www.independent.co.uk/arts-entertainment/music/features/what-if-elvis-had-never-been-born-45975.html, accessed 20 September 2020.

8   Bram van Splunteren, *Nick Cave: Stranger in a Strange Land*, VPRO Dutch Television, 1987. It may have surprised his own hardcore post-punk fan base, but Nick considered covering Springsteen's 1978 classic 'Racing in the Streets' for his covers album, *Kicking Against the Pricks* (1986).

9   Robert Brokenmouth, 'A Portrait of the Artist as He Begins to Figure Things Out', in Sam Kinchin-Smith, *Read Write [Hand]: A Multidisciplinary Nick Cave Reader*, Silkworms Ink, East Sussex, 2011.

10 Bruce Milne, interview with the author, Melbourne, 26 February 2010.

11 Phill Calvert, interview with the author, Sydney, 26 July 2012.

12 *Spurt!* (fanzine), No.4, 1978, in Nick Cave: The Exhibition, The Arts Centre collection, Melbourne.

13 Rowland S Howard had also witnessed Radio Birdman live on their first tour of Melbourne. He was so impressed he wrote a letter to join their fan club, enquiring as to why Deniz Tek had such an obsession with the TV-show *Hawaii Five-O*. During their tour of Sydney, The Saints' Chris Bailey chose to mock Radio Birdman's trademark insignia and crowd chants as proto-Nazi drivel. Naturally enough, Birdman took offence. Nick would toy with using the swastika in cover art for The Birthday Party, begging to offend people. Its

origins as a Sanskrit symbol of wellbeing were the stronger, if equally sarcastic, reference.

14 Clinton Heylin, *Babylon's Burning: From Punk to Grunge*, Penguin, London, 2008, p. 55. The Saints' guitarist Ed Kuepper was not unaware of his band's forceful use of volume from the start, serving up a back-hander to the sneering clichés of every punk pretender cranking out noises at the time: 'We [The Saints] don't use volume as a substitute for excitement, though we probably play twice as loud as most other local bands. It all boils down to *realism*. We haven't got the attitude of "Who gives a damn, man."' (Heylin, *Babylon's Burning*, p. 51.)

15 Ian Johnston, *Bad Seed: The Biography of Nick Cave*, Abacus, London, p. 46.

16 Michel Faber, 'Conversations with Boys Next Door', *Farrago – The Rock Edition*, 1979, p. 20.

17 Clinton Walker, *Stranded: The Secret History of Australian Independent Music 1977–1991*, Pan Macmillan, Sydney, 1996, pp. 42–43.

18 Mick Harvey, interview with the author, Melbourne, 23 November 2010.

19 Robert Brokenmouth, *Nick Cave: The Birthday Party and Other Epic Adventures*, Omnibus Press, London, 1996, p. 20.

20 Michel Faber, 'A Boy Next Door', in Mat Snow, *Nick Cave – Sinner Saint: The True Confessions*, Plexus, London, 2011, p. 16. Mick Harvey, however, questions Nick's description of the crowd at Ashburton Hall as 'Homesglen skinheads' and Michel Faber's attempts to define them. He says their audience was invaded by local 'sharpies', akin to but quite different from skinheads, and a distinct Australian suburban phenomenon of the era, most of all in Melbourne where they thrived. Along with crewcut hair at the front and longer hair at the back (a kind of aggressive precursor to the mullet), sharpies favoured tight-fitting Lee jeans, ultra-tight cardigans and jumpers that accentuated muscle tone and malice, home-made T-shirts with gang names written on them, and chisel-toed boots with Cuban heels. They were instantly recognisable, and had a reputation for street fights that could include knife use. Females were called 'brushes' and often wore halter necks. Among the sharpies' favourite bands were Lobby Loyde and The Coloured Balls and Billy Thorpe and The Aztecs, and early incarnations of AC/DC and Rose Tattoo. Sharpies had a special dance, an ape-like shuffle that was faintly comical and threatening. The criminal Chopper Read and the singer Bon Scott might be considered sharpie heroes. The gangs faded out as their membership was absorbed into other subcultures, from glam to skinheads to punks, of which they were a crude working-class amalgam and preview dating back to the

1960s. Greg Macainsh of Skyhooks' four-minute documentary *Sharpies* captures them having fun at the Summer Jam concert in 1974.

21 ibid., p. 18.

22 Julie and Dawn Cave, interview with the author, Melbourne, 21 October 2010.

23 Robert Brokenmouth, *Nick Cave – The Birthday Party and Other Epic Adventures*, Omnibus Press, London, 1996, p. 18.

24 Bruce Milne, interview with the author, Melbourne, 26 February 2010.

25 Mick Harvey, interview with the author, phone, 27 July 2020.

26 'Interview with Rowland S. Howard 24/11/94', *Prehistoric Sounds· Aussie Indie Music 1977–1990*, Vol. 1 Issue 2, 1995, p. 27.

27 Glass appeared in the Australian production of *Hair* when it ran in Kings Cross, Sydney, in 1969–70. He played the leading role of Berger, a free-spirited and anarchistic figure likened, in one song, to a hippie Lucifer seeking to bring down capitalism through a change in consciousness. Glass also sang on the recorded version of the production. His understudy, Reg Livermore, would succeed him in the role when the show opened in Melbourne in mid-1971.

28 Keith Glass, interview with the author, Sydney, 13 May 2010.

29 Deborah Thomas, interview with the author, phone, 8 March 2012.

30 Jenny Watson, interview with the author, Brisbane, 17 March 2010.

31 Tobsha Learner, interview with the author, phone, 30 November 2011. Learner makes an intriguing reference to Joris-Karl Huysmans' *Against Nature* (1884) as a seminal book affecting how people modelled themselves in St Kilda at the time. *Against Nature's* central character, Jean des Esseintes, is a French aristocrat who rejects society and immerses himself in solitary luxury, art, literature and sensuality. Huysmans wrote a new preface in 1903. It reflected on the controversy this decadent, story-less and amoral book had stirred during the late 1800s: 'There was undoubtedly, as I was writing *Against Nature*, a land-shift, the earth was being mined to lay foundations of which I was unaware. God was digging to set his fuses and he worked in the darkness of the soul, in the night. Nothing could be seen; it was only years later that the sparks began to run along the wires.'

32 Legend has it that Ross Wilson liked a young Nick Cave's song 'Big Future' so much, Nick sold it to him at the Tiger Lounge for a shake-hands deal and a stubby bottle of beer. Wilson never recorded the song.

33 Karen Marks, interview with the author, 21 August 2020.

34 Polly Borland, interview with the author, Melbourne, 6 April 2012.

35 Polly Borland and John Hillcoat, interview with the author, Brighton and Hove, England, 15 June 2010.

36 Ian Johnston, *Bad Seed: The Biography of Nick Cave*, Abacus, London, 1996, p. 37.

37 Dawn Cave, interview with the author, phone, 28 May 2015.

38 Ian Johnston, *Bad Seed: The Biography of Nick Cave*, Abacus, London, 1996, p. 47.

39 Dawn and Julie Cave, interview with the author, Melbourne, 21 November 2010.

40 Davina Davidson, email correspondence with the author, 6 January 2011.

41 Dawn and Julie Cave, interview with the author, Melbourne, 21 November 2010.

42 Pierre Voltaire, interview with the author, Melbourne, 25 March 2010.

43 Deborah Thomas, interview with the author, phone, 8 March 2012.

Boy Hero

1 Deborah Thomas, interview with the author, phone, 8 March 2012. Mick Harvey also remembers Blondie coming to see them. '[Clem] was one of those people we'd always bump into over the years. Great guy. Great drummer. Always really friendly. Mick Cocks from Rose Tattoo was like that too. He'd just turn up at all these places we'd be. Really nice guy, always encouraging. It's funny the people you meet.' (Mick Harvey, interview with the author, phone, 28 July 2020.)

2 Karen Marks, interview with the author, phone, 21 August 2020.

3 Michael Gudinski, interview with the author, phone, 7 March 2012.

4 Jon Savage, one of the most important music critics and cultural historians of the era, would describe The Saints' 'This Perfect Day' as 'the most ferocious single to ever grace the UK Top 40'. ('The Saints', *The J Files*, Triple J, 30 November 2000.)

5 Michael Gudinski, interview with the author, phone, 7 March 2012.

6 Keith Glass, interview with the author, Sydney, 13 May 2010.

7 Karen Marks, interview with the author, phone, 21 August 2020.

8 Greg Macainsh, interview with the author, phone, 9 May 2011.

9 ibid.

10 Aside from Michael Shipley's world-class credentials as an engineer, Mick Harvey says that he was Nick Cave's cousin. Harvey says Shipley would also do some work on the band's debut album, *Door, Door*, with producer Les Karski. 'So I wonder why Nick was

struggling so much with his singing in the studio when I think back on it.' Shipley would go on to be nominated for eight Grammy awards, working with The Damned, The Cars, Thomas Dolby, Blondie and a host of heavy metal bands. Def Leppard nicknamed him 'bat ears' due to his acute sonic abilities in the studio. Sadly, Shipley would commit suicide on 25 July 2013.

11 'The song is a joke, but Nick was obsessed with whether he was good-looking or not at the time. I don't know why.' (Mick Harvey, interview with the author, phone, 20 July 2020.)

12 Later versions of this story would raise the age to sixteen and change the instruction from 'fucks' to 'dates' in an effort to clean up, if not quite homogenise, the original advice. Rowland S Howard idolised Hazlewood's songwriting skills and would cover the Nancy and Lee hit 'Some Velvet Morning' in a duet with Lydia Lunch in 1982, transforming the faintly psychedelic, woozy sexual overtones of the original into a tribute to co-dependency and addiction.

13 See www.youtube.com/watch?v=zCbl5bfBw2I

14 Karen Marks, interview with the author, phone, 21 August 2020.

15 Anita Lane would do an extraordinary version of 'These Boots Are Made for Walkin'' in collaboration with Barry Adamson and The Thought System of Love in 1991. Their film clip is pretty cool too. It seems to shoot an arrow right through the heart of something that had begun years earlier and stomp all over it. It was commissioned for the American crime film *Delusion*, as part of Barry Adamson's score.

16 Tony Clark, interview with the author, Melbourne, 10 February 2010.

17 ibid.

18 These days Nick Cave prefers not to see his lyrical juvenilia on display anywhere if he can prevent it. The lines Anita Lane was laughing at concerned people becoming so insane they go bald. It's more than likely Nick was having a laugh and under the influence of his Ramones album when writing it, but on the page the joke perished.

19 Robert Brokenmouth, *Nick Cave: The Birthday Party and Other Epic Adventures*, Omnibus Press, London, 1996, p. 23.

20 Tony Clark, interview with the author, Melbourne, 10 February 2010.

21 ibid.

22 Jenny Watson, interview with the author, Brisbane, 17 March 2010.

23 Tony Clark, interview with the author, Melbourne, 10 February 2010.

24 Pierre Voltaire, interview with the author, Melbourne, 25 March 2010.

25 Clinton Walker, interview with the author, Sydney, 8 April 2011.

26 Tracy probably did like the soundtrack to *The Sting*. But Pew was always attracted to deflating pretentious moments with something ridiculous or uncool. He would have also been acutely aware of a misinformed cultural snobbery that valued Satie and Eno but condescended to Scott Joplin's early-twentieth-century ragtime music and a brilliant piano player, commercial film composer and conductor like Marvin Hamlisch.

27 Released in 1972, *Nuggets: Original Artyfacts from the First Psychedelic Era* was a double album of obscure 1960s garage rock and raw psychedelic band singles assembled by then record store clerk and music obsessive Lenny Kaye for Electra Records. It revived cult interest in groups like Strawberry Alarm Clock, The Kingsmen, The Electric Prunes, Count Five and others, providing a musical template for the punk explosion. Lenny would take his musical knowledge further with Patti Smith.

28 'List by Nick Cave', c. 1978, in Nick Cave, *Stranger Than Kindness*, Canongate Books, Edinburgh, 2020, p. 36.

29 Alan Yentob's 1975 BBC documentary *Cracked Actor: A Film About David Bowie* depicted the singer in a drugged-out and identity-troubled state during his Diamond Dogs tour of the United States in 1974. Bowie was transitioning radically away from his previous image, and was in the process of recording *Young Americans*. The documentary was given a late-afternoon screening in Australia on ABC TV to fill a pop-music program slot, providing sensational, even unforgettable, viewing for curious adolescents.

30 Mick Harvey, interview with the author, phone, 27 August 2020.

31 Jillian Burt, 'Boys Next Door', *Roadrunner*, June, 1978, p. 6.

32 Susanne Moore, 'New Breed of Boys Next Door', *Daily Mirror* (Sydney), 22 May 1978.

33 Ash Wednesday would go on to play with Einsturzende Neubaten as a touring member from 1997 till 2013.

34 It would be fair to attribute what became a trademark Melbourne sub-genre – a swaggering, urban swamp sound referred to sarcastically as 'the Caulfield Grammar Schoolboy Blues' because of its long-term associations with Nick Cave – to the defining bass sounds that Walsh and Pew originally mastered as Mount Waverley hoodlums. Walsh was always the kind of guy to work off negative energy, and his refusal to heed Barrie Earl's instructions to stand with his legs wide apart like English bass players fed into a natural antipathy that drove his aggressive and dark playing style. Whenever Walsh got in Nick's ear about the music industry, it was only to pour petrol on the fires of a siege mentality they would share for quite some time to come. Indeed, there was something about Walsh that arguably foreshadowed

the character of The Birthday Party itself, a mythic and annihilating machismo that partially inspired the subject matter for Nick's alcohol-charged song 'Fears of Gun'. When Tracy Pew was gaoled briefly in 1982 for drunk driving and petty theft, Chris Walsh would be called up to fill in for him in The Birthday Party.

35 Pierre Voltaire, interview with the author, Melbourne, 25 March 2010.

36 Robert Brokenmouth, *Nick Cave: The Birthday Party and Other Epic Adventures*, Omnibus Press, London, 1996, p. 23.

37 Jillian Burt, 'Gigs: Boys Next Door', *JUKE*, 20 May 1978, p. 16.

38 John Stapleton, 'The Boys Next Door', *Roadrunner*, December 1979, n.p.

39 Jillian Burt, 'Boys Next Door', *Roadrunner*, June, 1978, p. 6.

40 *Autoluminescent: Rowland S Howard*, directed by Lynne-Maree Milburn and Richard Lowenstein, Ghost Pictures, 2011.

41 'Interview with Rowland S Howard 24/11/94', *Prehistoric Sounds, Aussie Indie Music 1976–1999*, Vol. 1, Issue 2, 1995, p. 28.

42 Rowland S Howard and Ollie Olsen, *Music Around Us*, ABC TV, 1977, online at www.youtube.com/watch?v=5HfsSWTP7J8, accessed 24 September 2020.

43 Harry Howard, interview with the author, Melbourne, 19 November 2010.

44 *Autoluminescent: Rowland S Howard*, directed by Lynne-Maree Milburn and Richard Lowenstein, Ghost Pictures, 2011.

45 Clinton Walker, interview with the author, Sydney, 8 April 2011.

46 Jeffery Wegener, interview with the author, Sydney, 10 March 2010.

47 Mick Harvey, interview with the author, Melbourne, 23 November 2010.

48 Hutchence and Olsen first came together while working on Richard Lowenstein's *Dogs in Space*.

49 Tim Anstaett, 'The Birthday Party', *The Offense*, April 1983. Republished at *Rowland S Howard – Outta the Black:* https://rowland-s-howard.com/articles/1983-offense.php, accessed 5 August 2020.

50 'Ian', 'The Boys Next Door', *SPURT!*, No. 4, 1978.

51 Models would evolve out of their electronic-influenced art-pop beginnings to become one of the most successful Australian pop-rock bands of the 1980s. Legend has it that concerns about their barbed approach and arty eccentricities led to their new manager, Chris Murphy (who'd guided the career of INXS), calling them in and asking if they wanted to be like Michael Jackson or Talking Heads. Duffield was the only band member to excitedly say 'Talking Heads', thus marking himself as the man ready to be shown the 'out' door. Ironically,

Duffield would make his fortune writing advertising jingles. His most famous work is probably the theme song to globally popular children's fantasy show *Round the Twist*. One of the last songs Duffield worked on with Models was 'Barbados', a reggae-influenced singalong co-written with James Freud. Beneath its glistening eighties pop sound lies a tale of alcoholism and sunny surrender that some interpret as suicidal ideation, presaging Freud's personal struggles and his death in 2010.

52 Stephen Scott, 'He Hears Motion', *Medium*, 12 June 2017, https://medium.com/the-cultural-savage/andrew-duffield-he-hears-motion-by-stephen-scott-a56c0b95975, accessed 5 September 2020.

53 Ian Johnston, *Bad Seed: The Biography of Nick Cave*, Abacus, London, 1996, p. 55.

54 Janet Austin, interview with the author, phone, 7 September 2011.

55 Janet Austin, interview with the author, phone, 7 September 2011.

56 *Autoluminescent: Rowland S Howard*, directed by Lynne-Maree Milburn and Richard Lowenstein, Ghost Pictures, 2011.

57 'Interview with Rowland S Howard 24/11/94', *Prehistoric Sounds, Aussie Indie Music 1976–1999*, Vol. 1, Issue 2, 1995, p. 27.

58 Bruce Milne, interview with the author, Melbourne, 26 February 2010.

59 Mick Harvey, interview with the author, Sydney, 17 January 2012.

60 'Interview with Rowland S Howard 24/11/94', *Prehistoric Sounds, Aussie Indie Music 1976–1999*, Vol. 1, Issue 2, 1995, p. 28.

61 Jenny Valentish, 'Rowland S Howard: Storm Und Twang – The Prophet of St Kilda', *Australian Guitar*, May 2006; republished at Rowland S Howard – Outta the Black: https://rowland-s-howard.com/articles/2006-australian-guitar.php

62 Phill Calvert, interview with the author, 26 July 2012.

63 Mick Harvey, interview with the author, Sydney, 17 January 2012

64 Robert Brokenmouth, *Nick Cave: The Birthday Party and Other Epic Adventures*, Omnibus Press, London, 1996, p. 33.

65 Pierre Voltaire, interview with the author, Melbourne, 25 March 2010.

66 ibid.

67 Peter Milne, interview with the author, Brisbane, 17 March 2010.

68 Robert Brokenmouth, *Nick Cave: The Birthday Party and Other Epic Adventures*, Omnibus Press, London, 1996, p. 36.

69 Miranda Brown, 'Oz Punk Suicides', *RAM*, 6 October 1978, p. 32.

70 ibid.

71 Clinton Walker, interview with the author, Sydney, 13 May 2011.

72 Stephen Cummings, *Will It Be Funny Tomorrow, Billy?: A Kind of Music Memoir*, Hardie Grant Books, Melbourne, 2009.

73 Nick Cave, cited by Stephen Cummings in 'Good Bones', *Love Town*; see http://lovetown.net/discog/goodbones.html, accessed 21 September 2020.

74 Pierre Voltaire, interview with the author, Melbourne, 25 March 2010.

PART IV: GOD'S HOTEL
Shivers

1 Phill Calvert, interview with the author, Sydney, 19 February 2014.

2 Robert Brokenmouth, *Nick Cave: The Birthday Party and Other Epic Adventures*, Omnibus Press, London, 1996, p. 57.

3 Greg Perano, interview with the author, Sydney, 6 March 2012.

4 Robert Brokenmouth, *Nick Cave: The Birthday Party and Other Epic Adventures*, Omnibus Press, London, 1996, p. 57.

5 Pierre Voltaire, interview with the author, Melbourne, 25 March 2010.

6 Gillian Upton, 'Sinking', *The George: St Kilda Life and Times*, Venus Bay Books, Melbourne, 2001, p. 93.

7 Dolores San Miguel, interview with the author, Melbourne, 22 March 2010.

8 ibid.

9 Mick Harvey, interview with the author, phone, 27 July 2020.

10 ibid.

11 Jenny Watson, interview with the author, Brisbane, 17 March 2010.

12 Bannister was the inspiration for the title character in Luke Davies' thinly veiled autobiographical novel *Candy* (1997). The junkie love story – based on Bannister's relationship with Davies in Sydney in 1984 – was made into a 2006 film starring Abbie Cornish and Heath Ledger; see www.abc.net.au/news/2017-05-22/real-life-candy-megan-bannister-tells-her-story/8528798?nw=0.

13 Hank Cherry, 'Shivers', The Nervous Breakdown, 29 June 2011, http://thenervousbreakdown.com/hcherry/2011/06/shivers, accessed 28 August 2020.

14 Peter Milne, interview with the author, Brisbane, 17 March 2010.

15 Genevieve McGuckin, interview with the author, Sydney, 26 October 2011.

16 ibid.

17 Mick Harvey and Katy Beale began dating each other at age sixteen. They are together to this day.

18 Bronwyn Bonney (née Adams), interview with the author, Sydney, 28 March 2011.

19 Pierre Voltaire, interview with the author, Melbourne, 25 March 2010.

20 Dawn Cave, interview with the author, Melbourne, 21 October 2010.

21 St Kilda would become known through a series of coronial enquiries as the most brutal and corrupt police station in the state. Streetwise locals knew it as an evil place, to be avoided at all costs.

22 Phill Calvert, interview with the author, Sydney, 19 February 2014.

23 Dolores San Miguel, *The Ballroom: The Melbourne Punk and Post-Punk Scene – A Tell-All Memoir*, Melbourne Books, Melbourne, 2011, pp. 56–57. In her retelling in the book, Dolores gets her dates wrong for Colin Cave's death and the encounter with Nick, but she reiterated her story in an interview with me in Melbourne, 22 March 2010.

24 Mick Harvey, interview with the author, 11 February 2010.

25 Robert Brokenmouth, *Nick Cave: The Birthday Party and Other Epic Adventures*, Omnibus Press, London, 1996, pp. 33–34.

26 *Autoluminescent: Rowland S Howard*, directed by Lynne-Maree Milburn and Richard Lowenstein, Ghost Pictures, 2011.

27 The Boys Next Door, Storey Hall, 3RRR Xmas Party, RMIT Live to Air, 21 December 1978. A live recording of this show captures this young band at their best.

28 Tony Cohen, interview with the author, Sydney, 30 September 2010.

29 ibid.

30 Mick Harvey, interview with the author, 11 February 2010.

31 Tony Cohen, interview with the author, Sydney, 30 September 2010.

32 Phill Calvert, interview with the author, Sydney, 18 November 2010.

33 Harry Howard, interview with the author, Melbourne, 19 November 2010.

34 Clinton Walker, interview with the author, Sydney, 13 May 2011.

35 The British adult comic magazine *Viz* adopted a defiantly adolescent satirical style, including mock-tabloid news, toilet humour, stupid misunderstandings and an absurd helping of sex and violence. Long-running strips like 'Johnny Fartpants' and 'Buster Gonad' suggest the tone. Available from newsagents in Australia, its risqué and ridiculous material made it a schoolboy favourite.

36 Phill Calvert, interview with the author, Sydney, 19 February 2014.

37 *Autoluminescent: Rowland S Howard*, directed by Lynne-Maree Milburn and Richard Lowenstein, Ghost Pictures, 2011.

38 *We're Livin' on Dog Food*, directed by Richard Lowenstein, Ghost Pictures, 2009.

39 Nick's vocals on side two of *Door, Door* mark a real change in emotional delivery. His disgust with his singing on the album reflects his reaction to the initial influence of producer Les Karski on side one, but the shift to working with Tony Cohen and the trauma of Colin Cave's death undoubtedly influenced his delivery of songs like 'Shivers'.

40 *We're Livin' on Dog Food*, directed by Richard Lowenstein, Ghost Pictures, 2009.

41 Pierre Voltaire, interview with the author, Melbourne, 25 March 2010.

42 Jeffrey Wegener, interview with the author, Sydney, 10 March 2010.

43 Bruce Milne, interview with the author Melbourne, 26 February 2010.

44 Mick Harvey, interview with the author, Wombarra, 5 April 2013.

45 Clinton Walker, interview with the author, Sydney, 8 April 2011. Rowland S Howard would take years to find himself again after leaving The Birthday Party, but his output would be lean and spasmodic beside Nick's downpour of albums and ideas. Even so, a mysterious power and sadness radiates from his swaggering band, These Immortal Souls, and his only two solo albums, *Teenage Snuff Film* and *Pop Crimes*. On the set of the ABC music program *Studio 22*, some three decades after he first wrote 'Shivers', he was asked by host Clinton Walker if the song was 'an albatross or a Victoria Cross'. It was a brilliant question. Howard almost recoiled before recovering his typically amused poise and saying it was nearer an albatross because he wished people would ask him about a song he'd written in the last fifteen years. Rowland said something else that was even more telling: that playing 'Shivers' felt like playing a song that someone else had written – 'like a cover'.

46 *Autoluminescent: Rowland S Howard*, directed by Lynne-Maree Milburn and Richard Lowenstein, Ghost Pictures, 2011.

47 Mick Harvey says that none of the band wanted to thank Barrie Earl. It was Tracy Pew who insisted, also demanding they describe Earl as their mentor. 'We argued with Tracy but he just liked the idea of telling people we had a mentor.' (Mick Harvey, interview with the author, 27 August 2020.)

48 Mick Harvey, interview with the author, Wombarra, 5 April 2013.

49 Keith Glass, interview with the author, Sydney, 13 May 2010.

50 ibid.

51 Mick Harvey, interview with the author, Wombarra, 5 April 2013.

52 Keith Glass, interview with the author, Sydney, 13 May 2010.

53 Mick Harvey, interview with the author, Sydney, 17 January 2012.

54 Nick Cave on The Pop Group (1999), www.youtube.com/
watch?v=BUC2GmzJpGY, accessed 7 September 2020.

55 Jillian Burt, 'Suicide Survivors', *Roadrunner*, March 1979, p. 79.

56 Clinton Walker, *Stranded: The Secret History of Australian Independent Music
1977–1991*, Pan Macmillan Australia, Sydney, 1996, p. 52.

57 David Pestorius, curator, notes for exhibition Brisbane: Punk, Art and After,
The Ian Potter Museum of Art, Melbourne, 24 February – 15 May 2010.

58 Clinton Walker, interview with the author, Sydney, 13 May 2011.

59 *We're Livin' on Dog Food*, directed by Richard Lowenstein, Ghost
Pictures, 2009.

60 Pierre Voltaire, interview with the author, Melbourne, 25 March 2010.

61 Robert Brokenmouth, *Nick Cave: The Birthday Party and Other Epic
Adventures*, Omnibus Press, London, 1996, p. 51.

62 Jim Thirlwell, interview with the author, phone, 16 July 2011.

63 Ian McFarlane, 'Interview with Rowland S Howard 24/11/94', *Prehistoric
Sounds, Aussie Indie Music 1976–1999*, Vol. 1, Issue 2, 1995, p. 29.

64 Andrea Jones, 'Birthday Party Celebrate', *Rolling Stone Australia*, Sydney,
February 1982, p. 17.

65 *The Offense* was a 1980s post-punk fanzine from Colombus, Ohio
put together by Tim Anstaett. A history can be found here: https://
blurtonline.com/news/80s-ohio-fanzine-the-offense-gets-bookd-in-
fine-style. The quote from Nick Cave is in *The Offense*, April 1983
edition, republished here: https://rowland-s-howard.com/articles/1983-
offense.php, accessed 22 September 2020.

66 Tony Cohen, interview with the author, Sydney, 30 September 2010.

67 Barney Hoskyns, 'A Manhattan Melodrama Starring The Birthday
Party', *New Musical Express*, 17 October 1981.

68 Andrew McMillan, *RAM*, December 1979, n.p.

69 Ian Johnston, *Bad Seed: The Biography of Nick Cave*, Abacus, London, p. 57.

Flight from Death

1 Mick Harvey, interview with the author, Wombarra, 5 April 2013.

2 Jenny Watson, interview with the author, 17 March 2010.

3 Bronwyn Bonney (née Adams), interview with the author, Sydney,
28 March 2011.

4 ibid.

5 Ashley Crawford, 'Ballroom Mayhem (18.07.08)', *The Funeral Party*, City
of Port Phillip's Urban Art Strategy, 2009.

6 Bruce Milne, interview with the author, Melbourne, 26 February 2010.

7 Pierre Voltaire, interview with the author, Melbourne, 25 March 2010.

8 Robert Brokenmouth, *Nick Cave: The Birthday Party and Other Epic Adventures*, Omnibus Press, London, 1996, p. 46.

9 ibid.

10 Anne Tsoulis, interview with the author, iMessage, 12 June 2012: 'I have a theory that our generation were raised by traumatised parents – post-war freakout.'

11 Bruce Milne, interview with the author, Melbourne, 26 February 2010.

12 Ashley Crawford, 'Ballroom Mayhem (18.07.08)', *The Funeral Party*, City of Port Phillip's Urban Art Strategy, 2009. Crawford's recreation is supported by filmmaker Evan English's memories of the Crystal Ballroom as 'a wonderful venue, both very grand and deeply seedy. Its red floral carpet (from memory) was stained with beautiful excess and deep human misery' (https://nickcavefixes.wordpress. com/2010/01/25/boys-next-door-melbourne-punk-pics, accessed 22 September 2020).

13 Conrad Knickerbocker, 'The Art of Fiction – William Burroughs Interview', *The Paris Review*, Issue 35, Fall 1965, www.theparisreview. org/interviews/4424/the-art-of-fiction-no-36-william-s-burroughs, accessed 11 September 2020.

14 Greg Perano, interview with the author, Sydney, 6 March 2012.

15 Bronwyn Bonney (née Adams), correspondence with the author, iMessage, 16 August 2020.

16 Greg Perano, interview with the author, Sydney, 6 March 2012.

17 Genevieve McGuckin, interview with the author, Sydney, 26 October 2011.

18 Pierre Voltaire, interview with the author, Melbourne, 25 March 2010.

19 Greg Perano, interview with the author, Sydney, 6 March 2012.

20 Lisa Craswell died from a heroin overdose in 1985 – one year prior to the death of Tracy Pew – after an argument between the couple over Tracy's involvement with another woman.

21 Paul Goldman, interview with the author, Melbourne, 9 February 2010.

22 Bronwyn Bonney (née Adams), interview with the author, Sydney, 28 March 2011.

23 Robert Brokenmouth, *Nick Cave: The Birthday Party and Other Epic Adventures*, Omnibus Press, London, 1996, p. 32.

24 This wounded energy would be strangely repeated in the alienating struggle to complete the final Birthday Party record, which would see

Rowland pushed out of the band entirely. In Heiner Mühlenbrock's documentary *Mutiny! The Last Birthday Party*, you can see Nick becoming intolerant of Rowland's efforts to please as Blixa Bargeld emerges as Nick's new compatriot and guitar hero.

25 Paul Goldman, interview with the author, Melbourne, 9 February 2010.

26 Egon Schiele on his 1911 painting *Revelation (Composition with Figures)*. Schiele's painting has a very particular power balance: 'One half is supposed to represent the vision of a personality so great that the one who has just been influenced is overwhelmed, kneeling before the Great One, who observes him through closed eyelids' (http://egonschieleonline.org/works/paintings/work/p203, accessed 22 September 2020).

27 Laknath Jayasinghe, 'Nick Cave, Dance Performance and the Production and Consumption of Masculinity' in Karen Welbery and Tanya Dalziel (eds), *Cultural Seeds: Essays on the Work of Nick Cave*, Ashgate Publishing, London, 2009.

28 Bronwyn Bonney (née Adams), correspondence with the author, iMessage, 16 August 2020.

29 Jillian Burt, 'Suicide Survivors', *Roadrunner*, March 1979, p. 9.

30 John Stapleton, 'The Boys Next Door', *Roadrunner*, December 1979, n.p.

31 Pierre Voltaire, interview with the author, Melbourne, 25 March 2010.

32 Phill Calvert, interview with the author, phone, 2 September 2020.

33 'Boys Next Door; Melbourne Punk; Pics', https://nickcavefixes.wordpress.com/2010/01/25/boys-next-door-melbourne-punk-pics, accessed 11 September 2020.

34 Phill Calvert, interview with the author, Melbourne, 20 February 2010.

35 Article, *Sunday Mail*, Adelaide, 14 May 1979, from Nick Cave: The Exhibition, Newspaper Clippings 1978-79 H0000582.

36 Pierre Voltaire, interview with the author, Melbourne, 25 March 2010. It was on this same night that Julie Cave recalls a young male friend arriving, glancing at both Nick and Rowland and saying, 'I'm sorry, I did not know this was a fancy dress party.' 'He was being quite sincere and apologetic about it,' Julie says. 'Nick and Rowland were really pissed off.' (Dawn and Julie Cave, interview with the author, Melbourne, 21 November 2010.)

37 Pierre Voltaire, interview with the author, Melbourne, 25 March 2010.

38 Greg Perano, interview with the author, Melbourne, 6 March 2012.

39 Keith Glass, interview with the author, Sydney, 13 May 2010.

40 ibid.

41 Mick Harvey, interview with the author, Wombarra, 5 April 2013.

42 Ron Rude, email correspondence with the author, 19 June 2012.

43 In the United States, hog calling, or pig calling, is a competitive event at country fairs. Use of the actual word 'suey' may be derived from 'sow' but the origins are vague. No-one knows why pigs respond to such a call, but some people have a knack for it.

44 Ron Rude, email correspondence with the author, 19 June 2012.

45 Launched in 1979 as Australia's first commercial FM radio station, Eon FM changed its name to Triple M in 1980. Initially it had no playlist and an open agenda for the music it might play. It developed a tighter strategy, rejecting the album-oriented approach of other FM stations to focus on becoming a Top 40 station. The first song played on Eon was the Eagles' 'New Kids in Town'.

46 Phill Calvert, correspondence with the author, 15 June 2020.

47 Ron Rude continues to perform with his group Ron Rude's Renaissance, and is working on a novel: 'People have suggested that I write a memoir, but it involves too much reliving of the past to be palatable to me. My book is a novel about world government, and the plot serves as a framework to present a suite of ideas about political ideology and personal practices for growth and practicality. It's done as a conversation between two men, and so follows the paradigm of the Bhagavad Gita. It's a Bhagavad Gita for the Covid-19 era.' (Ron Rude, correspondence with the author, 12 August 2020.)

48 Phill Calvert, interview with the author, Melbourne, 20 February 2010.

49 Mick Harvey is equally adamant about this side of Pew: 'So many write-ups and people who never knew Tracy get him all wrong. He gets depicted as this looming, dark presence. His image on stage maybe adds to that idea, [as well as] some of the things Rowland said in interviews, but that's just Rowland. When I think of Tracy I always remember how funny he was. He was more naughty than dark. I'd have to say he is still to this day the funniest person I have ever known in my life. And I think anyone who really knew him will tell you the same thing.' (Mick Harvey, interview with the author, phone, 27 July 2020.)

50 Fred Negro, conversation with the author, phone, 14 September 2020. Fred's cartoon originally appeared, with the title 'One Nite After the Ballroom', on the inside cover of Dolores San Miguel, *The Ballroom: The Melbourne Punk and Post-Punk Scene – A Tell-All Memoir*, Melbourne Books, Melbourne, 2011.

51 Michel Faber, 'Conversation with Boys Next Door', *Farrago – The Rock Edition*, University of Melbourne, Melbourne, 1979, pp. 20-21.

52 John Stapleton, 'The Boys Next Door', *Roadrunner*, December 1979, n.p.

53 *Autoluminescent: Rowland S Howard*, directed by Lynne-Maree Milburn and Richard Lowenstein, Ghost Pictures, 2011.

54 Quote from *The Denial of Death* by Ernest Becker. Copyright © 1974 by The Free Press, a Division of Simon and Schuster, Inc. Copyright © renewed 2002 by Marie H. Becker. Reprinted with the permission of The Free Press, a division of Simon & Schuster, Inc. All rights reserved.

55 Tony Cohen, interview with the author, Sydney, 30 September 2010.

56 ibid.

57 In fact, the last album by Nick Cave and The Bad Seeds to fully make use of tape-recording in the studio was *Abattoir Blues/The Lyre of Orpheus* (2004). By the time of *Dig!!! Lazarus Dig!!!* (2008), they had moved to digital recording.

58 Tony Cohen, interview with the author, Sydney, 30 September 2010.

59 'The Red Clock' faintly references *A Clockwork Orange* (1971), an iconic film of the decade. Director Stanley Kubrick's depiction of a futuristic criminal gang of 'droogs' did not entirely have the moral impact he hoped for. Rowland and Nick could see how malice had an attractive power and – in the wake of punk rock – was something to be used artistically, in performances and in their image, which were taking on stylishly sinister overtones. The fact that Rowland was allowed lead vocal on 'The Red Clock' revived hopes of sharing singing duties when it came to his own material. Nick doing 'Shivers' had been a bitter pill to swallow. But the lyrics of 'The Red Clock' suggest another disturbing take on the night when the red chair was stolen and Nick cut his hand on the window. It's as if Nick's criminality is making its way into Rowland's dreams.

60 Phill Calvert, interview with the author, phone, 19 February 2014.

61 Keith Glass, interview with the author, Sydney, 13 May 2010.

62 Mick Harvey, interview with the author, Sydney, 17 January 2012.

63 Ian McFarlane, 'Interview with Rowland S Howard 24/11/94', *Prehistoric Sounds, Aussie Indie Music 1976–1999*, Vol. 1, Issue 2, 1995, p. 28.

64 ibid.

65 Ironically, the Clifton Hill Community Music Centre's leading light, Philip Brophy, was from Reservoir in Melbourne and probably more working-class than anyone in the communist-inspired enclave that surrounded the Primitive Calculators. As it was, the latter were already descending into amphetamine and heroin addictions that would merge with their nihilism and obliterate them. Primitive Calculators knew how to attack, but it seemed they had nothing left to defend.

66　Jenny Valentish, 'Rowland S Howard: Storm Und Twang – The Prophet of St Kilda', *Australian Guitar*, May 2006; republished at Rowland S Howard – Outta the Black, https://rowland-s-howard.com/articles/2006-australian-guitar.php

67　Robert Brokenmouth, *Nick Cave: The Birthday Party and Other Epic Adventures*, Omnibus Press, London, 1996, p. 34.

68　Mick Harvey, interview with the author, Wombarra, 5 April 2013.

69　Clinton Walker, 'Last Hee Haw from The Boys Next Door', *Inner City Sound*, Verse Chorus Press, Melbourne, 2005, p. 77.

70　ibid.

71　ibid.

Crime and Punishment

1　John Stapleton, 'The Boys Next Door', *Roadrunner*, December 1979, n.p.

2　Barney Hoskyns, 'A Manhattan Melodrama Starring The Birthday Party', *New Musical Express*, 17 October 1981; republished at Rowland S Howard – Outta the Black, https://rowland-s-howard.com/articles/1981-nme-2.php, accessed 22 September 2020.

3　ibid.

4　Tim Anstaett, 'The Birthday Party', *The Offense* April 1983; republished at *Rowland S Howard – Outta the Black:* https://rowland-s-howard.com/articles/1983-offense.php, accessed 5 August 2020.

5　Ian McFarlane, 'Interview with Rowland S Howard 24/11/94', *Prehistoric Sounds, Aussie Indie Music 1976–1999*, Vol. 1, Issue 2, 1995, p. 30.

6　Phill Calvert, interview with the author, Melbourne, 20 February 2010.

7　Mick Harvey, interview with the author, Sydney, 17 January 2012.

8　After graduating, Goldman and English would consolidate themselves as an innovative young production duo called The Rich Kids. They developed videos for The Birthday Party and Nick's early solo career, as well as forging the creative core behind the prison drama *Ghosts … of the Civil Dead* (1986), with John Hillcoat directing and Nick scriptwriting and taking a leading role. *Ghosts* would take everyone to the edge, souring English and Goldman's relationship with Hillcoat and Cave.

9　Polly Borland and John Hillcoat, interview with the author, Melbourne, 6 April 2012.

10　*We're Livin' on Dog Food*, directed by Richard Lowenstein, Ghost Pictures, 2009.

11 Phill Calvert, interview with the author, Sydney, 19 February 2014.

12 Jenny Watson, interview with the author, Melbourne, 17 March 2010.

13 Tony Clarke, interview with the author, Melbourne, 10 February 2010.

14 Bronwyn Bonney (née Adams), interview with the author, Sydney, 28 March 2011.

15 Ian McFarlane, 'Interview with Rowland S Howard 24/11/94', *Prehistoric Sounds*, Aussie Indie Music 1976–1999, Vol. 1, Issue 2, 1995, p. 30.

16 Harry Howard, interview with the author, Melbourne, 19 November 2010.

17 Ron Rude, correspondence with the author, email, 19 June 2012.

18 ibid.

19 Paul Goldman, interview with the author, Melbourne, 9 February 2010.

20 Ron Rude, correspondence with the author, email, 19 June 2012.

21 Kathleen Stewart, correspondence with the author, email, 3 September 2020.

22 Kathleen Stewart, *The After Life*, Random House, 2008, p. 175.

23 Phill Calvert, interview with the author, Sydney, 20 February 2010.

24 Kathleen Stewart, *The After Life*, Random House, 2008, p. 261.

25 Kathleen Stewart, correspondence with the author, email, 3 September 2020.

26 Phill Calvert, interview with the author, Melbourne, 20 February 2010.

27 Rowland S Howard would continue to play this guitar up until his death on 30 December 2009. So strongly did it define his sound that fan sites and tribute events would identify him as the 'Crown Prince of the Crying Jag'.

28 Keith Glass, interview with the author, Sydney, 13 May 2010.

29 ibid.

30 Helen Gillman, 'Boys Next Door: Monument in the Making', *Rolling Stone Australia*, January 1980, n.p.

31 Jane Simon, 'The Birthday Party', *Roadrunner*, June 1990, p. 19.

32 'Michael Hutchence of INXS Chooses His Top Ten Songs': number 2 is 'Anything by The Boys Next Door', clipping from unidentified publication.

33 Dolores San Miguel, interview with the author, Melbourne, 22 March 2010.

34 Ian McFarlane, 'Interview with Rowland S Howard 24/11/94', *Prehistoric Sounds, Aussie Indie Music 1976–1999*, Vol. 1, Issue 2, 1995, p. 29.

35 Keith Glass, interview with the author, Sydney, 13 May 2010.

36 Mick Harvey, interview with the author, Wombarra, 5 April 2013.

37 Robert Brokenmouth, 'Portrait of the Artist as He Begins to Figure Things Out', in Sam Kinchin-Smith (ed.), *Read Write [Hand]: A Multi-Disciplinary Nick Cave Reader*, Silkworm Ink, London, 2011, http://silkwormsink.com/nick/home.html

38 Bruce Milne, interview with the author, Melbourne, 26 February 2010.

39 *Autoluminescent: Rowland S Howard*, directed by Lynne-Maree Milburn and Richard Lowenstein, Ghost Pictures, 2011.

40 Clinton Walker, 'Back Home for the Birthday Party', *RAM*, Sydney, 24 Nov 1980, n.p.

41 *Autoluminescent: Rowland S Howard*, directed by Lynne-Maree Milburn and Richard Lowenstein, Ghost Pictures, 2011.

42 'Loverman'. Lyrics by Nick Cave. Published by Mute Song Limited. All Rights Reserved. International Copyright Secured. Reproduced by kind permission.

43 'There seems to be a view put forward in some quarters that were wasteful. We never wasted time. We were very aware of the money being spent. We worked hard in the studio. Our output shows this.' (Mick Harvey, interview with the author, phone, 27 August 2020.)

44 Phill Calvert, correspondence with author, email, 15 June 2020.

45 Dave Graney would arrive in Melbourne ready for action in 1980. The departure of The Boys Next Door had left a huge vacuum: the scene felt depressed and cynical after the Suicide debacle. Graney had formed The Moodists back in Adelaide with his partner, drummer Clare Moore. On arriving in Melbourne, they advertised for a bass player who could hum The Velvet Underground's 'White Light/White Heat', a song inspired by an amphetamine rush. They worked with a few bassists before Chris Walsh turned up and hummed himself into the band. Walsh's part in the evolution of their snaking, Mack-truck sound would soon make The Moodists the perfect support act for The Birthday Party: 'Chris was a very old friend of Tracy's and the two were mirror images in many ways. Cowboy hats, tattoos and that kind of bass sound … We were all into that post-punk sound with the bass being central and the guitars light and spindly. Like PiL and Ubu and the Pop Group.' (Dave Graney, interview with the author, iMessage, 9 August 2020.)

46 Phill Calvert, correspondence with author, Melbourne, 20 February 2010.

47 Mick Harvey, interview with the author, Wombarra 5 April 2013.

48 ibid.

49 ibid.

50 Fyodor Dostoyevsky, *Crime and Punishment*, translated by Constance Garnett, Part 1, Chapter 1.

51 Tim Anstaett, 'The Birthday Party', *The Offense*, April 1983. Republished at *Rowland S Howard – Outta the Black:* https://rowland-s-howard.com/articles/1983-offense.php, accessed 5 August 2020.

Epilogue: The Singer and the Song

1 Bleddyn Butcher, interview with the author, iMessage, 15 September 2020.

2 *Autoluminescent: Rowland S Howard*, directed by Lynne-Maree Milburn and Richard Lowenstein, Ghost Pictures, 2011.

3 Mick Harvey, interview with the author, phone, 27 July 2020.

SELECTED BIBLIOGRAPHY

Books and essays

John Barker (ed.), *The Art of Nick Cave: New Critical Essays*, Intellect, Bristol, 2013

Janine Barrand and James Fox, *Nick Cave Stories*, Nick Cave: The Exhibition, Victorian Arts Trust, Melbourne, 2007

Robert Brokenmouth, *Nick Cave: The Birthday Party and Other Epic Adventures*, Omnibus Press, London, 1996

Colin F Cave, 'Introduction', *Ned Kelly: Man and Myth*, Cassell Australia, Sydney, 1968

Nick Cave, *And the Ass Saw the Angel*, Blackspring Press, London, 1989

Nick Cave, *The Complete Lyrics 1978–2013*, Penguin Books, Melbourne, 2013

Nick Cave, 'Introduction', *The Gospel According to Mark*, Pocket Canon/Canongate, Edinburgh, 1998

Nick Cave, *The Secret Life of the Love Song/The Flesh Made Word: Two Lectures by Nick Cave*, King Mob, London, 1999

Nick Cave and Christina Back, *Stranger Than Kindness*, Canongate, Edinburgh, 2020

Maximilian Dax and Johannes Beck, *The Life and Music of Nick Cave: An Illustrated Biography*, Die Gestaltan Verlag, Berlin, 1999

Amy Hanson, *Kicking Against the Pricks: An Armchair Guide to Nick Cave*, Helter Skelter Publishing, London, 2005

Ian Johnston, *Bad Seed: The Biography of Nick Cave*, Abacus, London, 1996

Sam Kinchin-Smith (ed.), *Read Write [Hand]: A Multi-Disciplinary Nick Cave Reader*, Silkworm Ink, London, 2011

Peter Milne, *Juvenilia*, M.33/Perimeter Books, Melbourne, 2020

Dolores San Miguel, *The Ballroom – The Melbourne Punk and Post-Punk Scene: A Tell-All Memoir*, Melbourne Books, Melbourne 2011

Mat Snow (ed.), *Nick Cave – Sinner Saint: The True Confessions*, Plexus Books, London, 2011

Kathleen Stewart, *The After Life: A Memoir*, Vintage, Sydney, 2008

Gillian Upton, *The George: St Kilda Life and Times*, Venus Bay Books, Melbourne, 2001

Clinton Walker (ed.), *Inner City Sound: Punk and Post-Punk in Australia, 1976–1985*, Verse Chorus Press, Melbourne, 2005

Clinton Walker, *Stranded: The Secret History of Australian Independent Music 1977–1991*, Pan Macmillan Australia, Sydney, 1996

Karen Welberry and Tanya Dalziel (eds), *Cultural Seeds: Essays on the Work of Nick Cave*, Ashgate Publishing, Surrey, 2009

Documentaries

20,000 Days on Earth, directed by Ian Forsyth and Jane Pollard, Pulse Films, London, 2014

Autoluminescent: Rowland S Howard, directed by Lynn-Maree Milburn and Richard Lowenstein, Ghost Pictures, Melbourne, 2011

The Good Son, VPRO Dutch Television, 1997 (available on YouTube)

We're Livin' on Dog Food, directed by Richard Lowenstein, Ghost Pictures, 2009

The Boys Next Door: Discography

Lethal Weapons (Suicide, 1978) – compilation, three tracks: 'These Boots Are Made For Walking', 'Masturbation Generation', 'Boy Hero'

Door, Door (Mushroom, 1979) – debut album

Hee-Haw (Missing Link, 1979) – EP

'Scatterbrain' – giveaway single at Crystal Ballroom. 'Early Morning Brain' by Models on flipside – rare

'Happy Birthday' / 'Riddle House' (Missing Link, 1980) – single

The Birthday Party by The Boys Next Door (Missing Link, 1980) – compilation album of *Hee-Haw* material with unreleased Boys Next Door recordings and early singles by The Birthday Party